In Conversation with God

Meditations for each day of the year

Volume Five
Ordinary Time: Weeks 24 – 34

Francis Fernandez

In Conversation
with God
Meditations for each day of the year

Volume Five
Ordinary Time: Weeks 24 – 34

SCEPTER
London – New York

This edition of *In Conversation with God – Volume 5* is published:
in England by Scepter (U.K.) Ltd., 21 Hinton Avenue, Hounslow
  TW4 6AP; e-mail: scepter@pobox.com;
in the United States by Scepter Publishers Inc.; 800-322-8773; e-
  mail: info@scepterpublishers.org; www.scepterpublishers.org

This is a translation of *Hablar con Dios – Vol V*, first published in
1990 by Ediciones Palabra, Madrid, and in 1991 by Scepter.

With ecclesiastical approval

© Original — Fomento de Fundaciones (Fundación Internacional),
Madrid, 1990
© Translation — Scepter, London, 1991
© This edition — Scepter, London, 2019

British Library Cataloguing in Publication Data

Fernandez-Carvajal, Francis
In Conversation with God — Volume 5
Ordinary Time: Weeks 14 – 24.
1. Christian life — Daily Readings
I Title   II Hablar con Dios   *English*
242'.2

ISBN Volume 7   978-0-906138-36-6
ISBN Volume 6   978-0-906138-25-0
ISBN Volume 5   978-0-906138-24-3
ISBN Volume 4   978-0-906138-23-6
ISBN Volume 3   978-0-906138-22-9
ISBN Volume 2   978-0-906138-21-2
ISBN Volume 1   978-0-906138-20-5
ISBN Complete set 978-0-906138-19-9

Cover design & typeset in England by KIP Intermedia, and printed in
China.

CONTENTS

Contents

Contents

Scheduled Use of this Volume in *Ordinary Time*

Year	Cycle	24th Week begins on Sunday	First Sunday of Advent is on
2020	A	13 September	29 November
2021	B	11 September	28 November
2022	C	16 September	27 November
2023	A	17 September	3 December
2024	B	15 September	1 December
2025	C	14 September	30 November
2026	A	13 September	29 November
2027	B	12 September	28 November
2028	C	10 September	3 December
2029	A	9 September	2 December
2030	B	15 September	1 December

TWENTY-FOURTH SUNDAY: YEAR A

1. UNLIMITED FORGIVENESS

1.1 To forgive always, promptly and wholeheartedly.

God pardons those who pardon others. The mercy we show to others is the same mercy that will be shown to us. This is the measure we find in today's readings. The *First Reading* tells us: *He who exacts vengeance will experience the vengeance of the Lord, who keeps strict account of sin. Forgive your neighbour the hurt he does you, and when you pray, your sins will be forgiven. If a man nurses anger against another, can he then demand compassion from the Lord?*[1]

The Lord has perfected this command by extending it to every person and to every offence. Through his Death on the Cross, Christ has made all men brothers in a new creation. St Peter wondered aloud if this teaching was going too far when he asked Jesus how many times we must forgive another. The Lord responded: *I do not say to you seven times, but seventy times seven.*[2] This means *always*. It is not a question of mathematical calculations. Christ wants us to learn how to overcome evil through the power of his infinite love. In the *Our Father* prayer, Christ taught us to pray: *Forgive us our trespasses, as we forgive those who trespass against us.* Today's *Liturgy of the Hours* reminds us that when we pray the *Our Father* we have to be *united among ourselves and with Jesus Christ, well disposed to forgiving one another.*[3] This is the only

---

[1] Eccles 27:33; 28:1-9
[2] cf Matt 18:21-35
[3] *Liturgy of the Hours,* Evening prayer

way we will attract the infinite mercy of God.

To forgive from one's heart often requires true faith. Due to the intensity of their faith, holy souls who have lived their lives in imitation of Christ often do not see the need to forgive. They realize that the only real evil is sin. Injuries and calumnies are simply not so very important.

Let us examine our conscience today to see if we are holding on to any resentment, whether real or imaginary. Has our pardon been speedy, sincere, wholehearted and unreserved? *If they annoy you fifty thousand times, that's how often you have to forgive them ... Your patience has to get ahead of your bad feelings, wearing them out before they provoke more harm.*[4]

1.2 If we truly learn how to forgive others, we will find it to be almost unnecessary, since we no longer feel offended.

Frequently we can be offended by the most trivial things – a lack of gratitude perhaps, a sharp word in a moment of weakness or just a piece of bad luck. At other times, we can become upset from serious causes such as calumnies and twisted interpretations of what we have done with an upright conscience. Whatever be the provocation, if we are to forgive right away, and to the full, we need to have our hearts directed towards God. This grandeur of soul will lead us to pray for people who do us harm. A renowned Spanish author has posed the problem in these terms: *Is it not customary that the sick be treated with more affection than the healthy? Be then the doctor to your enemies. The good you do to them may enkindle worthy thoughts of love (Col 3:13). Think of the means of perfection that your enemies are giving to you ... Consider for a moment that it was Herod's hatred that made the 'Innocents' holy, not the*

---

[4] St John of Avila, *Sermon 25, for the 25th Sunday after Pentecost* in *Obras Completas,* Madrid 1970

love which they had from their parents.[5]

Our practice of Christian pardon and legitimate self-defence can bring many souls to the Faith. This was how the first Christians behaved in the face of calumnies and persecution. As he prepared for his martyrdom, St Ignatius of Antioch counselled the early church at Ephesus: *But pray unceasingly also for the rest of men, for they offer ground for hoping that they may be converted and win their way to God. Give them an opportunity therefore, at least by your conduct, of becoming your disciples. Meet their angry outbursts with your own gentleness, their boastfulness with your humility, their revilings with your prayers, their error with your constancy in the faith, their harshness with your meekness; and beware of trying to match their example. Let us prove ourselves their brothers through courtesy. Let us strive to follow the Lord's example and see who can suffer greater wrong, who more deprivation, who more contempt. Thus no weed of the devil will be found among you; but you will persevere in perfect chastity and sobriety through Jesus Christ, in body and soul.*[6]

The Lord is ready to forgive everyone. St Paul takes up this theme in his letter to the Thessalonians: *See that none of you repays evil for evil, but always seek to do good to one another and to all.*[7] To the Colossians he writes: *Bear with one another and forgive one another, if anyone has a grievance against any other; even as the Lord has forgiven you, so also do you forgive.*[8] If we truly learn how to forgive others, we will find it to be almost unnecessary to do so, since we no longer feel offended. We are not following Christ's way if our charity becomes cold to

---

[5] F. de Osuna, *The Law of saintly love,* 40-43, in *Franciscan mystics,* vol. I, pp. 580-610

[6] St Ignatius of Antioch, *Epistle to the Ephesians,* 10, 1-3

[7] 1 Thess 5:15

[8] Col 3:13

someone in the family, in the workplace, in our school. On those occasions when it is more difficult to forgive, we need to repeat the Lord's words on Calvary: *Father, forgive them, for they do not know what they are doing.*[9] In most cases, however, it is enough that we smile, or return a greeting, or do some small favour in order to resume a friendship. The little frictions of each day should not lead us to lose our peace and joy. We can not allow our pride to get the better of us in this regard.

1.3 The Sacrament of Penance helps us to be merciful towards others.

The Lord gives Peter a memorable explanation of the nature of Christian pardon in the parable of the two debtors. One debtor owed ten thousand talents while the other owed a hundred denarii. The difference in value is enormous. It took six thousand denarii to make a single talent. The lesson is that God's mercy is immensely greater than our own. True mercy belongs to those humble souls who understand how much they have been forgiven. *Just as the Lord is always ready to forgive us, so we must always be ready to forgive one another. And how great is the need for forgiveness in our world today – indeed in our communities and families, in our very own hearts! That is why the special sacrament of the Church for forgiveness, the Sacrament of Penance, is such a precious gift from the Lord.*

In the Sacrament of Penance, God extends his forgiveness to us in a very personal way. Through the ministry of the priest, we come to our loving Saviour with the burden of our sins. We confess that we have sinned against God and our neighbour. We manifest our sorrow and ask for pardon from the Lord. Then, through the priest, we hear

---

[9] Luke 23:34

Christ say to us: 'Your sins are forgiven' (Mark 2:5); 'Go, and do not sin again' (John 8:11). Can we not also hear him say to us as we are filled with his saving grace: 'Extend to others, seventy times seven, this same forgiveness and mercy'?[10] Confession is a magnificent school of love and generosity. The sacrament renews the soul and vivifies its capacity for pardon.[11] *The Church must profess and proclaim God's mercy in all its truth, as it has been handed down to us by revelation.*[12] This task belongs to every Christian. It seems especially urgent in our times.

Let us ask Our Lady for a magnanimous heart like her own. She can help us to avoid brooding over disappointments and injuries. In addition, we must continually grow in our spirit of reparation to the merciful Heart of Jesus.

---

[10] St John Paul II, *Angelus,* 16 September 1984
[11] cf F. Sopena, *Confession,* Madrid 1957
[12] St John Paul II, Encyclical, *Dives in misericordia,* 30 November 1980, 13

TWENTY-FOURTH SUNDAY: YEAR B

2. WITH JESUS

2.1 Our life is intimately related to the life of Christ.

It was the third year of Jesus' public ministry and the feast of Pentecost was drawing near. The Lord had gone up to Jerusalem on the two previous celebrations to preach the Good News. On this occasion, however, he seemed reluctant to go to the Holy City. Perhaps he wanted to shield his followers from the hostility of his enemies. He led them instead to the tranquil villages around Caesarea Philippi.[1] St Luke relates that after praying for some time, the Lord put his famous query to the Apostles: *Who do men say that I am?*[2] With remarkable simplicity they responded: *John the Baptist; and others say, Elijah; and others one of the prophets.* Then Jesus asked with more insistence: *But who do you say that I am?*

There are many questions in this life which we can safely ignore without consequence. There are other questions which have a more important relation to ourselves and to our society. One thinks of the dignity of the human person, the ultimate impermanence of temporal goods, the fleeting nature of our life on earth ... There is still a more momentous question which touches upon the meaning of our existence. It is the question which Christ posed to the Apostles at Caesarea Philippi almost twenty centuries ago: *But who do you say that I am?* There is only one valid answer. *You are the Christ,* the Anointed One, the Messiah, the Only-Begotten One of God. He is the person who is of

---

[1] cf Matt 8:22
[2] cf Luke 9:18

the greatest importance to my destiny, my happiness, my successes and failures in this life and hereafter.

Our happiness is not in our health, our worldly successes or our ability to get what we want. Our life will have been worth something if and when we fall in love with Christ. All our problems can be resolved if we are close to him. There is no satisfactory solution to any of these problems of ours without reference to the Lord.

Through the testimony of Peter, the Apostles give Jesus their summary of what the two years of being next to him have meant. *In our case also, in order to make a more conscious profession of faith in Jesus Christ, we must, like Peter, listen attentively and carefully. We must follow in the school of the first disciples, who had become his witnesses and our teachers. At the same time we must accept the experience and testimony of no less than twenty centuries of history marked by the Master's question and enriched by the immense chorus of responses of the faithful of all times and places.*[3] We should seriously ask ourselves whether Christ has an important place in our hearts. Let us pray with St Paul: *But whatever gain I had, I counted as loss for the sake of Christ. Indeed I count everything as loss because of the surpassing worth of knowing Christ Jesus my Lord. For his sake I have suffered the loss of all things, and count them as refuse, in order that I may gain Christ ...*[4]

2.2 To imitate Christ is to live his Life. Divine filiation.

Following Peter's confession, Jesus revealed to his disciples for the first time that *the Son of man must suffer many things, and be rejected by the elders and chief priests and the scribes, and be killed, and after three days rise again. And he said this plainly.*[5] These seemed very strange

---

[3] St John Paul II, *Address,* 7 January 1987
[4] Phil 3:7-8
[5] Mark 8:31-32

words to those who had witnessed so many marvels. *And Peter took him, and began to rebuke him.* The Lord thereupon addressed Peter in such a way that all might pay heed: *Get behind me, Satan!* It was with these same words that Jesus rejected the Devil's temptations in the desert.[6] Jesus will not be thwarted either by friend or foe in his determination to fulfil the Will of the Father. In today's *First Reading,* Isaiah utters his prophecy of the Passion that awaits the *Servant of the Lord*: *I gave my back to the smiters, and my cheeks to those who pulled out the beard; I hid not my face from shame and spitting.*[7]

God proved his love for mankind by sending us his Only-Begotten Son *that we may live through him.*[8] With his Death He brought us Life. Christ is the only path to the Father. As Jesus said at the Last Supper: *No one comes to the Father, but by me.*[9] Without him we can do nothing.[10] The primary concern of every Christian ought to be living the life of Christ, to become one with him as the vine is with its branches. The branch depends upon the vine for its very life. Remove the branch from the vine and it is useless, fit only for the fire.[11] The Christian's goal is to become through grace a child of God. This is the fundamental aim of Christian life: to imitate Jesus, especially in his divine filiation. Christ himself has told us as much: *I am ascending to my Father and your Father, to my God and your God.*[12]

Jesus looks to encourage us in a thousand ways through the circumstances and events of our ordinary lives.

---

[6] cf Matt 4:10
[7] Is 50:5-10
[8] 1 John 4:9
[9] John 14:6
[10] cf John 15:5
[11] cf John 15:1-6
[12] John 20:17

He wants successes and failures to bring us closer to him.
There are many times when we resist his call.

> *What have I that makes you seek my friendship?*
> *What could lead you O my Jesus,*
> *To stand at my door covered with frost,*
> *Through the dark winter nights.*
> *Oh, how hard my heart was*
> *In not opening its door to you! What strange madness*
> *That the cold ice of my ingratitude*
> *Should dry the wounds of your poor feet!*
> *How many times has my Angel told me:*
> *'Soul, look out of your window right now*
> *And you'll see how lovingly he keeps knocking!'*
> *And how many times, sovereign beauty,*
> *I answered, 'Tomorrow we will open to him,'*
> *Only to answer the very same thing the next day!*[13]

2.3 Following Christ by carrying the Cross.

*We recognize in fact that in the presence of Jesus we
cannot be satisfied with a merely human sympathy, however legitimate and valuable, nor is it sufficient to consider
him solely as a personage worthy of historical, theological,
spiritual and social interest, or as a source of artistic inspiration.*[14] Jesus Christ complicates our life in a way no
other person can. He asks us to follow him through a
complete identification of our will with his own. This is
why, following his sharp words to Peter, He told his
Apostles: *If any man would come after me, let him deny
himself and take up his cross and follow me. For whoever
would save his life will lose it; and whoever loses his life
for my sake and the gospel's will save it.*[15]

The Lord spoke openly about his Passion. He uses the

---

[13] Lope de Vega, *Sonnet to the Crucified Christ*
[14] St John Paul II, *loc cit*
[15] Mark 8:34-35

image to *take up his cross* and follow him. Pain and suffering acquire with Christ a new meaning full of love and redemptive significance. Pain allows us to accompany Christ on the cross. Suffering and contradiction purify us. Sickness, failure, ruin ... in the company of Christ these become *divine caresses* for which we should be thankful. Let us thank the Lord when times are bad and the going gets rough. He will take away the most grievously troublesome part of any adversity. Let us not abandon the cross by grumbling and moaning, complaining or giving in to sadness.

Contradictions, be they large or small, physical or moral, can be made to serve as reparation for our past faults. They can be transformed into a real contribution to the apostolate. With that attitude in mind, contradictions lose their sting. Quite contrariwise, they the more effectively dispose us to prayer, to conversation with God throughout the day. A Christian who regularly flees from sacrifice will not find Christ along his way. Nor will he find any lasting form of happiness, which is so intimately linked to love and self-denial. How many Christians end their day's work with a long face, worn out not by great contradictions but by the day's minor pinpricks, small setbacks which they failed to sanctify!

Let us tell Jesus that we want to follow him. He will help us to carry our cross with refinement. We ask him to include us among his closest disciples. *Lord, take me as I am, with my defects, with my shortcomings, but make me become as You want me to be,*[16] just as you did with St Peter!

---

[16] John Paul I, *Address,* 13 September 1978

TWENTY-FOURTH SUNDAY: YEAR C

3. THE PRODIGAL SON

3.1 The limitless mercy of God.

Have mercy on me, God, in your kindness. In your compassion blot out my offence. O wash me more and more from my guilt and cleanse me from my sin. A pure heart create for me, O God, put a steadfast spirit within me ... a humbled, contrite heart you will not spurn.[1]

The liturgy brings to our consideration once again the limitless mercy of God. This is a God who forgives and takes delight in the conversion of a single sinner. We see in the *First Reading* how Moses interceded with God on behalf of the Chosen People.[2] They had strayed from the Covenant even while Moses was conversing with God on top of Mount Sinai. Moses makes no attempt to excuse the people's sin. He relies instead on the ancient promises of the Lord and his great mercy. Many centuries later, St Paul understood his personal experience in a similar light. He wrote to Timothy these words in today's *Second Reading*: *This saying is true and worthy of acceptance, that Christ Jesus came into the world to save sinners. And I am the foremost of sinners; but I received mercy for this reason, that in me, as the foremost, Jesus Christ might display his perfect patience.*[3] We all share this same experience. God never tires of forgiving us, of helping us to come closer to him.

In the Gospel of today's Mass[4] St Luke relates Christ's

---

[1] *Responsorial Psalm,* Ps 50:3-4; 12; 19
[2] Ex 32:7-11; 13-14
[3] 1 Tim 1:15-16
[4] Luke 15:1-32

parables about divine compassion. God is overjoyed at the recovery of a single sinner. The central figure in these parables is God himself. He does everything He can to recover those of his children who have succumbed to temptation. He is the Good Shepherd who goes out in search of the lost sheep. Once He has found it, He brings it home on his shoulders since it is trembling with exhaustion, worn out as a result of its disobedience. God is represented as the woman who, having lost a drachma, lights a lamp and sweeps the house in a careful search for it. Finally, He is seen as the loving father who goes out every day to await the return of his dissolute son. He strains his eyes to see if the newest figure on the horizon is his youngest son. Clement of Alexandria has written: *God's great love for humanity is similar to the care shown by the mother-bird for the chick that has fallen from the nest. If a serpent should threaten to devour the little creature, she hovers over it, spreading her wings to protect it (cf Deut 32:11). This is how God paternally seeks out his fallen creature, curing him from his lapse, warding off the savage beast that would attack him and recovering his own. God beckons the soul to fly once again and return to the nest.*[5]

Just so, I tell you, there is joy before the angels of God over one sinner who repents. Given the prospect of such heavenly delight, how can we fail to make the most of Confession? Should we not do our utmost to bring our friends to this sacrament of mercy? There they will recover their inner peace, their joy, their transcendent dignity. The incredible mercy of God should be our greatest motivation for repentance, even when we have wandered off a great distance. Before we manage to stretch out our hand for help, God's own outstretched hand is already extended towards us.

---

[5] Clement of Alexandria, *Protrepticus,* 10

3.2 Dignity restored.

Sin, so clearly described in the behaviour of the prodigal son, consists in rebellion against God, or at least in indifference or forgetfulness of him and his love.[6] This reckless desire to live apart from God is symbolized by the escape to a *distant country. This 'flight from God' causes the person to be in a state of deep confusion about his own identity, as well as a bitter experience of impoverishment and desperation; the prodigal son, the parable tells us, after all this, began to find himself in dire need, and he hired himself out as a servant – he who was born in freedom – to one of the local citizens.*[7] How terrible it is to be far from God! St Augustine poses this poignant question: *When will one find goodness without Christ? When will a person find evil with him?*[8]

The parable of the prodigal son is an invitation for us to meditate upon God's great love for us. When the younger son at long last makes the decision to return to his home as a labourer, his father runs out to meet him on the road. The father showers on his humbled son many tokens of love. *But while he was yet at a distance, his father saw him and had compassion, and ran and embraced him and kissed him.* He wastes no time in welcoming the prodigal back as truly his son. *That's what the sacred text says: he covered him with kisses. Can you put it more humanly than that? Can you describe more graphically the paternal love of God for men?*

When God runs toward us, we cannot keep silent, but with St Paul we exclaim: 'Abba, Pater': Father, my Father!, for, though he is the creator of the universe, he doesn't mind our not using high-sounding titles, nor worry about our not acknowledging his greatness. He wants us to call

---

[6] St John Paul II, *Homily,* 17 September 1989
[7] *ibid*
[8] St Augustine, *Commentary on St John's Gospel,* 51, 11

him Father; he wants us to savour that word, our souls filling with joy.[9] Father, my Father, we have called upon you so many times and you have filled us with your peace and consolation ...

Up until this moment the father has not said a word. Now he is filled with joy. He does not lay conditions on his son. He has no wish to dwell upon the past. He is already thinking of the future. He wants to restore right away his son's lost dignity. This is why he does not even allow him to finish his apology. *Bring quickly the best robe, and put it on him; and put a ring on his hand, and shoes on his feet; and bring the fatted calf and kill it, and let us eat and make merry; for this my son was dead, and is alive again; he was lost, and is found.* The best robe would make his son the guest of honour. The ring would symbolize the restoration of a loved and respected son's dignity. The shoes would show him to be a free man.[10] *This love is able to reach down to every prodigal son, to every human misery, and above all to every form of moral misery, to sin. When this happens, the person who is the object of mercy does not feel humiliated, but rather found again and 'restored to value'.*[11]

In the sacrament of Confession the Lord acts through the priest to restore us to grace and to the dignity of sons of God. Christ instituted this sacrament so that we might return over and over again to the father's house. The Lord fills us with his grace and, if our repentance is genuine and sincere, places us even higher in his favour than we have previously been. *Our Father God, when we come to him repentant, draws, from our wretchedness, treasure; from our weakness, strength. What then will he prepare for us, if*

---

[9] St. J. Escrivá, *Christ is passing by,* 64
[10] cf St Augustine, *Sermon 11,* 7
[11] St John Paul II, Encyclical, *Dives in misericordia,* 30 November 1980, 6

*we don't forsake him, if we go to him daily, if we talk
lovingly to him and confirm our love with deeds, if we go to
him for everything, trusting in his almighty power and
mercy? If the return of a son who had betrayed him is
enough for him to prepare a banquet, what will he have in
store for us, who have tried to remain always at his side?*[12]

3.3 To serve God is a great honour.

And they began to make merry ... With this reconciliation of father and son, it would seem that the parable has
ended. Yet at this moment the Lord chooses to introduce a
new character into the story. He is the elder son. *Now his
elder son was in the field; and as he came and drew near
to the house, he heard music and dancing. And he called
one of the servants and asked what this meant.* The servant
said to him: *Your brother has come, and your father has
killed the fatted calf, because he has received him safe and
sound.* His brother had returned home!

But he was angry and refused to go in. St Augustine
comments: *Are you not moved by the celebration in the
father's house? The banquet with the fatted calf, has this
not given you pause? No one will exclude you from the
banquet. All is for nought, however. The elder son becomes
furious and will not go in.*[13] In his fit of pique, he reveals
his deepest motivation: *Lo, these many years I have served
you, and I never disobeyed your command; yet you never
gave me a kid, that I might make merry with my friends.
But when this son of yours came, who has devoured your
living with harlots, you killed for him the fatted calf!*

The Father is God. He always has his arms outstretched, being full of mercy. The younger son is the image of
the sinner who converts to God. And the elder son? He is
the worker who has laboured in the fields, but without joy.

---

[12] St. J. Escrivá, *Friends of God,* 309
[13] St Augustine, *Sermon 11,* 10

He has served because he had to serve. Over the course of time, his heart has grown cold. His sense of charity has evaporated. His brother has become *this son of yours*. What a striking contrast there is between the magnanimity of the father and the meanness of the elder son! Serving God and enjoying his friendship should be a continual feast. *To serve is to reign.*[14] The elder son represents those who forget that serving God is a tremendous honour. In the act of service is to be found a good measure of the compensation. *'Omnia bona mea tua sunt': Son, you are always with me, and all that is mine is yours. Therefore, all honour and glory are ours if we are really of God.*[15] God himself will give us of his riches. What more can we ask for?

Each one must do as he has made up his mind, not reluctantly or under compulsion, for God loves a cheerful giver.[16] There are always many reasons for us to celebrate if we truly live in the presence of God. We have a special opportunity to be magnanimous in our dealings with those closest to us. *How sweet a joy it is to think that God is just; that, in other words, He makes allowances for our weaknesses and understands perfectly the frailty of our humanity. So what have I to be afraid of? If God, who is perfectly just, shows such mercy in forgiving the prodigal son, must He not also be just to me 'who am always with Him'?*[17]

---

[14] cf Second Vatican Council, *Lumen gentium*, 36
[15] St Augustine, *Sermon 11*, 13
[16] 2 Cor 9:7
[17] St Therese of Lisieux, *Autobiography of a Soul*, 8

TWENTY-FOURTH WEEK: MONDAY

4. THE FAITH OF THE CENTURION

4.1 Humility, the prerequisite to belief.

We may speculate that the scene narrated in today's Gospel took place in the late afternoon. Having finished his preaching for the day, Our Lord was entering the town of Capharnaum. Two elders of the Jewish community approached Jesus on behalf of a Roman centurion with a sick servant who *was dear* to him.[1] This Gentile officer is presented to us as a man of great virtue. He is someone who knows how to lead others. *I say to one, 'Go,' and he goes; and to another, 'Come,' and he comes.* At the same time he has a great heart. He knows how to care for those around him, like this sick servant of his. He is a generous man. He does everything in his power to help his servant. He himself had built the local synagogue though not himself a Jew. The elders point out to Jesus: *He is worthy to have you do this for him, for he loves our nation.*

Above all, the most striking characteristic of this centurion is his humility. When Jesus had already started out for the centurion's house, the centurion sent a messenger saying: *Lord, do not trouble yourself, for I am not worthy to have you come under my roof; therefore I did not presume to come to you. But say the word, and let my servant be healed.*

This faith and humility take Jesus by surprise. *When Jesus heard this he marvelled at him, and turned and said to the multitude that followed him, 'I tell you, not even in Israel have I found such faith'.*

---

[1] Luke 7:1-10

Humility is the prerequisite to belief, to coming close to Christ. This virtue is the narrow road that leads to faith and to growth in the supernatural life. Humility allows us to understand Jesus. In his commentary on this passage, St Augustine notes that humility served as the door through which the Lord would enter into the life of this just man.[2] Today let us ask the Lord for a true humility which will lead us closer to Christ. *You told me, in confidence, that in your prayer you would open your heart to God with these words: 'I think of my wretchedness, which seems to be on the increase despite the graces you give me. It must be due to my failure to correspond. I know that I am completely unprepared for the enterprise you are asking of me. And when I read in the newspapers of so very many highly qualified and respected men, with formidable talents, and no lack of financial resources, speaking, writing, organizing in defence of your kingdom ... I look at myself, and see that I'm a nobody: ignorant, poor: so little, in a word. This would fill me with shame if I did not know that you want me to be so. But Lord Jesus, you know how gladly I have put my ambition at your feet ... To have Faith and Love, to be loving, believing, suffering. In these things I do want to be rich and learned: but no more rich or learned than you, in your limitless Mercy, have wanted me to be. I desire to put all my prestige and honour into fulfilling your most just and most lovable Will'.*[3]

4.2 To grow in faith.

I tell you, not even in Israel have I found such faith. What an incredible compliment! How much Our Lord must have been delighted for him to utter these words! Let us meditate today on the quality of our own faith, asking Jesus to grant us the grace for it to increase day by day.

---

[2] cf St Augustine, *Sermon 46,* 12
[3] St. J. Escrivá, *The Forge,* 822

St Augustine gave this definition of faith: *Deo credere, Deum credere, in Deum credere.*[4] *Deo credere* means: to believe that what God says is true ...; thus we also believe a man, whereas we do not believe 'in' a man. *Deum credere* means: to believe that He is God. *In Deum credere* means: believingly to love, believingly to go to Him, believingly to cling to Him and be joined to His Members. Progress in faith is to believe in these three aspects. To believe in God we need to have a serious desire for doctrinal formation. How is our effort to understand God and his Revelation going? How is our interest in our *spiritual reading*? How is our attendance and participation in means of formation such as retreats? Our longing to know God better is also manifested in our loyalty to revealed truth as proclaimed by the Church.

To believe in God we have to grow in our personal friendship with him. We have to deal with God on a daily basis in loving prayer. We should meet him in daily Mass. We should find him in our successes and our failures. Believing in God leads us to see him close up in our daily life.[5]

To believe God himself is the crowning of the other two aspects. This is the love which brings with it the true Faith. *Lord, I believe in you and I love you. I speak with you like a friend, not a stranger. It is impossible to get to know you and not end up loving you. He that loves you knows that he has to struggle to identify with your Will.*[6]

4.3 Humility is indispensable for perseverance.

And when those who had been sent returned to the house, they found the slave well. All of the miracles worked by Jesus were manifestations of his loving and

---

[4] St Augustine, *Sermon 144, 2*
[5] cf P. Rodriguez, *Faith and life of Faith,* Pamplona 1974
[6] *ibid*

merciful heart. He never performed a miracle that hurt anyone. Nor did he ever work a miracle for its own sake. We see him suffering hunger and he does not ask for bread. At Jacob's Well he is thirsty and he asks the Samaritan woman to give him to drink.[7] When Herod asks for a sign, he keeps silence. The purpose of the miracles is that people will believe in him, *that they may believe that thou didst send me.*[8] He transforms the corporal works of mercy into means of spiritual growth. This is the reason why the curing of the servant had the effect of bringing the centurion closer to the Lord. We might suppose that he was one of the first Gentiles to seek baptism after the feast of Pentecost.

Our faith unites us to Christ the Redeemer with his dominion over all creation. It gives us a security greater than any human activity can provide. Yet to have this faith we need the humility of that centurion. We need to see ourselves as nothing before Jesus. We resolve always to follow his lead, no matter what our feelings may be.

St Augustine stated that all the gifts of God could be reduced to this: *Receive the Faith and persevere in it to the end of your life.*[9] Humility will teach us to beware of our inherent weakness. The true obstacle to faith is pride. *God resists the proud, but gives grace to the humble.*[10] We have to ask often for humility.

We find in Our Lady the perfect synthesis of faith and humility. Her cousin Elizabeth, moved by the Holy Spirit, greets Mary with these words: *Blessed is she who believed.* Similarly inspired, Mary responds with her *Magnificat*: *My soul magnifies the Lord, and my spirit rejoices in God my Saviour; for he has regarded the low estate of his*

---

[7] cf John 4:7
[8] John 11:42
[9] St Augustine, *On the gift of perseverance,* 17, 47; 50, 641
[10] Jas 4:6

handmaiden. For behold, henceforth all generations will call me blessed. Mary does not take credit for this divine favour. God has seen her great humility and has decided to fill her with grace.[11] Let us go to Mary so that she may teach us how to grow in humility, which is the best foundation for our faith. *The Handmaid of the Lord is today the Queen of the Universe. 'Whoever humbles himself shall be exalted' (Matt 23:12). If we give ourselves to the service of God without condition, we will be elevated to great heights. We will partake of the intimate life of God. We will be 'like gods' as we follow the road of humility and docility to the Will of God.*[12]

---

[11] cf Luke 1:45 ff
[12] A. Orozco, *Looking to Mary,* Madrid 1981

5. RETURNED TO LIFE

5.1 Going to the most merciful Heart of Jesus with all our material and moral petitions.

Jesus was approaching a small town called Naim.[1] With him were his disciples and a large crowd. At the entrance to Naim, they met a funeral procession. A widow was to bury her only son. Perhaps Jesus and his followers waited by the side of the road for the procession to pass. It was then that Jesus noticed the bereaved mother. *And when the Lord saw her, he had compassion on her.* The Evangelists are accustomed to point out Christ's reactions to suffering. On another occasion St Matthew writes of Jesus: *When he saw the crowds, he had compassion for them, because they were harassed and helpless, like sheep without a shepherd.*[2] When a leper with great faith implores the Lord's help, *moved with pity, he stretched out his hand* and cured him.[3] Before the great crowd that has no food, he tells his disciples: *I have compassion on the crowd.* He thereupon multiplied the loaves and the fishes.[4] In response to the insistent cries of two blind men, *Jesus in pity touched their eyes* and they received their sight.[5]

Mercy is *proper to God,* according to St Thomas Aquinas.[6] Mercy has its most perfect manifestation in Jesus Christ. *Especially through his life-style and through his*

---

[1] cf Luke 7:11-17
[2] Matt 9:36
[3] Mark 1:41
[4] Mark 8:2
[5] Matt 20:34
[6] St Thomas, *Summa Theologiae,* 2-2, q. 30, a. 4

actions, Jesus revealed that love is present in the world in which we live – an effective love, a love that addresses itself to man and embraces everything that makes up his humanity. This love makes itself particularly noticed in contact with suffering, injustice and poverty – in contact with the whole historical 'human condition', which in various ways manifests man's limitation and frailty, both physical and moral.[7] The Gospels should inspire us to rely on the merciful Heart of Jesus in our every physical and moral petition. He awaits our loving plea.

Hear my prayer, O Lord; let my cry come to thee! Do not hide thy face from me in the day of my distress! Incline thy ear to me; answer me speedily in the day when I call! This prayer is read by priests today in the *Liturgy of the Hours.*[8] The Lord hears our every word. He is there to help us immediately.

5.2 The mercy of the Church.

Seeing the widow of Naim, Jesus *had compassion on her and said to her, 'Do not weep.' And he came and touched the bier, and the bearers stood still. And he said, 'Young man, I say to you, arise.' And the dead man sat up, and began to speak. And he gave him to his mother.*

Many Fathers of the Church have seen in the widow of Naim an image of the Church, inasmuch as she welcomes home sinners through the merciful intercession of Christ. The Church is a Mother *who intercedes for each one of her children like the widow for her only son.*[9] St Augustine comments that she *rejoices every day at the conversion of sinners. The 'only son' had been dead according to the flesh, but these sinners had been dead according to the spirit.*[10] If

---

[7] St John Paul II, Encyclical, *Dives in misericordia,* 30 November 1980, 3
[8] *Liturgy of the Hours,* Ps 102:1-2
[9] St Ambrose, *Commentary on St Luke's Gospel,* V, 92
[10] St Augustine, *Sermon 98,* 2

the Lord is moved by a crowd which is hungry, how much more will He be moved to assist someone who has a spiritual affliction?

The Church lives an authentic life when she professes and proclaims mercy – the most stupendous attribute of the Creator and of the Redeemer – and when she brings people close to the sources of the Saviour's mercy, of which she is the trustee and dispenser.[11] This mission is realized when she leads people to *conscious and mature participation in the Eucharist and the Sacrament of Penance or Reconciliation. The Eucharist brings us ever nearer to that love which is more powerful than death ... It is the Sacrament of Penance or Reconciliation that prepares the way for each individual, even those weighed down with great faults. In this sacrament each person can experience mercy in a unique way, that is, the love which is more powerful than sin.*[12]

Christ is present in today's world. He continues to *have compassion on the crowd.* He is most concerned about those individuals who are weighed down by the burden of their sins. He says to all: *Follow me ...* He invites us to throw off the weight of sin. Through the sacrament of Confession, he cures the wounds caused by sin with his great mercy. This sacrament has been made for us because of the likelihood of our many falls. It is the sacrament of divine patience. This is where our Father God awaits the return of his prodigal children.

How well do we appreciate this sacrament of mercy which Christ has given us? It not only frees us from sin, but also strengthens us for our interior struggle.

5.3 Divine mercy as revealed in the Sacrament of pardon. Conditions for a good confession.

The mercy of God is limitless. *Also infinite therefore*

---

[11] St John Paul II, Encyclical, *Dives in misericordia,* 13
[12] *ibid*

and inexhaustible is the Father's readiness to receive the prodigal children who return to his home. Infinite are the readiness and power of forgiveness which flow continually from the marvellous value of the sacrifice of the Son. No human sin can prevail over this power or even limit it. On the part of man only a lack of good will can limit it, a lack of readiness to be converted and to repent, in other words persistence in obstinacy, opposing grace and truth.[13] We ourselves are the only ones who can get in the way of the efficacy of this divine medicine.

As we grow in our knowledge of and adherence to the Lord, we grow in our desire for interior purification. We need to avoid routine in our confessions, filling them with the sorrow of love. We should approach each confession as if it were our last confession. Let us recall those five conditions for a good confession which we probably learned in childhood. First should come our *examination of conscience,* to make a thorough review of our sins and bad habits. Second should come *sorrow for sins,* so as to be truly contrite. Third, we should have a *true purpose of amendment,* so that we can seriously resolve to sin no more. Fourth, there has to be *confession of our sins,* to seek Christ's pardon in a personal encounter. Fifth is *to do penance,* to fulfil the penance imposed by the confessor. This penance is not merely a work of piety. It serves as an act of reparation and satisfaction for the sins committed.

We should make sure to go to Confession frequently. In this way, we will avoid any separation from the Lord, even in little things. Let us ask the help of Our Lady, *Refuge of sinners,* that we may constantly improve the quality of our confessions. We should think also of the splendid work of mercy involved in bringing a friend, relative or colleague to this Sacrament and to a renewal of supernatural life.

---

[13] *ibid*

6. SPEAKING WELL OF OTHERS

6.1 The gift of speech comes to us from God. It should not be used in a bad way.

By making reference to the behaviour of local children, Jesus responds to those who were twisting the meaning of his teaching: *They are like children sitting in the market place and calling to one another, 'We piped to you, and you did not dance; we wailed, and you did not weep'*. He then goes on to speak of how John the Baptist was treated. *For John the Baptist has come eating no bread and drinking no wine; and you say, 'He has a demon.' The Son of man has come eating and drinking; and you say, 'Behold, a glutton and a drunkard, a friend of tax collectors and sinners!'*[1] *The baptist's fasting they interpret as the work of the devil; whereas they accuse Jesus of being a glutton. The evangelist has to report these calumnies and accusations spoken against our Lord; otherwise, we would have no notion of the extent of the malice of those who show such furious opposition to him who went about doing good.*[2]

Divine wisdom is manifested in different ways by John and Jesus. John prepared the way for the Lord through his life of penance. Jesus, perfect God and perfect man, is the realization of the Promise. St John Chrysostom comments: *Through both roads one reaches the Kingdom of Heaven.*[3] The Lord concludes his commentary on public opinion with these words: *Yet wisdom is justified by all her*

---

[1] Luke 7:31-35
[2] cf *The Navarre Bible,* note to Matt 11:16-19
[3] St John Chrysostom, *Homilies on St Matthew's Gospel,* 37, 4

children. Many of the Pharisees and Doctors of the Law proved unable to discover the wisdom facing them. Instead of singing the praises of the long-awaited Messiah, they speak ill of him and maliciously distort his words. Their eyes can not see the wonders in front of them. Their hearts are closed to God. How different is their reaction from that of the simple people who seem so eager to celebrate the Messiah's arrival! Our Lord does not allow any public demonstrations of his importance until the eve of the Passion. *As he was now drawing near, at the descent of the Mount of Olives, the whole multitude of the disciples began to rejoice and to praise God with a loud voice for all the mighty works that they had seen, saying, 'Blessed is the King who comes in the name of the Lord! Peace in heaven and glory in the highest!* [4] When some of the Pharisees asked Jesus to silence his disciples, Jesus responded: *I tell you, if these were silent, the very stones would cry out.*

The gift of speech comes from the hands of God. It should be used to sing his praises and to speak well of others. It should never be used to do harm. *Acquire the habit of speaking about everyone and about everything they do in a friendly manner, especially when you are speaking of those who labour in God's service. Whenever that is not possible, keep quiet. Sharp or irritated comment may border on gossip or slander.* [5]

6.2 Imitating Christ in his friendly conversation with others. Our speech should strengthen and console our neighbour.

Jesus enjoyed the company of his disciples. He *found solace in conversation; to ascertain this, you have only to read in St John the confidences disclosed to his disciples during the Last Supper. Jesus often made conversation the*

---

[4] Luke 19:37-38
[5] St. J. Escrivá, *Furrow,* 902

vehicle of his apostolate: He spoke as they walked along the roads, as He strolled under the arches of Solomon's Temple; He spoke in houses, with people around him – like Mary, seated at His feet, like John, who rested his head against the Lord's bosom.[6] He never refused to speak to anyone. We need but recall the cases of Nicodemus who came by night, the Samaritan woman at Jacob's Well, and the 'good thief' on Calvary. Jesus opens his arms to everyone. He has words of comfort for all who seek him with a sincere heart. We should imitate Our Lord in this regard. Perhaps we need to overcome a tendency to say things without due consideration. This is a great opportunity to do battle with egoism, a contest that yields immediate benefits to those who live with us.

Our speech should be at the service of the good – to console those who suffer; to teach those who are ignorant; to correct in a courteous manner those who are in the wrong; to strengthen those who are weak. Holy Scripture reminds us that *the tongue of the wise is health.*[7] We can use our speech to show the right path to those who may have strayed from the truth. A Spanish author has written some wise words on this theme: *Once while travelling with some friends in the Pyrenees, we became lost about the middle of the day ... We were surrounded by howling winds when all of a sudden we heard the clanging of cow-bells in the distance. We discerned a mare grazing on a bit of grass. We set out in that direction with hopes of securing assistance ... There we found a man who seemed to be made of rock. We asked him for directions and he pointed the way, saying, 'That waterway ...' The wind was so terrific that we could not make out anything else. Those two words were all we could hear because of the force of the wind ... The 'waterway' was the road formed by the*

---

[6] A. Luciani, *Illustrissimi*, pp. 214-215
[7] Prov 12:18

melting waters. It was not just any stream or canal, but 'that waterway.' Do you get my point? This is what I mean by communication.[8] *I also find that, in conversing, I am enriched. To hold firm convictions, in fact, is a beautiful thing; to hold them in such a way that you can communicate them and see them shared and appreciated is even more beautiful.*[9]

There are many people in our lives who are victims of their own pessimism, ignorance and lack of purpose. Our words can lead them to the path of joy, peace and the realization of their proper vocation. It is along *that waterway* that they will find the Lord.

6.3 Directing our conversation to the good of others. Never speaking badly of anyone.

Speech is *one of the most precious talents ever bestowed on men by God, a most beautiful gift for the expression of deep thoughts of love and friendship towards the Lord and his creatures.*[10] We should not use this gift in an inconsiderate or frivolous way. We should always keep in mind the warning of St James that *the tongue is a fire, the very world of iniquity.*[11] The damage it does can come from useless arguments, sarcasm, calumnies, etc. How many friendships have been ruined by tongues out of control!

Jesus took care in what he said to other people. *I tell you, on the day of judgment men will render account for every careless word they utter.*[12] Idle words spring from an impoverished spirit. An unwillingness to control one's speech is a clear symptom of spiritual lukewarmness. *The*

---

[8] J. Maragall, *Praise to the word,* Madrid 1970

[9] A. Luciani, *op cit,* p. 214

[10] St. J. Escrivá, *Friends of God,* 298

[11] Jas 3:6

[12] Matt 12:36

*good man out of his good treasure brings forth good; and
the evil man out of his evil treasure brings forth evil.*[13]

Our Lord will judge us on how we have used his gifts.
*After seeing how many people waste their lives (without a
break: gab, gab, gab – and with all the consequences!), I
can better appreciate how necessary and lovable silence is.
And I can well understand, Lord, why you will make us
account for every idle word.*[14] The road from sarcasm to
calumny is all too short. It is difficult to control one's
tongue if one is not trying to live in the presence of God.
The Christian ought never to be found saying anything bad
about anybody. On the contrary, the Christian should act
like Christ, who *went about doing good.*[15] Part of this
doing good is speaking well of others. This behaviour
should reach into the simplest details such as our manner
of greeting others. Our attitude should be: What a joy it is
to have met you on my way!

---

[13] Matt 12:35
[14] St. J. Escrivá, *The Way,* 447
[15] Acts 10:38

7. RECEIVING JESUS WELL

7.1 A Pharisee invites Jesus for a meal.

Today's Gospel shows Jesus going to dinner at the home of a wealthy Pharisee named Simon.[1] When the banquet has already begun, suddenly a woman comes into the room. This woman is publicly known to be a sinner. Here we have another example of the greatness of Christ's Heart. Despite her many faults, this woman will be understood and pardoned by Christ. We may wonder whether she has already listened to him preach. Her resolution to sin no more has now come to fruition. Her love for Christ has given her the daring to interrupt the banquet, contrary to all the Jewish customs of the time. Surely those attending the meal will be shocked and taken aback by this unexpected arrival. The woman becomes the centre of attention. Maybe this is why there is no regret for the lack of hospitality that has been shown to the Master.

Yet Jesus is aware of the slight offered him by his host. The Lord says that he has noticed the absence of the normal tokens of welcome, just as he had missed the gratitude of the nine lepers who failed to thank him for their cure. The bad manners of Simon are in marked contrast to the behaviour of the public sinner. Having *brought an alabaster flask of ointment, and standing behind him at his feet, weeping, she began to wet his feet with her tears, and wiped them with the hair of her head, and kissed his feet, and anointed them with the ointment.*

In the face of the negative feelings of those present at

---

[1] Luke 7:36-50

the meal, Jesus deliberately moves to reveal the supernatural lesson to be derived from the incident. *Then turning toward the woman he said to Simon: 'Do you see this woman? I entered your house, you gave me no water for my feet, but she has wet my feet with tears and has wiped them with her hair. You gave me no kiss, but from the time I came in she has not ceased to kiss my feet. You did not anoint my head with oil, but she has anointed my feet with ointment'.* Jesus now proclaims the reward for her loving service: *Therefore I tell you, her sins, which are many, are forgiven, for she loved much.* Then follow those few words which are of such consolation to us sinners: *But he who is forgiven little, loves little.* Our daily falls can, with God's grace, be a means of bringing us closer to Christ.

He then addresses the woman: *Your sins are forgiven.* And the woman leaves the scene with great joy, a clean soul and a new life.

7.2 The Lord comes to our soul.

When Jesus reproaches Simon for his lack of hospitality, there is a trace of sadness in his words: *I entered your house, you gave me no water for my feet.* We are reminded of how Jesus was disappointed by the lepers who failed to give thanks for their cure.[2] The Lord is prepared to undergo any suffering and humiliation for our salvation. Yet how he misses the details of respect involved in common courtesy. How well do we ourselves receive the Lord in our reception of Holy Communion?

To illustrate this point, a catechism teacher often used the following example. He would tell his young charges that whenever a famous person stays somewhere overnight, people like to hang some kind of plaque or memorial. For

---

[2] cf Luke 17:17-18

example, *Cervantes lived here* or *Pope 'X' slept here*. This is why every Christian who has received Holy Communion should imagine himself wearing the sign, *Jesus Christ stayed here.*[3]

If we want, we can have the Lord in our house each and every day. *O Godhead hid, devoutly I adore thee ...*[4] We greet Christ into our souls with these words. We try to give Christ a better reception than we would give to the most important person on earth. We do not wish to incur his reproach: *I entered your house, you gave me no water for my feet ...* You have not given me your heart and your soul. You have your attention focused on other things. *We should receive Our Lord in the Eucharist as we would prepare to receive the great ones of the earth, or even better: with decorations, with lights, with new clothes ... And if you ask me what sort of cleanliness I mean, what decorations and what lights you should bring, I will answer you: cleanliness in each one of your senses, decoration in each of your powers, light in all your soul.*[5] Let us resolve today to receive the Lord the best we can.

Have we ever thought about how we would behave if we could only receive him once in a lifetime? St Josemaría Escrivá once recalled: *When I was a child, frequent communion was still not a widespread practice. I remember how people used to prepare to go to communion. Everything had to be just right, body and soul: the best clothes, hair well-combed – even physical cleanliness was important – maybe even a few drops of cologne ... These were manifestations of love, full of finesse and refinement, on the part of manly souls who knew how to repay Love with love.*[6]

---

[3] cf C. Ortuzar, *The Catechism illustrated with examples*
[4] Hymn, *Adoro te devote*
[5] St. J. Escrivá, *The Forge*, 834
[6] St. J. Escrivá, *Christ is passing by*, 91

7.3 Preparation for Communion.

St John of the Cross preached about preparation for Communion using this analogy: *How joyful would a man become if he were to be told, 'The king is coming to stay in your house and show you his favour!' I believe that he would not be able to eat or sleep at all. He would be constantly thinking about his preparations for the royal visit. Brothers and sisters, I say to you on behalf of the Lord God that he wants to come into your souls and establish his kingdom of peace.*[7] This is great news! It should fill us with joy.

Christ himself, He who reigns in glory from Heaven, wants to be sacramentally present in our soul. *He comes in love, receive him with love.*[8] True love presupposes desires for purification. This means going to Confession when necessary.

Jesus greatly desires to be with us. He repeats to every Christian his memorable words at the Last Supper: *I have earnestly desired to eat this passover with you ...*[9] The inn he wants to stay at is the soul of each individual. The inn has to be in very good shape, very clean. Nothing could be more gratifying than to have Jesus accept accommodation in our soul. He comes to us with love, therefore with love we should receive him.*[10] This is the most important moment of our day! The angels are full of wonder at our blessed opportunity to receive Jesus. As the moment approaches, we should be fostering greater and greater acts of love.

Alongside our spiritual preparations we should also be attentive to physical details such as the fast which the

---

[7] St John of Avila, *Sermon 2 for the Third Sunday of Advent,* vol. II, p. 59
[8] St John of Avila, *Sermon 41, in the octave leading to Corpus Christi,* vol. II, p. 654
[9] Luke 22:15
[10] St John of Avila, *loc cit*

Church has imposed as a sign of respect and reverence, our posture at Mass and our dress, all of which express our dignity as children of the Father. When Jesus has entered our heart, we speak to him:

> *O loving Pelican! O Jesu Lord!*
> *Unclean I am but cleanse me in Thy Blood;*
> *Of which a single drop, for sinners spilt,*
> *Can purge the entire world from all its guilt.*
>
> *Jesu! whom for the present veiled I see,*
> *Whom I so I thirst for, oh, vouchsafe to me:*
> *That I may see Thy countenance unfolding,*
> *And may be blest Thy glory in beholding. Amen.*[11]

Our Blessed Mother will teach us how to give her Son a good reception. No other creature has taken better care of Jesus than she, or can receive him more graciously, or with such love.

---

[11] Hymn, *Adoro te devote*

TWENTY-FOURTH WEEK: FRIDAY

8. SERVING JESUS

8.1 The holy women of the Gospels.

Soon afterward he went on through cities and villages, preaching and bringing the good news of the kingdom of God. And the twelve were with him, and also some women who had been healed of evil spirits and infirmities: Mary, called Magdalene, from whom seven demons had gone out, and Joanna, the wife of Chuza, Herod's steward, and Susanna, and many others, who provided for them out of their means. [1]

St Luke tells us in today's Gospel of the work of these holy women who made such an important contribution to the Lord's public life. It is impressive that the Lord wanted to rely on their generosity. We can only imagine how the Lord would return such great kindness! During the hours of the Passion it seems as if these women proved to be more faithful to Jesus than the Apostles themselves, with the exception of John. The holy women were present at the foot of the Cross. They heard Christ's last words to mankind. When Christ was brought down from the Cross, these women were already planning for his embalming on the first day of the week, following the sabbath rest.

The Lord made a point of first appearing to these women on the morning of his Resurrection, instead of going straight to his disciples. The women were the only ones to see the angels. John and Peter verified that the tomb was empty, but they did not see any angels. Perhaps the women were favoured with this visit because they were

---
[1] Luke 8:1-3

better prepared than the men to receive it. The women also shared in the angel's mission of nurturing the faith of the nascent Church. *From the beginning of Christ's mission, women show to him and to his mystery a special sensitivity which is characteristic of their femininity. It must also be said that this is especially confirmed in the Paschal Mystery, not only at the Cross but also at the dawn of the Resurrection.*[2] The holy women were very conscientious about telling the disciples whatever happened, while never failing to remind the disciples of the content of Christ's message. They are present at the final appearances of the Resurrected Lord. Without a doubt, the sisters of Lazarus were in attendance from Bethany on, along with Mary, the Mother of Jesus.[3]

The example of these holy women should be an inspiration for every Christian to serve the Lord without conditions. Our attitude has to be to serve the Lord and others with supernatural spirit, not expecting any reward for our generosity. We should serve even that person who probably will not thank us. Every action we do on behalf of others ought to be thought of as a direct service for Christ. *Truly, I say to you, as you did it to one of the least of these my brethren, you did it to me.*[4] How many opportunities to serve the Lord come before us every day! *Serviam!* I will serve you, my Lord, all the days of my life. Help me to persevere in this intention.

8.2 Serving the Lord according to our given nature. The contribution of women to the life of the Church and society.

If any one serves me, he must follow me; and where I

---

[2] St John Paul II, Apostolic Letter, *Mulieris dignitatem,* 15 August 1988, 16
[3] cf Indart, *Jesus in his world,* Barcelona 1963
[4] Matt 25:40

*am, there shall my servant be also; if any one serves me,
the Father will honour him.*[5]

In the history of the Church, even from earliest times,
there were side by side with men a number of women, for
whom the response of the Bride to the Bridegroom's
redemptive love acquired full expressive force. First we see
those women who had personally encountered Christ and
followed him. After his departure, together with the
Apostles, they 'devoted themselves to prayer' in the Upper
Room in Jerusalem until the day of Pentecost. On that day
the Holy Spirit spoke through 'the sons and daughters' of
the People of God, thus fulfilling the words of the prophet
Joel (cf Acts 2:17). These women, and others afterwards,
played an active and important role in the life of the early
Church, in building up from its foundations the first
Christian community – and subsequent communities –
through their own charisms and their varied service.[6]

We would do well to recall that Christianity began in
Europe because of the apostolate of one dedicated woman
named Lydia.[7] She initiated the conversion of a continent
from the confines of her home. Something similar occurred
with regard to the Samaritans. It was the Samaritan woman
who brought the first news of the Redeemer to her
kinsfolk.[8] At that time the Apostles themselves were
probably a little afraid of preaching to these people, of
telling them that the Messiah was at Jacob's Well.
Throughout the centuries the Church has been mindful of
the profound importance of women to Christianity as
mother, wife and sister in the propagation of the Faith. The
apostolic writings provide ample testimony of women who
made great sacrifices for the Church: Lydia of Philippi,

---

[5] John 12:26
[6] St John Paul II, *loc cit,* 27
[7] cf Acts 16:14-15
[8] cf John 4:39

Priscilla and Chloe of Corinth, Phoebe of Cenchreae, the mother of Rufus who cared for Paul as if he were her own son, the daughters of Philip of Caesarea, etc.

Every Christian is called to serve the Lord according to his or her nature and qualities. *Women are called to bring to the family, to society and to the Church their gentle warmth and untiring generosity, their love for detail, their quick-wittedness and intuition, their simple and deep piety, their constancy ...*[9] The Church is counting on the contribution of women to restore society's awareness of the dignity of the person. *The Church is constantly enriched by the witness of the many women who fulfil their vocation to holiness. Holy women are an incarnation of the feminine ideal; they are also a model for all Christians, a model of the 'sequela Christi', an example of how the bride must respond with love to the love of the Bridegroom.*[10]

The Lord wants everyone to serve him, the Church and society, with all the talents at our disposal. Then we will come to understand the wisdom of that truth: *To serve is to reign.*[11]

8.3 Giving ourselves to the service of others.

Man, who is the only creature on earth which God willed for itself, cannot fully find himself except through a sincere gift of himself.[12] St John Paul II applied these words of the Second Vatican Council to the identity of woman: *Woman can find herself only by giving love to others.*[13] It is in love, in giving, in service to others that people realize their dignity. Perhaps this is particularly true

---

[9] *Conversations with Monsignor Escrivá,* 87

[10] St John Paul II, *loc cit,* 27

[11] cf Second Vatican Council, *Lumen gentium,* 36

[12] Second Vatican Council, *Gaudium et spes,* 24

[13] St John Paul II, *loc cit,* 30

for women when they live out their vocation to holiness. *To fulfil this mission, a woman has to develop her own personality and not let herself be carried away by a naive desire to imitate which, as a rule, would tend to put her in an inferior position and leave her unique qualities unfulfilled. If she is a mature person, with a character and mind of her own, she will indeed accomplish the mission to which she feels called, whatever it may be. Her life and work will be really constructive, fruitful and full of meaning, whether she spends the day dedicated to her husband and children or whether, having given up the idea of marriage for a noble reason, she has given herself fully to other tasks.*

Each woman in her own sphere of life, if she is faithful to her divine and human vocation can and, in fact, does achieve the fullness of her feminine personality. Let us remember that Mary, Mother of God and Mother of men, is not only a model but also a proof of the transcendental value of an apparently unimportant life.[14]

As we consider the generosity and fidelity of these holy women, let us examine our own lives as Christians. Are we making a serious effort to extend the Reign of Christ? If we are truly generous, our lives will be filled with God's peace. Let us remember that the holy women spent a lot of time in the company of Our Lady. They were closer to Mary than even the disciples were. Here we have the secret of being generous with Our Lord. We go to Mary to help us be faithful souls with a keen sense of detachment. Next to our devotion to Mary, we will find plenty of occasions to serve others. In this way we will surely forget about ourselves.

---

[14] *Conversations with Monsignor Escrivá, loc cit*

9. THE GOOD GROUND

9.1 Hearts which have become hardened due to a lack of contrition are incapable of receiving the divine word.

A great crowd came together and people from town after town came to him.[1] Jesus took advantage of this opportunity to teach people about the mysterious action of grace on souls. Since his audience was made up largely of farmers, Jesus used an agricultural parable. *A sower went out to sow his seed* ... The sower is Christ himself. He works all the time to extend his kingdom of peace and love in souls. In this effort, he depends on the freedom and personal response of each person. God can be found in souls in the most diverse circumstances, as diverse as the types of soil on a farm. *And as he sowed, some seed fell along the path, and was trodden under foot, and the birds of the air devoured it.* The seed was completely lost without having given any fruit. Later on, Jesus explained to his disciples the parable and the reason for this loss: *The devil comes and takes away the word from their hearts.* Hearts which have become hardened through a lack of contrition are incapable of receiving the divine word. This bad ground represents *the heart which has become accustomed to unclean thoughts, so 'parched' as it were that it cannot receive and sustain the seed.*[2] The devil finds in souls of this kind a source of resistance to God's saving grace.

On the other hand, a soul which reacts to imperfections

---

[1] Luke 8:4-15
[2] St Gregory the Great, *Homilies on the Gospels, in loc.*

and transgressions by sincere repentance actually attracts divine mercy. True humility allows God to sow his seed and have it bear abundant fruit. This is why we should use this parable to examine our spirit of reparation for the falls of every day, even in the least serious things. Do we go to Confession frequently and with a sincere yearning for divine assistance?

Let us ask Jesus to help us to avoid any and all sin, to keep away from whatever might separate us from his friendship. *You have reached a level of real intimacy with this God of ours, who is so close to you, so deeply lodged in your soul. But what are you doing to increase and deepen this intimacy? Are you careful not to allow silly little hindrances to creep in which would upset this friendship? Show courage! Don't refuse to break with every single thing, no matter how small, which could cause suffering to the One who loves you so much.*[3]

9.2 Our need for prayer and sacrifice if grace is to bear fruit in the soul.

And some fell on the rock; and as it grew up, it withered away, because it had no moisture. This signifies those who, *when they hear the word, receive it with joy; but these have no root, they believe for a while and in time of temptation fall away.* At 'the moment of truth' they succumb because their allegiance to Christ has been rooted solely in feeling and not in prayer. They have therefore been unable to endure difficult moments unscathed, or take in their stride the trials of life and periods of spiritual dryness. *Many people are pleased by what they hear, and sincerely resolve to pursue the good. Yet when adversity and suffering come, they soon abandon their good works.*[4] How many good resolutions have come to nought when the

---

[3] St. J. Escrivá, *The Forge,* 417
[4] St Gregory the Great, *op cit,* 15, 2

spiritual life has become a struggle! These souls were seeking themselves rather than God. As St Augustine pointed out, *Some act for one reason. Others act for another. The fact is that few look for Jesus for the sake of Jesus.*[5] To look for Jesus is to follow his footsteps wherever they may lead, no matter if the trail is smooth and easy or uphill and arduous. The key thing is to have the firm desire to reach Christ, to *look for Jesus for the sake of Jesus.* We can accomplish this only if we are faithful to our daily prayer, whether it comes to us easily or is more of a sacrifice.

And some fell among thorns; and the thorns grew with it and choked it. This represents those people who, having heard the word of God, are *choked by the cares and riches and pleasures of life.* It is impossible to follow Christ unless we lead a life of mortification. If we don't, little by little the attractions of the world will overcome the things of God. In the end, the soul abandons the spiritual struggle for the sake of worldly things. St Basil has written: *Do not be surprised that Jesus calls the pleasures of the world 'thorns.' No matter where thorns catch us, they always bloody our hands. So too the pleasures of the world harm the feet, hands, head and eyes ... When a person has his heart set on temporal things, he deadens the acuteness of his sensitivity and weakens reason ...*[6]

Prayer and mortification prepare the soul to receive the divine seed and then give fruit. Without these means, life remains sterile. *The system, the method, the procedure, the only way to have a life abundant and fertile in supernatural fruits, is to follow the Holy Spirit's advice, which comes to us via the Acts of the Apostles: 'omnes erant perseverantes unanimiter in oratione' – all these with one accord devoted themselves to prayer. Nothing can be done*

---

[5] St Augustine, *Commentary on St John's Gospel*, 25, 10
[6] St Basil, *Homily on St Luke*, 3, 12

without prayer![7] All roads that lead to God have to pass through prayer and sacrifice.

9.3 Prayer and perseverance: beginning again with humility.

Jesus first describes the circumstances that will result in failure before going on to the promise of the good ground. He does not allow himself to be disappointed, however, but fosters the hope that everyone might eventually become good ground.[8] *And some fell into good soil and grew, and yielded a hundredfold ... They are those who, hearing the word, hold it fast in an honest and good heart, and bring forth fruit with patience.*

All are capable of giving abundant fruits to the Lord, regardless of their past history. God is always sowing the seed of his grace. *The most important thing is not to become like a much-trodden path, like outcrop rock, like thistles .... We have to become good ground ... The heart cannot be fair game for birds and passers-by. It has to provide enough ground for the seed to take root. The sun of human passions and a dissolute life should not scorch the seedlings of divine promise.*[9]

There are three prerequisites for our becoming good ground: to listen with a contrite and humble heart, to be earnest in prayer and mortification, and, finally, to be disposed to begin and begin again in the interior struggle. We cannot let ourselves become discouraged if the fruits of our struggle are not readily apparent, even after many years of effort.

A new heart I will give you, and a new spirit I will put within you; and I will take out of your flesh the heart of

---

[7] St. J. Escrivá, *op cit,* 297
[8] St John Chrysostom, *Homilies on St Matthew's Gospel,* 44
[9] St Augustine, *Sermon 101,* 3

stone and give you a heart of flesh.[10] This passage comes from today's reading in the *Liturgy of the Hours*. If we are willing to change our ways, the Lord is more than willing to transform us into 'good ground.' He will bring this about in the deepest recesses of our being. The grace of God is all-powerful. The crucial thing is to return again and again to his side. St Augustine teaches: *God is a farmer, and if he abandons man, man becomes a desert. Man is also a farmer and if he leaves God, he turns himself into a desert as well.*[11] Let us resolve never to become separated from the Lord. We have to go to his merciful Heart many times during the day.

---

[10] *Liturgy of the Hours, Lauds,* Ez 36:26
[11] St Augustine, *Commentary on Psalm 145,* 11

TWENTY-FIFTH SUNDAY: YEAR A

10. THE LORD'S VINEYARD

10.1 The plans of the Lord. The honour of working in his vineyard.

There are times in the life of all of us when God grants special graces to help us find him. The imminent return of the Chosen People from exile was one such moment of divine intervention.

Many of the Jews seemed content with the idea of simply seeing the Holy City of Jerusalem once again. That is where they placed their hope and joy. But God wanted more from his people. He wanted them to leave behind their attachment to sin through a conversion of heart. God speaks through his prophet Isaiah in today's *First Reading* of the Mass: *For my thoughts are not your thoughts, neither are your ways my ways, says the Lord. For as the heavens are higher than the earth, so are my ways higher than your ways and my thoughts than your thoughts.*[1] How many times have our expectations fallen short of the wonderful plans which God has prepared for us!

In the liturgy of today's Mass the Church reminds us of the mystery of God's wisdom which is intimately united to his redemptive mission: *I am the salvation of the people, says the Lord. Should they cry to me in any distress, I will hear them, and I will be their Lord for ever.*[2] Today's Gospel from St Matthew concerns the parable of the vineyard.[3]

---

[1] Is 55:6-9
[2] *Entrance Antiphon*
[3] Matt 20:1-16

Working in the vineyard is symbolic of the Lord's salvific will. *For the kingdom of heaven is like a householder who went out early in the morning to hire labourers for his vineyard.* He promised to pay the workers one denarius a day. He sent them off into the vineyard. As the day wore on, the householder went out to hire more workers. He even hired people at the eleventh hour. When day was done, the first workers expected to be paid more than the last group which had been hired. When everyone got the same pay, the first workers complained to the householder, who replied: *Friend, I am doing you no wrong; did you not agree with me for a denarius? Take what belongs to you, and go; I choose to give to this last as I give to you. Am I not allowed to do what I choose with what belongs to me?*

The Lord does not mean this parable to be a strict lesson in labour relations. He wants us to understand that his grace is a pure gift. Whoever is called to follow Christ as a youth does not thereby enjoy precedence over someone called during maturity or in life's final moments. People who are near death should not think it is too late to follow Our Lord. The day's wages for every person is God's grace. That gift will always be infinitely greater than whatever anyone has done in life. The greatness of God's plans for us is always superior to our short-range, human designs.

Although we have been called by the Lord at different hours of the day, we should be one in our spirit of thanksgiving. The call to work in the vineyard is an immense honour. St Bernard affirms: *Each one can find reasons to thank God in his life. We should feel particularly moved to thank God because he has called us to serve him and him alone.*[4]

---

[4] St Bernard, *Sermon 2 for the Sixth Sunday after Pentecost,* I

10.2 There is work for everyone in the vineyard of the Lord.

Go you also into the vineyard. Among the many problems facing the world, there is one that stands out from the rest, namely, how few people there are who really know Christ on a personal basis. Many people live and die without even knowing the fact that Christ has brought salvation to the world. There are many people who will or will not find Christ because of our example. *Since the work that awaits everyone in the vineyard of the Lord is so great, there is no place for idleness. With even greater urgency the 'householder' repeats his invitation: 'You go into the vineyard too'.*[5] How can we remain indifferent when so many people do not know the Lord? St Gregory the Great exhorts us: *Each one should examine themselves to see how energetically they are working in the vineyard of the divine Sower. Perhaps we have not dedicated everything we have to the service of the Lord. The people who really work for him ... are those who are anxious to win souls and bring others to the vineyard.*[6]

There is room for everyone in the vineyard of the Lord: young and old, rich and poor, men and women, be they in the prime of life or in their sunset years, whether they have time to spare or no time at all ... The Second Vatican Council pointed out that *children too have an apostolate of their own. In their own measure they are true living witnesses of Christ among their companions.*[7] Sick people are also called to the apostolate. *On all Christians, accordingly, rests the noble obligation of working to bring all men throughout the whole world to hear and accept the divine message of salvation.*[8]

---

[5] St John Paul II, Apostolic Exhortation, *Christifideles laici,* 30 December 1988, 3

[6] St Gregory the Great, *Homilies on the Gospels,* 19, 2

[7] Second Vatican Council, *Apostolicam actuositatem,* 12

[8] *ibid,* 3

No one who has crossed our path in this life should be able to say that he was not encouraged, by our example and word, to love Christ more. None of our friends, none of our relatives, should be able to say at the end of their lives that that they had no one who was concerned about them.

10.3 Positive meaning of the circumstances in which we find ourselves.

In commenting on this parable,[9] St John Paul II wrote that the urgency of this call has increased since the days of the Second Vatican Council.[10] He emphatically states: *This then, is the vineyard; this is the field in which the faithful are called to fulfil their mission. Jesus wants them, as he wants all his disciples, to be the 'salt of the earth' and the 'light of the world' (cf Matt 5:13-14).*

The Lord is not interested in useless complaining which shows a lack of faith. Nor does he want us to have a negative or pessimistic outlook on the people and circumstances around us. *This is the vineyard; this is the field* where the Lord wants us to work, inserted into the middle of the world. It is in our very own family and no other that we have to become saints. Likewise, it is in our job that we meet God and introduce others to him. This is the vineyard. We must not wait for imaginary 'better opportunities.' We have the graces necessary to do an effective apostolate wherever we are. This fact should be the basis for our optimism. *God calls me and sends me forth as a labourer in his vineyard. He calls me and sends me forth to work for the coming of his Kingdom in history. This personal vocation and mission defines the dignity and the responsibility of each member of the lay faithful and makes up the focal point of the whole work of formation, whose purpose is the joyous and grateful recognition of this dignity and*

---

[9] cf St John Paul II, *loc cit*, 3

[10] cf Second Vatican Council, *Gaudium et spes*

the faithful and generous living-out of this responsibility.

In fact, from eternity God has thought of us and has loved us as unique individuals. Every one of us he called by name, as the Good Shepherd *'calls his sheep by name'* (John 10:3). However, only in the unfolding of the history of our lives and its events is the eternal plan of God revealed to each of us. Therefore, it is a gradual process; in a certain sense, one that happens day by day.[11] God gives us special graces so that our circumstances can be an occasion for loving him more and doing a genuine apostolate.

In the *Second Reading* of today's Mass, St Paul tells the Christians of Philippi: *I am caught in this dilemma: I want to be gone and be with Christ, which would be very much the better, but for me to stay alive in this body is a more urgent need for your sake.*[12] How great was Paul's longing for Christ! Paul writes from prison. He suffers because of people who out of jealously want to undermine his apostolic work. Nevertheless, all this does not take away his peace. He continues to work in the vineyard of the Lord with the means at his disposal. We ought to throw off pessimism and sadness whenever we are disappointed in the apostolate. *Don't let discouragement enter into your apostolate. You haven't failed, just as Christ didn't fail on the Cross. Take courage! ... Keep going, against the tide, protected by Mary's Immaculate and Motherly Heart: 'Sancta Maria, refugium nostrum et virtus'!, you are my refuge and my strength.*

Hold your peace. Be calm ... God has very few friends on earth. Don't yearn to leave this world. Don't shy away from the burden of the days, even though at times we find them very long.[13]

---

[11] St John Paul II, *loc cit,* 58
[12] Phil 1:20-24; 27
[13] St. J. Escrivá, *The Way of the Cross,* Thirteenth Station, 3

TWENTY-FIFTH SUNDAY: YEAR B

11. THE MOST IMPORTANT OF ALL

11.1 To command is to serve.

The *First Reading* for today's Mass concerns the sufferings of the children of God who are unjustly persecuted because of their upright behaviour. *Let us lie in wait for the righteous man, because he is inconvenient to us and opposes our actions; he reproaches us for sins against the law, and accuses us of sins against our training. He professes to have knowledge of God, and calls himself a child of the Lord. He became to us a reproof of our thoughts; the very sight of him is a burden to us ... Let us test him with insult and torture, that we may find out how gentle he is, and make trial of his forbearance. Let us condemn him to a shameful death, for, according to what he says, he will be protected.*[1] The liturgy applies this description of the *righteous man* to Jesus Christ. He was condemned to a most brutal chastisement and an *ignominious death.*

St Mark tells us in today's Gospel of how Jesus strove to prepare his disciples for his impending death and resurrection. As they were passing through Galilee, He spoke to them in very clear terms: *The Son of man will be delivered into the hands of men, and they will kill him; and when he is killed, after three days he will rise.*[2] The Lord's disciples were dismayed by this news, for they were dreaming of an earthly kingdom. *But they did not understand the saying, and they were afraid to ask him.*

---

[1] Wis 2:12-20
[2] Mark 9:29-36

Despite the Master's warning, the disciples continued to debate the make-up of their future regime and *who was the greatest.* Upon their arrival at Capharnaum, Jesus asked them, *What were you discussing on the way?* Perhaps more than a little ashamed, they fell silent. *And he sat down and called the twelve; and he said to them, 'If anyone would be first, he must be last of all and servant of all'.* To better illustrate this teaching, *He took a child, and put him in the midst of them; and taking him in his arms, he said to them, 'Whoever receives one such child in my name receives me; and whoever receives me, receives not me but him who sent me'.*

The Lord wants everyone who exercises authority to realize that theirs is a work of service. *To demonstrate to his Apostles the obligation and humility needed in their ministry, he takes a child in his arms and explains the meaning of this gesture: if we receive for Christ's sake those who have little importance in the world's eyes, it is as if we are embracing Christ himself and the Father who sent him. This little child whom Jesus embraces represents every child in the world, and everyone who is needy, helpless, poor or sick – people who are not naturally attractive.*[3]

11.2 Love for Christ is the basis for all authority and obedience in the Church.

In this Gospel passage, the Lord wants to teach *the Twelve* how they are to govern the Church. He shows them that to exercise authority is an act of service. The word *authority* proceeds from the Latin word *auctor,* that is to say, the author, promoter, or source of something.[4] It suggests the function of one who watches over the interests

---

[3] *The Navarre Bible,* note to Mark 9:36-37
[4] cf J. Corominas, *Spanish and Castillian Critical Etymological Dictionary,* Madrid 1987

or development of a social grouping. As a consequence, authority and obedience are not to be understood as contradictory concepts. In the Church they both have their origin in the same love for Christ. One commands for the love of Christ, while the other obeys for the love of Christ.

Authority is necessary for every society, and in the case of the Church it has been willed expressly by the Lord. When authority is absent in society, or when authority is abused, damage is done to the members. If the purpose of the group is essential to the welfare of its members, then such harm can prove quite serious. *There is a great love of comfort, and at times a great irresponsibility, hidden behind the attitude of those in authority who flee from the sorrow of correcting, making the excuse that they want to avoid the suffering of others.*

They may perhaps save themselves some discomfort in this life. But they are gambling with eternal happiness – the eternal happiness of others as well as their own – by these omissions of theirs. These omissions are real sins.[5]

In the Church, authority has to be exercised as Christ exercised it, as one who did not come to be served, but to serve: *non veni ministrari sed ministrare.*[6] His service to humanity is directed toward salvation, since he came for all *to give his life as a ransom for many.*[7] The Lord said these words in response to a situation much like the one described in today's Gospel. Jesus told his Apostles on that occasion: *You know that the rulers of the Gentiles lord it over them, and their great men exercise authority over them. It shall not be so among you; but whoever would be great among you must be your servant, and whoever would be first among you must be your slave.*[8] The Apostles were

---

[5] St. J. Escrivá, *The Forge,* 577
[6] Matt 20:28
[7] *ibid*
[8] Matt 20:24-27

just beginning to understand the Master's teaching. They
would come to understand it fully after the coming of the
Holy Spirit at Pentecost. Years later, St Peter would write
to the bishops that they were obliged to care for the flock
entrusted to them by God. They were not to dominate
people, but, instead, to serve by example.[9] St Paul too
would affirm that, since he was not under anyone's
particular authority, he would be the servant of all so as to
win all.[10] The *higher* one is in the Church hierarchy, the
greater is one's obligation to serve others. This truth is
reflected in the title which has long been reserved for the
Roman Pontiff: *Servus servorum Dei,* the servant of the
servants of God.[11]

Let us pray that the Church will always be blessed
with good shepherds who know to serve all, especially
those in greatest need. The shepherds of the Church must
know *how to combine all the qualities of a father of a
family with the loving intuition of a mother who treats each
of her children in a different way, according to their needs.*[12]

We should pray every day for the Roman Pontiff, for
the bishops, for priests, for whoever has been set in
authority over us, for those who depend on our good
example. This prayer will greatly please Our Lord.

11.3 Authority in the Church is a great blessing. To obey as Christ did.

When a person exercises authority in imitation of
Christ, then that person truly serves. Jesus taught us that
service means obedience. He became *obedient unto death,
even death on a cross.*[13] This is the context for how we

---

[9] cf 1 Pet 5:1-3
[10] cf 1 Cor 9:19 ff; 2 Cor 4:5
[11] C. Burke, *Authority and Freedom in the Church,* p. 114
[12] Bl. A. del Portillo, *On Priesthood,* p. 18
[13] Phil 2:8

should understand authority. Authority is a good. Authority in the Church is more than a good; it is a blessing. Without authority, the Church could not possibly exist according to the desire of her Founder.

A community of people realize that they cannot achieve their common goals except under the guidance and coordination of some authority. Authority itself is regarded as a task of service. People look to authority. If it is lacking they set it up. The tendency to accept authority within the community is not the product of a servile or a collectivized mentality. It is precisely the natural tendency of each individual reflective conscience. Each one, because he wants to belong to that particular community with its concrete goals, freely and personally looks to the common authority. His tendency is to accept it. He would only resist authority if he felt it was no longer serving the common good. To resist it simply because it seems to be contrary to his personal interests would show a loss of sense of community; an individualistic and selfish approach that would estrange him from the community, putting what he regards as his own personal good above the common good...

Ordinary life provides countless examples of this tendency of community to seek authority: from social or sports clubs to trade-unions, to professional associations; down to the spontaneous on the spot organization that emerges once a group of boys comes together for a football game.[14]

We should look upon authority in the Church with eyes of faith. Christ himself comes to meet us in the instructions we are given by ecclesiastical authorities.

The great enemy of authority and community is self-love. This is something which we all suffer from. It is our shared inheritance of Original Sin. We have to be humble.

---

[14] C. Burke, *op cit*, p. 117

A proud person will seek any excuse to avoid obedience. Let us resolve to obey God's commands wholeheartedly and cheerfully. *Nowadays the world we live in is full of disobedience and gossip, of intrigue and conspiracy. So, more than ever we have to love obedience, sincerity, loyalty and simplicity: and our love of all these will have a supernatural significance, which will make us more human.*[15]

Let us conclude this meditation by going to the protection of our holy Mother Mary. She was the one who wanted to be *the handmaiden of the Lord, 'ancilla Domini'.*[16] She will teach us the full meaning of that glorious Christian motto: *to serve is to reign.*[17]

---

[15] St. J. Escrivá, *op cit,* 530
[16] Luke 1:38
[17] cf Second Vatican Council, *Lumen gentium,* 36

Twenty-Fifth Sunday: Year C

12. THE SONS OF LIGHT

12.1 The parable of the unfaithful steward.

The Prophet Amos thunders against the exploitation of the poor by ruthless profiteers in the *First Reading* of today's Mass.[1] These immoral merchants despise the needy and make money off of them. They tamper with the scales and sell defective goods. They raise prices by taking advantage of shortages ... Through their unscrupulous behaviour, they insure their own.

In the Gospel of the Mass, the Lord tells the parable of the unjust steward who is forced to give an accounting to his master.[2] The cunning steward thinks to himself, *What shall I do, since my master is taking the stewardship away from me? I am not strong enough to dig, and I am ashamed to beg. I have decided what to do, so that people may receive me into their houses when I am put out of the stewardship.* The steward calls in his master's debtors and awards each one of them favourable settlements. To the first debtor he says, *How much do you owe my master?* He replies, *A hundred measures of oil.* The steward responds, *Take your bill, and sit down quickly and write fifty.* Then the steward asks another debtor, *And how much do you owe?* He answers, *A hundred measures of wheat.* The steward tells him, *Take your bill, and write eighty.*

When the owner discovers what his steward had done, he wryly commends this shrewd behaviour. And Jesus, perhaps with a tinge of sadness, adds, *The sons of this*

---

[1] cf Amos 8:4-7
[2] Luke 16:1-13

world are wiser in their own generation than the sons of light. The Lord does not mean to praise the dishonesty of this administrator who prepared for his future security. *Why did the Lord propose this parable?* asks St Augustine, *Not because that servant was a model for us to imitate. Nonetheless, the worldly-wise steward had an eye to the future. So too should the Christian have this determination to secure his eternal reward. If not, the steward puts him to shame.*[3] The Master praised the quick-wittedness, the decisiveness, the shrewdness, the firm resolve of the steward who made the most of a difficult situation. He did not give in to discouragement.

We are well accustomed to seeing people make unbelievable sacrifices in order to improve their *life-style* or standard of living. At times we may be taken aback by the lengths people will go to acquire more wealth, power or fame. The media frequently trains a spotlight on ambitious people and their accomplishments. Well, we Christians must put the same amount of zeal into the service of God. This undertaking has both a material and a spiritual dimension. In the material realm, our society should manifest an authentic concern for the needs of the poor that is shown in education, just remuneration, meaningful social security benefits and programmes directed for the public welfare. In the spiritual realm, we have to make a heroic effort to win Heaven. *What zeal men put into their earthly affairs! Dreaming of honours, striving for riches, bent on sensuality! Men and women, rich and poor, old and middle-aged and young and even children: all of them alike.*

When you and I put the same zeal into the affairs of our soul, then we'll have a living and working faith. And there will be no obstacle that we cannot overcome in our apostolic works.[4]

---

[3] St Augustine, *Sermon 359*, 9-11
[4] St. J. Escrivá, *The Way*, 317

12.2 Making full use of our resources for the service of God.

At times, it seems as if the children of this world are more resolute in the pursuit of their goals than we Christians. They live as if there existed only what is here below, and they single-mindedly focus their attention on that end. The Lord wants us to put ourselves entirely into his concerns – personal sanctity and apostolate – with at least the same determination as that with which others engage in worldly concerns. Jesus wants us to have a real interest in his things. This is the only objective that is truly worthwhile. No ideal is comparable to that of serving Christ, of using the talents we have been given as means to that everlasting goodness.

At the conclusion of the parable the Lord reminds us of an ineluctable fact: *No servant can serve two masters; for either he will hate the one and love the other, or he will be devoted to the one and despise the other. You cannot serve God and mammon.* We have only one Lord. We must serve him with all our heart, with the natural gifts He himself has given us, using every licit means throughout our entire life. We must direct everything toward him: our work, our plans, our leisure, without holding anything back. The coherent Christian does not devote one part of his attention to God and another to the business of this world. He must convert both into the service of God and neighbour by struggling to have rectitude of intention, by living the virtues of justice and charity.

In order to be a good steward of the talents he has received, the Christian must know how to prudently direct his actions towards the promotion of the common good. He should initiate or collaborate in enterprises focussed on the service of others. Surely, this kind of activity is worth more than the most flourishing and 'profitable' business. It is the laity *who must contend with those issues that relate to the*

Church's presence in the world: education, the defence of life, the protection of the environment, the protection of religious liberty, the effective witness of the Christian message in the media. The lay faithful ought to play their full role as citizens in all the legitimate avenues of social development. Christians should make their voices heard. And they should make their just rights prevail.[5]

We cannot allow money to become our god, or let the objective of our life become the accumulation of the greatest number of goods and the highest level of comfort. God calls us to the most transcendent destiny. We need to work *with renewed enthusiasm and energy to remake what has been destroyed by the culture of hedonism and materialism. Let us give new life to those remnants of Christian culture which still remain. The challenge, however, is not just to invigorate the roots. In many instances, in all too many environments, the challenge is to begin from scratch, practically from zero. This explains why we can speak today of our being engaged in a 'new' Evangelization.*[6] St John Paul II has summarized this challenge with these stirring words: *Humanity is loved by God! This very simple yet profound proclamation is owed to humanity by the Church. Each Christian's words and life must make this proclamation resound.*[7] The Master has said it already: *if only we children of the light were to put at least as much effort and obstinacy into doing good as the children of darkness put into their activities!*

Don't complain. Work instead to drown evil in an abundance of good.[8]

---

[5] Cardinal A. Suquía, *Address to Spanish Episcopal Conference*, 19 February 1990

[6] *ibid*

[7] St John Paul II, Apostolic Exhortation, *Christifideles laici*, 30 December 1988, 34

[8] St. J. Escrivá, *The Forge*, 848

12.3 Human and supernatural means.

Although it is grace that converts hearts, the Lord wants us to use human means in the apostolate. St Thomas Aquinas teaches[9] that it would be tempting God if we omitted to do what we could and expected everything to be done by him. This principle certainly applies to the apostolate, where the Lord expects from his disciples a wise, effective and complete cooperation. We are not inert instruments. Together with the supernatural means, the *children of light* must also apply their human capacity, their ingenuity and their zeal to the work of winning a soul for Christ. Without a doubt, in the apostolic works of formation and teaching we will need material means, just as our Lord himself told the disciples: *When I sent you out with no purse or bag or sandals, did you lack anything?* They replied, *Nothing.* Then Jesus said, *But now, let him who has a purse take it, and likewise a bag. And let him who has no sword sell his mantle and buy one.*[10] There were many occasions when Jesus chose to use earthly means such as a few pieces of bread and some fish, a handful of clay, the goods provided by several pious women ...

Clearly, the apostolic mission exceeds our own ability and the capacity of any human means. Therefore, we will not put to one side, as if they were secondary, the supernatural means. We have not placed our trust in our personal talents and energy, or in any of the other means which support an apostolic enterprise. Our hope rests on divine grace. We can rest assured that God will perform incredible miracles with inadequate means. Let us believe in the power of his grace and never become daunted by apparently insurmountable obstacles. *Don't let the lack of*

---

[9] St Thomas, *Summa Theologiae*, 2-2, q. 53, a. 1 ad 1
[10] Luke 22:35-37

'instruments' stop your work. Begin as well as you can.[11] Let us ask Jesus to give us whatever we lack.

I was amused by your vehemence. Faced by the lack of material resources to set to work, and with no one to help you, you said: 'I have only two arms, but I sometimes feel impatient enough to become a monster with fifty arms to sow and reap the harvest'.

Ask the Holy Spirit for that effectiveness, for he will grant it to you![12]

---

[11] cf St. J. Escrivá, *The Way*, 488
[12] *idem, Furrow*, 616

13. THE LIGHT UPON THE LAMPSTAND

13.1 Christians have to give light to their surroundings.

In today's Gospel, the Lord speaks to us about our apostolic responsibility: *No one after lighting a lamp covers it with a vessel, or puts it under a bed, but puts it on a stand, that those who enter may see the light.*[1]

Whoever follows Christ – whoever lights up a lamp – not only has to work for his own sanctification, but also for that of others. The Lord illustrates this duty by using images which were readily understandable to the ordinary people who listened to him. In every house the lamp gives light when darkness falls. Everyone knows where it is normally placed and why: the lamp is there to illuminate. For that reason, it may be placed quite high. Perhaps it would hang from a hook. It would not occur to anyone to hide their lamp so that its light would be obscured. What purpose would that serve?

Jesus said to his disciples: *You are the light of the world.*[2] The light of the disciple is a reflection of the light of the Master himself. In the absence of this light of Christ, society becomes engulfed in the most impenetrable darkness. When one walks in darkness, one soon stumbles and falls. Without Christ, the world is a perilous minefield that is barely inhabitable.

Christians are to illuminate the environment in which they live and work. A follower of Christ necessarily gives light. If he did not do so, he would be like a lamp hidden

---

[1] Luke 8:16-18
[2] Matt 5:14

beneath a vessel. The Second Vatican Council emphasized the faithful's right and duty to do apostolate. This responsibility originates in the Sacrament of Baptism and is reaffirmed at Confirmation.[3] As a consequence, each and every Christian belongs to the Mystical Body of Christ. *Between the members of this body there exists, further, such a unity and solidarity (cf Eph 4:16) that a member who does not work at the growth of the body to the extent of his possibilities must be considered useless both to the Church and to himself.*[4]

The apostolate is manifested in many different forms. It is a continuous action somewhat comparable to the constant flow of light from a lamp. It is neither a flashing light nor an oscillating light. It is on all the time. *The very witness of a Christian life, and good works done in a supernatural spirit, are effective in drawing men to the faith and to God.*[5] In addition, those who still do not believe in Christ can see their own way illuminated by the example of those who follow the Master. *All Christians by the example of their lives and the witness of the word, wherever they live, have an obligation to manifest the 'new man' which they put on in Baptism, and to reveal the power of the Holy Spirit by whom they were strengthened at Confirmation, so that others, seeing their good works, might glorify the Father (cf Matt 5:16) and more perfectly perceive the true meaning of human life and the universal solidarity of mankind.*[6]

Let us ask ourselves today about our effect on those who live side by side with us, those who have dealings with us for professional or social reasons. Do they see this light which illumines the way that leads to God? Do these

---

[3] cf Second Vatican Council, *Lumen gentium,* 33

[4] *idem, Apostolicam actuositatem,* 2

[5] *ibid,* 6

[6] *idem, Ad gentes,* 11

same people feel themselves moved, by their contact with us, to lead better lives?

13.2 Professional prestige.

What is the lamp from which the light of Christ may shine forth into our environment? It is our top quality work and the professional prestige that comes with it. For what good would the apostolate be of a mother who did not conscientiously care for her family? How can a student who does not study speak about human and supernatural virtues to his friends? How can a Catholic businessman who does not practice the Church's social doctrine talk about high ideals with his employees? If a Christian were to ignore the practice of the human virtues, his life would be nothing but wishful thinking. Apparently pious but nonetheless sterile desires in the realm of personal sanctity can have little positive influence on other people.

Yet Christ and his Church command us to have a real impact on the world around us. Consequently, *every Christian should make Christ present among men. He ought to act in such a way that those who know him sense 'the fragrance of Christ' (cf 2 Cor 2:15). Men should be able to recognize the Master in his disciples.*[7] Following Jesus Christ means that religious principles should be actualized in ordinary life. A Christian should not only be different, but should be seen to be different. The sick person can give light if he bears his own infirmity with a supernatural sense. The Lord wants the Catholic pharmacist to be knowledgeable and perfectly competent with the medicines he sells, and equally, when it is necessary, He expects that he will know how to give good human and supernatural advice. Similarly, the taxi driver should be thoroughly familiar with the streets of a big city,

---

[7] St. J. Escrivá, *Christ is passing by,* 105

the bus driver should show his concern for his passengers by driving carefully ...

From the very first moments of his public life, the Lord was known as *the carpenter, the son of Mary.*[8] At the time of his miracles the people exclaim, *He has done all things well;*[9] and *all things* means absolutely everything: *not only the great miracles, but also the little everyday things that didn't dazzle anyone, but which Christ perform-ed with the accomplishment of one who is 'perfectus Deus, perfectus homo' (Athanasian Creed), perfect God and perfect man.*[10] As a sign of his respect for human work, Jesus frequently used examples from the most varied occupations in his teaching. *It can indeed be said that he looks with love upon human work and the different forms that it takes, seeing each one of these forms a particular facet of man's likeness with God, the Creator and Father.*[11]

If we are to have professional prestige, we must aim at mastering our occupation or craft or profession. We need to dedicate the necessary time for learning, for practice or study, by setting goals in order to perform better in our chosen avocation each day, even after we have completed our formal course of study or training. More often than not, the student's report card will be a good indicator of his love of God and neighbour: *Deeds are love.*

As a logical consequence of this commitment, the faithful Christian will be respected by his colleagues as a good worker or a good student. This kind of reputation is indispensable for anyone who wants to carry out a serious apostolate in the middle of the world.[12] Almost without

---

[8] Mark 6:3
[9] Mark 7:37
[10] St. J. Escrivá, *Friends of God,* 56
[11] St John Paul II, Encyclical, *Laborem exercens,* 14 September 1981, 26
[12] cf Second Vatican Council, *Lumen gentium,* 36

realizing it, he or she will show how the doctrine of Christ can become a reality in ordinary life. This fact bears out something which was pointed out by St Ambrose many centuries ago, namely, that things appear less difficult to us once we see them done by others.[13] Everyone has a right to this good example from us.

13.3 Beacons in the middle of the world.

It is a truth of our Faith that Christ's message has not been spread by human means, but under the impulse of divine grace. However, it is also true that a meaningful and lasting apostolate must needs be founded on people who embody the human virtues. Otherwise, people would be repulsed by the disparity between what Christians practice and what Christians preach. The Second Vatican Council has declared in this regard: *One of the gravest errors of our time is the dichotomy between the faith which many profess and the practice of their daily lives ... The Christian who shirks his temporal duties shirks his duties towards his neighbour, neglects God himself, and endangers his eternal salvation. Let Christians follow the example of Christ who worked as a craftsman; let them be proud of the opportunity to carry out their earthly activity in such a way as to integrate human, domestic, professional, scientific and technical enterprises with religious values, under whose supreme direction all things are ordered to the glory of God.*[14]

Whatever one's profession or occupation may be, the more expertise we acquire, the more we will be respected by our colleagues and companions. This professional standing is of such vital importance that a good Christian should not conceal his high competence and should not avoid the recognition which is his due. For those who are

---

[13] cf St Ambrose, *Treatise on Virginity*, 2, 2
[14] Second Vatican Council, *Gaudium et spes*, 43

determined to live their Christian vocation seriously, work is a paramount obligation. Therefore, the well respected doctor will not abandon his efforts to keep abreast of new scientific and clinical developments. The good teacher will be sure to periodically revise his teaching materials and techniques. He cannot become satisfied with repeating the same old lectures year after year.

Our competence and our unity of life will be a beacon that sheds its light on colleagues, friends, and perhaps our whole community. Then Christian charity will be visible from a distance with the light of sound doctrine illuminating everyone's way. *The sanctification of ordinary work is, as it were, the hinge of true spirituality for people who, like us, have decided to come close to God while being at the same time fully involved in temporal affairs.*[15]

St Paul exhorted the first Christians at Philippi to be faithful *in the midst of a crooked and perverse generation, among whom you shine as lights in the world.*[16] Their heroic example drew so many people to the Faith that an early Christian writer concluded: *What the soul is for the body, the Christians are in the midst of the world.*[17]

If we are to bring the light of Christ to all, together with the supernatural means we have to practice the human virtues and the social graces. Many people practice good manners only because they make business dealings run more smoothly. For us Christians they also have to be the fruit of charity, external manifestations of a genuine interest in other people. This conduct is another aspect of the divine light we must carry with us and transmit to others. We have many opportunities to live these social graces with the people whom God has put by our side.

---

[15] St. J. Escrivá, *Friends of God,* 61
[16] Phil 2:15
[17] Diognetus, *Epistle,* VI, 1

14. THE SILENCE OF MARY

14.1 The Virgin pondered in her heart the events of her life.

How often we have wished that the Gospels would tell us more about the life of Our Lady and the things that she said! Love makes us want to know more about our Mother in Heaven. Nevertheless, God has seen fit to reveal only what we need to know of Our Lady's life here on earth. It is in this context that the Magisterium of the Church progressively reveals to us the pivotal role which Mary has played in salvation history.

Our Lady's silence in history corresponds to her silence as an ordinary female inhabitant of Palestine. The Virgin did not reveal the mystery of the Incarnation to her cousin Elizabeth. At the moment of the Visitation, Elizabeth discovered the secret thanks to divine inspiration. Nor did Our Lady reveal her secret to Joseph. It was an angel in a dream who told Joseph the news. When the Messiah was born in Bethlehem, Mary also kept silent. The shepherds found out about this central event in human history from angelic messengers. *And when they saw it they made known the saying which had been told them concerning this child; and all who heard it wondered at what the shepherds told them.*[1] When Joseph and Mary took the child to the Temple for the Presentation, they did not give advance notice about Jesus to Simeon or to Anna, the prophetess. They went simply as one more married couple with their first-born son. Later on, during their

---

[1] Luke 2:17-18

residence in Egypt and then Nazareth, Mary told no one
about the divine mystery which fulfilled the historic
yearnings of the Chosen People. She said nothing about it
to her parents or neighbours. Mary *kept all these things in
her heart.*[2] As a consequence of her discretion, people
sometimes reacted to Jesus in the manner of Nathaniel who
quipped, *Can anything good come out of Nazareth?*[3] *The
Virgin did not seek, as you and I do, the glory men give to
one another. It is enough for her to know that God knows
everything. And he doesn't need spectacular declarations
to inform man of his prodigies. After all, 'the heavens are
telling the glory of God; and the firmament proclaims his
handiwork. Day to day pours forth speech, and night to
night declares knowledge' (Ps 18:1-2). We praise the Lord
'who makest the winds thy messengers, fire and flame thy
ministers' (Ps 103:4).*[4]

As the Gospel wonderfully demonstrates, Mary lived
in a beautiful state of recollection, of presence of God. She
kept all these things in her heart. Her contemplative spirit
has a certain enchantment.[5] In the intimacy of her soul,
Mary penetrated more and more deeply into the mystery
that had been revealed to her. Dear Mary, Mother of
prayer, teach us to discover God who is so close to our
lives! Help us to find him in the silence and peace of our
hearts. *Only he who ponders things in his heart with a true
Christian spirit can discover the immense riches of the
interior world, the world of grace, that hidden treasure
which is within us all ... It was by pondering things in her
heart that Mary, as time went on, grew in understanding of
the mystery, in sanctity and in unity with God.*[6] The Lord

---

[2] Luke 2:51
[3] John 1:46
[4] S. Munoz Iglesias, *The Gospel of Mary,* Madrid 1973
[5] Ch. Lubich, *Meditations,* Madrid 1989, p. 14
[6] F. Suarez, *Mary of Nazareth,* p. 154

invites us to cultivate this same interior recollection. We will then be able to converse with the Master. St Teresa has written that recollection *is nothing else, in my opinion, but being on terms of friendship with God, frequently convers- ing in secret with Him Who, we know, loves us.*[7]

14.2 Mary's silence during the three years of her Son's public life.

Certainly the Annunciation is the culminating moment of Mary's faith in her awaiting of Christ, but it is also the point of departure from which her whole 'journey towards God' begins, her whole pilgrimage of faith.[8] Mary's faith was growing from fullness to fullness, since Our Lady did not understand everything at once in its entirety. We may imagine that with the passing of time she came to smile at the memory of her dialogue with the Angel Gabriel at the Annunciation, or her plaintive words upon discovering the young Jesus at the Temple, though He was only doing his Father's business. She could see how God was revealing her vocation in a progressive manner.[9]

Silence is an indispensable condition for keeping things and pondering them in one's heart. Profundity of thought can develop only in a climate of silence. Too much chatter exhausts our inner strength; it dissipates everything of any value in our heart, which becomes like a bottle of perfume left open for a long time: only water remains with a slight touch of its former fragrance.[10]

The Virgin kept a discreet silence during the three years of her Son's public life. She was not unduly affected by his departure from home, the enthusiasm of the crowds or the sensational reports of his miracles. Then again, Mary

[7] St Teresa, *Life*, 8, 7
[8] St John Paul II, Encyclical, *Redemptoris Mater*, 25 March 1987, 14
[9] cf J. Guitton, *The Virgin Mary*, Madrid 1964
[10] F. Suarez, *op cit*, p. 155

certainly did miss the company of Jesus. It seems most
likely, though, that she did not travel with her Son about
Palestine. The Evangelists do take note of the generous
women who accompanied the Master and his disciples,[11]
but they say nothing of Mary in this regard. Whenever it
was possible, of course, Mary would go to see her Son, to
listen to him, to speak with him. The Gospel of today's
Mass tells us of one of these encounters: *Then his mother
and his brethren came to him, but they could not reach him
for the crowd.*[12] Someone then got the message to Jesus
that his mother wanted to see him. According to the
account given by St Matthew, Jesus replied in this manner:
*Stretching out his hand toward his disciples, he said, 'Here
are my mother and my brethren!'*[13] St Mark relates that
Jesus reacted to the news by asking, *'Who are my mother
and my brethren?' And looking around on those who sat
about him, he said, 'Here are my mother and my brethren!
Whoever does the will of God is my brother, and sister, and
mother'.*[14]

The Virgin was not upset by this answer. She knew
that this was, in fact, the greatest praise that Jesus could
give of her. Because of her life of faith and prayer, Mary
understood that Jesus was praising her exemplary life,
insofar as no one has ever been more united to Jesus than
his Mother Mary. The Second Vatican Council teaches us:
*In the course of her Son's preaching she received the
words whereby, in extolling a kingdom beyond the
concerns and ties of flesh and blood, he declared blessed
those who heard and kept the word of God as she was
faithfully doing.*[15] Jesus loves Mary more because of the

---

[11] cf Luke 8:2-3
[12] Luke 8:19-21
[13] Matt 12:49
[14] Mark 3:34
[15] Second Vatican Council, *Lumen gentium,* 58

ties of grace rather than those of nature. Mary kept silent on that occasion also, and did not try to explain to anyone that the words of the Master referred especially to herself. Afterwards, maybe a few minutes later, Mary was in the company of her beloved Son. Perhaps she took the opportunity to thank him for his extraordinary compliment.

Jesus approaches us in many different ways. If we are to properly understand his message, we must needs be souls of prayer. Like any artist or man of letters, the Christian must know how to temper his *impatience and anxiety to the slow plodding of time. He learns the lesson, perhaps with some pain, that every seed needs time to germinate in the earth, take root and break forth from the soil. A person may find this process extremely dull and taxing. That is no matter, for it is essential to a plant's growth. As the ancients were wont to say, a tree will spread out its limbs in accordance with the depths of its roots.*[16]

14.3 The interior recollection of the Christian.

Every Christian should do his or her level best to bring a spirit of prayer to family life, to the workplace, to the whole gamut of social activities. We should develop a sense of *interior recollection* which is compatible with all the comings and goings of our everyday life. *We children of God have to be contemplatives: people who, in the midst of the din of the throng, know how to find silence of soul in a lasting conversation with Our Lord, people who know how to look at him as they look at a Father, as they look at a Friend, as they look at someone with whom they are madly in love.*[17]

Human life has a profound meaning which is ultimately expressed in God. Therefore, we cannot allow our lives to be dominated by frivolity, vanity or sensuality.

---

[16] F. Delclaux, *The silent creator,* Madrid 1969
[17] St. J. Escrivá, *The Forge,* 738

God teaches us the true importance of events and the real value of things. To be recollected is to join what is separated, to re-establish a lost order. If we want to be recollected souls, we have to guard our senses from hazardous dissipation. Otherwise, we shall find it impossible to be contemplatives in the middle of the world, no matter how tranquil our immediate surroundings may be.

We need to habitually remind ourselves that we are in the presence of God. It will be a great help to us, perhaps an indispensable one, to have many of these moments of personal conversation with the Lord. *Each day try to find a few minutes of that blessed solitude you need so much to keep your interior life going.*[18] We should combine with our time of prayer the practice of voluntary mortification in all that can separate us from God. We can also mortify ourselves in things that are themselves licit, so that we might offer this sacrifice up to the Lord.

In our world of almost constant external distraction, we need *this esteem for silence, this admirable and indispensable condition for our spirit, assaulted as it is by such a deafening clamour ... O blessed silence of Nazareth! Teach us recollection; teach us interior life; teach us to be docile to good inspirations and trustworthy spiritual guides. Teach us the value of study, of meditation, of interior life, of the secret prayer that is only heard by God.*[19]

The Blessed Virgin will show us how to have more and more esteem for this blessed silence of the heart. This silence is by no means an emptiness of spirit. Quite the opposite, it is an interior richness. Far from separating us from other people, it brings us closer to them, and helps us to understand their problems and worries.

---

[18] *idem, The Way,* 304
[19] Bl. Paul VI, *Address in Nazareth,* 5 January 1964

15. TO VISIT THE SICK

15.1 To imitate Christ in his compassion for the sick and the suffering.

The Church has always recommended that the faithful engage in corporal works of mercy, particularly that of visiting the sick. It is to be hoped that our interest and charity may partially alleviate another person's suffering. We may even be able to encourage the sick to sanctify their condition. The Church encourages us to imitate the Master who showed so much solicitude for the sick during his life on earth. Corporal works of mercy can do an immense amount of good for the sick person as well as the benefactor himself. *Whether we are dealing with children in the womb, old people, accident victims, the physically or mentally ill, we are always dealing with our fellow human beings whose credentials of nobility are to be found on the very first page of the Bible: 'God created man in his own image' (Gen 1:27). On the other hand, it has often been said that it is possible to judge a civilization by the way it deals with the defenceless, with children, with the sick, et cetera.*[1] Wherever you have a sick person, there has to be *a supremely human environment where each one is treated with dignity. One experiences in such circumstances the closeness of brothers and friends.*[2]

The Evangelists make frequent reference to Christ's love and mercy for people who are in pain. The Gospels are full of his miraculous cures. It was St Peter who summed up

---

[1] Bl. Paul VI, *Address,* 24 May 1974
[2] *ibid*

the life of Jesus of Nazareth with these words: *He went about doing good and healing ...*[3] *His actions concerned primarily those who were suffering and seeking help. He healed the sick; consoled the afflicted; fed the hungry; freed people from deafness, from blindness, from leprosy, from the devil and from various physical disabilities; three times He restored the dead to life. He was sensitive to every human suffering, whether of the body or of the soul.*[4] Jesus was not content to heal only those who came to him, He also went out in search of the sick. When he saw the paralytic by the pool, a man who had been there for thirty-eight years, He asks him without hesitation, *Do you want to be healed?*[5] On another occasion He offered to travel to the house of the centurion to heal his servant.[6] Jesus did not avoid people afflicted with contagious diseases. For example, he went right up to the leper outside of Capharnaum, though He surely could have cured him from a distance, *and he stretched out his hand and touched him.*[7] As we read in the Gospel for today's Mass, Jesus sent his Apostles out *to preach the kingdom of God and to heal,* giving them *power and authority over all demons and to cure diseases.*[8]

Our Lord taught his disciples to see the sick in a new way: *I was sick and you visited me.*[9] Whenever we take care of a person who is suffering, we are taking care of Jesus Christ himself: *Truly, I say to you, as you did it to one of the least of these my brethren, you did it to me.* You helped me to bear that illness, that sadness, that tiredness, that loneliness ...

Let us take a closer look today at the attention we give

---

[3] Acts 10:38
[4] St John Paul II, Apostolic Letter, *Salvifici doloris,* 11 February 1984, 16
[5] John 5:6
[6] cf Matt 8:7
[7] Matt 8:3
[8] Luke 9:1-6
[9] cf Matt 25:36-44 ff

to those who suffer in our surroundings. How much time do we make available? How much interest? *Children ... the sick ... As you write these words, don't you feel tempted to write them with capitals?*

The reason is that in little children and in the sick a soul in love sees Him![10]

15.2 To do what He would do in these circumstances.

Mercy is one of the fruits of charity. Mercy is *a certain compassion for the misery of one's neighbour, born in one's heart, and by which, if we can, we try to help him.*[11] It is of the very essence of mercy to pour oneself out, to expend oneself for the one who suffers pain or need, and to take on the other's pain or need as one's own in order to remedy them as best one can. Consequently, when we visit a sick person, we are not fulfilling a mere precept of courtesy. On the contrary, we are making his pain into our pain. We try to alleviate it, perhaps with a kind conversation concerning news of interest to him, perhaps providing some small material assistance. We should encourage sick people to sanctify this treasure which God has placed in their hands. We can join together in prayer. We can read from a good spiritual book, whatever seems appropriate ... We will then be acting as Christ would act. We will act as if we were going to visit Jesus Christ himself.

When we make the sacrifice to visit a sick person, or one who is in some way needy, we make the world more human. We come close to the heart of man and at the same time pour over him the charity of Christ. St John Paul II wrote: *We could say that suffering, which is present under so many different forms in our human world, is also present in order to unleash love in the human person, that unselfish gift of one's 'I' on behalf of other people,*

---

[10] St. J. Escrivá, *The Way,* 419
[11] St Augustine, *The City of God,* 9, 5

*especially those who suffer. The world of human suffering
unceasingly calls for, so to speak, another world: the world
of human love; and in a certain sense man owes to
suffering that unselfish love which stirs in his heart and
actions.*[12] How much good we can accomplish by being
merciful towards those who are suffering! How much
grace is produced in our soul as a result! The Lord enlarges
our heart and makes us understand those words He once
said: *It is more blessed to give than to receive.*[13] For Jesus
is generous beyond our wildest dreams.

15.3 Charity sharpens our spiritual vision.

St Augustine states that mercy is *the showpiece of the
soul* since it makes it appear good and beautiful[14] and
covers a multitude of sins.[15] *He who begins to suffer over
the miseries of others begins to abandon sin.*[16] For this
very same reason, when we go to visit the sick we should
bring along a friend. This should be a natural part of our
apostolate. The soul that partakes of another's sufferings is
rewarded with a richer understanding of the love of God. St
Augustine points out that by loving one's neighbour we
purify the sight of our eyes in such a way as to be able to
see God.[17] Our vision is sharpened in the perception of
divine goods. Egoism hardens the heart, while the exercise
of charity enables us to rejoice in God. Hence, charity is a
foretaste of eternal life.[18] Eternal life itself may be
understood as an uninterrupted act of charity.[19] What better

---

[12] St John Paul II, *loc cit,* 29
[13] Acts 20:35
[14] St Augustine, in *Catena Aurea,* VI, p. 48
[15] cf 1 Pet 4:8
[16] St Augustine, *loc cit*
[17] *idem, Commentary on St John's Gospel,* 17, 8
[18] 1 John 3:14
[19] cf St Thomas, *Summa Theologiae,* I, q. 114, a. 4

reward could Our Lord give to us than the gift of himself? What better prize than for Christ to increase our ability to love the others? *No matter how much you may love, you will never love enough. The human heart is endowed with an enormous coefficient of expansion. When it loves, it opens out in a crescendo of affection that overcomes all barriers. If you love Our Lord, there will not be a single creature that does not find a place in your heart.*[20]

In our modern world, one cannot help but notice that there are a growing number of people who require the assistance of Christians: the elderly, the sick, the depressed, the homeless ... *There are many people who suffer in their own homes the difficulties of sickness or the disgrace of poverty, though there may be fewer of these people than there once were. Today we have many nursing homes and residences for old people. There are many organizations and programmes dedicated to people in need. Yet despite the best of intentions, these institutions often harbour multitudes of lonely individuals who live in great spiritual want. Deprived of the affection of friends and relatives, these sorry people may find themselves completely abandoned.*[21] When we provide companionship to those who suffer in this way, we bring upon ourselves the mercy of the Lord. This is something which we need as much as anyone else.

In today's *Liturgy of the Hours,* we find this prayer to the Lord: *Bring it about that we might know how to discover you in all of our brothers and sisters, above all in those who are poor and those who are suffering.*[22] Close by the side of those who suffer we will find Mary, *Comforter of the afflicted.* She will make our heart sensitive to the needs of others. Then we will never ignore sick people or keep at a distance from anyone who is suffering in body or soul.

---

[20] St. J. Escrivá, *The Way of the Cross,* Eighth Station, 5

[21] J. Orlandis, *The Eight Beatitudes,* Pamplona 1982, p. 105

[22] *Liturgy of the Hours,* Morning Prayer

16. TO WANT TO SEE THE LORD

16.1 Purifying one's sight in order to contemplate Jesus in the midst of our everyday tasks.

St Luke tells us in the Gospel for today's Mass that King Herod Antipas wanted to see the Lord. *'Et quaerebat videre eum,' And he sought to see him.*[1] So much news had reached the tetrarch that it had aroused his fickle curiosity.

Throughout the Gospels we find many people who wanted to see Jesus. For example, the Magi travelled a great distance to this end. They went into Jerusalem and asked people, *Where is he who has been born king of the Jews?*[2] The Magi declared their intentions quite openly: *For we have seen his star in the East, and have come to worship him.* At long last, the Magi found Jesus in the arms of Mary his Mother. Years later, St John relates how certain Greeks asked to see the Lord. They approached Philip with their request, saying, *Sir, we wish to see Jesus.*[3] On another occasion the Blessed Virgin, accompanied by some relatives, went down from Nazareth to Capharnaum with the hope of seeing her Son. There were so many people in the house that she had to send a message in to him: *Your mother and your brethren are standing outside, desiring to see you.*[4] We can only imagine how eager Mary was to be with her Son once more.

We too share this desire to see Jesus, to contemplate

---

[1] Luke 9:7-9
[2] Matt 2:3
[3] John 12:21
[4] Luke 8:20

him, to know him personally. This is indeed our greatest desire and our greatest hope. Nothing can compare with the joy of being in his presence. On Good Friday Herod Antipas had Jesus standing right in front of him, but he did not appreciate his good fortune. Only a few months previously, Herod had been listening to the words of his captive, John the Baptist. The Precursor spoke of nothing other than the coming of the Messiah. As we all know, Herod did not heed the Baptist but, instead, had him executed on a whim. Herod manifested the same blind obstinacy which Jesus had found in the Pharisees: *With them indeed is fulfilled the prophecy of Isaiah which says: 'You shall indeed hear but never understand, and you shall indeed see but never perceive. For this people's heart has grown dull, and their ears are heavy of hearing, and their eyes they have closed'.*[5]

It was the Apostles who had the immense good fortune of the Messiah's company for almost three years. The Master reminded them, *Blessed are your eyes, for they see, and your ears, for they hear.*[6] Many centuries before, Moses beheld the burning bush as a symbol of the living God.[7] After his struggle with that mysterious man in the desert, Jacob declared, *For I have seen God face to face.*[8] The Prophet Gideon later said something similar: *I have seen the angel of the Lord face to face.*[9] But these visions were obscure and imprecise compared with the experience of seeing the Lord in person. *Truly, I say to you, many prophets and righteous men longed to see what you see, and did not see it, and to hear what you hear, and did not hear it.*[10] The

---

[5] Matt 13:14-15
[6] Matt 13:16
[7] cf Ezek 3:2
[8] Gen 32:31
[9] Judg 6:22
[10] Matt 13:17

Lord blessed the first martyr, St Stephen, with this glorious vision. While he was being stoned to death, the Proto-martyr exclaimed, *Behold, I see the heavens opened, and the Son of man standing at the right hand of God.*[11]

Jesus is present in our everyday affairs, but we have to purify our sight in order to contemplate him. Our life should always be aimed at this supreme objective. Let us say to him many times each day in the words of the Psalmist, *'Vultum tuum Domine requiram.' Thy face, Lord, do I seek.*[12]

16.2 The sacred humanity of the Lord, source of love and fortitude.

He who seeks finds.[13] The Virgin and St Joseph looked for Jesus for three days, and they finally found him.[14] Zacchaeus also wanted to see the Lord. Because he made a sincere effort, the Master anticipated his petition and entered into his house.[15] The multitudes went about in search of the Lord and they had the great fortune to be in his company.[16] No one who ever sought Jesus with a sincere heart was ever deceived or frustrated in his or her quest. In the course of the Lord's Passion, Herod Antipas wanted to see the Lord to satisfy his curiosity. This explains why he did not really find Jesus. *When Herod saw Jesus, he was very glad, for he had long desired to see him, because he had heard about him, and he was hoping to see some sign done by him. So he questioned him at some length; but he made no answer.*[17] Love has nothing to say

---

[11] Acts 7:56
[12] Ps 26:8
[13] Matt 7:8
[14] cf Luke 2:48
[15] Luke 19:1 ff
[16] cf Luke 6:9 ff
[17] Luke 23:8-9

to a person wholly taken up with frivolity and corruption. Jesus is ready to meet us if we are ready to correspond to his infinite Love.

We see Jesus present in our Tabernacles. He is close to us in the Sacrament of Confession. He is present in our effort to be detached from the things of this world, even things that may be licit in themselves. We must needs be watchful that the means do not become our end. St Augustine teaches us: *Love for the shadows ends up making the eyes of the soul weaker and weaker. The eyes become unable to see the face of God. Therefore, the more a man gives in to his weakness, the more he slips into darkness.*[18]

'Vultum tuum, Domine, requiram.' Thy face, Lord, do I seek. The contemplation of the sacred humanity of the Lord is an inexhaustible source of love and strength amidst life's difficulties. Time after time we should renew our acquaintance with those scenes of the Gospel. We should meditate slowly on this Jesus of Bethany, of Jerusalem, of Capharnaum – how he receives everyone so graciously! Perhaps at this very moment, he is only a few feet away from us in the Tabernacle. Statues or images of Christ can help us to have a living remembrance of his presence. This has always been the experience of the saints. St Teresa of Avila writes: *It came to pass one day, when I went into the oratory, that I saw a statue which they had put there ... It was a representation of Christ most grievously wounded; and so devotional, that the very sight of it, when I saw it, moved me – so well did it show forth that which He suffered for us. So keenly did I feel the evil return I had made for those wounds, that I thought my heart was breaking. I threw myself on the ground beside it, my tears flowing plenteously, and implored him to strengthen me once for all, so that I might never offend him any more.*[19]

---

[18] St Augustine, *On Free Will*, I, 16, 43

[19] St Teresa, *Life*, 9, 1

This love, which in some way is necessary to nurture the senses, is of enormous benefit to the soul. What could be more natural than to want a portrait of our beloved! St Teresa herself exclaimed: *Wretched are they who, through their own fault, have lost this blessing; it is clear enough that they do not love Our Lord – for if they loved him, they would rejoice at the sight of his picture, just as men find pleasure when they see the portrait of one they love.*[20]

16.3 Jesus awaits us in the Tabernacle.

Jesu, quem velatum nunc aspicio ...
Jesu! whom for the present veiled I see,
Whom I so I thirst for, oh, vouchsafe to me:
That I may see Thy countenance unfolding,
And may be blest Thy glory in beholding. Amen.[21]

We pray these words in the *Adoro te devote* hymn.

One day, with the help of God's grace, we will see Christ in all his glory and majesty. He will receive us into his kingdom. We will recognize him as the Friend who never failed us. He was, in fact, with us all along in the details and difficulties of our ordinary life. This is why we should say with St Augustine, *I have this tremendous thirst to see the face of God. I feel this thirst in the course of my journey; I suffer thirst along the way. But my thirst will be quenched when I arrive at long last.*[22] Our heart will only be satisfied by union with God.

Happily, we already have Jesus with us in the Tabernacle. Following the priest's words of consecration, the Lord is fully present in the Eucharist in his Body, Soul and Divinity. His sacred humanity is hidden beneath the eucharistic 'accidents' of bread and wine. His Body and Blood, although in a glorious state, are especially

---

[20] *ibid*, 9, 7
[21] Hymn, *Adoro te devote*
[22] St Augustine, *Commentary on the Psalms*, 41, 5

accessible to us under the species of bread and wine, those most commonplace of foods. We take advantage of this accessibility at the moment of Communion or when making a *Visit to the Blessed Sacrament.* Let us go with a great desire to see Jesus, following the example of Zacchaeus, the blind men, the lepers and all those crowds who put their trust in him. Better yet, we should seek Jesus with the same earnest zeal that Mary and Joseph showed in Jerusalem as they looked about everywhere for him. There will be times when our miseries or lack of faith will make it difficult to discern the loveable face of Jesus. It is precisely then that we should ask Our Lady for a clean heart, for a purified vision. Let us learn from the behaviour of the Apostles in those days following the Resurrection. *Now none of the disciples dared ask him, 'Who are you?' They knew it was the Lord.*[23] What a joy it must have been for them to find Jesus alive, their Jesus of Nazareth, after the tragedy of the Cross! It is equally wonderful to find Jesus living in the Tabernacle where He eagerly awaits us!

---

[23] John 21:12

17. THE TIME AND THE MOMENT

17.1 To live in the present moment.

We have a lot to do if we are to present ourselves before our Father God with our hands full of fruit. Sacred Scripture teaches us in one of the readings for today's Mass that *for everything there is a season.*

People frequently become engrossed in activities that have little to do with the responsibilities which they have at hand. For example, despite an apparent physical proximity, a father can be far away from his children when they are in most need of his attention. A student may allow his imagination to range far beyond the subject matter before him. He thereby fails to use his study time to good advantage and wastes his energies on chimerical pursuits and worries. *Time is very precious because time quickly passes away. It is a testing ground for our eternal destiny. Our fate depends to a large extent on our fidelity to our duties in life.*

Time is a gift from God. He invites us to prove our love for him in a free and determined fashion. We should therefore be miserly in our use of time. We should use it well by working with love and intensity. A Christian should never give in to sloth or boredom. It is fine for us to rest whenever necessary (cf Mark 6:31), but we should always have our eyes fixed on our final resting place in Heaven.[1]

One of the readings of today's Mass invites us to live our life in the presence of God. Everything has its proper time: *a time to be born, and a time to die; a time to plant, and a time to pluck up what is planted; a time to kill, and a*

---

[1] Bl. Paul VI, *Address*, 1 January 1976

*time to heal, a time to break down, and a time to build up;
a time to weep, and a time to laugh; a time to mourn, and a
time to dance ... a time to keep silence, and a time to speak
...*[2] We can waste our time by doing whatever we want
instead of what God wants. For example, we might spend
time at our place of work when we are needed at home.
Conversely, we might choose to read the newspaper when
we should be working. The life of each man and woman
exists in the *present moment.* These are the only moments
which we can truly sanctify. The past and the future only
exist in our imagination. The memory of our past can
inspire us to acts of contrition or thanksgiving, yet even
these prayers take place in the reality of the present.

We should not become overwrought by future events
because they may not come to pass. In any event, we will
have the grace of God when we need it. *The secret to
building the city of God within us is this: we have to build
on a brick by brick basis in the reality of the present
moment.*[3] This is the only time which God gives us to sanctify. *Hodie, nunc.* We must live the present moment with
love, with full concentration. What a wonderful offering
this will be to the Lord! Let us not miss this opportunity.

17.2 To give the tasks we have at hand our full attention.

By not fulfilling the duty of the moment, by putting
things off until tomorrow, we often end up omitting them
altogether. St Paul reminded the first Christians to make
the best use of their time.[4] In like manner, we should put
some order into our day. We should draw up a schedule or
plan and then stick to it as best we can. Thus, by
overcoming laziness on a regular basis, we can help others,

---

[2] *First Reading,* Year II, Eccles 3:1-11
[3] Ch. Lubich, *Meditations,* p. 61
[4] cf Gal 6:10

and therefore *raise all of society, and even creation itself,
to a better mode of existence.*[5] Laziness may be personified
by someone who accomplishes absolutely nothing, but also
by the person who is busy doing everything except what is
his responsibility. Such a person will give in to any and all
distractions. He has a great love for beginning things but
little experience of persevering. *A hardworking person
makes good use of time, for time is not only money, it is
glory, God's glory! He does as he ought and concentrates
on what he is doing, not out of routine nor to while away
the passing hours, but as the result of attentive and
pondered reflection.*[6]

Living in the present moment is an aspect of living in the
presence of God. We should become convinced that the
offering of our work requires our complete attention, as if it
were the last thing we would be able to offer him. This attitude
will lead us to finish our tasks well, no matter how insignificant they may appear to be. We will behave in this way
because we have become thoroughly convinced that these
tasks will be converted into something great by the Lord.

If we resolve to concentrate in this way on the present
moment, we will be relieved of much useless worry about
our health, our career, our finances, whatever. *Sometimes
we allow other things to scare us, things that come from
far away – fears about future dangers. We are afraid of
things or of dangers which at present do not exist and we
don't know if they will ever happen; but in our imagination
we see them as present, and this makes them appear even
more terrible. A simple supernatural reasoning process
will get rid of them: since these dangers which you imagine
possible are not actual dangers and this fear you have has
not been verified, then clearly you do not have the grace of
God necessary to overcome them, to accept them. If your*

---

[5] Second Vatican Council, *Lumen gentium,* 41
[6] St. J. Escrivá, *Friends of God,* 81

fears were verified, if things did turn out as you expect, then you would have divine grace; with that grace and your response to it you would win out and have peace.

It's quite natural that at present you do not have God's grace to overcome those obstacles and to accept crosses which exist only in your imagination. What you have to do is base your spiritual life on a serene, objective realism.[7] By living with a true sense of our divine filiation, we will be spared all manner of anxieties. As a result, we will be able to make better use of our time. Imagine all the awful things which we have dreaded at one time or another which have never come to pass! Our Father God takes wonderful care of his children – far beyond what we might ever expect.

17.3 Avoiding useless worries.

Making good use of our time means that we will live in the present moment. We will not retreat into the past which is gone forever, nor escape into the future which may never materialize outside of our imagination. It is the present moment which can be offered to the Lord, none other. This is the context where we can enrich our spiritual life (faith, hope and charity) and progress in the human virtues (industriousness, order, optimism, affability, spirit of service). *Now is the time of mercy; then, there will be only the time of justice. This is why we have to live in the present moment and transform it into the moment of God.*[8]

The Lord himself invites us to live each day with serenity and intensity. He warns us of succumbing to useless worries over the past or the future. *Do not be anxious about tomorrow, for tomorrow will be anxious for itself. Let the day's own trouble be sufficient for the day.*[9]

---

[7] S. Canals, *Jesus as Friend*, p. 72
[8] St Thomas, *About the Creed*, 7
[9] Matt 6:34

The Lord's words are a combination of guidance and consolation. Let us firmly resolve to live the present moment and to sanctify our actual circumstances. We should avoid carrying any unnecessary and burdensome loads. This is the behaviour which is proper to children of God, men and women who know that they are in his loving hands. This approach is also confirmed by common sense. As the inspired author tells us in the *Book of Ecclesiastes*: *He who observes the wind will not sow; and he who regards the clouds will not reap.*[10]

What really matters is that we live by faith, that we sanctify our ordinary work. *Conduct yourself well 'now,' without looking back on 'yesterday' which is really gone, and without worrying about 'tomorrow,' which for you may never come.*[11] Our longing for Heaven and our meditation on the last things should inspire us to work with more supernatural spirit, not less. We must work here on earth as if we had a long life ahead of us. At the same time we should work as if we were going to die this very afternoon. Our approach to the task of the present moment has a lot to do with our future reward. Now is the *time to build up.* For here on earth, God's work must truly be our own. Let us not deceive ourselves by putting our sanctification off to some distant future.

---

[10] Eccles 11:4
[11] St. J. Escrivá, *The Way,* 253

18. MEDIATRIX OF ALL GRACES

18.1 Mediatrix before the Mediator.

St Paul teaches us, *For there is one God, and there is one mediator between God and men, the man Christ Jesus, who gave himself as a ransom for all.*[1]

The Blessed Virgin cooperated in an extraordinary way in her Son's work of redemption. It was her free consent to the Angel Gabriel at the Annunciation which brought about the Incarnation. According to St Thomas Aquinas, it was as if God the Father had been waiting for humanity's assent through the voice of Mary.[2] By reason of her divine maternity, Mary is intimately united to the mystery of the Redemption, right up to its consummation on the Cross. There on Calvary Mary participated in the suffering and death of her Son in a unique way. From his throne on the Cross, Jesus deigned to give Mary to the Apostle John who was a representative of all mankind. This explains the reasoning behind the constant teaching of the Church, as most recently defined by the Second Vatican Council: *The maternal duty of Mary toward men in no wise obscures or diminishes this unique mediation of Christ, but rather shows his power.*[3] She is the *Mediatrix* before the *Mediator.* St John Paul II stated: *Mary's mediation is intimately linked with her motherhood. It possesses a specifically maternal character, which distinguishes it from the mediation of the other creatures who in*

---

[1] 1 Tim 2:5-6
[2] St Thomas, *Summa Theologiae,* 3, q. 30, a. 1
[3] Second Vatican Council, *Lumen gentium,* 60

various and always subordinate ways share in the one medi-
ation of Christ, although her own mediation is also a shared
mediation.[4] *In no way does it impede, but rather does it*
foster the immediate union of the faithful with Christ.[5]

Mary already exercised this work of mediation when
John the Baptist leaped with joy in the womb of Elizabeth.[6]
Years later, at the marriage feast of Cana, Mary was
responsible for the first miracle performed by her Son.[7] In
that situation, Mary wanted to be of service to her hosts so
that they would not be humiliated. St John points out that
this miracle had spiritual consequences as well: *and his*
disciples believed in him. As in the case of all mothers, the
Virgin interceded with her Son on any number of occasions
which are not recorded in the Gospels. And her motherly
solicitude continued after the Assumption. *Taken up to*
Heaven she did not lay aside this salvific duty, but by her
constant intercession continued to bring us the gifts of
eternal salvation. By her maternal charity, she cares for
the brethren of her Son, who still journey on earth
surrounded by dangers and difficulties, until they are led
into the happiness of their true home. Therefore the
Blessed Virgin is invoked by the Church under the titles of
Advocate, Helper, Benefactress, and Mediatrix.[8]

Mary's prayers are always heard by her Son. Are we to
imagine that Jesus could deny his mother anything? She
engendered him, carried him in her womb for nine months,
nurtured him and remained true to him without fail. The
Church teaches us that Mary is the best guarantee for our
every need. Pope Leo XIII has written, *It is by the express*
Will of God that no good is given to us but through Mary.

---

[4] St John Paul II, *Redemptoris Mater,* 25 March 1987, 38
[5] Second Vatican Council, *loc cit,* 60
[6] cf Luke 1:14
[7] cf John 2:1 ff
[8] Second Vatican Council, *loc cit,* 62

Just as no one can reach the Father except through the Son, generally speaking, no one can reach Jesus except through Mary.[9] Let us not be bashful in appealing to her as our trusted and most influential advocate. She listens to our every prayer.

We should entrust Mary with the resolution of our various difficulties and problems, be they great or small: family tensions, financial worries, examinations, professional concerns ... Let us also ask her help in matters of the spiritual life: the grace to respond to one's vocation, the strength to overcome a serious contradiction, the humility to pray better ...

Holy Mary, Mother of God, pray for us ... Mary is in Heaven. She is very close to her Son. She will direct our prayer to him. She will make it better, that is to say, more pleasing in God's sight.

18.2 All graces come to us through Mary.

The Church teaches that all graces come to us through Mary. *No one is saved, most holy one, if not through your intercession. No one is freed from evil, except through your help ... Neither does anyone receive the divine gifts without benefit of your mediation ... Apart from your Son, who is it that has more concern for the human race than you? Who else protects us without fail when we are in trouble? Who frees us so rapidly from the temptations that befall us? Who seeks more earnestly to protect sinners? Who comes to their defence no matter how hopeless their situation? ... For these many reasons, the afflicted seek refuge in you ... The very invocation of your name puts to flight the enemy and his servants. It is a safe refuge. You free those who invoke you from every need and you forewarn them against every temptation.*[10]

---

[9] Leo XIII, Encyclical, *Octobri mense,* 22 September 1891
[10] St Germanus of Constantinople, *Homily on St Mary Zonam*

We Christians have recourse to the Mother of Heaven for all kinds of assistance, both temporal and spiritual. Among our many spiritual requests, we ask Our Lady for the conversion of anyone who has become separated from her Son. For ourselves we ask a state of *continuous conversion,* in other words, an ongoing disposition to improve, to weed out any obstacles that could impede the action of the Holy Spirit. We also need Mary's constant assistance in the apostolate. She is the one who can change hearts. It is for this very reason that Christians of every age have called Mary *Health of the sick, Refuge of sinners, Comforter of the afflicted, Queen of Apostles and Queen of Martyrs* ... Mary generously dispenses every grace imaginable, *even in a certain sense the graces of the sacraments, because she has merited them for us by her union with the Lord on Calvary. She prepares us with her prayer to better approach the sacraments, to receive them well. At times she even sends the priest to us, without whose involvement there would be no sacrament.*[11]

Let us place our worries in her hands. We should resolve to go to Mary many, many times each day with everything that concerns us.

18.3 A continuous prayer goes up to the Mother of Heaven.

Raised to the glory of heaven, she accompanies your pilgrim Church with a mother's love and watches in kindness over the Church's homeward steps, until the Lord's Day shall come in glorious splendour.[12] We seek Mary's protection each and every day. In the *Hail Mary,* we ask for her help: *Holy Mary, Mother of God, pray for us sinners, now and at the hour of our death* ... This *now* is repeated throughout the world by people of every age and race who

---

[11] R. Garrigou-Lagrange, *The Three Ages of the Interior Life,* I, 6
[12] *Roman Missal,* Preface of the Mass for Mary, Mother of the Church

desire the *grace of the present moment*.[13] This is a most personal grace, one that varies according to each person and each situation. Although we may occasionally be distracted from our prayers, Our Lady never loses her attention. She knows our every need. She prays for us and wins for us what we should have. A continuous prayer rises up to our Mother in Heaven: *Pray for us sinners, now ...* How can she not fail to hear us? Could she possibly ignore our pleas?

Every time we seek Mary, we come closer to her Son. *Mary is always the road that leads to Christ. Each encounter with Mary, therefore, turns out to be an encounter with Christ himself: through her, with her and in her. For what other purpose could we have in mind by going to her than to find her Son and our Saviour? He is there in her arms.*[14]

We have countless reasons to go to Mary. We know that she will always hear our prayers. *Remember, O most gracious Virgin Mary, that never was it known that anyone who fled to your protection, implored your help or sought your intercession, was left unaided. Inspired by this confidence, I fly to you, O Virgin of virgins, my Mother. To you I come, before you I stand, sinful and sorrowful. O Mother of the Word Incarnate, despise not my petitions, but, in your mercy, hear and answer me.*[15]

In this month of October, the month which the Church has dedicated to the Holy Rosary, we go to Mary with filial confidence. The Rosary is Our Lady's favourite prayer.[16] We should pray it with renewed devotion. Let us be really ambitious in our petitions, because Our Blessed Mother will be attentive to every single one of them.

---

[13] cf R. Garrigou-Lagrange, *loc cit*
[14] Bl. Paul VI, Encyclical, *Mense maio,* 29 April 1965
[15] The *Memorare* Prayer
[16] cf Bl. Paul VI, *loc cit*

19. THE VIRTUE OF OBEDIENCE

19.1 The parable of the two sons sent out into the vineyard. True obedience is born of love.

The Lord was teaching in the Temple when he told this parable: *What do you think? A man had two sons; and he went to the first and said, 'Son, go and work in the vineyard today.' And he answered, 'I will not'; but afterward he repented and went. And he went to the second and said the same; and he answered, 'I go, sir,' but did not go.* Jesus asks his listeners, *Which of the two did the will of his father?* They said the first son was the one. Jesus then reveals the supernatural significance of the lesson: *Truly, I say to you, the tax collectors and the harlots go into the kingdom of God before you. For John came to you in the way of righteousness, and you did not believe him, but the tax collectors and the harlots believed him.*[1]

John the Baptist had shown the way of salvation, yet the Scribes and Pharisees, the people who were supposedly dedicated to God's service, did not take the Precursor seriously. They are symbolized by the son who said, *I go, sir,* but did not go to the vineyard. As far as anyone could tell, these officials were very rigorous in their observance of the Law. Yet when the moment of truth arrived, that being the testimony of John the Baptist, these religious leaders showed their true colours. They were not docile to the divine Will and the fulfilment of the Law. On the other hand, a great number of tax collectors and sinners responded to the Baptist's call for repentance. They are

---

[1] Matt 21:28-32

represented by the son who at first said *I will not*, but in the event went to work in the vineyard. He obeyed, and thereby pleased his father enormously.

The Lord himself teaches us by example: *To carry out the Will of the Father, Christ inaugurated the Kingdom of Heaven on earth and revealed to us the mystery of that kingdom. By his obedience He brought about redemption.*[2] In the *Second Reading* for today's Mass, St Paul emphasizes how Jesus revealed his love for us through obedience: *He humbled himself and became obedient unto death, even death on a cross.*[3] The Romans and the Jews considered crucifixion to be the most degrading form of execution. Consequently, it was a punishment reserved for slaves and the worst of criminals. What a profound mystery lies in the fact that God the Son chose to do the Will of God the Father even to this utterly humiliating extent!

Christ obeyed out of love. This is the Christian meaning of obedience: that which we owe to God, that which we give to the Church, that which we give to our parents and those in authority over us. God does not want to be served by slaves or by robots. God wants to be served by his sons and daughters. He desires a willing and cheerful obedience that comes straight from the heart. St Teresa recalled how she once became envious of the penances done by a woman she knew. St Teresa would have done the same penances but her confessor prohibited her from doing so. She wondered whether it would be better to emulate her penitent friend rather than to obey her confessor. After a while, Jesus told her: *My daughter, you are heading the right way. Do you see how much penance this woman does? Know that I have an even greater esteem for your obedience.*[4]

---

[2] Second Vatican Council, *Lumen gentium,* 3
[3] Phil 2:1-11
[4] St Teresa, *Stories of Conscience,* 20

19.2 The example of Christ. Obedience and freedom.

As we have just heard from St Paul, the obedience lived by Christ was not a matter of mere submission to the Will of the Father. Christ became obedience itself. He became perfectly united to the plans of the Father for the salvation of the human race. Christ practiced an active obedience.

A very good sign of one's being on the right road in the spiritual life is one's willingness to obey others.[5] *Pride inclines us to do our own will and to seek what exalts us, not to wish to be directed by others, but to direct them. Obedience is opposed to this pride. The only Son of the Father came down from Heaven to save us, to cure our pride, becoming obedient unto death, and even to the death of the cross.*[6] Jesus wants to teach us the path of self-denial: *Thy word is a lamp to my feet and a light to my path.*[7] This *Psalm* appears in today's *Liturgy of the Hours.*

Obedience springs from freedom, while at the same time leading us to greater freedom. When a person obeys with all his heart, he is actually conserving his freedom by choosing the good. This truth is somewhat analogous to the situation of a person going on a trip. Without a doubt, he does not feel restricted by the markings on the highway. Similarly, a mountain climber does not feel constrained by the rope that ties him to his companions. There are many such examples which can be taken from ordinary life.

Love is essential to Christian obedience. Christ obeyed the Will of the Father not because he *had* to, but, rather, because he *wanted* to. *Love is what makes our obedience fully free. For the person who wants to follow Christ, the law is never a burden. It becomes a burden only insofar as one fails to discern the call of Christ. Therefore, if the law*

---

[5] St Thomas, *Commentary on the Epistle to the Philippians*, 2, 8
[6] R. Garrigou-Lagrange, *The Three Ages of the Interior Life*, II, p. 129
[7] *Liturgy of the Hours*, First Vespers, Ps 118:105

*sometimes seems burdensome, it may not be the law so much
as our keenness to follow Christ that needs amending.*

'If you love me, you will keep my commandments'
(John 14:15). *That is why I want to obey you, and your
Church, Lord; not primarily because I see the reasonableness of what is commanded (though that reasonableness is
often so evident). No; primarily because I want to love you,
and to show you my love. And also because I am convinced
that your commandments come from love and set me free.
'I will run in the way of thy commandments when thou
enlargest my understanding! ... And I shall walk at liberty,
for I have sought thy precepts' (Ps 118:32; 45).*[8]

19.3 Desires to imitate Jesus.

Behold, to obey is better than sacrifice.[9] St Gregory
the Great has commented on this verse from the *First Book
of Samuel*: *It is fitting that obedience be juxtaposed to the
sacrificial victims. For just as the animal meat is immolat-
ed, so too obedience involves the immolation of our will.*[10]
This sacrifice is the most difficult one to perform because
it concerns our inmost being. That is why it is so pleasing
to the Lord. To a certain extent, this may explain why Jesus
was so emphatic about the indispensable nature of this
virtue. Let us not forget that our teacher in obedience is the
One whom even the winds and sea obey.[11]

All interior progress relates to growth in this key virtue.
This concept is stressed throughout the Old Testament, as
in the *Book of Proverbs* where we read: *'Vir obediens
loquetur victoriam.' An obedient man shall speak of
victory.*[12] He who obeys will triumph. He will obtain grace

---

[8] C. Burke, *Authority and Freedom in the Church*, p. 49
[9] 1 Sam 15:22
[10] St Gregory the Great, *Morals*, 14
[11] cf Matt 8:27
[12] Prov 21:28

and light from God. As St Peter told the high priest and the council: *We are witnesses to these things, and so is the Holy Spirit whom God has given to those who obey him.*[13] St Teresa has exclaimed, *Oh, virtue of obedience! It can do everything!*[14] Because this virtue is so important to our pursuit of sanctity, the devil tempts us with all manner of excuses so that we might disobey.[15]

The practice of Christian obedience unites us to the mystery of the Cross and our Redemption.[16] The person who sets limits on his obedience is consequently setting limits on his union with Christ. A disobedient person will not be able to imitate the Lord. *Have this mind among yourselves, which was in Christ Jesus, who, though he was in the form of God, did not count equality with God a thing to be grasped, but emptied himself, taking the form of a servant ...*[17]

We should make a good examination of conscience about the quality of our obedience. Am I doing what God wants me to do? Do I give in to my vanity, my moods, my whims? Do I listen to the Lord's voice in spiritual direction? Do I practice true Christian obedience which is interior, prompt, cheerful, humble and discreet?[18]

Let us ask Our Lady to inspire us to imitate Christ through our humble obedience. *Obey without so much useless brooding. Appearing sad or reluctant when asked to do something is a very considerable fault. But just to feel like this is not only no fault, but can in fact be the opportunity for a great victory, for crowning an act of heroic virtue.*

---

[13] Acts 5:32
[14] St Teresa, *Life,* 18, 10
[15] *idem, Foundations,* 5, 10
[16] cf St Thomas, *Commentary on the Epistle to the Romans,* V, 8, 5
[17] Phil 2:5-7
[18] cf St Thomas, *Summa Theologiae,* 2-2, qq. 104 and 105, aa. 5 and 8

I have not invented this. Remember the Gospel tells us that a father asked his two sons to do the same job. And Jesus rejoices in the one who, despite raising difficulties, does it! He rejoices because discipline is the fruit of Love.[19]

---

[19] St. J. Escrivá, *Furrow,* 378

TWENTY-SIXTH SUNDAY: YEAR B

20. WORK FOR EVERYONE

20.1 Different apostolic modes. Unity on the essentials. Rejecting any sign of the 'one-party mentality' in the Church.

Today's *First Reading* from the Old Testament relates how Moses asked the Lord to give his spirit to other elders of the tribe.[1] Moses did not feel that he had sufficient strength to carry all the responsibility by himself. The Lord *took some of the spirit that was on him and put it on the seventy elders.* These men congregated at the Tent and began to prophesy right away. *Two men had stayed back in the camp; one was called Eldad and the other Medad. The spirit came down on them; though they had not gone to the Tent, their names were enrolled among the rest. These began to prophesy in the camp.* Joshua asked Moses to forbid them from doing so. Moses responded: *If only the whole people of the Lord were prophets, and the Lord gave his Spirit to them all!*

The Gospel for today's Mass concerns a somewhat similar event.[2] John approaches Jesus to report that the apostles have seen a man casting out demons in the name of Jesus. Since he does not belong to the Master's circle, the apostles try to stop him. But Jesus corrects John by saying: *You must not stop him: no one who works a miracle in my name is likely to speak evil of me.*

Jesus reproves the exclusive mentality of his disciples. He opens their eyes to an apostolate of wide-ranging

---

[1] Num 11:25-29
[2] Mark 9:38-41

dimensions. Christians should not have a *'one-party' mentality* which would lead them to reject legitimate diversity in apostolic activities. All that matters is unity in the essentials, in that which forms the foundations of the Church. St John Paul II affirmed that through Baptism all Christians have a right of association. He has listed the fundamental criteria for determining whether a particular association is in union with the Church.[3] Such associations are to be evaluated, first of all, according to *the primacy given to the call of every Christian to holiness* which is the best expression of the fulness of Christian life. It is in this regard that each association of this kind should act as an *instrument leading to holiness.*

The Pope also emphasizes certain criteria relating to the *apostolate*: *The responsibility of professing the Catholic faith, embracing and proclaiming the truth about Christ, the Church and humanity, in obedience to the Church's Magisterium as the Church interprets it. For this reason every association of lay faithful must be a forum where the faith is proclaimed as well as taught in its total content.* Every Christian has a part to play in the Church's apostolic work. The Lord wants there to be apostles in the factory, the office, the university, in the home ... As a consequence of their faith, Christians should live a filial unity with the Pope and the Bishops. Catholic associations should be loyal to the teachings of the Church and follow the directions that come from the hierarchy. *Church communion demands both an acknowledgment of a legitimate plurality of forms in the associations of the lay faithful in the Church and at the same time, a willingness to cooperate in working together.*

If we are *full-time* Christians, then we will have to take our faith into the workplace. We will want to light up our

---

[3] St John Paul II, Apostolic Exhortation, *Christifideles laici*, 30 December 1988, 30

conduct by becoming familiar with the social doctrine of the Church. *Therefore, associations of the lay faithful must become fruitful outlets for participation and solidarity in bringing about conditions that are more just and loving within society.*

If we have the heart of Christ, how easy it will be to accept the apostolic activities of others! This diversity in unity will give us cause for rejoicing. The absolutely essential thing is that Christ be known and loved.

The Good News has to reach every corner of the earth. For this work the Lord counts on everyone to contribute: men and women, priests and laity, young and old, widowers, married people, members of religious orders, associations inspired to do the work of the Holy Spirit ... No Christian is exempt.

20.2 All of life's circumstances are good for apostolate.

Every Christian is called to extend the Kingdom of Christ. Every social circumstance is a good opportunity for bringing this about. *Wherever God opens a door for the word in order to declare the mystery of Christ, then the living the God, and He whom He has sent for the salvation of all, Jesus Christ, are confidently and perseveringly proclaimed to all men.*[4] In the face of cowardliness, laziness or excuses, we have to keep in mind that many people depend on our word and example if they are to receive the grace to follow Christ more closely. We can never stop doing apostolate with the people whom God has placed by our side. The means used may differ, but the end is always the same. There are many, many different ways for people to be drawn to the Lord.

Let us maintain, therefore, our fervour of spirit. Let us preserve the sweet and heartfelt joy of evangelizing, even

---

[4] Second Vatican Council, Decree *Ad gentes*, 13

when we have to sow in tears.[5] We can not give in to thinking that adverse circumstances are an obstacle to the apostolate. Difficulties can serve as a means for extending Christ's teaching – as was shown by the first Christians and by so many others who have suffered for the Faith. St Paul wrote to the Philippians from his prison cell: *Most of the brethren have been made confident in the Lord because of my imprisonment, and are much more bold to speak the word of God without fear.* Even though some had been preaching out of envy, with a lack of right intention, the Apostle exclaims: *What then? Only that in every way, whether in pretence or in truth, Christ is proclaimed; and in that I rejoice. Yes, and I shall rejoice.*[6] Our most important goal is that we draw closer to Christ from day to day. The Lord invites everyone to this work. There is no room for a *'one-party' mentality* in this divine progress. The Church has never wanted to force her children into one specific spirituality. On the contrary, she has always valued the great variety of spiritual paths and apostolates available to her children.

There is no doubt that work, rest, social life, sport, can all provide chances to bring people to God. Contradictions and even downright persecution can also teach us to treat others with charity. These conditions can train us how to love our enemy. St Polycarp, bishop and martyr, wrote about this form of education in his *Letter to the Philippians* which appears in today's *Liturgy of the Hours.* He asks the faithful to abstain from *critical spirit and false accusations, thereby returning evil for evil, insult for insult, blow for blow. Remember instead the words of the Lord who taught us: 'Do not judge and you will not be judged; forgive and you will be forgiven; have compassion and you will be understood. The measure you use will be used against you.*

---

[5] Bl. Paul VI, *Evangelii nuntiandi,* 8 December 1975, 80
[6] Phil 1:14-18

Blessed are those who suffer persecution, for theirs is the kingdom of God.[7] We ought not to respond in kind to ill-treatment. If we need to defend ourselves we should by all means do so, but always with respect for the person involved. We must teach others that our actions are inspired by the charity of Christ. All apostolate that takes place in the shadow of the Cross is fruitful.

20.3 Charity is the bond of unity and the foundation of the apostolate.

Whatever form our apostolate takes and whatever reception it gets, charity must always inform our activities. The Lord made this very clear when he said: *By this all men will know that you are my disciples, if you have love for one another.*[8]

When St Paul wrote to the Thessalonians and recalled his visit with them, he made a point of reminding them: *For you know how, like a father with his children, we exhorted each one of you and encouraged you and charged you to lead a life worthy of God, who calls you into his own kingdom and glory.*[9] *Each one of you,* he writes. Every one. The Apostle did not limit himself to preaching in the synagogues and public places as was certainly his custom. He made sure that he paid attention to each and every individual in the Christian community. He gave friendly encouragement and guidance to every single one. This is how we should behave with our neighbours at work, at home, in the classroom, in the community. We should become good friends with those around us. Friendship is the basis of all apostolate. We should really care for our neighbours, even though this may take some effort at first. Defects should not be a cause of alienation. *The ministry of*

---

[7] *Liturgy of the Hours,* Second Reading
[8] John 13:35
[9] 1 Thess 2:11-12

evangelization requires of the evangelizer a fraternal and ever-increasing love for those whom he is evangelizing.[10] We have to see in each person his or her value as a child of God. This realization will lead us to a true esteem for our neighbour which will be stronger than any defects or difficulties.

We who have received the gift of faith should feel the need to share it with others. This effort should be the prime motivation of our life. The apostolic mission is not exclusively the responsibility of the clergy and religious, or of specially-commissioned and *ad hoc* groups. It is the task of every Christian. With the lives of the first Christians as our model, we should examine the actuality of our apostolate in the middle of the world. Let us not forget those moving words of Jesus from today's Gospel: *For truly, I say to you, whoever gives you a cup of water to drink because you bear the name of Christ, will by no means lose his reward.* What will be the Lord's reward for us if we bring many souls to him?

---

[10] Bl. Paul VI, *loc cit,* 79

21. SHARING

21.1 The parable of the rich man and Lazarus.

In the *First Reading* for today's Mass[1] we meet the Prophet Amos on his return from the desert of Samaria. He finds the leaders of the chosen people wholly given over to the pleasures of the world. *Lying on ivory beds and sprawling on their divans, they dine on lambs from the flock, and stall-fattened veal ... They drink wine by the bowlful, and use the finest oil for anointing themselves, but about the ruin of Joseph they do not care at all.* Amos then declares what is to be their destiny: *That is why they will be the first to be exiled.* This prophecy was fulfilled a few years afterwards.

Today's liturgy warns us that an excessive concern for comfort and the things of this world will inevitably lead to a neglect of God and neighbour. The Gospel records Christ's parable about a man who fell into this very trap.[2] Instead of winning Heaven through the use of his wealth, he lost it forever. The story concerns *a rich man who used to dress in purple and fine linen and feast magnificently everyday.* Meanwhile, at his door there was *a poor man called Lazarus, covered with sores, who longed to fill himself with the scraps that fell from the rich man's table.*

The Lord contrasts two extreme conditions in this parable: vast wealth in one case, tremendous need in the other. Jesus says nothing about the rich man's possessions themselves. He puts his entire emphasis on how they have

---

[1] Amos 6:1; 4-7
[2] Luke 16:19-31

been used, mentioning only expensive clothes and sumptuous daily banquets. Lazarus was not even given the left-overs.

The rich man did nothing wrong as he amassed his fortune. He was not responsible for the wretched poverty of Lazarus, at least not in any direct way. He did not take advantage of the situation to exploit Lazarus. Nevertheless, the rich man had a definite lifestyle. It might be summed up with the words *he feasted magnificently*. He lived for himself as if God did not exist. He had completely forgotten the fact that we are not owners of what we have, but only administrators.

The rich man had a good time to himself. He was not against God, nor did he oppress his impoverished neighbour. He was simply blind to the existence of the needy person on his doorstep. He lived for himself and spared himself no expense. What was his sin? He did not see Lazarus. He could have cared for Lazarus if he had not been so selfish. He did not use his wealth in a way that was in conformity with God's desires. He did not know how to share. St Augustine comments: *Lazarus was received into Heaven because of his humility and not because of his poverty. Wealth itself was not what kept the rich man from eternal bliss. His punishment was for selfishness and disloyalty.*[3]

Selfishness can be manifested in an insatiable desire to possess more and more material goods. It can make people blind to the needs of their neighbours. Selfish people come to treat others as if they were objects without value. Let us remember today that we all have needy people living alongside of us – people like Lazarus. We cannot forget to administer what we have with generosity. In addition to the sharing of material goods, we should also be sowers of understanding, sympathy, friendship ...

---

[3] St Augustine, *Sermon 24,* 3

21.2 How well we use the goods of this life may determine whether we win or lose entrance to Heaven.

Our life on earth is a testing-ground for our generosity. The Lord reminds us: *It is better to give than to receive.*[4] Paradoxically, one gets more from giving than from receiving: what one gets is Heaven. If we are generous, we will come to discover that other people are really children of God who need us. We will then be happy on this earth and also for eternity. Charity itself is the realization of the Kingdom of God. It is one commodity of which there can never be an excess. We have to be alert for the Lazarus in our home, in our office or place of work ...

In the *Second Reading,* St Paul teaches Timothy that *covetousness is the root of all evils.*[5] Then Paul reminds him: *As a man dedicated to God, you must aim to be saintly and religious, filled with faith and love, patient and gentle. Fight the good fight of the faith and win for yourself the eternal life to which you were called ...*[6]

All Christian men and women have been chosen by God to be the leaven that transforms and sanctifies temporal realities. We should help to save people from eternal death much as the first Christians did in their communities. When we witness the worldly concerns of so many of our neighbours, we have to remember that the power of our *fermentation* as yeast will depend a great deal on our sense of detachment. We will not be able to influence our surroundings if we permit ourselves to become attached to things we don't need, and if we acquire wasteful spending habits. We need to teach people by our example that happiness and salvation will not come from the possession of material things, but only from living a holy life.

---

[4] Acts 20:25

[5] 1 Tim 6:10

[6] 1 Tim 6:11-16

Sobriety, temperance and detachment will create the conditions for us to be generous with others, to be attentive to the needs of the poor, to comfort the sick. We will then find that we are freed from the snares set by our selfish nature, from a disordered desire for things. In this way *we will be able to live solidarity with those who suffer, with the poor and the sick, with the marginalized and the oppressed. Our sensitivity will grow. It will not be so hard for us to see Jesus Christ in the needy person in front of us. It is Christ who speaks to us those memorable words: 'As long as you did it for these the least of my brethren, you did it for me' (Matt 25:40). These will be our credentials on the day of judgment. We will all understand at that time that Heaven is reserved for those who loved their brothers in deeds and in truth.*[7]

21.3 Detachment. Sharing with others what we ourselves have been given.

Be not conformed to this world ...[8] This was St Paul's message to the first Christians in Rome. When we lead selfish lives we find it very difficult to see the needs of others. We also find it increasingly difficult to see God. *The rich man was condemned because he did not pay attention to the other man. Because he failed to take notice of Lazarus, the person who sat at his door and who longed to eat the scraps from his table.*[9] We should be willing to give away a great deal while teaching others also to be generous.

Christians must not sit idly by as the tide of materialism sweeps over our entire culture. Nor should we become entrapped by a purely economic vision of the world. *Solidarity is a direct requirement of human and*

---

[7] A. Fuentes, *The Christian Meaning of Wealth*, Madrid 1988

[8] Rom 12:2

[9] St John Paul II, *Homily at Yankee Stadium*, 2 October 1979

supernatural brotherhood.[10] This attitude will lead us to live that personal poverty which Jesus called *blessed*. This poverty consists of detachment, of confidence in God, of temperance and generosity, of a longing for justice, of hunger for the kingdom of heaven, of docility to the word of God and perseverance in the truth (cf '*Libertatis conscientia*', 66). This is quite different from the poverty that oppresses most of our brothers in this world, impeding their integral development as persons. Before this type of poverty and privation, the Church lifts up her voice to promote the solidarity which is so urgently required.[11]

We have got to see the people around us as our brothers. They are brothers in need of the great treasure of the Faith which we possess. They need our joy, our friendship and sometimes our economic assistance. We can not remain indifferent to conditions in parts of the world when so many are suffering from want of food, lack of education and ignorance of the truth about man and God.

We should examine ourselves to see whether our detachment is a real detachment. Does it lead to any practical consequences? Our life should be a model of temperance as far as our use of material goods is concerned. Do we have our heart focussed on the treasure that lasts forever, which neither thief can take away nor moth destroy?[12] If we are faithful, we can have Christ for all eternity. St Augustine records the story of his conversion in these words: *How lovely I suddenly found it, to be free from the glamour of those vanities, so that now it was a joy to renounce what I had been so much afraid to lose. For you cast them out of me, O true and supreme Loveliness, you cast them out of me and took their place instead, you*

---

[10] Congregation for the Doctrine of the Faith, Instruction *Libertatis conscientia,* 22 March 1986, 89
[11] St John Paul II, *Homily,* 7 May 1990
[12] cf Luke 12:33

who are sweeter than all pleasure, yet not to mere flesh and blood; brighter than all light, yet deeper within than any secret; loftier than all honour, but not to those who are high and mighty in their own estimation. [13] What a shame if we should ever fail to appreciate the treasure of divine love!

---

[13] St Augustine, *Confessions,* 9, 1, 1

22. THE CHRISTIAN MEANING OF SUFFERING

22.1 The trials and tribulations of Job.

During the course of this week we read from the *Book of Job* about the subject of suffering and disgrace.[1]

This is the inspired story of a God-fearing man named Job who lived in the land of Hus. He had received countless blessings during his life. He was a prosperous farmer with abundant sheep, livestock and crops. He was the father of a large family. According to the beliefs of the time there was a direct relationship between leading a virtuous life and enjoying worldly prosperity. Job's material prosperity would have been seen as a reward from God for his saintly life. The story indeed begins with the fact that God is pleased with Job. Satan comes before God to challenge the sincerity of Job's fidelity. He predicts that Job will abandon God when put to the test: *Job is not God-fearing for nothing, is he? Have you not put a wall round him and his house and all his domain? You have blessed all he undertakes, and his flocks throng the countryside. But stretch out your hand and lay a finger on his possessions: I warrant you, he will curse you to your face.*[2]

With God's permission the devil strips Job of all possessions. Then his numerous children perish in a disaster. Faithful to his beliefs, Job reacts with submission to divine providence: *Naked I came from my mother's womb, naked I shall return. The Lord gave, the Lord has*

---

[1] *First Reading,* Year II, Job 1:6-22
[2] Job 1:9-11

taken back. Blessed be the name of the Lord![3] Job gives his complete acceptance to God's Will in both prosperity and adversity. He converts his misery into a wonderful spiritual treasure.

God then allows Satan to put Job through an even greater trial. His body is afflicted with loathsome sores from head to foot. To lose one's physical well-being can be even worse than the loss of material goods. Job's faith, however, remains steadfast despite his ailments and in spite of sharp words from his wife. He tells her: *Shall we receive good at the hand of God, and shall we not receive evil?*[4]

Today is a good time to examine what our feelings towards God are when we experience disgrace or suffering, or both. God is always our loving Father, even when we are sorely afflicted. Do we behave as grateful sons and daughters in good times and bad times alike, in sickness and in health?

22.2 The sufferings of the just.

Three of Job's friends, each from a different tribe, learn of his fate and join together to provide some consolation. Their names are Eliphaz, Bildad and Zophar. When they find Job in such a lamentable state they are convinced that God has cast a curse upon him. These men believe that prosperity is God's reward for virtue. Tribulation, they hold, is God's punishment for iniquity. The conduct of these men combined with the prolongation of his suffering makes Job feel very lonely. He breaks his silence with a lengthy lamentation. His 'comforters' have some harsh words for their friend, who has surely offended God in some grievous way. Job is convinced of his fundamental innocence even though he has committed

---

[3] Job 1:21
[4] Job 2:10

minor offences like any other person.[5] He also recalls the
many good works he has done. A great conflict erupts in
the depths of his soul.

Job knows that God is just, but he is totally unable to
make sense of the injustice he is going through. He also
believes that God treats man according to some system of
merit. Yet how is he to reconcile divine justice with his
tragic fate? His friends are ready with an answer to his
problem, but he rejects this answer of theirs. There appears
to be an insoluble contradiction between divine justice and
Job's innocence. This conflict gives Job still more anguish
than even his physical sufferings and material disaster.[6]
Seen without the eyes of faith, the suffering of innocent
people is always disturbing – children who die in infancy,
babies who are born with serious defects, upright people
who experience economic catastrophe or grave illness ... all
this, while others who seem indifferent to God live and
prosper without a care in the world.

The *Book of Job with complete frankness presents the
problem of the suffering of an innocent man: suffering
without guilt. Job has not been punished, there was no
reason for inflicting a punishment on him, even if he has
been subjected to a grievous trial.*[7] As a consequence of
this test, Job emerges strengthened in virtue. His loyalty
does not, after all, depend on temporal blessings received
from God. *The Book of Job is not the last word on this
subject in Revelation. In a certain way it is a foretelling of
the Passion of Christ*[8] which is the only satisfactory
explanation for the mystery of human suffering, especially
for the pain experienced by those who have done no

---

[5] cf Job 13:26; 14:4
[6] cf B. Orchard, *Verbum Dei,* Barcelona 1960, II, pp. 104 ff
[7] St John Paul II, Apostolic Letter, *Salvifici doloris,* 11 February 1984,
11
[8] *ibid*

wrong.

For God so loved the world that he gave his only Son, that whoever believes in him should not perish but have eternal life.[9] One can say that with the Passion of Christ all human suffering has found itself in a new situation. And it is as though Job had foreseen this when he said: *'I know that my Redeemer lives ...' (Job 19:25)*, and as though he had directed towards it his own suffering, which without the Redemption could not have revealed to him the fullness of its meaning. In the Cross of Christ not only is the Redemption accomplished through suffering, but also human suffering itself has been redeemed. Christ – without any fault of his own – took on himself 'the total evil of sin'.[10] The sufferings of Jesus were the price of our salvation.[11] From that moment on, our suffering could be united with the suffering of Christ. In this way we can participate in the Redemption of all mankind. *The great Christian revolution has been to convert pain into fruitful suffering and to turn a bad thing into something good. We have deprived the devil of this weapon; and with it we can conquer eternity.*[12]

22.3 Pain and the Passion of Christ.

The experience of pain always leaves one a different person than before. Pain can purify and elevate the soul. It can move us to intensify our union with the divine Will. It can inspire us to become detached from worldly goods and from excessive concern for our health. Pain can make us co-Redeemers with Christ. Pain can do all this ... or it can lead us away from the Lord, leaving the soul alienated from the supernatural life. When Simon of Cyrene was

---

[9] John 3:16
[10] St John Paul II, *loc cit,* 19
[11] cf 1 Cor 6:20
[12] St. J. Escrivá, *Furrow,* 887

picked out of the crowd to help Jesus carry his Cross, he did what he was told to do without enthusiasm. He was *forced,* writes the Evangelist.[13] The first thing he saw was the cross, just heavy wooden planks. Later on, his thoughts turned from the wood to the condemned prisoner, that very unusual man. It was then that his attitude was transformed. He helped Jesus out of love. He won the prize of faith for himself and for his two sons, Alexander and Rufus.[14] We too should look for Christ in the midst of our trials and tribulations. By so doing, we will pay less attention to the Cross and more attention to our Beloved. We will discover that *carrying the Cross* has true meaning when we walk alongside the Master. *His most fervent desire is to inflame our hearts with that same fire of love and sacrifice which burns in his own heart. No matter how little we correspond with this wish, our heart will become a furnace powerful enough to burn away the dross of our accumulated faults. We will be changed into sacrificial offerings, blessed by suffering until we attain to a greater purity and a closer union with our Beloved. We will complete, as He wants us to do, the Passion of the Saviour for the good of the Church and all souls (Col 1:24). It is at the feet of the Crucified Lord that we will come to an understanding of the true nature of the love that lies in sacrifice. Yet sacrifice is sweet to him who is in love.*[15]

As we finish our meditation, let us contemplate the scene of Our Lady on Calvary in union with the sufferings of her Son. *Marvel at the courage of Mary – at the foot of the cross, in the greatest of human sorrow (there is no sorrow like hers), filled with fortitude. And ask her for that same fortitude, so that you, too, will know how to remain*

---

[13] Matt 27:32

[14] cf Mark 15:21

[15] A. Tanquerey, *The divinization of suffering,* Madrid 1955

close to the cross.[16] Next to Mary we can well understand how *sacrifice is sweet to him who is in love.* We will put before her most sweet Heart all of our failures, mistakes, misunderstandings, family problems, headaches and setbacks at work, sickness and pain ... *Once the offering has been made we should try not to think about that particular trouble any more. We should concentrate our mind on fulfilling whatever is God's Will for us, there where we are – in the family, in the factory, in the office, at school ... Above all, we will seek to love those whom God has placed by our side.*

If we do this we will have a wonderful surprise: our soul will be filled with peace, with love, with pure joy, with light. We will find ourselves lifted up by a new energy. We shall see how we can participate in the work of the Resurrected Lord by our union with the Cross.

Revitalized by this discovery, we will be able to help our friends to find solace amidst their tears. We will become instruments of joy for many, many people. We will be spreading a happiness that knows no limit.[17]

---

[16] St. J. Escrivá, *The Way,* 508
[17] Ch. Lubich, *Words which give life,* Madrid 1990

TWENTY-SIXTH WEEK: TUESDAY

23. ON THE ROAD TO JERUSALEM

23.1 We should not become discouraged at the sight of our defects. The Lord has taken them into account. He wants us to make the effort to overcome them.

As the time drew near for him to be taken up to heaven, Jesus resolutely took the road for Jerusalem. Upon his entering a Samaritan village *the people would not receive him because He was making for Jerusalem.*[1] The Lord takes no action against the Samaritans for their inhospitable behaviour. He does not even speak ill of them. He prefers to lead his company to another village. The Apostles react in a different manner. James and John ask the Lord: *Do you want us to call down fire from heaven to burn them up?* The Lord takes advantage of this opportunity to teach his disciples to be understanding towards everyone, even towards those who do not understand them.

The Gospels are replete with examples of the personal defects of the Apostles. James and John and the others had their shortcomings even as they took in the words and example of the Master. God knows that spiritual growth takes time. He has no illusions about the weaknesses and defects of his disciples in every period of history. It was this same indignant John who would write many years later: *He who does not love does not know God; for God is love.*[2] He has been converted into the one we remember as the Apostle of charity and love! Without ever losing his identity, John was transformed by the workings of the Holy

---

[1] Luke 9:52-56
[2] 1 John 4:8

Spirit. The central theme of his letters is charity. St Augustine has commented – on the first letter of John – that *he said many things. Practically all of them were related to charity.*[3] It is John who has given us Christ's *new commandment*, the *mandatum novum* that is the distinguishing characteristic of his disciples.[4] John learned a fundamental lesson from the Master – that *if we love one another, God abides in us and his love is perfected in us.*[5]

Tradition has preserved for us a number of details about the final years of John's life. He always insisted on the importance of fraternal love. St Jerome relates that when the disciples took John to prayer services, the Apostle would repeat again and again: *Little children, love one another.* When the disciples asked him why he always said the same thing, John answered: *This is the Lord's commandment. If you follow that commandment, it is enough.*[6]

Whenever we have a glimpse of our many defects we should meditate on the lives of the saints. They had their defects as well. But they struggled against their defects with humility and ultimately achieved sanctity. This has been true despite personal faults that have led to un-Christian behaviour, as we once saw in the case of St John.

23.2 The continual assistance of the Holy Spirit.

In the wake of Pentecost, the Holy Spirit completed the formation of those who had been chosen to be the supporting pillars of the Church, in spite of their frailties. Since that time the Holy Spirit has not ceased to operate in the souls of Christians of every epoch. The inspirations of the Holy Spirit occasionally affect us as fast as lightning: that we be generous in some small mortification, that we be

---

[3] St Augustine, *Commentary on the First Letter of St John,* prologue
[4] cf John 13:34-35
[5] 1 John 4:12
[6] St Jerome, *Commentary on the Epistle to the Galatians,* III, 6

patient in the face of adversity, that we control our senses ... At other times the Holy Spirit acts directly to inspire some good. He speaks to us through the advice we receive in spiritual direction, through events in our lives, through the impressive example of another person, through reading a good book ... The Holy Spirit wants to *lay in the edifice of my life the stone which is there and then needed.*[7] God has great plans for us, but they will only be realized with our docile cooperation. Everything has been ordered, permitted, decreed by our Father God so that we may achieve holiness. It is for this very reason that we have been created. This is the way in which we are to find happiness on earth and in heaven. Pain, suffering and failure are permitted by God so that we might never lose sight of our last end: *For this is the Will of God, your sanctification.*[8]

God never stops loving us, whether He gives us consolations or permits us to experience affliction, suffering, poverty, or failure ... Even more, *God never loves me more than when He sends me suffering.*[9] This is a *divine caress* for which we should be grateful. In today's Gospel, St Luke reminds us of how determined Jesus was to go up to Jerusalem where the Cross awaited him.

St John did not change in an instant, not even after receiving the rebuke of the Lord. But he did not become discouraged by his failings. He stayed by the side of the Lord and grace did the rest. This is what God asks of each one of us. With the passing of years, the Apostle remembered this event, as well as other occasions when he was far from being in tune with the spirit of the Master. He recalled the patience Jesus had with him. How many times he had to begin again! This recognition served to deepen his love for Jesus.

---

[7] J. Tissot, *The Interior Life,* p. 184
[8] 1 Thess 4:3
[9] J. Tissot, *op cit,* p. 188

23.3 The dominant defect.

God granted St John a profound grasp of the meaning of charity both in his writings and his personal life. The Lord chose him to watch over Our Lady! Inspired by the Holy Spirit, John wrote these words of great wisdom: *By this it may be seen who are the children of God, and who are the children of the devil: whoever does not do right is not of God, nor he who does not love his brother.*[10] We can not become discouraged at the thought of our faults and failures. The Lord knows full well what we are made of. He relies on time and grace along with our desires to improve.

According to many authors of spiritual books, progress in our life of piety depends a good deal on our recognition and understanding of our *dominant defect*. This is the defect which has the biggest influence on our behaviour and thinking.[11] It typically becomes evident in what we do, what we want, what we think: it can be vanity, laziness, impatience, pessimism, a critical spirit ... Each person has his or her own path to holiness. Some people require more fortitude. Others need more hope or joy. *If we think of the interior life as a little fortress, then the dominant defect is the weak point in the wall. The enemy of souls looks precisely for this area of vulnerability so that he can enter the fortress with relative ease. As a result, we would do well to know this weakness.*[12] We ought to ask ourselves: What do we habitually have our hearts set on? What worries us most? What leads us to suffer or lose our peace or fall into sadness? Most of the temptations we experience will be related in some way to this dominant defect. This strategy is completely logical from the enemy's point of view.

Progress in the interior life requires knowledge of this defect. Let us ask God for his grace in overcoming it: *Lord,*

---

[10] 1 John 3:10

[11] cf R. Garrigou-Lagrange, *The Three Ages of the Interior Life,* I

[12] *ibid*

keep away from me whatever keeps me away from you. We can repeat this prayer many times a day. We should build up the firm resolution never to make a compromise with our defects. The *particular examination* should be focussed on the wearing down of the dominant defect. *In your particular examination you have to go straight toward the acquisition of a definite virtue or toward the rooting out of the defect which is dominating you.*[13] We will find the strength to wage this life-long struggle in personal spiritual direction.

Mary, our Mother, will forever offer peace and joy to all those who resolve to follow the Lord. *Our step should be lively like that of the Virgin's. Like Mary too, we will experience pain, exhaustion from work, difficult moments of faith.*

We walk hand-in-hand with Mary, who is full of grace. God the Father, God the Son, God the Holy Spirit have showered her with gifts. She has been made the most perfect creature. She is a person like us. Her mission is to give out good things. More than that, she has become herself our life, our sweetness and our hope.

Mary, Mother of Jesus, 'sign of consolation and sure hope' (Second Vatican Council, Lumen gentium, 68). She is the guiding light that goes before the pilgrim People of God. She is our Mother. She is the way to reach the Lord. Mary will fill our lives with joy.[14]

---

[13] St. J. Escrivá, *The Way,* 241
[14] J. Urteaga, *The Defects of the Saints,* Madrid 1982

TWENTY-SIXTH WEEK: WEDNESDAY

24. FOLLOWING CHRIST

24.1 Following Christ requires detachment. The material goods of this world as means to that end. Learning to live Christian poverty.

Today's Gospel tells of a time Jesus decided to cross over to the other side of the Sea of Galilee.[1] A scribe approached him and declared: *I will follow you wherever you go.* Jesus then explained in a few words what following him would entail – the renunciation of comfort, detachment from things, complete abandonment to the divine Will: *Foxes have holes, and birds of the air have nests; but the Son of man has nowhere to lay his head.*

Jesus asks of disciples, of all of us, a radical and habitual detachment: the firm resolve to be the master of the things we use. We can never become attached to possessions. Those who have been called to live their vocations in the world need to give this struggle serious attention and keep it up. This struggle is all the more important nowadays when the desire for having, for owning and enjoying things has become the ultimate aim of many lives.[2]

To live the poverty which Christ asks of his disciples requires a great interior sense of detachment, in the mind and in the will, in the imagination. It is necessary to live the same spirit as the Lord did.[3] One of the first manifestations of evangelical poverty is the use of goods as

---

[1] Luke 9:57-62
[2] cf Second Vatican Council, *Gaudium et spes,* 63
[3] cf St Francis de Sales, *Introduction to the Devout Life,* III, 15

means instead of as ends in themselves.[4] Let us ask the
Lord that we may never become carried away by a
disordered desire for more and more wealth. Material
means are *goods* insofar as they are ordered to a higher
end: to support a family, to educate one's children, to
acquire a better education for the elevation of society, to
help works of apostolate and assist those people who are in
need ... This is not so easy to implement in those critical
situations where the heart of man becomes mistakenly
attached. We have to learn how to avoid in real life
attachments to people or places or things that can impede our
progress to the Lord. This training is necessary whether we
own great wealth or hardly any at all. We should not confuse
the attitude of poverty with the condition of poverty: *It is this
sort of poverty, made up of detachment, trust in God,
sobriety and a readiness to share, that Jesus declared
blessed.*[5] This is the poverty required of those who intend to
sanctify themselves in the middle of the world.

St Paul relates how much he depended on this
education in detachment when he wrote to the Philippians:
*I know how to be abased, and I know how to abound; in
any and all circumstances I have learned the secret of
facing plenty and hunger, abundance and want. I can do
all things in him who strengthens me.*[6] He placed all his
trust in God.

24.2 Living poverty: the proper use of money, avoiding unnecessary expenses, luxury, caprice ...

Let us continue our contemplation of the Christ who
had *nowhere to lay his head*. If we are going to follow
Christ we have to imitate his life. We need to use material

---

[4] A. Tanquerey, *The Spiritual Life,* Baltimore 1930
[5] Congregation for the Doctrine of the Faith, *Instruction on Christian
Freedom and Liberation,* 22 March 1986, 66
[6] Phil 4:12-13

means to fulfil our vocation on earth, but we cannot allow these means to cheapen or slacken our dedication.

Authentic Christian poverty is incompatible with ambition for superfluous goods, as distinct from things that are really necessary. If someone who is dedicated to serving God were to become consumed with such worries, this would be a sign of lukewarmness in his interior life. The soul, in this case, is vainly trying to serve two masters.[7] If we readily accept the privation and discomfort that poverty entails we will become more united to Jesus Christ.

One clear aspect of Christian poverty has to do with the proper use of money. Some things are altogether disproportionately expensive. How can a Christian aspire to such extravagance when there are so many people living in abject penury? These are the objects, the creature comforts, the caprices which have no place in the life of a follower of the Master. Going without these attractions may lead us to run counter to contemporary fashion in our environment. Our example of living Christian poverty may help many others to forego and reject the values of practical materialism.

What could be more opposed to the spirit of Christian mortification than spending-sprees motivated by capriciousness? We have to be honest with ourselves when it comes, for example, to our use of corporate expense accounts and similar perquisites and privileges. The heart can very easily become attached to the things of this earth. The heart can become quite incapable of understanding or seeking supernatural goods. There is a great deal more to reality than what delights the senses.

No matter whether we are rich or poor we need to be poor in spirit for love of Christ. We use material goods in many different ways, but we should always make use of them with the same interior approach. *I copy these words*

---

[7] cf Matt 6:24

*for you because they can bring peace to your soul. 'My
financial situation is as tight as it ever has been. But I
don't lose my peace. I'm quite sure that God, my Father,
will settle the whole business once and for all. I want,
Lord, to abandon the care of all my affairs into your
generous hands. Our Mother – your Mother – will have let
you hear those words, now as in Cana: 'They have none!' I
believe in you, I hope in you, I love you, Jesus. I want
nothing for myself: it's for them'.*[8] Perhaps there are many
times when we need to make this prayer our own.

24.3 Further aspects of Christian poverty: rejecting superfluous and false needs ... The joyful acceptance of scarcity and want.

We want to follow Christ very closely, to live as He
lived in the middle of the world. One way to live poverty is
to take good care of what we have so that it lasts a long
time. This approach to things requires real mortification. It
consists of very small sacrifices made over and over again.
It is much easier and more comfortable to leave one's
belongings lying about all over the place and carelessly
looked after, to put off a small repair that could preclude a
major one later at greater expense.

If we can live without superfluous goods we will be to
that extent closer to Christ's own life of detachment. Let us
ask ourselves frequently: Do I really need this? For
example, do I need two fountain pens? St Augustine
teaches: *What is superfluous for the rich is the necessity of
the poor. When we have superfluous possessions, we
possess objects that harm us.*[9] Do I have many things I
don't really need? Shoes, utensils, sportswear, clothing ...
One clear sign of detachment is genuinely not to consider

---

[8] St. J. Escrivá, *The Forge*, 807
[9] St Augustine, *Commentary on Psalm 147*

anything as one's own.[10] Do I truly live out the consequences of Christian detachment?

Christian poverty is certainly compatible with the tasteful decoration of a Christian home. The home should be a place where everyone in the family can relax in pleasant surroundings from the day's work. People should look forward to reviving their energies at home. Yet the home should not be a setting for non-stop entertainment. Giving up superfluous needs means, above all, not creating needs for oneself. *We have to make demands on ourselves in our daily lives. In this way we will not go about inventing false problems and ingenious needs which, in the last analysis, are prompted by conceit, capriciousness and a comfort-loving and lazy approach to life. We ought to be striding towards God at a fast pace, carrying no dead weights or impedimenta which might hinder our progress.*[11]

While we struggle to be free of false attachments we should be growing in our gratitude to the Lord for what we have. We should thank God for the goods we have at our disposal at work, which allow us to support our families and collaborate in apostolic activities. We are prepared to be separated from these good things should God so desire. We will not complain when we lack even what we need. We will not lose our interior joy, because we know ourselves to be in the hands of our loving Father. He knows best.

The Blessed Virgin will help us to put into practice this first-class piece of advice: *Do not fix your heart on anything that passes away. Imitate Christ, who became poor for us, and had nowhere to lay his head. Ask him to give you, in the midst of the world, a real detachment, a detachment that has nothing to soften it.*[12]

---

[10] St. J. Escrivá, *op cit,* 524
[11] *idem, Friends of God,* 125
[12] *idem, The Forge,* 523

25. THE HARVEST IS PLENTIFUL

25.1 The urgent need for new apostles to re-evangelize the world.

Among the crowds that followed Jesus there was a large number of disciples.[1] They included many who accompanied Our Lord from the time of the baptism of John to the Ascension. The *Acts of the Apostles* gives us further news about some of these people, especially Joseph called Barsabbas, and Matthias.[2] Christ appeared to two of these disciples, Cleopas and his companion, on the road to Emmaus.[3] None of these disciples was called to be one of the original twelve Apostles, but they were nevertheless an important and highly dedicated group of followers.[4] They formed the nucleus of the primitive Church after Pentecost. The Gospel of today's Mass tells of the time when Jesus appointed seventy-two of these disciples to prepare the people for his arrival. *The harvest is plentiful,* he told them, *but the labourers are few.*[5]

In our day the apostolic panorama is equally immense – traditionally Christian countries which need to be re-evangelized, nations which have suffered many years of religious persecution, entire peoples thirsting for doctrine ... We need only look about us at our surroundings – our place of work or study, the means of communication – in order to grasp the dimensions of what needs to be done.

---

[1] cf Mark 2:15
[2] cf Acts 1:21-26
[3] cf Luke 24:13-35
[4] cf P. R. Bernard, *The Mystery of Jesus,* Barcelona 1965
[5] Luke 10:1-12

The harvest is plentiful ... Whole countries and nations where religion and the Christian life were formerly flourishing and capable of fostering a viable and working community of faith are now put to a hard test, and in some cases are even undergoing a radical transformation as a result of a constant spreading of an indifference to religion, of secularism and atheism. This particularly concerns countries and nations of the so-called First World in which economic well-being and consumerism, even if coexistent with a tragic situation of poverty and misery, inspires and sustains a life lived 'as if God did not exist.' This indifference to religion and the practice of religion devoid of true meaning in the face of life's very serious problems are not less worrying and upsetting when compared with declared atheism. Sometimes the Christian faith as well, while maintaining some of the externals of its tradition and rituals, tends to be separated from those moments of human existence which have the most significance, such as birth, suffering and death. In such cases, the questions and formidable enigmas posed by these situations, if remaining without responses, expose contemporary people to an inconsolable delusion or to the temptation of eliminating the truly humanizing dimension of life implicit in these problems.[6]
Now is the time to spread the divine seed and to harvest as well. There are places where it is difficult to sow the seed for lack of means. There are harvests which are being lost because there are not enough labourers. *The harvest is plentiful, but the labourers are few.*

Early Christianity grew up in a world which seems very much like our own. It boasted abundant material means but suffered from great spiritual poverty. The early Church had the necessary vigour to protect itself from paganizing influences. It was also vibrant enough to

---

[6] St John Paul II, Apostolic Exhortation, *Christifideles laici*, 30 December 1988, 34

transform a worldly civilization from within. The world today seems no more difficult to evangelize. At first sight it may appear to be closed to Christ. Yet if we are firmly united to the Lord as the first Christians were, we can be sure that the transformation will take place once again. How well are we succeeding in our efforts to transform the people around us, the members of our family, our friends, our colleagues at work?

The world is in need of many things. But there is no doubt that it is in great need of apostles who are holy, cheerful, loyal to the Church and eager to make Christ known. The Lord is calling for us to work in his fields: *Pray, therefore, the Lord of the harvest to send out labourers into his harvest. Prayer is the most effective means of winning new apostles.*[7] Our apostolic zeal has to be manifested, first of all, in a continuous prayer of petition for new apostles. Prayer always comes first.

That cry of the Son of God, lamenting that the harvest is plentiful but the labourers are few, is always relevant. How it tears at our heartstrings. That cry came from Christ's mouth for you to hear too. How have you respond-ed to it up to now? Do you pray at least daily for that intention of his?[8]

25.2 Charity, the foundation of the apostolate.

The harvest is plentiful ... St Gregory the Great has commented on this passage: *It is indeed regrettable that the harvest is plentiful but the labourers are few. There is no shortage of people to hear the Good News. What is missing are people to spread it.*[9] Our Lord wants us now to join with his disciples in the work of evangelization.

Before sending out his disciples into the world the

---

[7] St. J. Escrivá, *The Way*, 800
[8] *idem*, *The Forge*, 906
[9] St Gregory the Great, *Homilies on the Gospels*, 17, 3

Master revealed to them the Father and his wonderful love for them. *As the Father loved me, so have I loved you; abide in my love.*[10] *No longer do I call you servants, for the servant does not know what his master is doing; but I have called you friends ... I chose you and appointed you that you should go and bear fruit.*[11] With this clear vision we should go to all the corners of the earth *to reveal and communicate the love of God to all men and to all peoples.*[12] The Christian will be an apostle insofar as he or she is a friend of God. This friendship with God needs to be a daily affair. This attitude will stand in marked contrast to the pervasive distrust and aggressiveness of our environment. When those around us see that we are trustworthy, that we are ready to be of service, that we do not harbour resentment, that we do not speak ill of anyone ... They should find that Christians are different because we follow Christ. We may have different opinions one from another, but we do not attack other people personally. When no one is excluded from our apostolate and assistance, then we are giving true testimony to Christ.

25.3 Joy ought to accompany the message of Christ.

Alongside our charity we have to also show the world our joy. This is the joy the Lord promised us at the Last Supper.[13] It springs from our effort to put aside personal worries and enter into friendship with God. Joy is essential to the apostolate. Who will be attracted by a sad and negative critic or a gloomy complainer? The apostolic fruitfulness of the first Christians was the result, in good part, of their joy at being the heralds of the Good News. They were the messengers of the One who had brought

---

[10] John 15:9
[11] John 15:16
[12] Second Vatican Council, Decree *Ad gentes,* 10
[13] cf John 16:22

salvation to the world. They shone forth as a happy people in the middle of a world in anguish. Their happiness spread abroad their faith in Christ. It was a special gift that they shared in their families and among their friends ... at every moment, since it was their very reason for living.

Christian joy has a solid foundation in the reality of divine filiation. This is the recognition that one is a son or daughter of God at all times. *As Chesterton suggests, it is joy not because we are in the right place, but because we are in the wrong place. We were lost, but Someone has found us and is leading us home. It is joy not because we are alright – we are not – but because Someone can put us right. Christian joy comes from facing up to the one really sad fact of life, which is sin; and countering it with a joyful fact that is even realer and stronger than sin: God's love and mercy.*[14]

Let us ask ourselves whether we reflect Christian joy in our ordinary life. We have so many reasons for being happy: the wonder of our divine filiation, the comfort of divine mercy, the knowledge that we are on the road to heaven ..., the joy of being able to receive communion so often! *The first step towards bringing others to the ways of Christ is for them to see you happy and serene, sure in your advance towards God.*[15]

In combination with the joy and charity of Christ, we have to be able to express the truths of the faith which will make others happy. *Only convinced Christians have any chance of convincing others. Half-convinced Christians won't even half-convince anybody. They won't convince at all.*[16]

---

[14] C. Burke, *Authority and Freedom in the Church*, p. 143
[15] St. J. Escrivá, *The Forge*, 858
[16] C. Burke, *op cit*, p. 141

TWENTY-SIXTH WEEK: FRIDAY

26. PREPARING THE SOUL

26.1 The cities which would not be converted.

Jesus had spent a great deal of time in the cities along the shores of Lake Gennesareth. He had granted countless miracles and favours to these people and yet they would not be converted. They did not know how to receive the Messiah they had heard so much about in their synagogues. This is the reason for the Lord's complaint: *Woe to you, Chorazin! Woe to you, Bethsaida! For if the mighty works done in you had been done in Tyre and Sidon, they would have repented long ago, sitting in sackcloth and ashes ... And you, Capharnaum, will you be exalted to heaven? You shall be brought down to Hades.*[1] Jesus had sown abundant seed and precious little of it had borne fruit in these places. Truly incredible signs had been multiplied one on top of the other, but the people were not moved to penance. Without this conversion and a life of sacrifice it was unlikely that they would recognize Christ in their midst. Tyre and Sidon were burdened with less responsibility since they had received fewer graces.

Therefore, as the Holy Spirit says, 'Today, when you hear his voice, do not harden your hearts ...[2] God speaks to men and women throughout the ages. Christ continues to pass through our cities and towns, showering innumerable blessings upon us. To know how to listen to his Will and fulfil it right away is of capital importance in our lives. Nothing is more important. We need to listen with great

---

[1] Luke 10:13-15
[2] Heb 3:7-8

docility to the invitations Christ gives in the heart of each individual. *God is not to blame when the faith fails to spring up among men. The reason is to be found in the unreadiness of those who have heard the divine word.*[3] Holy Scripture calls this resistance to grace *hardness of heart.*[4] Men sometimes pose intellectual difficulties as inhibiting their growth in faith when the real problem lies in their lack of desire. Perhaps they just do not want to abandon some bad habit. They may not be willing to struggle seriously to overcome some defect that impedes their friendship with the Lord.

Mortification prepares the soul to listen to the Lord and to follow his Will: *If we want to reach God we will have to mortify the soul and all its powers.*[5] Mortification can convert our souls into the good soil that will bring the divine seed to fruition. We have to weed out and burn those thorns that tend to flourish in the soul – laziness, egoism, envy, curiosity ... This is why the Church recommends that we review our spirit of penance and mortification on Fridays. This spirit will lead us to be more generous in our imitation of Christ on the Cross. Closely related to mortification is that happiness which we all find so necessary.

26.2 Motives for penance. Passive mortifications.

Anyone who intends to live his Christian faith seriously needs to *put off the old nature with its practices.*[6] This *old nature* consists in *the variety of bad inclinations we have inherited from Adam. It is the triple concupiscence which we need to control through the exercise of mortification.*[7]

---

[3] St Gregory Nazianzen, *Oratio catechetica magna,* 31
[4] Ex 4:21; Rom 9:18
[5] St Jean Vianney, (The Curé d'Ars), *Sermon on Ash Wednesday*
[6] Col 3:9
[7] A. Tanquerey, *The Spiritual Life,* 323

Mortification is not recommended as a negative action. On the contrary, it is meant to rejuvenate the soul. Mortification makes the soul better disposed to receive supernatural gifts. It also helps us to make reparation for our past sins. This is why we frequently pray to the Lord to grant us *emendationem vitae, spatium verae paenitentiae,* a time of true penance and reformation of life.[8] By means of the Communion of Saints we give help and strength to other members of the Mystical Body which is the Church.

There are three main areas for daily mortification in our ordinary lives. First of all, there is the heartfelt and serene acceptance of the contradictions each day brings. In most cases this refers to the very small things that crop up unexpectedly, and that force us to change our plans or adjust our expectations. One example might be a minor illness that interferes with our performance at work or affects family life. Other examples would include having to put up with inclement weather, heavy traffic, the difficult personality of a colleague at work ... These circumstances are beyond our personal control. We have got to see them as providing opportunities to love God even more. None of these problems should take away our peace and joy.

If these small contradictions are not accepted for the sake of Love, they will only succeed in making people become frustrated and irritable. The great majority of our frustrations come from small contradictions which we have not accepted rather than from major disasters. The person who lies awake at night, who is gloomy, who is in a bad humour, has usually not suffered some great blow. He has simply been unable to turn small setbacks into encounters with God.[9] Such a one loses many chances to grow in virtue. In addition, when the soul gets into the habit of accepting small reverses as divine favours it becomes

---

[8] cf *Roman Missal, Formula intentionis Misae*
[9] A. G. Dorronsoro, *Time to Believe,* Madrid 1976, p. 142

better prepared to face more serious trials in union with the Lord.

God came into the world *to provide a healing remedy for the root of all our rebellion and misery. He destroyed many things as useless obstacles but chose to leave pain intact. He did not take away pain, but gave it a new meaning. He could have chosen a thousand different ways to accomplish the Redemption of the human race, but he chose the Cross. It was by this path that He has led his Mother Mary, Joseph, the Apostles and all the sons of God. The Lord allows evil to exist and he draws out good for our souls from it.*[10] Let us be sure to convert setbacks into occasions of interior growth.

26.3 Voluntary mortifications and those that spring from the faithful fulfilment of our duties.

Another area of daily mortification lies in the conscientious carrying out of our duties, the basic material in our struggle for sanctity. Here we find God's Will for us each day. We need to fulfil our duties with hard work, high standards and much love. The mortification which is most pleasing to God *is to be found in order, in punctuality, in care for the small details in whatever we do. It has to do with the faithful performance of the most insignificant aspects of our vocation – even when it hurts. We need to struggle against the temptation to prefer comfort. We persevere in our work not because we feel like it but because we know it has to be done. When we work in that frame of mind we will work with enthusiasm and joy.*[11] The mother of a family will find a thousand reasons to give her home a warm and cheerful atmosphere. The student will offer up his efforts to study well. In this way, tiredness will become one more offering to the Lord. Let us examine our

---

[10] J. Urteaga, *The Defects of the Saints,* pp. 222-223
[11] St. J. Escrivá, *Letter,* 15 October 1948

conduct to see whether we complain about our work, grumbling about something that should be leading us to God.

The third area of our mortifications consists in those sacrifices that we make voluntarily in order to please Our Lord, to make ourselves better souls of prayer, in order to overcome temptation, in order to help our friends come closer to God. We should be looking for ways to help others seek sanctity. *Bring out your spirit of mortification in those nice touches of charity, eager to make the way of sanctity in the midst of the world attractive for everyone. Sometimes a smile can be the best proof of a spirit of penance.*[12] Let us resolve to overcome our moods and our weariness with the help of our Guardian Angel. *A spirit of penance is to be found first of all in taking advantage of the many little things – deeds, renunciations, sacrifices, services rendered and so on – which we find daily along our way and we then convert into acts of love and contrition, into mortifications. In this way we shall be able to gather a bouquet at the end of each day – a fine display which we can offer to God.*[13]

---

[12] *idem, The Forge,* 149
[13] *ibid,* 408

TWENTY-SIXTH WEEK: SATURDAY

27. THE REASON FOR OUR JOY

27.1 Being 'open' to joy.

Today's Gospel records the joy of the seventy-two disciples after they had preached the Kingdom of God throughout the countryside. With complete simplicity they exclaim to Jesus: *Lord, even the demons are subject to us in your name!*[1] The Master joins in their delight: *I saw Satan fall like lightning from heaven.* But then He warns the disciples: *Behold, I have given you authority to tread upon serpents and scorpions, and over all the power of the enemy; and nothing shall hurt you. Nevertheless do not rejoice in this, that the spirits are subject to you; but rejoice that your names are written in heaven.*

Jesus speaks these words with great joy. He begins a canticle of praise and thanksgiving: *I thank thee, Father, Lord of heaven and earth, that thou hast hidden these things from the wise and understanding and revealed them to babes; yea, Father, for such was thy gracious Will.*

The disciples would never forget this extraordinary moment with the Master when they told him of their first apostolic ventures. How blessed they were to be instruments of the Lord! How happy Jesus was to hear of their apostolate! Then there were those remarkable words: *Rejoice that your names are written in heaven.* If we are faithful to the end we too will hear those sweet words: *Enter into the joy of your master.*[2]

Here on earth each step we take brings us closer to

---

[1] Luke 10:17-24
[2] Matt 25:21

Christ and to true happiness. There is no lasting happiness apart from God. The Christian's joy presupposes the *natural joys* which the Lord sets before us, *the joy of life itself, the joy of honest and holy love, the joy of nature and silence, the austere joy to be found in dedicated work, the joy of a job well done, the transparent joy of holy purity, of sharing, of self-sacrifice. The Christian can purify, fulfil and be identified with these joys. He can not despise them. Christian joy is granted to those who understand natural joys.*[3] There were many occasions when the Lord took advantage of earthly joys to announce the joys of his Kingdom: the joy of the sower and the reaper, of the man who finds a treasure, of the shepherd who discovers his lost sheep, of those invited to a banquet; the joy of marriage, the joy of a father receiving back his son, that of a woman who has just given birth to a child ...

The disciple of Christ is not a de-humanized being. He should not separate himself or allow himself to be separated from what is human. This was not the Master's way. Our friends and acquaintances should find us increasingly welcoming and open to them. We should become better and better able to make life pleasant for others. At times this will require sacrifice and mortification if we are to overcome moodiness and tiredness.

27.2 The essence of joy. Where it is to be found.

Joy is the fruit of love. It is, in fact, the first fruit.[4] The greater our love, the greater will be our joy. St John teaches us that *God is love,*[5] a love without measure, an eternal Love that gives itself to us. Sanctity is love, corresponding to this gift of God to the soul. The disciple of Christ is a joyful man or woman, even in the midst of great

---

[3] Bl. Paul VI, Apostolic Exhortation, *Gaudete in Domino,* 9 May 1975
[4] St Thomas, *Summa Theologiae,* 1-2, q. 24, a. 5
[5] 1 John 4:89

contradictions. Here we find the fulfilment of those words of the Master: *I will see you again, and your hearts will rejoice, and no one will take your joy from you.*[6] Perhaps it is in joy that we distinguish true virtue from false virtue.

The Lord tells us in the First Commandment to love him with our whole heart, our whole soul and our whole being. This is a call to joy and happiness. He himself will come to us: *If a man loves me, he will keep my word, and my Father will love him, and we will come to him and make our home with him.*[7] Without the joy that comes from this self-giving, all the other commandments become difficult or impossible to fulfil.[8]

The Lord wants us to make the effort to overcome our tendency to react badly to things or to hold back an intemperate word. *Yet joy is not something we can order up. Joy is the fruit of love. There is no human love that can sustain a lasting joy. It often seems that human love is the source of more sorrow than joy ... This is not the case in the Christian religion. A Christian who does not love God is a contradiction in terms. A Christian who does not radiate joy because of his love for God needs to take a closer look at his spiritual life. For the Christian, joy is something natural since it springs from the most important Christian virtue – love. Christian life and joy are essentially bound up together.*[9] There is also a relationship between sadness and lukewarmness, between sadness and egoism, between sadness and loneliness.

Joy can be increased or even recovered, if it is temporarily lost, with true prayer face to face with Jesus. This prayer ought to be personal and selfless. Frequent

---

[6] John 16:22
[7] John 14:23
[8] cf P. A. Reggio, *Supernatural spirit and good humour*, Madrid 1966
[9] *ibid*, pp. 35-36

confession is *the privileged source of holiness and peace.*[10] *Authentic joy is based on this foundation: that we want to live for God and want to serve others because of God. Let us tell the Lord that we want nothing more than to serve him with joy. If we behave in this way we shall find that our inner peace, our joy, our good humour will attract many souls to God. Give witness to Christian joy. Show to those around you that this is our great secret. We are happy because we are children of God, because we deal with him, because we struggle to become better for him. And when we fail, we go right away to the Sacrament of joy where we recover our sense of fraternity with all men and women.*[11]

27.3 Holy Mary, Cause of our joy.

For twenty centuries the source from which joy has sprung has been the Church. It arrived with Jesus and remained in the form of his Mystical Body. In our day the happiest creatures ought to be those who are closest to Christ. This explains why no one is more joyful than Mary, the Mother of Jesus and our Mother. She who is *full of grace*[12] is consequently full of joy. To be close to Mary is to live a blessed life. She overflows with joy and spreads it throughout creation. *What must the voice and words of Mary be like to generate such an ever-renewing joy? They are like a divine music that resounds in the depths of souls, filling them with peace and love. How often do we pray the Holy Rosary and in the Litany call her Cause of our joy.* This she is, because she is the gate of Heaven, the doorway to God. Daughter of God the Father, portress to his infinite love. Mother of God the Son, she is gatekeeper of the Love that gave itself up to death. Spouse of God the Holy Spirit,

---

[10] Bl. Paul VI, *loc cit*
[11] Bl. A. del Portillo, *Homily,* 12 April 1984
[12] Luke 1:28

she it is who admits at the portal of divine fire and joy. As she goes by, the environment is transformed. Sadness is banished. Shadows give way to light. Hope and love are ignited ... It is not the same to be with the Virgin as it is to be without her! Praying the Rosary is not the same as not praying it! ...[13] Let us resolve to pray the Rosary well during this month of October that is dedicated to Our Mother in Heaven and to this Marian devotion. In the company of so many other Christians, let us pray to Mary with an increased devotion on this and every Saturday. We might want to offer up some small mortification in her honour today. Through our joy let us bring our friends and relatives to God. Mary, *Cause of our joy,* will help us to spread peace and joy, *gaudium cum pace,* wherever we go. This is one of our greatest treasures as Christians. It is what the world is really searching for in its misguided quest for happiness in the possession of material things.

---

[13] A. Orozco, *Looking to Mary*

28. IN THE VINEYARD OF THE BELOVED

28.1 The parable of the vineyard.

Today's Liturgy speaks to us in very beautiful allegories about God's love for his people and of their failure to correspond. In the *First Reading*[1] we read the Prophet Isaiah's *love song* of the vineyard. Israel is symbolized by God's plantation which is full of promise. *Let me sing for my beloved a love song concerning his vineyard: My beloved had a vineyard on a very fertile hill. He dug it well and cleared it of stones, and planted it with choice vines; he built a watchtower in the midst of it, and hewed out a wine vat in it; and he looked for it to yield grapes, but it yielded wild grapes.* Even though the vines had been planted in good ground they bore sour fruit. The Prophet Isaiah continues: *And now, O inhabitants of Jerusalem and men of Judah, judge, I pray you, between me and my vineyard. What more was there to do for my vineyard, that I have not done in it? When I looked for it to yield grapes, why did it yield wild grapes?*

Palestine was a land of vineyards. The prophets of the Old Testament returned again and again to this popular image of the chosen people. Israel is the vineyard of God, the work of the Lord, the joy of his heart.[2] *Yet I planted you a choice vine, wholly of pure seed.*[3] *Your mother was like a vine in a vineyard transplanted by the water ...*[4] In

---

[1] Is 5:1-7
[2] cf St John Paul II, Apostolic Exhortation, *Christifideles laici*, 30 December 1988, 8
[3] Jer 2:21
[4] Ex 19:10

today's Gospel the Lord makes reference to the words of Isaiah in the parable of the vineyard.[5] Jesus reveals to us the infinite patience of God, the owner of the vineyard, who sends one messenger after another in search of fruit. These are the prophets of the Old Testament. The Father finally sends his *beloved son* and the tenants murder him: *And they took him and cast him out of the vineyard, and killed him.* Here is an unmistakable reference to the coming crucifixion outside the walls of Jerusalem.

The vineyard is Israel. She did not live up to her divine calling. The vineyard is also a symbol of the Church and therefore of each one of us. *Yet the true vine is Christ who gives life and fruitfulness to the branches, that is, to us, who through the Church remain in Christ without whom we can do nothing (John 15:1-5).*[6]

Let us meditate today about whether the Lord can find abundant fruits of sanctity and apostolate in our life. They should be abundant, since we have received so much already. The fruits can come in the form of acts of charity, of work well done, of apostolate with friends and family, of acts of love and reparation to God and of contradictions accepted with faith. Are we producing instead wild grapes that represent sins, lukewarmness, spiritual mediocrity, faults, etc.?

28.2 The bitter fruits.

There was a householder who planted a vineyard, and set a hedge around it, and dug a wine press in it.. St Ambrose comments: *The hedge is meant to represent divine protection for the vineyard against spiritual predators ... The wine press is for extracting the vintage of the divine grape.*[7] We have received so many spiritual favours. The

---

[5] Matt 21:33-43
[6] Second Vatican Council, *Lumen gentium,* 6
[7] St Ambrose, *Commentary on St Luke's Gospel,* 20, 9

hedge, the *wine press* and the *watchtower* signify that God has invested a great deal of care in the cultivation of his vineyard. *When I looked for it to yield grapes, why did it yield wild grapes?*

Sin is the sour and bitter fruit of our lives. The experience of mankind and that of every individual is replete with the reality of sin. *No one is freed from sin by himself or by his own efforts, no one is raised above himself or completely delivered from his own weakness, solitude or slavery; all have need of Christ who is the model, master, liberator, saviour, and giver of life.*[8] Our sins are intimately related to the death of the *beloved son,* who is Jesus: *And they took him and cast him out of the vineyard, and killed him.*

If we are to produce good fruit for the Lord we need to ask him for a strong aversion from all sin, including venial sin. Faults of lack of charity, of critical spirit towards others, of impatience, festering resentment, dissipation of the senses, work poorly done ... *Venial sins do great harm to the soul. That's why Our Lord says in the 'Canticle of Canticles' – 'Capite nobis vulpes parvulas, quae demoliuntur vineas' – Catch the little foxes that destroy the vines.*[9] Time and time again we need to reject whatever displeases Our Lord. The soul that abhors deliberate venial sin will come to a deeper friendship with the Master.

Our weaknesses ought to help us to make more acts of reparation and true contrition. Just as we seek pardon from someone we have offended by doing a good deed, so much the more effort should we put into repairing our friendship with Christ. He will smile on our efforts and give peace to our souls. We will therefore recover the fruit that had been lost. *Ask the Father, the Son and the Holy Spirit, and your Mother, to make you know yourself and weep for all those*

---

[8] Second Vatican Council, *Ad gentes,* 8
[9] St. J. Escrivá, *The Way,* 329

foul things that have passed through you, and which, alas, have left such dregs behind ... And at the same time, without wishing to stop considering all that, say to him: Jesus, give me a Love that will act like a purifying fire in which my miserable flesh, my miserable heart, my miserable soul, my miserable body may be consumed and cleansed of all earthly wretchedness. And when I have been emptied of myself, fill me with yourself. May I never become attached to anything here below. May Love always sustain me.[10]

28.3 The fruits that God expects.

In today's *Second Reading* we read these words of St Paul to the Philippians: *Finally, brethren, whatever is true, whatever is honourable, whatever is just, whatever is pure, whatever is lovely, whatever is gracious, if there is any excellence, if there is anything worthy of praise, think about these things.*[11]

The things of this world are good in themselves. They can come to have a divine worth. As St Irenaeus has written: *Through the action of the Word of God, everything has come within his salvific work. The Son of God has been crucified for everyone. He has placed the sign of the Cross above all things.*[12] Our everyday activities need to be transformed into good fruit for God. *We cannot say that there are things – good, noble or indifferent – which are exclusively worldly. This cannot be, after the Word of God has lived among the children of men, felt hunger and thirst, worked with his hands, experienced friendship and obedience and suffering and death.*[13] Every noble human reality should be sanctified and offered up to God.

---

[10] *idem, The Forge,* 41
[11] Phil 4:6-9
[12] St Irenaeus, *Example of apostolic preaching*
[13] St. J. Escrivá, *Christ is passing by,* 112

Each day of our lives we encounter many opportunities to give good fruit to the Lord. In the first moment of the morning we can offer to him that *heroic minute* of getting up on time. We can give him our serene acceptance of frustrating traffic jams or a slight illness. There are many, many occasions during the day when we can offer up a smile, a friendly word, an act of pardon ... In our work the Lord looks for that good fruit to be found in work well done, in punctuality, in order, in concentrated attention ... We will need to have a lively presence of God if we are to persevere in these offerings throughout the day. Glances at an image of Our Lady or a crucifix can help. We can keep in mind Our Lord in whichever Tabernacle is closest to us ... *He who abides in me, and I in him, he it is that bears much fruit, for apart from me you can do nothing ... By this my Father is glorified, that you bear much fruit, and so prove to be my disciples.*[14]

Our Mother Mary will teach us how important it is that we produce good fruit for God. She will help us to avoid giving bad fruit to the Lord.

---

[14] John 15:5-8

TWENTY-SEVENTH SUNDAY: YEAR B

29. HOLY MATRIMONY

29.1 The unity and indissolubility of marriage.

Jesus was teaching in Judaea on the banks of the Jordan to a great multitude.[1] They were listening closely to his every word. Today's Gospel[2] reports that Jesus was then approached by some Pharisees who wanted *to test him*. They asked Jesus to pass judgment on the Mosaic Law. *Is it lawful for a man to divorce his wife?* Moses had permitted divorce because of the hardness of heart of the chosen people. The condition of woman was at that time ignominious. She could be put aside by her husband for virtually any reason. Moses required that the husband give the wife a certificate of repudiation ('a bill of divorce') so that she might be free to marry again.[3] The Prophets spoke out against divorce when they came to the Promised Land.[4]

Jesus takes this opportunity to affirm the indissolubility of marriage, as God originally intended at Creation. He quotes the words of *Genesis* which we find in today's *First Reading*.[5] *But from the beginning of creation, 'God made them male and female.' 'For this reason a man shall leave his father and mother and be joined to his wife, and the two shall become one.' So they are no longer two but one. What therefore God has joined together, let not man put asunder.* The Lord declares that the unity and

---

[1] Mark 10:1
[2] Mark 10:2-16
[3] cf J. Dheilly, *Biblical Dictionary,* Barcelona 1970, see *Divorce*
[4] cf Mal 2:13-16
[5] Gen 2:18-24

indissolubility of marriage had been established *from the beginning*. This teaching was so surprising to the disciples that once they had left the crowd they asked Jesus to explain it again. *And he said to them: 'Whoever divorces his wife and marries another, commits adultery against her; and if she divorces her husband and marries another, she commits adultery'*. It would be hard to express the matter more clearly. His words were of an unmistakable clarity. How is it possible that there are Christians who call into doubt this teaching on marriage and continue to consider themselves followers of Christ?

It is a fundamental duty of the Church to reaffirm strongly ... the doctrine of the indissolubility of marriage. To all those who, in our times, consider it too difficult, or indeed impossible, to be bound to one person for the whole of life, and to those caught up in a culture that rejects the indissolubility of marriage and openly mocks the commitment of spouses to fidelity, it is necessary to reconfirm the good news of the definitive nature of that conjugal love that has in Christ the foundation and strength (Eph 5:25).

Being rooted in the personal and total self-giving of the couple, and being required by the good of the children, the indissolubility of marriage finds its ultimate truth in the plan that God has manifested in his revelation: He wills and He communicates the indissolubility of marriage as a fruit, a sign and a requirement of the absolutely faithful love that God has for man and that the Lord Jesus has for the Church.[6] This bond can be broken only by death. It is an image of the bond between Christ and his Mystical Body.

The dignity and stability of marriage is of the greatest importance to the future of families, of children and of society itself. The moral health of peoples is closely tied to

---

[6] St John Paul II, Apostolic Exhortation, *Familiaris consortio*, 22 November 1981, 20

the condition of matrimony. When matrimony is corrupted, then society itself is sick, perhaps gravely ill.[7] This is why we need to pray for and take care of families. Scandal can be converted into an opportunity to give good doctrine, to overcome evil with an abundance of good.[8] *In national life there are two things which are really essential: the laws concerning marriage and the laws to do with education. In these areas God's sons have to stand firm and fight with toughness and fairness, for the sake of all mankind.*[9]

29.2 A way of holiness.

When Jesus elevated matrimony to the dignity of a sacrament He was doing something completely unprecedented. The transformation might be likened to the time in Cana when he changed the water into wine. *Behold, I make all things new.*[10] Christ elevated the natural reality of Christian marriage to a supernatural plane. Marriage between non-Christians was also filled with grandeur and dignity. *The ideal proposed by Christ to married couples is infinitely greater than that of human perfection. It is a totally new concept. It literally means that the spouses receive divine life through the sacrament. This is what sustains their work of mutual perfection. This is what has to inspire their children from the moment of Baptism.*[11]

Those who marry begin a new life in the company of the Lord. God himself has called man and wife to follow this path to holiness. *For a Christian marriage is not just a social institution, much less a mere remedy for human weakness. It is a real supernatural calling. A great sacrament,*

---

[7] cf F. J. Sheed, *Society and Sanity,* p. 137
[8] cf Rom 12:21
[9] St. J. Escrivá, *The Forge,* 104
[10] Rev 21:5
[11] J. M. Martinez Doral, *The holiness of conjugal life, Scripta Theologica,* Pamplona, IX-XII 1989, pp. 869-870

in Christ and in the Church, says St Paul (Eph 5:32) ... It is a permanent contract that sanctifies in cooperation with Jesus Christ. He fills the souls of husband and wife and invites them to follow him. He transforms their whole married life into an occasion for God's presence on earth.[12]

Pope John Paul I spoke of the greatness of matrimony to a group of newlyweds. He told them the following story: *Last century there was in France a great professor, Frederick Ozanam. He taught at the Sorbonne, and was so eloquent, so capable! His friend Lacordaire said: 'He is so gifted, he is so good, he will become a priest; he will become a great bishop, this fellow!' But no! He met a nice girl and they got married. Lacordaire was disappointed and said: 'Poor Ozanam! He too has fallen into the trap!' But two years later, Lacordaire came to Rome and was received by Pius IX. 'Come, come, Father,' the Pope said, 'I have always heard that Jesus established seven sacraments. Now you come along and change everything. You tell me that He established six sacraments, and a trap! No, Father, marriage is not a trap − it is a great sacrament!'*[13] We should never forget that the first thing Jesus chose to sanctify was the home. Christian sobriety leads to happy, generous families which, in turn, produce vocations of total dedication to God, the very crown of the Church.

God often calls the children of generous parents to lead lives of virginity or celibacy. These vocations are real treasures which the parents can present to the Lord in Heaven.

29.3 The family, school of virtues.

God took great care to prepare the family which would

---

[12] St. J. Escrivá, *Christ is passing by*, 23
[13] John Paul I, *Address*, 13 September 1978

receive his Son: Joseph, *of the house and lineage of David*,[14] would serve as the earthly father on equal terms with Mary, the virginal Mother. The Lord wanted to show in his own family a shining model of formation, protection and love.

The family is *the primary vital cell of society*[15] and, in a certain manner, of the Church itself.[16] The family has a sacred status which deserves the veneration and attention of all its members, of civil society itself, and of the entire Church. St Thomas compares the mission of parents to that of priests. Just as priests contribute to the supernatural growth of the People of God by the administration of the sacraments, the Christian family provides corporal and spiritual support. *Through the sacrament of matrimony, the man and the woman come together to give birth to children and educate them in the worship of God.*[17] By means of the generous collaboration of the parents, God himself *will increase and enrich his family from day to day.*[18] This generosity increases both the number of the members of the Church and the Church's supernatural glory.

God has wanted the family to be a *school of virtues*[19] where children are formed as good citizens and good sons and daughters of God. It is in the midst of family life that each person finds his or her own vocation. *You should be full of wonder at the goodness of our Father God. Are you not filled with joy to know that your home, your family, your country, which you love so much, are the raw material which you must sanctify?*[20]

---

[14] Luke 2:4
[15] Second Vatican Council, *Apostolicam actuositatem*, 11
[16] cf St John Paul II, Apostolic Exhortation, *Familiaris consortio*, 22 November 1981, 3
[17] St Thomas, *Summa contra gentiles*, IV, 58
[18] Second Vatican Council, *Gaudium et spes*, 50
[19] St John Paul II, *Address*, 28 October 1979
[20] St. J. Escrivá, *The Forge*, 689

30. TO GROW IN FAITH

30.1 Continually renewing one's love for God.

The liturgy this Sunday focuses on the virtue of faith. In the *First Reading* the Prophet Habakkuk complains to the Lord about the apparent triumph of evil over good.[1] He laments the mistreatment of the chosen people by invaders who flaunt their scandalous behaviour. *How long, Lord, am I to cry for help while you will not listen.? ... Why do you set injustice before me, why do you look on where there is tyranny? Outrage and violence, this is all I see, all is contention, and discord flourishes.* The Lord answers the Prophet with a call to patience and hope. The day will come when the evil ones will be punished: *See how he flags, he whose soul is not at rights, but the upright man will live by his faithfulness.* Even when it seems that evil has triumphed, as if God did not exist, we need to remember that God and his followers will triumph in the end. Living by faith means realizing that God calls us to live as his children in every moment of the day. We must be patient and place our hope in him.

In the *Second Reading,* St Paul exhorts Timothy to remain firm in his vocation, to preach the truth without being inhibited by human respect: *I am reminding you to fan into a flame the gift that God gave you when I laid my hands on you. God's gift was not a spirit of timidity, but the Spirit of power, and love, and self-control.*[2] St Thomas teaches that *the grace of God is like a fire that loses its*

[1] Hab 1:2-3; 2:2-4
[2] 2 Tim 1:6-8; 13-14

brilliance when the ashes are covered over.[3] This is what happens when charity is almost smothered by lukewarmness or human respect. The fortitude needed to advance the Faith springs from the furnace of our interior life, which must never be allowed to go out. This is what we must ask from the Lord, *who in the abundance of your kindness surpass the merits and the desires of those who entreat you, pour out your mercy upon us to pardon what conscience dreads.*[4] *Give what prayer does not dare to ask.*[5] Give us a strong faith so that we may overcome our defects and give proper testimony to others. *There are men who have no faith, who are sad and hesitant because of the emptiness of their existence, and exposed like weathercocks to 'changeable' circumstances. How different that is from our trusting life as Christians, which is cheerful, firm and solid, because we know and are absolutely convinced of our supernatural destiny!*[6] What inspiration we can derive from faith! With this source of energy we can overcome the obstacles of difficult circumstances or personal weaknesses.

30.2 Asking the Lord for a firm faith.

There is such a thing as a dead faith which does not save. It is a faith without works.[7] It is to be found wherever life is separated from belief. There is also such a thing as a *dormant faith. This cowardly lifestyle is also known as 'lukewarmness.' Practically speaking, lukewarmness is the worst thing that can infect a Christian. It can contaminate even those who think themselves very good Christians.*[8] We need to develop a firm faith which will enable us to go

---

[3] St Thomas, *Commentary on the Second Letter to the Corinthians*, 1:6
[4] *Roman Missal, Collect*
[5] *ibid*
[6] St. J. Escrivá, *Furrow*, 73
[7] cf Jas 2:17
[8] P. Rodriguez, *Faith and Life of Faith*, p. 138

beyond our own abilities in the apostolate. If we truly live by faith we will gain a true understanding of our circumstances. We will also be able to judge things with rectitude of intention. *Only the light of faith and meditation on the Word of God can enable us to find everywhere and always the God 'in whom we live and exist' (Acts 17:28); only thus can we seek his will in everything, see Christ in all men, acquaintance or stranger, make sound judgments on the true meaning and value of temporal realities both in themselves and in relation to man's end.*[9]

On a number of occasions Jesus called his Apostles *men of little faith.*[10] There was the time when they were sailing in a great storm and the Master himself was aboard.[11] The Apostles tended to worry a great deal about 'the future,' about what was going to happen.[12] The Gospel for today's Mass shows us that the Apostles were well aware of their far-from-perfect faith. They ask the Lord: *Increase our faith.*[13] This is precisely what He did. And the Apostles gave their lives for Christ and his teachings. The Lord's words were fulfilled: *Were your faith the size of a mustard seed you could say to this mulberry tree, 'Be uprooted and planted in the sea,' and it would obey you.* An even greater miracle was the transformation of the souls they came into contact with.

Much like the Apostles, we frequently find ourselves lacking in faith in the face of difficulties or lack of means ... We need to increase our faith. God will grant us more faith if we keep asking him for it. *We lack faith. The day we practise this virtue, trusting in God and in his Mother, we will be daring and loyal. God, who is the same God as*

---

[9] Second Vatican Council, *Apostolicam actuositatem*, 4

[10] Matt 8:26; 6:30

[11] cf Matt 8:26

[12] cf Matt 6:30

[13] Luke 17:5

*ever, will work miracles through our hands. Grant me,
dear Jesus, the faith I truly desire. My Mother, sweet Lady,
Mary most holy, make me really believe.*[14]

30.3 Acts of faith.

Lord, increase our faith! What a wonderful prayer to
repeat to the Lord many times a day! We also should
practise this virtue frequently: whenever we find ourselves
in need or in danger, when we come up against our
weaknesses, when we are in pain, when we encounter
difficulties in the apostolate, when souls don't seem to
respond ..., whenever we pray in front of the Blessed
Sacrament.

We need to make many acts of faith in our prayer and
during Holy Mass. It is said of St Thomas that when we
looked upon the host at the moment of the Consecration, he
would pray: *Tu rex gloriae, Christe; tu Patris sempiternus
es Filius.* You are the king of glory. You are the eternal
Son of the Father. St Josemaría Escrivá had the custom of
praying at that moment of the Mass: *Adauge nobis fidem,
spem et caritatem.* Increase our faith, our hope and our
love. Whenever he made a genuflection he would pray:
Adoro te devote, latens deitas. I adore you with devotion,
hidden God.[15] Many of the faithful have the custom of
praying at the moment of Consecration those words of the
Apostle Thomas: *My Lord and my God!* We should not let
this opportunity pass without showing the Lord our faith
and our love.

Even though we are filled with a great desire for
formation and closer union with Christ, it is possible that
our faith may at times weaken. We may give in to human
respect in our apostolate. Faith is a gift of God that we
sometimes fail to live up to. The occasion may be as

---

[14] St. J. Escrivá, *The Forge,* 235

[15] cf A. Vazquez de Prada, *The Founder of Opus Dei,* Madrid 1983

unimportant as a grain of mustard seed. We should not be surprised at our weaknesses. God has already taken them into account. Let us imitate the Apostles, who were conscious of their defects as well as conscious of the infinite power of the Almighty. Let us ask their help along with Our Lady's to increase our faith that we may be faithful to the end of our days. Let us pray that we bring many others to Christ in the process.

Our Mother Mary will always be a tremendous source of faith and hope, especially when we are in direst need. *We, sinners, know that she is our Advocate who never gets tired of lending us a hand again and again, as often as we fall and make an effort to rise again; we who go through life fumbling and faltering, who are weak to the point of not being able to avoid the pains inherent to our human condition, know that she is the comforter of the afflicted, the refuge where as a last resort we may find a bit of peace, a bit of serenity (that special consolation that only a mother can give and that makes everything all right again). We know also that in those moments when our helplessness reaches almost exasperation or despair, when nobody can do anything anymore and we feel utterly forlorn with our sorrow or our shame, up against the wall, she is still our hope, our beacon light; she can still be appealed to when there is no longer anyone to appeal to.*[16]

---

[16] F. Suarez, *The Narrow Gate*, p. 126

31. TAKING CARE OF ONE ANOTHER

31.1 Christ is the Good Samaritan who comes down from Heaven to heal and help us.

In today's Mass we read the parable of the Good Samaritan as recorded by St Luke.[1] It is one of the most beautiful and moving stories in the Gospels. The Lord teaches us who our neighbour is, and how we should live fraternal charity towards others. It may have been that the Lord was not far from the road referred to in the parable. He would often associate his teachings with his surroundings. *A man was once on his way down from Jerusalem to Jericho and fell into the hands of brigands; they took all he had, beat him and then made off, leaving him half dead.*

Many Fathers of the Church and early Christian writers have identified Christ himself as the Good Samaritan.[2] The man who falls into the hands of thieves is a symbol of humanity wounded by original sin and personal sin. St Augustine has commented: *These offences robbed mankind of immortality. They covered him with wounds and made him susceptible to sin.*[3] St Bede has written that sins are called *wounds* because they destroy the integrity of human nature.[4] The thieves represent the devil, unrestrained human passions, scandal ... The Levite and the priest symbolize the Old Covenant, which cannot cure these wounds. The inn is a symbol of the Church. *What*

---

[1] Luke 10:25-37
[2] cf St Augustine, *Sermon about the words of the Lord,* 37
[3] *idem,* in *Catena Aurea,* V, p. 513
[4] cf St Bede, *Commentary on St Luke's Gospel, in loc*

would have happened to this poor Jew if the Samaritan had stayed at home? What would have happened to our souls if the Son of God had not undertaken his journey?[5] Jesus is moved with compassion for man and heals his wounds, making them his own.[6] St John wrote to the early Christians: *In this the love of God was made manifest among us, that God sent his only Son into the world, so that we might live through him ... Beloved, if God so loved us, we also ought to love one another.*[7]

To the Gospel of suffering there also belongs – and in an organic way – the parable of the Good Samaritan.[8] Christ's entire life was a continual approach to man so as to remedy both his material and spiritual needs. We should exercise the same kind of compassion towards others. We should never pass by a suffering person with indifference. We have to learn from Jesus to stop and spend time with one who may be in need of physical or spiritual solace. Through this attention to others, people will see Christ himself present in his disciples.

31.2 Compassion for the needy that is both effective and practical.

The parable was inspired by the question, *Who is my neighbour?* In order to make his point as clearly as possible, the Lord examines the behaviour in a particular situation of different types of people: *Now a priest happened to be travelling down the same road, but when he saw the man, he passed by on the other side. In the same way a Levite who came to the place saw him, and passed by on the other side. But a Samaritan traveller who came*

---

[5] R. A. Knox, *Pastoral Sermons*, p. 140
[6] Is 53:4; Matt 8:17; 1 Pet 2:24; 1 John 3:5
[7] 1 John 4:9-11
[8] St John Paul II, Apostolic Letter, *Salvifici doloris,* 11 February 1984, 28

upon him was moved with compassion when he saw him. He went up and bandaged his wounds, pouring oil and wine on them. He then lifted him on to his own mount, carried him to the inn and looked after him.

Jesus wants to teach us that our neighbour is whoever happens to be near us, without regard to race, political beliefs, age ... And it may happen that our neighbour needs help. The Master has given us an example of how we should behave. *This Samaritan (Christ) washed our sins, suffered for us and carried the half-dead man who is our sinful self to the inn which is the Church. The Church is open to everyone. She never closes her doors or denies her assistance to anyone. It was Jesus who said: 'Come to Me ...' (Matt 11:28). Once the Samaritan has taken the traveller to the inn he does not leave the rescued victim immediately. He stays with him all day to watch over his recovery ... When the Samaritan leaves the following day, he makes sure he pays the inn-keeper in advance for the traveller's lodgings. He entrusts the inn-keeper, the angels of his Church, with the care of the traveller. This help will, the Samaritan hopes, lead the traveller to Heaven.*[9]

The Lord encourages us to live a compassion which is both effective and practical. We should provide the proper remedy for our neighbours in need. They may be suffering for different reasons: their wounds may be caused by loneliness or lack of love or abandonment; their needs may be needs of the body – hunger, clothing, shelter, employment ...; perhaps they are suffering the grave wound of ignorance ...; maybe their hurt is the moral wound of sin which can be cured by the Sacrament of Penance. The Church *is the inn located along the road of life. She receives those travellers who are worn out from their journey who bring with them the baggage of their past sins.*

---

[9] Origen, *Homily 34 on St Luke*

Here travellers can be freed from the weight of sin so that they may rest and take nourishment to enable them to continue on their way.[10]

We should do what we can to alleviate poverty, just as Christ did in his earthly life. What better way to identify ourselves with the Master than through the exercise of charity and compassion! *In its various forms – material deprivation, unjust oppression, physical and psychological illnesses, and finally death – human misery is the obvious sign of the natural condition of weakness in which man finds himself since original sin and the sign of his need for salvation. Hence it drew the compassion of Christ the Saviour to take it upon himself (Matt 8:17) and to be identified with the least of his brethren (cf Matt 25:40; 45). Hence also those who are oppressed by poverty are the object of a love of preference on the part of the Church, which since her origin and in spite of the failings of many of her members has not ceased to work for their relief, defence and liberation.*[11]

Whenever we draw near to someone in need we have to do so with great empathy, making their misfortune our very own. The Venerable Louis of Granada has pointed out that something more than just sympathy is often required: *Without doubt, therefore, he who desires to please God must fulfil this great precept of charity, not only in word but also in deed.*[12] He later adds: *Among the works comprising charity to our neighbour the following are the most important: advice, counsel, succour, forbearance, pardon, edification. These are so strongly linked with charity that the practice of them indicates the progress we*

---

[10] St John Chrysostom, in *Catena Aurea*, VI, p. 519
[11] Congregation for the Doctrine of the Faith, *Instruction on Christian Freedom and Liberation*, 22 March 1986, 68
[12] Venerable Louis of Granada, *The Sinner's Guide*, p. 344

have made in the practice of this greatest of virtues.[13]

31.3 Charity with our closest neighbours.

The parable of the Good Samaritan teaches *what the relationship of each of us must be towards our suffering neighbour. We are not allowed to 'pass by on the other side' indifferently; we must 'stop' beside him. Everyone who stops beside the suffering of another person, whatever form it may take, is a Good Samaritan.*[14] God places us next to people in need whom we encounter along our way. Love should move us to do whatever we can. It is not always a matter of heroic deeds. Many a time all that is necessary is a smile, a word of encouragement, good advice, the willingness to bite one's tongue in the face of an insult or injury, visiting a friend who is sick or experiencing loneliness, the exercise of social virtues such as warm greetings and words of thanks ... St John Paul II wrote that certain professions are a continual work of mercy – such as the medical professions, for example.[15] Yet every profession involves serving or attending to other people in one way or another. We should make an effort to deal with our colleagues with affection, compassion and respect. We should struggle to see Christ in the persons closest to us.

We should be concerned with the welfare of every person but it is only natural that our concern should be focussed especially on those whom God has placed by our side. Charity should be ordered so that we are attentive to our brothers and sisters in the Faith, members of our family, friends, colleagues ... St John Chrysostom put the question this way: *If the Samaritan was so solicitous in the case of a perfect stranger, how should our behaviour be*

---

[13] *ibid*
[14] St John Paul II, *loc cit,* 28
[15] *ibid,* 29

with our closer neighbours in need? We should not make excuses for not doing anything just because others have been remiss in their conduct. You have to work the cure without making vain comparisons the negligence of other people. If you were to find a gold coin, would you ask yourself, 'Why has no one else found it?' Of course not. You would not hesitate to take it as your own. Likewise, whenever you find a brother in need, realize that you have found something more valuable than any treasure – the opportunity to care for another.[16] Let us not fail to do so.

---

[16] St John Chrysostom, *Contra Iudeos*, 8

TWENTY-SEVENTH WEEK: TUESDAY

32. IN BETHANY

32.1 Ordinary life is a means of and an occasion for meeting God.

In his Gospel, St Luke relates that while Jesus was making his way to Jerusalem He took time out to rest with friends at Bethany.[1] His friends were Lazarus, Martha and Mary, a brother and two sisters; they enjoyed a wonderful friendship with the Lord as is evident from various references in the Gospels.[2] The Master was at ease in their home, surrounded thus as he was by friends. Martha busied herself with preparing some refreshment for Jesus and his disciples, just arrived from their dusty and demanding travels. *Martha was distracted with much serving.* Meanwhile, Mary *sat at the Lord's feet and listened to his teaching.*

For many years Martha has been held up as a symbol of the active life while Mary has been thought of as a symbol of the contemplative life. Perhaps this is not a very helpful distinction for the many, many Christians who seek to sanctify themselves through their work in the middle of the world. How is one's life at work, in the university, in the kitchen to make any sense if it has no connection with God? Conversely, how meaningful can one's life of prayer be if it bears no fruit in deeds of charity, loyal friendship and work well done? Work, study, life's ordinary trials, all have to become a means of and an occasion for meeting

---

[1] Luke 10:38-42
[2] cf John 11:1-45; 12:1-9

God.[3] *In this life, the contemplation of supernatural reality, the action of grace in our souls, our love for our neighbour as a result of our love for God – all these are already a foretaste of heaven, a beginning that is destined to grow from day to day. We Christians cannot resign ourselves to leading a double life – our life must be a strong and simple unity into which all our actions converge ... Let us be contemplative souls, carrying on an unceasing dialogue with our Lord at all hours – from the first thought of the day to the last, turning our heart constantly toward our Lord Jesus Christ, going to him through our Mother, Holy Mary, and through him to the Father and the Holy Spirit.*[4]

Our conversation with Jesus should be nourished by our professional concerns, our noble hopes, our worries ... If we were not to act in this way, what indeed would we have to talk about? Our Lord's friends at Bethany told the Lord all about their mundane concerns. The Apostles acted in the same manner. A few of these dialogues have been recorded in the Gospel, as when the Apostles raised this matter with Jesus: *Master, we saw a man casting out demons in your name, and we forbade him, because he does not follow with us ...* The Apostles would reveal to Jesus their most heartfelt longings: *Who can be saved? ... We have left everything and followed you.* Life itself was their topic of conversation with Jesus. We should make this way our own.

As we pray more about our daily concerns, we will find those realities to be increasingly filled with prayer. With Jesus by our side we will learn how to become better friends, better citizens, better workers. We will be more human, especially open and attentive to the needs of others.

---

[3] cf *The Navarre Bible, in loc*
[4] St. J. Escrivá, *Christ is passing by,* 126

32.2 Unity of life.

It is very understandable how Martha could have become unduly concerned about the work involved in being hospitable. She became so caught up in what she was doing that she seemed to forget the Guest himself. It also seems that Martha is really concerned about Mary's behaviour. *She went to him and said, 'Lord, do you not care that my sister has left me to serve alone? Tell her then to help me'.* We can well imagine how the Lord responded affectionately to his friend, *Martha, Martha, you are anxious and troubled about many things; one thing is needful.* Only one thing is necessary: that we love God, that we seek personal sanctity. When Christ is our primary concern all day long, then we will find ourselves working harder and better. This orientation should serve as a source of unity for our entire day. Then we will avoid leading a *double life*: one life for God and another life dedicated to worldly affairs, business, politics, rest and so on ...

St John Paul II wrote about unity of life: *In discovering and living their proper vocation and mission, the lay faithful must be formed according to the union which exists from their being members of the Church and citizens of human society. There cannot be two parallel lives in their existence: on the one hand, the so-called 'spiritual' life, with its values and demands; and on the other, the so-called 'secular' life, that is, life in a family, at work, in social relationships, in the responsibilities of public life and in culture. The branch, engrafted to the vine which is Christ, bears its fruit in every sphere of existence and activity. In fact, every area of the lay faithful's lives, as different as they are, enters into the plan of God who desires that these very areas be the 'places in time' where the love of Christ is revealed and realized for both the glory of the Father and service of others. Every activity, every situation, every precise responsibility – as, for*

*example, skill and solidarity in work, love and dedication
in the family and the education of children, service to
society and public life and the promotion of truth in the
area of culture – are the occasions ordained by Providence
for a 'continuous exercise of faith, hope and charity'
(Apostolicam actuositatem, 4).*[5]

The ordinary business of living, the demands of
professional life, social relations, these all provide the
circumstances which allow us to exercise both human and
supernatural virtues. Like Martha, we have Jesus close by
our side. He accompanies us at home, in the office, in the
laboratory, on our travels. We should offer up to Christ all
the events of our day. With this approach we will be able to
pray to Jesus even while we are fully engrossed in our
daily tasks. United with the readings from today's *Liturgy
of the Hours,* we will pray with the Psalmist: *Oh, how I
love thy law! It is my meditation all the day. Thy commandment makes me wiser than my enemies, for it is ever with
me. I have more understanding than all my teachers, for
thy testimonies are my meditation.*[6]

32.3 Only one thing is necessary: personal sanctity.

One thing is needful: an ever-increasing friendship
with the Lord. *This should be the constant object of our
heart ... Everything that separates us from this goal, no
matter how important it may appear, has to take second
place to that which is our ultimate end. Distractions from
this goal may even be seen as doing us positive harm.*[7] The
greatest good we can offer to our family, our colleagues,
our friends, – to society itself – is our union with the Lord.
The means to this union include keeping presence of God

---

[5] St John Paul II, Apostolic Exhortation, *Christifideles laici,* 30
December 1988, 59
[6] *Liturgy of the Hours,* Ps 118:97-99
[7] Cassian, *Conferences,* 1

during the day, a serious effort at daily prayer, frequent Confession ... The greatest harm would come if we were to neglect precisely these means that lead us to Jesus. This neglect might come about through disorder, lukewarmness, and yielding to the temptation to spend our energies on other, more attractive activities. St Ignatius of Antioch wrote to St Polycarp that we have to desire friendship with God: *As a pilot calls on winds and a storm-tossed mariner looks havenward, so the times call on you to win your way to God.*[8]

Real friendship with the Lord will unfailingly enrich all our actions. The absence of that friendship will devalue and impoverish whatever we do. Whenever we notice that life's concerns seem to be crowding out the time we have reserved for the Lord, then we need to hear again the Lord's words to Martha: *One thing is needful.* Our pursuit of holiness should be the highest priority in our life. *But seek first his kingdom and his righteousness, and all these things shall be yours as well.*[9]

Thank the Lord for the enormous gift He has granted you by making you understand that 'only one thing is necessary.' And along with that thanksgiving may no day go past without your offering a prayer of petition for those who as yet have no idea of this duty or do not understand it.[10] What a joy it is to know that the purpose of our existence is to grow in love for Jesus Christ! What a joy to share this Good News with others! Let us ask Our Lady to help us never to lose sight of the Lord while we struggle to perform our daily work to perfection for his glory.

---

[8] St Ignatius of Antioch, *Epistle to St Polycarp,* 2, 3
[9] Matt 6:33
[10] St. J. Escrivá, *Furrow,* 454

33. THE *OUR FATHER*

33.1 The Lord's prayer.

There were many occasions when the disciples saw Jesus retire in order to pray. Sometimes He would pray throughout the night. As we read in today's Gospel,[1] the disciples approached Jesus one day when he had finished his prayer. They asked him with all simplicity: *Lord, teach us to pray.*

Jesus taught them the *Our Father,* a prayer which millions of people of every language have repeated for twenty centuries. It is a prayer that unites various petitions which the Lord had taught them at different times. Perhaps this is the reason why the prayer is not exactly the same in the Gospels of St Luke and St Matthew.[2] What is the same, however, is the prayer's entirely new way of dealing with God. The seven requests have *such a simplicity in them that even a child can learn them, but at the same time such a depth that a whole life can be spent meditating on their meaning.*[3]

The first words of the Lord's prayer are *Abba, Father.* The early Christians did their best to preserve the Aramaic word which Jesus used: *Abba.* It is very likely that this word was used in the liturgies of the nascent Church.[4] This word sets the tone for the rest of the prayer. We find

---

[1] Luke 11:1-4
[2] cf Matt 6:9 ff
[3] St John Paul II, *Address,* 14 March 1979
[4] cf W. Marchel, *Abba! Father. The prayer of Christ and Christians,* Rome 1963

ourselves immediately in a relationship of trust and
filiation. The Catechism of the Council of Trent teaches
that the Lord omitted other words *which might have
induced awe or fear in us. He wanted to use a word which
would inspire love and confidence in those who were
praying. What word could be more agreeable than 'father',
so full is it of tenderness and affection?*[5] Jesus chose the
word Jewish children used to address their fathers. This
was the word He found most suitable for invoking the
Creator of the entire Universe. *Abba! Father!*

It is not easy to take this in. The same God who
transcends all things is a Father wholly interested in the
lives of his children! Even though we are often weak and
ungrateful, the Father wants us to spend eternity with him.
We have been born so as to attain Heaven. St Thomas
teaches that *God granted other creatures little gifts; to us
men and women He has given his entire patrimony. We are
his heirs because we are his sons and daughters. By the
fact of our being children, we are the beneficiaries of his
Will. 'For you did not receive the spirit of slavery only to
fall back into fear, but you have received the spirit of
sonship. When we cry, Abba! Father! it is the Spirit himself
bearing witness with our spirit that we are children of God
...' (Rom 8:15).*[6]

When we pray the Our Father we should take care to
savour those sweet words, *Abba, Father, my Father ...* This
prayer will then have a decisive influence on our daily life
*because if we really mean that God is our father, we will
struggle to behave as his worthy children.*[7]

33.2 Divine filiation and prayer.

A good many people look for God in a hesitant and

---

[5] *Catechism of the Council of Trent*, IV, 9, 1
[6] St Thomas, *Commentary on the Lord's Prayer*
[7] St Cyprian, *Treatise on the 'Our Father'*, 11

blindly groping manner, as if they were in a dense fog. We Christians know with confidence that God is our Father and that He watches over us. *The expression 'our Father-God' had never been revealed to anyone. When he asked God to identify himself, the name Moses was given was different from this. This completely new name has been revealed to us by none other than God's Son.*[8] Every time we approach God, He tells us: *Son, you are always with me, and all that is mine is yours.*[9] He is interested in every one of our needs and problems. Should we happen to fall, He is there to support us and help us get back on our feet. *Everything comes to us from God. If at first something should happen to us that seems either good or bad, we have only to recall that it has been sent to us, or permitted, by a loving Father who is wiser than any physician. God knows what is good for us.*[10]

The spirit of divine filiation gives life a whole new meaning. It is not an impossible riddle. It is a participation in the building up of the house of the Father which is Creation itself. God calls to each one of us: *My son, you go into my vineyard too.*[11] Life is no longer filled with anxiety. Death can be faced with serenity and peace since it leads to our long-awaited encounter with Christ. If we can live every moment of our lives as sons and daughters of God we will be souls of prayer. This attitude of piety disposes us *promptly to give and spend ourselves generously in whatever relates to the service of the Lord.*[12] Since children ought to give respect, veneration and love to their parents, our lives will give praise and honour to God Almighty. *The piety which is born of divine filiation is a profound attitude*

---

[8] Tertullian, *Treatise on prayer,* 3
[9] Luke 15:31
[10] Cassian, *Conferences,* 7, 28
[11] Matt 20:1
[12] St Thomas, *Summa Theologiae,* 2-2, q. 8, a. 1, c

of the soul which eventually permeates one's entire existence. It is there in every thought, every desire, every affection.[13]

Through the course of his earthly life Our Lord taught us how to deal with our Father God. In Jesus we find the highest expression of filial love for the Father. The Gospels recount how on many occasions Jesus would withdraw from the multitude to unite himself in prayer with the Father.[14] Jesus teaches us the importance of spending some time in daily prayer with God in the midst of our ordinary activities. There are times when the Lord prays for his own intentions. This is the prayer of filial abandonment to the Will of his Father which we witness at Gethsemane[15] and on Calvary.[16] Many times too Jesus prays for others, particularly for the Apostles and his future disciples, including ourselves.[17] Jesus advises us that filial prayer is necessary if we are to resist temptation,[18] to obtain material goods[19] and final perseverance.[20]

This filial conversation has to be personal. *When you pray, go into your room and shut the door and pray to your Father who is in secret.*[21] This prayer ought to be discreet.[22] It needs to be a humble petition like that of the publican.[23] Our prayer should be constant and unflagging like that of the importunate friend or the stubborn widow.[24]

---

[13] St. J. Escrivá, *Friends of God,* 146
[14] Matt 14:23; Luke 6:12
[15] cf Mark 14:35-36
[16] cf Mark 15:34; Luke 23:34-36
[17] cf Luke 22:32; John 17
[18] cf Matt 26:41
[19] cf John 4:10; 6:27
[20] cf Luke 21:36
[21] Matt 6:5-6
[22] cf Matt 6:7-8
[23] cf Luke 18:9-14
[24] cf Luke 11:5-8; 18:1-8

It should be filled with trust in God's goodness.[25] Surely God the Father knows the needs of his children. He provides spiritual goods as well as material goods for them.[26] *My Father – talk to him like that, confidently – who art in heaven, look upon me with compassionate Love, and make me respond to thy love. Melt and enkindle my hardened heart, burn and purify my unmortified flesh, fill my mind with supernatural light, make my tongue proclaim the Love and Glory of Christ.*[27] *Our Father* ... teach us, teach me to deal with you with filial trust.

33.3 Prayer and fraternity.

Prayer is certainly a personal act, but it also involves other people. Recollection and interior peace are not an obstacle to including others in our prayer life. The Lord teaches us to say *Our Father* because we share the dignity of children of God with all our brothers and sisters.

Our Father. The Lord has told us[28] that before we begin our prayer we should be sure that no one has an outstanding complaint against us. Once we have been reconciled with our brethren, then the Lord will accept our offering.

We have a right to call God our Father if we treat other people as our brothers and sisters, especially those who are closest to us and those who are most in need. St John points out: *If any one says, 'I love God,' and hates his brother, he is a liar; for he who does not love his brother whom he has seen, cannot love God whom he has not seen.*[29] St John Chrysostom has written along the same lines: *We cannot call God our Father in all sincerity if we*

---

[25] cf Mark 11:23
[26] cf Matt 7:7-11; Luke 11:9-13
[27] St. J. Escrivá, *The Forge*, 3
[28] cf Matt 5:23
[29] 1 John 4:20

harbour in ourselves a hardened heart. If this is the case, we do not share in the spirit of goodness of our celestial Father.[30]

When we say to God, *Our Father*, we do not restrict ourselves to solely personal concerns. We should be presenting him with the adoration of all peoples. A never-ending prayer rises up to God through the action of the *Communion of Saints*. We pray for all men and women, for those who never learned to pray and for those who knew how to, but failed to practice prayer. We lend our voice to that of those who have forgotten the existence of their Father in Heaven. We give thanks in place of those who have neglected to give thanks. We ask for the needs of those who do not realize how close they are to the source of graces. In our prayer we should be so bold as to make petition for the needs of the entire world. We have to develop the sense of being advocates to God for those who are in need, especially those whom God has put by our side.

It should serve as some consolation to us that we have a place in the prayers of our brethren. In Heaven we will have the joy of meeting all of our intercessors. We will meet those Christians who have taken our place whenever we have neglected to pray as we should. How many services to be thankful for!

The prayer of a Christian is personal, but it should not be isolated. Whenever we pray the *Our Father* we immediately increase and amplify the *Communion of the Saints*. Our prayer is united with that of all the just: with the mother of a sick child, with the student struggling to pass an exam, with that girl helping her friend to make a good Confession, with that labourer who offers up his work, with that person who offers his unemployment.

---

[30] St John Chrysostom, *Homily on the narrow gate*

During the Holy Mass the priest prays with the faithful the *Our Father*. If we take into account the different timetables of different countries, we can be aware that the Holy Mass is being celebrated virtually continuously all around the world. Without ceasing, the Church prays this prayer for her children and for all mankind. The world takes on the appearance then of a great altar from which goes up unending praise to God the Father through his Son Jesus Christ in the Holy Spirit.

34. THE NAME OF GOD AND HIS KINGDOM

34.1 Ways of sanctifying the name of God. The first petition in the Our Father.

As soon as we have realized our dignity as children of God, we will experience the tenderness for our Parent that is felt by all true sons and daughters. We will no longer be thinking about our own interests. We will be fired with zeal for the glory of our Father. We will say to him: 'Hallowed be thy name.' By this statement we affirm that all of our desires depend upon his glory.[1]

In this, the first of seven petitions of the *Our Father* prayer, *we ask that God be known, loved, honoured, and served by the whole world, especially by ourselves.*[2] Jesus teaches us the right order of priority in our prayers. The first thing we should be praying for is the glory of God. This is truly the most important thing for us creatures who are so generally preoccupied by worldly concerns. Jesus told St Catherine of Siena: *Be you concerned about me, and I will be concerned about you.* The Lord will not leave us uncared for.

Hallowed by thy name. In Holy Scripture names have great significance. The name is related to the deepest identity of the person. It is for this reason that Jesus at the end of his earthly life summarized his teachings with these words: *I have manifested thy name to the men whom thou*

---

[1] Cassian, *Conferences*, 9, 18
[2] *Catechism of St Pius X*, 290

gavest me out of the world.[3] He revealed to mankind the mystery of God. In the *Our Father* we pray that God will be known and revered by all peoples. We also express our sorrow for the times when God's name has been profaned, silenced or used with disrespect. *When we say 'hallowed be thy name' we confirm our desire that the holy name of the Lord will be upheld and revered as sacred among men. We pray that his name will never be abused.*[4]

There are some places where it seems that men do not want to mention the name of God. Instead of referring to the Creator, they speak of 'divine wisdom.' Rather than speak of divine Providence, they speak of 'destiny.' At times these are no more than figures of speech. There are other occasions when we find that the name of God has been intentionally erased. We may have to overcome human respect to honour our Father intentionally. Without doing anything extraordinary, we should resolve to keep up christian customs of speech. These customs do add the presence of God to our conversation. Good examples are 'Thank God' and 'God willing.'[5] Yet we should not be the ones to bring God's name into daily affairs in a negative way. The Second Commandment prohibits us from taking the Lord's name in vain.

If we really love God, then we will sincerely love his holy name. We will never utter it in a disrespectful manner when we are impatient or surprised. This love for the name of God also extends to the name of Mary, his Mother, to the names of the saints and of all things consecrated to his service.

We honour God in our hearts whenever we pray an *act of reparation*. We should offer this type of prayer when we encounter disrespect for God's name, when someone has

---

[3] John 17:6
[4] St Augustine, *Letter 130, to Proba*
[5] Jas 4:15

committed a sacrilege, when we get news of events that
offend our Father in Heaven. We should take to our prayer
those words of praise from the *Benediction of the Most
Blessed Sacrament*: *Blessed be God, Blessed be his holy
name* ... We can say these prayers at any time during the
course of the day, especially when some act of reparation is
called for.

Our reverence for the holy name of God will lead us to
a deeper love for those prayers of praise, the *Gloria* and the
Sanctus in the Holy Mass.

St Teresa has written: *Take care not to miss this
wonderful opportunity. Say the 'Our Father' slowly without rushing. He is listening very close to you. This is the
best way to praise and honour his name.*[6]

There are many short prayers which can help us to
remain in the presence of God during the day: *Father,
hallowed be thy name, Blessed be God, Blessed be his holy
name, Blessed be the name of Jesus, Blessed be the name
of Mary, Virgin and Mother* ...

34.2 The Kingdom of God.

Thy kingdom come. St John Chrysostom has commented that the Lord *wants us to desire that which will
accelerate our heavenward pace. While we are living here
on the earth, He wants us to strive to embody the life of
Heaven.*[7]

The expression *kingdom of God* has a triple significance. It refers to the Kingdom of God present in our
souls in grace, the Kingdom of God on earth which is the
Church, and the Kingdom of God in Heaven. We ask God
to reign in our hearts as a king in his court. We ask his help
that we may remain united to him through the virtues of
faith, hope and love. We pray that these virtues reign in our

---

[6] St Teresa, *The Way of Perfection,* 31, 13
[7] St John Chrysostom, *Homilies on St Matthew's Gospel,* 19, 5

minds, our hearts and our wills.[8] When we pray each day for the coming of the Kingdom of God, we pray also that He will help us to overcome temptation. The reign of God in our soul will endure as long as we correspond with the graces He offers us.

The parables of the Kingdom should be fulfilled in our hearts. The Kingdom of God begins its action like the grain of wheat hidden in the earth. It grows to be a stalk of wheat in full ear, ripe for the harvest. The Kingdom is also like the leaven that transforms the entire heart until it becomes one with God. The Kingdom also resembles the grain of mustard seed which has a tiny beginning but grows to a great size. The Kingdom of God is present in our soul through grace while it awaits the definitive encounter with God that immediately follows death. The Kingdom of God is here, at hand, Jesus said. *The kingdom of God is in the midst of you.*[9] We can perceive its presence in our soul by the action of the Holy Spirit.

When we say *thy kingdom come* we pray that God will enter into us more fully, that we will be completely his. We pray that He will help us to overcome the obstacles we put in the way of divine grace. *Before, we were slaves, but today we are empowered to reign under the protection of Christ.*[10]

If our prayer is trusting, constant and sincere, it will be heard by God. As we read in today's Gospel: *For every one who asks receives, and he who seeks finds, and to him who knocks it will be opened. What father among you, if his son asks for a fish, will instead of a fish give him a serpent?*[11] How much confidence we can draw from these words of Jesus!

---

[8] cf *Catechism of St Pius X,* 294-295
[9] Luke 17:21
[10] St Cyprian, *Treatise on the 'Our Father',* 13
[11] Luke 11:5-13

34.3 The spreading of the Kingdom of Heaven.

When we pray *thy kingdom come* we ask that the Church may grow throughout the world for the salvation of souls. We are praying for the apostolate she carries out on earth. We commit ourselves to do what we can to extend the Kingdom of God. *It is not enough to pray for the Kingdom of God if we do not match our prayers with deeds.*[12] These deeds are the apostolic initiatives which we put into effect, no matter how small they may appear.

We cannot become discouraged because the world seems to be regressing to paganism. The Second Vatican Council challenges us: *On all Christians, accordingly, rests the noble obligation of working to bring all men throughout the whole world to hear and accept the divine message of salvation.*[13]

Our first obligation lies with those whom God has placed by our side, those with whom we have regular dealings. We cannot excuse ourselves from this apostolate. What is at stake is the eternal salvation of our neighbours. We should also be concerned about orienting the world to Christ: the dignity of persons, the rights of conscience, the respect due to work and to the payment of just wages, the sincere desire for peace among peoples – all of these are proper concerns for Christians in the middle of the world. They should unite with all men and women of good will to realize these ideals.

Thy kingdom come. Jesus reminds all of us: 'And I, if I be lifted up from the earth, I will draw all things to myself' (John 12:32). If you put me at the centre of all earthly activities, he is saying, by fulfilling the duty of each moment, in what appears important and what appears unimportant, I will draw everything to myself. My kingdom among you will be a reality! ...

---

[12] *Catechism of the Council of Trent*, IV, 10, 2
[13] Second Vatican Council, Decree *Apostolicam actuositatem*, 3

That is the calling of Christians, that is our apostolic task, the desire which should consume our soul: to make this kingdom of Christ a reality, to eliminate hatred and cruelty, to spread throughout the earth the strong and soothing balm of love. Let us ask our king today to make us collaborate, humbly and fervently, in the divine task of mending what is broken, of saving what is lost, of fixing what man has put out of order, of bringing to his destination whoever has gone off the right road, of reconstructing the harmony of all created things.[14] Let us begin, as always, with the little things of each day which are within our reach.

---

[14] St. J. Escrivá, *Christ is passing by,* 183

35. THE WILL OF GOD

35.1 Fulfilling the Will of God.

Thy will be done on earth as it is in heaven. This is our third petition to God in the *Our Father.* We want to draw down from the Lord the graces necessary so that we may do his Will on earth, just as the blessed do his Will in heaven. The best prayer is that which transforms our desire into his desire. Then we will be able to tell Jesus with joy: *Not my will, but thine be done.* I want only what you want. This indeed is the principal purpose of all prayer, that we identify ourselves entirely with the divine Will.

If we pray with this spirit we can always be sure our prayer is answered. Surely there is no one more interested in our welfare and happiness than the Lord is. Sometimes without our even realising it we may want our own will to be done. We may pray fervently that the divine Will coincide with our own ... St James writes: *You do not have, because you do not ask. You ask and do not receive, because you ask wrongly, to spend it on your passions.*[1]

Whenever we say: Lord, *thy will be done,* we need to be fully open to God's loving Providence. Even when God's plans at first sight seem to portend nothing but disaster, we have to see things with supernatural vision. There is a higher plane of existence which we do not fully appreciate. That ominous turn of events will perhaps serve as the necessary shadow in a beautiful work of art. After all, is not God's wisdom infinitely greater than our own? If we ask him for bread, will He give us a stone? Is not God

---

[1] Jas 4:3

our Father? *Abba, Father* ... True prayer is possible only when there is trust and confidence. *Lord, if it pleases you, grant me* ... God knows best. He is infinitely good. He wants the best for us, although there may be times when what we want is something different. Let us recall the example of Mary of Bethany. She sent an urgent message to Jesus to come and cure her brother Lazarus, who was on the point of death. Jesus did not cure him. He chose instead to bring him back to life. He is wisdom itself, and we are the ignorant ones. Jesus has an all-encompassing view of creation, of our entire life and of that of our friends. In comparison, we creatures can scarcely comprehend the complex nature of what is going on at this very moment. What we see in our impatience and in an incomplete manner, God sees in all its totality ... We do not really know how to pray for what are in fact our best interests. The Holy Spirit gently leads us in the right direction.[2] We cannot so much as pray *God willing* without his guidance and support.[3]

Our challenge is for us to want the Will of God in everything, to accept it with joy, to love it no matter how difficult or incomprehensible it appears. *This is not the capitulation of the weak before the strong. It is a manifestation of the trust between a son and his Father. The Father's goodness teaches us to become fully human, to discover the grandeur of our divine filiation.*[4]

35.2 Purifying the will and its self-centred tendencies.

Thy will be done ...

There are times when our will coincides with that of God's Will. Everything moves along smoothly. We make satisfactory progress along our way with little difficulty.

---

[2] cf Rom 8:20
[3] cf St Augustine, *Sermon on the Mount,* 2, 6, 21
[4] G. Chevrot, *In Secret,* p. 164

Yet we must not forget that the path to sanctity requires the purification of our will and of its self-centred tendencies. Even when we are engaged in the noblest of activities, we have to make the effort to identify our will with the divine Will. God's Will has to serve as our Pole Star, guiding our every step towards beatitude. This will sometimes mean that we must abandon our own plans which we have so carefully fashioned and mapped out. Perhaps the Holy Spirit will whisper in the depths of our heart: *For my thoughts are not your thoughts, neither are your ways my ways ...*[5]

Jesus is the perfect example of how to adapt ourselves to the Will of God in everything. This is his constant teaching throughout the Gospels. We may recall the scene in Samaria when, after a long day's journey, the Apostles brought him some food to eat. He told them: *My food is to do the Will of him who sent me, and to accomplish his work.*[6] Our ability to live as children of God will depend upon our fidelity to the Will of God even in the smallest details of ordinary life. Jesus himself emphasises this point: *I seek not my own will but the Will of him who sent me.*[7] If only we could always say the same! Let us tell Jesus: 'Lord, I do not want what my senses and my intelligence prompt me to desire, even if they yearn for good things. I want what you want, whatever it may cost.' If we should find it hard to accept the Will of God we should go to the Tabernacle and talk it over with Jesus. There we will come to understand that our deepest longing is to accept and love the Will of God. If we find a sacrifice to be especially difficult, this may be the moment to unite ourselves with Christ's prayer at Gethsemane: *Father, if thou art willing, remove this cup from me; nevertheless not my will, but*

---

[5] Is 55:8
[6] John 4:34
[7] John 5:30

thine, be done.[8] *Not my will* ... Let us repeat these words slowly.

In the earliest days of the Church the Apostles were faithful to this teaching of the Master: *Not every one who says to me, 'Lord, Lord,' shall enter the kingdom of heaven, but he who does the Will of my Father who is in heaven.*[9] *For whoever does the Will of my Father in heaven is my brother, and sister, and mother.*[10] The creature finds true happiness in the fulfilment of the Creator's Will. The divine Will is always oriented towards our true happiness on earth as well as our eternal happiness in Heaven. St Cyprian teaches: *Whoever possesses God lacks nothing ... if he does not let God down.*[11]

In the light of this, our will has only one purpose: to do what God wants us to do. Ordinary life becomes a theatre of action for pleasing God rather than for pleasing ourselves. Since God wants what is best for us, even though we may not understand at the time, we are exercising in this way of living our freedom to choose to do the good.[12] Through our free identification with the divine Will we are transforming our existence into a continual act of love.

35.3 Loving the Will of God in whatever happens.

Father, thy Will be done on earth as it is in heaven ... We should be disposed to do the Will of God and to love what God does or permits. When we find ourselves in circumstances that are outside of our control, we should look for God's loving presence. If our situation is difficult, humanly speaking, we should pray in a spirit of

---

[8] Luke 22:42
[9] Matt 7:21
[10] Matt 12:50
[11] St Cyprian, *Treatise on prayer,* 21
[12] cf C. Cardona, *Metaphysics of good and evil,* Pamplona 1987

abandonment: *Is that what you want, Lord? ... Then it's what I want also!*[13] These are wonderful opportunities for us to trust more and more in God. The divine Will may present itself to us in the form of suffering, of sickness or the death of a loved one. It may appear to us in the simplest of daily circumstances such as the gradual weakening and aging of the body, an insufficient salary or a professional commitment we cannot get out of. It could appear as some failure due to a simple mistake or misunderstanding. It might manifest itself in the grating personality of a co-worker, the frustration of unrealised ambitions and noble dreams, the acceptance of one's limitations or simply the lifelong struggle to grow in virtue. We may want to say with St Teresa of Avila:

Give me wealth or poverty,
give me comfort or discomfort,
give me joy or sorrow ...
What do you want to make of me?[14]

What do you want from me, Lord, in this present, actual, concrete situation?

If we accept the divine Will, God will give peace to our soul. We will also avoid useless human suffering, though we will still experience pain. Christ himself wept like one of us. In the *Letter to the Hebrews* we read: *In the days of his flesh, Jesus offered up prayers and supplications, with loud cries and tears.*[15] Our cries do not offend God, but move him to compassion. *You said to me: Father, I am having a very rough time. In answer I whispered in your ear: Take upon your shoulders a small part of that cross, just a tiny part. And if you can't manage that then ... leave it entirely on the strong shoulders of Christ. And from this moment on, repeat with me: 'My*

---

[13] cf St. J. Escrivá, *The Way,* 762
[14] St Teresa, *Poems,* 5
[15] Heb 5:7

Lord and my God: into your hands I abandon the past and the present and the future, what is small and what is great, what amounts to a little and what amounts to a lot, things temporal and things eternal.' Then, don't worry any more.[16]

The Lord wants us to accept his Will in everything. He also wants us to do whatever we can to improve a bad situation, if that is possible. If this is not to be or if we have to be more patient, let us hold on to our Father God's hand with renewed trust. As St Paul said in the midst of a great trial: *With all our affliction, I am overjoyed.*[17] Nothing can take away our joy.

Our Lady is a model for us to imitate. *Be it done unto me,* she said, *according to thy word.* May your Will be done, Lord, whenever it may please you.

---

[16] St. J. Escrivá, *The Way of the Cross,* Seventh Station, 3
[17] 2 Cor 7:4

36. PRAYERS TO THE MOTHER OF JESUS

36.1 The Virgin always brings us to her Son.

Jesus was speaking to a crowd of people one day when a woman cried out: *Blessed is the womb that bore you, and the breasts that you sucked!*[1] Jesus remembered very well the loving attention of his Mother. *These words of praise for Jesus and Mary spring from the simple faith of an unknown woman. Moved to the very depth of her heart by the teachings and gentle figure of Jesus, she could no longer contain her admiration. In her words we recognize a genuine example of the popular piety that has always been alive among Christians throughout the centuries.*[2] On that very day the words of the *Magnificat* came to life: *Henceforth all generations will call me blessed.* That unknown woman had begun a litany of praise that would continue until the end of time.

Jesus took these words of praise and made them even more profound: *Blessed, rather, are those who hear the word of God and keep it!* Undoubtedly, Mary is blessed for having borne in her womb the Son of God, for having nursed him and brought him up to manhood. But she is much more blessed for having fulfilled the word of God to perfection. *In the course of her Son's preaching she received the words whereby, in extolling a kingdom beyond the concerns and ties of flesh and blood, he declared blessed those who heard and kept the word of God as she*

---

uke 11:27-28

John Paul II, *Address*, 5 April 1987

was faithfully doing (cf Luke 2:19; 51).[3]

Today's Gospel reading[4] gives us an excellent prayer with which to honour the Son of God by venerating his Mother. Jesus is delighted to hear praises of Mary. This is why we pray the Holy Rosary with such devotion. In the words of St John Paul II: *As the woman in the Gospel cried out full of admiration and blessing for Jesus and his Mother, you too usually unite Jesus and Mary in your devotion and love. You understand that the Blessed Virgin leads us to her divine Son, and that he always listens to his Mother's requests.*[5] Having recourse to the Virgin is the shortest road to Jesus, and through him to the Holy Trinity. When we honour Mary we act as faithful children. We imitate Christ and in this we become like him. *Having entered deeply into the history of salvation, Mary, in a way, unites in her person and re-echoes the most important doctrines of the faith: and when she is the subject of preaching and worship she prompts the faithful to come to her Son, to his sacrifice and to the love of the Father.*[6] If we are with Mary we are certain to be on the sure path.

36.2 The Holy Rosary, the Virgin's favourite prayer.

Let us join our voices to that great chorus of voices of those who have praised Our Lady down through the centuries. We too want to learn how to go to Jesus through Mary. In this month we can follow the custom of the Church by putting more effort into the way we pray the Holy Rosary. The Roman Pontiff has strongly encouraged us: *I want to recommend to you in a special way the Rosary, a source of profound Christian life. Try to pray it every day, alone or with your family, repeating with great*

---

[3] Second Vatican Council, *Lumen gentium,* 58
[4] Luke 11:27-28
[5] St John Paul II, *loc cit*
[6] Second Vatican Council, *loc cit,* 65

*faith those basic prayers of the Christian: the Our Father,
the Hail Mary and the Glory be to the Father. Meditate on
those scenes of the life of Jesus and Mary of which the
joyful, sorrowful and glorious mysteries remind us. Thus
you will learn in the joyful mysteries to think of Jesus who
became poor and lowly, a child, for our sake, to serve us;
you will feel encouraged to serve your neighbour in his
needs. In the sorrowful mysteries you will realize that
accepting the sufferings of this life with docility and love,
like Christ in his Passion, leads to happiness and joy which
is expressed in the glorious mysteries of Christ and Mary
in the hope of eternal life.*[7]

The Rosary is Our Lady's favourite prayer.[8] It always
reaches her motherly heart. As a result, she obtains
countless graces and benefits for us. This devotion has
been compared to a ladder that goes up rung by rung. *We
therefore come closer and closer to Our Lady, which
inevitably means a meeting with Christ her Son. This is one
of the characteristics of the Rosary, the most beautiful and
important characteristic of all. This Marian devotion
brings us to Christ. Christ is the goal of this long and
repeated invocation to Mary. We speak to Mary so as to
reach Christ himself.*[9]

What peace the slow repetition of the *Hail Mary* gives
us! We can stop, perhaps, to savour each one of its parts:
Hail Mary ... That salutation which we have prayed so
often with filial love: *Holy Mary, Mother of God! ... pray
for us ... now!* She looks upon us with maternal affection.
*Just as with people in love, the pious Christian never tires
of repeating the same words over and over again, because
the fire of charity makes their content always new.*[10]

---

[7] St John Paul II, *loc cit*
[8] Bl. Paul VI, Encyclical, *Mense maio,* 29 April 1965
[9] *idem, Address,* 10 May 1964
[10] Pius XI, Encyclical, *Ingravescentibus malis,* 29 September 1937

36.3 The fruits of devotion to Our Lady.

True devotion to the Blessed Virgin can never consist in *sterile or transitory affection, nor in a certain vain credulity.*[11] The Second Vatican Council teaches us that true devotion *proceeds from true faith, by which we are led to recognize the excellence of the Mother of God, and we are moved to a filial love towards our Mother and to the imitation of her virtues.*[12] Our love for the Blessed Virgin inspires us to imitate her in the faithful fulfilment of our ordinary duties. She will move us to reject all sin, including venial sin. She will encourage us to struggle against our defects. To contemplate Mary's docility to the Holy Spirit is to be inspired to do God's will no matter what the cost. It is through this kind of love that we will overcome weakness and temptations to pride and sensuality.

Whenever we make a pilgrimage or visit a Marian shrine we build up a great reserve of hope. She is *Spes nostra,* our hope! When we pray the Holy Rosary with attention we will find the strength to seek sanctity. *It is not so much a matter of repeating formulas, but rather of speaking as living persons with another living person. Even though you do not see this person with the eyes of the body, you are able to see her with the eyes of faith. In fact, Our Lady and her Son Jesus live in heaven a life more 'alive' than our mortal life here below on earth.*

The Rosary is a confidential conversation with Mary, a way of speaking to her with confidence and abandonment. In it we entrust to her our sorrows, reveal our hopes and open our hearts. It is a way of declaring ourselves at her disposition for anything that she asks of us in the name of her Son. A way of promising her fidelity in every circumstance, even the most painful and difficult, sure of her protection, sure that if we ask her, she will always obtain

---

[11] Second Vatican Council, *loc cit,* 67

[12] *ibid*

for us from her Son all the graces necessary for our salvation.[13]

Let us resolve on this Saturday, Mary's day of the week, to offer her a *crown of roses* with greater affection. This is where the name 'Rosary' comes from. So let us not offer roses which have wilted or been soiled by neglect. *The Holy Rosary: the joys, the sorrows, and the glories of the life of Our Lady weave a crown of praises, repeated ceaselessly by the Angels and the Saints in Heaven – and by those who love our Mother here on earth. Practise this holy devotion every day, and spread it.*[14]

Through this devotion Our Lady will lift us up with hope whenever we experience our weaknesses. *'Immaculate Virgin, I know very well that I am only a miserable wretch, and all I do is increase each day the number of my sins ...' You told me the other day that was how you spoke to Our Mother. And I was confident in advising you with assurance to pray the Holy Rosary. Blessed be that monotony of Hail Marys which purifies the monotony of your sins!*[15]

---

[13] St John Paul II, *Address,* 25 April 1987
[14] St. J. Escrivá, *The Forge,* 621
[15] *idem, Furrow,* 475

TWENTY-EIGHTH SUNDAY: YEAR A

37. THE INVITED GUESTS

37.1 Heaven awaits us. Corresponding to the call from our Lord. Helping others to answer the invitation.

Today's liturgy represents salvation in terms of a royal banquet. The Lord invites us to attend the feast. *On this mountain, the Lord of hosts will prepare for all people a banquet of rich food, a banquet of fine wines, of food rich and juicy ... He will remove the mourning veil covering all peoples ... He will destroy Death for ever. The Lord will wipe away the tears from every cheek ...*[1] From the earliest of days the Prophets had spoken of Heaven using symbols from ordinary life. God himself leads us to this *holy mountain.* Today's *Responsorial Psalm* expresses this reality in moving terms: *The Lord is my shepherd ... Near restful waters he leads me ... He guides me along the right path ... If I should walk in the valley of darkness no evil would I fear. You are there with your crook and your staff; with these you give me comfort ... Surely goodness and kindness shall follow me all the days of my life. In the Lord's own house shall I dwell for ever and ever.*[2]

Jesus is our Shepherd. He invites us to follow him in a thousand different ways. Yet He wants to respect our freedom. This then is the mystery of evil: men and women can refuse God's invitation. The Gospel for today's Mass speaks to us of such a refusal. *The kingdom of heaven may be compared to a king who gave a feast for his son's wedding.*[3] According to the customs of the times, the king would have

---

[1] *First Reading,* Is 25:6-10
[2] *Responsorial Psalm,* Ps 22:1-6
[3] Matt 22:1-14

sent his servants to remind the previously invited guests that all was in readiness. The king was waiting for their arrival. And then to the king's surprise the guests declined to attend. Then the king sent more servants to demonstrate his concern. *Next he sent some more servants. 'Tell those who have been invited,' he said, 'that I have my banquet all prepared ...'* God's goodness is shown by the king's insistence and the worthiness of the feast: *my oxen and fattened cattle have been slaughtered, everything is ready.* Despite all this solicitude, the guests *were not interested: one went off to his farm, another to his business, and the rest seized his servants, maltreated them and killed them.* In other parables we have seen the Lord asking for what was his. For example, in the parable of the vineyard the Lord allows the tenants to use his land. But in this parable we have the Lord offering a free gift. And it is refused! The Lord offers us the most wonderful things which we only too frequently do not really appreciate. Jesus must have told this parable with deep sorrow. It is the saga of the love of God which has been rejected throughout time.

The invited guests represent those who are totally absorbed in their own activities. They think they have no need of God. When they are advised that God is calling them, they fulfil the parable by reacting with violence. *You have a duty to reach those around you, to shake them out of their drowsiness, to open wide new horizons for their selfish, comfortable lives, to make their lives more complicated (in a holy way, that is), to make them forget about themselves and show understanding for the problems of others. If you do not, you are not a good brother to your brothers in the human race. They need that 'gaudium cum pace,' that joy and peace, which maybe they do not know or have forgotten.*[4] Many will in fact respond to our apostolate and reach the banquet in time.

---

4 St. J. Escrivá, *The Forge*, 900

37.2 The call to participate in God's interior life. There are no good excuses for missing the Lord's banquet.

The image of a banquet is used throughout Holy Scripture to represent intimacy of relationship and salvation. *Behold, I stand at the door and knock; if any one hears my voice and opens the door, I will come in to him and eat with him, and he with me.*[5] God repeats over and over again his desire to engage in a loving dialogue with his creatures, a dialogue which will take definitive form in Heaven. *Open to me, my sister, my love, my dove, my perfect one; for my head is wet with dew, my locks with the drops of the night.*[6] What so far has been our response to the thousand invitations we are constantly receiving from the Lord? How is our prayer? Are we entering into close friendship with the Lord? Do we excuse ourselves from leading lives of greater dedication? Do we feel responsible for bringing the divine invitation to others? Are we concerned about the salvation of the people we know?

It is a very serious matter to reject the Lord's invitation, to live as if God were of little relevance and not prepare for his coming. There are no good excuses for missing the Lord's banquet – neither lands, nor possessions, nor health, nor any kind of well-being. The excuses people give in the parable are essentially the same sort of excuses people come up with today. The problem lies in our contemporaries' giving priority to earthly realities over eternal realities. *This rejection – which is an exclusion from God's kingdom – is unalterable beyond death, because previously there has been on the part of those invited a decisive negative response, no matter how courteously expressed, to the offer of salvation by God. They will have renounced their salvation in favour of other things they freely opted for and desired much more to*

---

[5] Rev 3:20
[6] Song 5:2

possess.[7] How dismaying it is to find so many people rejecting intimacy with God and eternal salvation for the sake of worldly interests!

But the Lord wants to fill his house. He never desists from his salvific effort: *'Go to the crossroads in the town and invite everyone you can find to the wedding.'* So these *servants went out onto the roads and collected together everyone they could find, bad and good alike.* No one is omitted from the divine call to salvation. The only one excluded is the person who chooses to ignore the Lord's repeated invitations.

St Augustine exclaims: *Help us, Lord, to disown our vain excuses. We want to attend the banquet ... Don't allow our pride or sensuality or attachments or idle curiosity to get in the way of our attendance. Make sure that we show up ... Who, after all, is going to be there? Beggars, the sick, the crippled, the blind ... We will arrive as the poor people that we are. We have been invited by the wealthy one who became poor for our sake, thereby enriching the poverty of the poor. We will come as sick people, since we need the divine doctor to cure our ills. We will come as lame people, and we will tell him: 'Keep steady my steps according to thy promise' (Ps 118:133). We will come as blind people and we will ask him: 'Lighten my eyes, lest I sleep the sleep of death' (Ps 12:4).*[8]

37.3 Christ's saving will. Our apostolic desires should be open to all souls.

Go to the crossroads in the town and invite everyone you can find to the wedding ... The Lord directs these words to every Christian because his saving will is universal in scope.[9] It encompasses all men and women of every race and condition and belief from every century. Christ patiently

---

[7] F. Suarez, *The Afterlife*, p. 132
[8] St Augustine, *Sermon 112*, 8
[9] cf 1 Tim 2:4

awaits the conversion of each individual soul. This is why He endured the agony of death on the Cross. Each person might say concerning Jesus: *I have been crucified with Christ ... who loved me and gave himself for me.*[10] If we are true disciples, we have to become united to the saving Will of the Lord. *So these servants went out on to the roads and collected together everyone they could find ...* Like Jesus, we have to be interested in the salvation of all souls – that of the elevator operator, the family doctor, a person getting onto our bus, the boys and girls in a schoolyard, a professor in the university ... Everyone is the focus of an immense divine love. Everyone should share some part of our apostolic concerns.

Just think, there are so many men and women on earth, and the Master does not fail to call every single one. He calls them to a Christian life, to a life of holiness, to a chosen life, to life eternal.[11]

It is very important that we bring souls to the Lord one by one. We ought to have the same concern for the people we work with every day. *Bear with all, just as the Lord does with you.*[12] We should open new horizons for our friends who may suffer from a limited human outlook. We should show them the need to approach God with confidence. Let us encourage them to offer their work to the Lord. Let us help them get to the root of that interior emptiness they experience from time to time ... No one should pass close to us without growing in the knowledge of God through our words and example. We will seek occasion to speak to them about eternal life and earthly happiness with patience.

Our Mother Mary will teach us how to treat each person with the concern and interest and respect that she showed for her Son.

---

[10] Gal 2:20

[11] St. J. Escrivá, *op cit,* 13

[12] St Ignatius of Antioch, *Epistle to St Polycarp,* 1, 2

TWENTY-EIGHTH SUNDAY: YEAR B

38. THE LOOK OF JESUS

38.1 The greatest wisdom lies in finding Jesus Christ.

The texts of today's Mass speak to us of divine wisdom. We should value it above any other good. In the *First Reading* we listen to the prayer of Solomon: *I called upon God, and the spirit of wisdom came to me. I preferred her to sceptres and thrones, and I accounted wealth as nothing in comparison with her. Neither did I liken to her any priceless gem, because all gold is but a little sand in her sight, and silver will be accounted as clay before her.*[1] Nothing can compare with the knowledge of God that gives meaning to our lives: *I loved her more than health and beauty, and I chose to have her rather than light, because her radiance never ceases. All good things came to me along with her, and in her hands uncounted wealth.*

Jesus Christ, the Son of God Incarnate, is divine Wisdom that has been hidden from all eternity in the bosom of the Father. He is now accessible to all men and women who are disposed to open their hearts to him. Next to Jesus, *all gold is but a little sand, and silver accounted as clay.* To possess Christ is to possess everything. That is why we commit the greatest folly whenever we choose some worldly good in place of Christ, be it honour, wealth, good health, anything at all. Nothing is worth more than the Master.

My Lord, thank you for coming to earth. You could have saved us without coming. It was sufficient that you wanted to save us. The Incarnation was not necessary. Yet

---

[1] Wis 7:7-11

you wanted to leave an example for us of total perfection ...
Thank you, my Master, for having come into the midst of
the world, a man among men, the Man among men, like
one of us ... and yet this Man would 'draw all things to
himself,' since there has existed nothing so perfect before
or since or ever shall. Thank you for coming to earth
because now I can look upon you and sustain my life on
you.[2] The greatest wisdom lies in finding you, my Lord, in
following you.

38.2 The encounter with the rich young man.

In today's Gospel St Mark recounts the story of the
young man who preferred worldly goods to Christ
himself.[3] Jesus and his disciples were about to set off on
their way to Jerusalem when a young man ran up and knelt
before the Master.[4] *Good Teacher,* he said, *What must I do*
to inherit eternal life? The Lord replied that he should
follow the Commandments as a sure path to salvation. The
young man answered that he had followed the Law ever
since he was a child. Jesus then looked at him, taking stock
of the purity of this heart and the potential for generosity
within it. *And Jesus looking upon him, loved him.* He loved
him with a love of predilection. He invited the youth to
follow him, setting aside and forsaking all that he
possessed.

We may recall that St Mark is recording the catechesis
of St Peter. He would have received all of the details from
the lips of the Apostle. This explains the Evangelist's
reference to the way Jesus looked at the young man. Peter
would never forget the look of Jesus that changed the course
of his own life! *Jesus looked at him, and said, 'So you are*

---

[2] J. Leclerq, *Thirty Meditations on Christian Life,* Bilbao 1958
[3] Mark 10:17-30
[4] cf Matt 19:16

Simon the son of John? You shall be called Cephas'.[5] Peter's life was never the same after that. Wouldn't it be wonderful to contemplate the look of Jesus! At times it is lofty and winning; or pained and sorrowful, as when he faced the incredulity of the Pharisees.[6] There was his look of compassion for the deceased son of the widow of Naim.[7] His look invited Matthew to rise up and follow him.[8] It was able to move the heart of Zacchaeus to conversion.[9] This was the look of love that beheld the poor widow in the Temple who gave all that she had.[10] This penetrating look brings the soul face to face with God himself, inspiring contrition. That was the effect the look of Jesus had on the woman found in adultery[11] and on Peter himself.[12] On Holy Thursday night a mere glance caused Peter to weep bitterly for his cowardice.

Jesus looked with great affection at this bold young man: *Iesus autem intuitus eum dilexit eum.* And he beckoned to him: *'Follow me.' Walk in my path! Stand by my side! Remain in my love!*[13] This is the invitation that perhaps we ourselves have received ... and we have followed him! *Man needs this loving look. He needs to know that he is loved, loved eternally and chosen from eternity (cf Eph 1:4). At the same time, this eternal love of divine election accompanies man during life as Christ's look of love. And perhaps most powerfully at the moment of trial, humiliation, persecution, defeat, when our humanity is as it were blotted out in the eyes of other people, insulted*

---

[5] John 1:42
[6] cf Mark 2:5
[7] cf Luke 7:13
[8] cf Matt 9:9
[9] cf Luke 19:5
[10] cf Mark 12:41-44
[11] cf John 8:10
[12] cf Luke 22:61; Mark 14:72
[13] St John Paul II, *Homily on Boston Common,* 1 October 1979

and trampled upon. At that moment the awareness that the Father has always loved us in his Son, that Christ always loves each of us, becomes a solid support for our whole human existence. When everything would make us doubt ourselves and the meaning of our life, then this look of Christ, the awareness of the love that in him has shown itself more powerful than any evil and destruction, this awareness enables us to survive.[14]

Each person receives a personal call to follow the Master. If we respond to Christ's invitation we will be filled with peace and true joy. Authentic wisdom consists in saying 'yes' to each one of Christ's invitations in the course of our life. *Open your own hearts to Jesus and tell him your story. I don't want to generalise. But one day, perhaps, an ordinary Christian, just like you, opened your eyes to horizons both deep and new, yet as old as the Gospel. He suggested to you the prospect of following Christ earnestly, seriously, of becoming an apostle of apostles. Perhaps you lost your balance then and didn't recover it. Your complacency wasn't quite replaced by true peace until you freely said 'yes' to God, because you wanted to, which is the most supernatural of reasons. And in its wake came a strong, constant joy, which disappears only when you abandon him.*[15] This is the joy of giving one's self. What a contrast this is to the sadness of the rich young man who didn't want to heed the Lord's call!

38.3 Jesus invites us to follow him.

Go, sell what you have, and give to the poor, and you will have treasure in heaven; and come, follow me. This was the Lord's advice to the youth who *had great possessions.* The words of Jesus should have served as a cause for joy to the young man, but they made him sad. *At*

---

[14] *idem, Letter to Youth,* 31 March 1985, 7

[15] St. J. Escrivá, *Christ is passing by,* 1

*that saying his countenance fell, and he went away
sorrowful. The sadness of the young man makes us reflect.
We could be tempted to think that many possessions, many
of the goods of this world, can bring happiness. We see
instead in the case of the young man in the Gospel that his
many possessions had become an obstacle to accepting the
call of Jesus to follow Him. He was not ready to say 'yes'
to Jesus, and 'no' to self, to say 'yes' to love and 'no' to
escape. Real love is demanding.*[16] If we should notice a
trace of sadness in our heart, perhaps it is because the Lord
is asking from us something which we do not want to
relinquish. Maybe we have not yet freed our heart from
some earthly attachment. This is the moment to remember
those words of Jesus at the close of this roadside
encounter: *Truly, I say to you, there is no one who has left
house or brothers or sisters or mother or father or children
or lands, for my sake and for the gospel, who will not
receive a hundredfold now, in this time, houses and
brothers and sisters and mothers and children and lands,
with persecutions, and in the age to come eternal life.*

Come and follow me ... How must everyone there have
been eagerly expecting, or hoping for, the right answer
from the young man! With these same words Jesus called
his closest disciples. This invitation is a calling to
accompany the Lord in his own ministry, to listen to his
doctrine and to digest it, to imitate his way of life ... After
the Lord's Ascension into Heaven this 'following' no
longer means being with the Lord in Palestine. Our
challenge is to be with Christ in the middle of the world,
right where he found us. We need to make his life and his
teaching part of our very being, of the very air we breathe.
We need to communicate Christ's message in all the
circumstances of our daily life. St Josemaría Escrivá has

---

[16] St John Paul II, *Homily on Boston Common*, 1 October 1979

written: *I have distinguished as it were four stages in our effort to identify ourselves with Christ: seeking him, finding him, getting to know him, loving him. It may seem clear to you that you are only at the first stage. Seek him then, hungrily; seek him within yourselves with all your strength. If you act with determination, I am ready to guarantee that you have already found him, and have begun to get to know him and to love him, and to hold your conversation in heaven.*[17] Jesus is alive today and He is calling his disciples – the same Jesus who walked the roads of Palestine. We cannot let slip the wonderful opportunity He offers us.

---

[17] St. J. Escrivá, *Friends of God*, 300

TWENTY-EIGHTH SUNDAY: YEAR C

39. BEING GRATEFUL

39.1 The cure of the ten lepers.

The *First Reading* for today's Mass tells of the cure by the Prophet Elisha of Naaman the Syrian's leprosy.[1] The Lord used this miracle to attract Naaman to the true religion. This was a much greater gift than health of the body. As soon as Namaan realised he was cured, he exclaimed: *Behold, I know that there is no God in all the earth but in Israel.* Today's Gospel from St Luke records a similar event.[2] Our Lord cures a Samaritan of his leprosy, and then rewards his gratitude with the gift of faith. Like the Syrian, the Samaritan was a stranger. He did not belong to the people of Israel.

On his final journey to Jerusalem Jesus was passing between Samaria and Galilee. Entering a village there He was met by ten lepers. They *stood at a distance* from Jesus and his followers. The Law forbade lepers from coming into close contact with other people.[3] Among this group of lepers there was a Samaritan, although Jews and Samaritans normally avoided one another.[4] Segregation and disgrace had brought traditional enemies together. They *lifted up their voices* in a petition that must have immediately moved the Heart of Jesus: *Jesus, Master, have mercy on us.* They threw themselves at God's mercy. Christ took pity on them. He told them to go and show

---

[1] 2 Kings 5:14-17
[2] Luke 17:11-19
[3] cf Lev 13:45
[4] cf 2 Kings 17:24 ff: John 4:9

themselves to the local priests. The Law laid down that such cures had to be verified in this way.[5] The lepers obeyed the Lord and went on their way, as if they had already been healed. Because of their faith and docility, they were freed from their infirmity.

The lepers are teachers of prayer. They had recourse to divine mercy, which is the source of all graces. They demonstrate the road to healing, a road which is open to all of us, no matter what kind of leprosy we may carry in our souls. The lesson is to have faith and to be docile to those who speak in the name of the Lord. We will hear Our Lord's voice especially through the means of spiritual direction.

39.2 The Lord waits for us to give thanks for his countless gifts.

And as they went they were cleansed. We can easily imagine their amazement and joy. In the midst of all this excitement, they forgot all about Jesus. Only one of the group, the Samaritan, turned back to where the Lord was with his disciples. He probably went back running. The Evangelist has him *praising God with a loud voice.* He fell at the feet of the Master to give thanks for the cure. What a beautiful and profoundly human reaction! *What better words may we carry in our heart, pronounce with our mouth, write with a pen, than the words, 'Thanks be to God'? There is no phrase that may be said so readily, that can be heard with greater joy, felt with more emotion or produced with greater effect.*[6] Gratitude is a wonderful virtue.

Surely the Lord was delighted by the gratitude of this Samaritan. At the same time, he was disappointed at the absence of the other nine. *Were not ten cleansed? Where*

---

[5] cf Lev 14:2
[6] St Augustine, *Letter* 72

are the nine? Jesus shows us his surprise at the turn of events: *Was no one found to return and give praise to God except this foreigner?* How many times has Jesus asked this about us? Today in our prayer let us try to make up for all the times we have been remiss and ungrateful. Certainly our lives have been full of divine cures, invitations and encounters. St John Chrysostom wrote that the gifts we receive from God greatly exceed the grains of sand on the seashore.[7]

It is only human that we should have a clearer sense of what we need over and above what we have received. Perhaps this would go some way to explaining why we typically do not appreciate what we have, and why our gratitude can be insufficient. Maybe we think that we are somehow owed a pleasant existence. We tend to forget the message St Augustine drew from today's Gospel narrative: *What is our own but the sins which we have committed? 'What do you have that you did not receive?' (1 Cor 4:7).*[8]

Our lives should be a continual act of thanksgiving. We should frequently bring to mind the many natural gifts and graces the Lord has granted us. We should not lose our joy when we are in need. This experience of poverty, when things are going badly, may be a preparation for our receiving some greater good. The Psalmist reminds us: *Remember the wonderful works that He has done.*[9] Let us not forget that the Samaritan came to know Jesus Christ by means of his dreadful disease. Because of his gratitude the Samaritan won Christ's friendship and the priceless gift of faith: *Rise and go your way; your faith has made you well.* The other nine who were cured deprived themselves of the best part of the generosity of the Lord. St Bernard teaches that *he who humbly acknowledges his indebtedness will*

---

[7] cf St John Chrysostom, *Homilies on St Matthew's Gospel,* 25, 4
[8] St Augustine, *Sermon 176,* 6
[9] Ps 104:5

naturally be promised even more. Whoever is faithful in a few things will justly be entrusted with many things. Conversely, he who is ungrateful for present favours has probably been ungrateful for past ones.[10]

Let us thank the Lord for everything. We should live with joy in the knowledge that God has overwhelmed us with blessings. *Have you seen the gratitude of little children? Imitate them, saying to Jesus when things are favourable and when they aren't, 'How good you are! How good!'*[11] Do we thank Jesus for the opportunity to have our sins cleaned away in the Sacrament of Penance? Are we grateful for the immense gift of having Jesus Christ with us in the same city, perhaps even on the same street, present in the Tabernacle?

39.3 Being grateful to other people.

Today's *Responsorial Psalm* proclaims: *O sing to the Lord a new song, for he has done marvellous things!*[12] When we live by faith we will find only reasons for thanksgiving. *There is no one who, with a little bit of thought, cannot but discover many reasons for being grateful to God ... Once we have come to an appreciation of all He has given to us, we will have abundant cause to give thanks continually.*[13]

We receive many gifts from the Lord at the hands of those we habitually have contact with in ordinary life. In these cases, our thanksgiving to the Lord should be routed to him through these same persons. We should do our best to make their lives less difficult. When we give thanks to them in this way, we will be giving thanks to God himself, for He is present in all men and women. We can be

---

[10] St Bernard, *Commentary on Psalm 50*, 4, 1
[11] St. J. Escrivá, *The Way*, 894
[12] *Responsorial Psalm*, Ps 97:1-4
[13] St Bernard, *Sermon for the Sixth Sunday after Pentecost*, 25, 4

confident that God will amply reward our efforts. *We do not believe that our commerce with men and women is restricted only to material goods and services. The truth is that other people can and do give us something more than material benefit. Teachers have opened to us the treasures of our intelligence. Doctors have contributed their knowledge and training to our health and that of our loved ones. Such services could never be invoiced in any satisfactory way since they come from the heart. We may also consider that coal or heating fuel is the product of other men's labour. Bread comes to us thanks to the exertions of farmers. We are receiving little pieces of their lives. Our lives, therefore, are involved in the lives of our brothers and sisters, and we are indebted to them. It is not a question of financial remuneration. All of these people have put their whole being into the fulfilment of their daily work, their social duties: they have the right to expect our heartfelt gratitude.*[14] We should direct particular gratitude to those who help us on our path to God.

The Lord is pleased by the gratitude we show to the people who in so many ways help us in our ordinary lives. Sometimes it takes only a smile or a friendly word of thanks to express appreciation ... It is possible that those nine lepers who were cured thanked Jesus in their hearts, but the fact remains that they did not turn back like the Samaritan, and we are conscious of something missing here. Jesus would have liked them to do so. Maybe they had it in mind to turn back ... Maybe they meant to, and the Lord was left with that.

Not a day goes by without our receiving some special and extraordinary grace from God. Let us make sure to end our examination of conscience each night with the prayer: *Thank you, Lord, for everything.* We cannot let a day pass

---

[14] G. Chevrot, *But I say to you ...*, Madrid 1981

without praying for blessings upon those who are around us, and who are our benefactors in all sorts of ways. Prayer is, after all, a most efficacious form of thanksgiving: *I thank you, my Lord, for the good resolutions, affections and inspirations which you have communicated to me ...*

40. OUR DAILY BREAD

40.1 What we are asking for with the words our daily bread.

Give us this day our daily bread ...

A certain Asian legend tells of a king and his son. The king bestowed upon the prince a royal endowment that would enable him to live in a worthy fashion for all twelve months of the year. But the king decided that rather than give these things away all at once he would distribute them in daily allotments. In this way the king was able to see his son every day of the year and vice versa.

This legend is somewhat analogous to our relationship with God. 'Our daily bread' depends upon the prayers we offer each day. The fact that we ask only for today's needs implies that we will have another encounter with our Father God tomorrow. This is the way the Father encourages us to be steadfast in saying his prayer.

The Lord taught us to ask for *bread,* that is, for everything we need to live as children of God – faith, hope, love, joy, food for the body and food for the soul, docility to the Will of God in everyday life, a heart big enough to understand other people and be of service to them ... Bread is a symbol of all the many gifts that come to us from God.[1] In the first place we ask for whatever we need in a material sense; then our request is for whatever we need for the health of our soul.[2]

The Lord wants us to ask him for temporal goods. If

---

[1] cf Ex 23:25; Is 33:16
[2] cf *Catechism of the Council of Trent,* IV, 13, 8

their use is well-ordered, they can certainly help us to attain Heaven. We find many examples of this truth in the Old Testament. The Lord himself moves us to ask for what we require in this life. We should not forget that the first miracle worked by Jesus was to change water into wine at a wedding feast. On another occasion he fed a great crowd of people who had followed him into a deserted place ... When Jesus had brought the daughter of Jairus back to life, he asked that she be given something to eat ... [3]

When we ask for *our daily bread* we are acknowledging the fact that our entire existence depends on God. The Lord wants us to ask the Father for whatever we need. As a consequence, we are constantly reminding ourselves that we are children who depend entirely on our Father God. We can do nothing by ourselves. To pray the *Our Father* well, with devotion, is to recognize our radical poverty before the loving eyes of God. He will make sure that we have what we need each day. God will never let us down.

When we pray for *our bread,* the Lord wants us also to keep in mind the intentions and needs of our brothers and sisters, especially those who have been entrusted to our care and those who suffer deprivation of any kind.

40.2 The bread of life.

The Fathers of the Church have interpreted the bread in the Lord's Prayer in a material sense, but also as the *bread of life,* the Holy Eucharist. This holy food is indispensable for our spiritual life.

I am the bread of life. Your fathers ate the manna in the wilderness, and they died. This is the bread which comes down from heaven, that a man may eat of it and not die. I am the living bread which came down from heaven;

---

[3] cf John 2:1 ff; Matt 14:13-21; Mark 5:22-43

if any one eats of this bread, he will live for ever; and the bread which I shall give for the life of the world is my flesh.[4] St John remembered this lengthy discourse for the rest of his days as well as its exact location: *This he said in the synagogue, as he taught at Capharnaum.*[5]

Christ's words have an impact of such tremendous realism that they simply cannot be interpreted in a figurative way. Jesus reveals that the *manna* of the Exodus was an anticipation, a prefiguring, of the Bread with which he would nourish Christians in their progress to Heaven. Communion is the 'sacrum convivium', the wonderful banquet at which Christ gives himself to us, and gives himself up for us. So by receiving Holy Communion we are sharing in the sacrifice of Jesus Christ. This is why the Church sings in the *Liturgy of the Hours* on the feast of Corpus Christi: *O sacred feast in which we partake of Christ, in which his sufferings are remembered, our minds are filled with his grace and we receive a pledge of the glory that is to be ours.*[6]

Christ's hearers understand perfectly well that He means exactly what He says; but they cannot believe that what He says could be true; if they had understood him in a metaphorical, figurative or symbolic sense there would be no reason for them to be so surprised and nothing to cause an argument.[7] The Jews then disputed among themselves, saying, 'How can this man give us his flesh to eat?'[8] Jesus clearly states that his Body and Blood are food for the soul, the pledge of eternal life, the guarantee of the resurrection of the body.

Our Lord uses a stronger word than just 'eating' (the

---

[4] John 6:48-52
[5] cf John 6:60
[6] *Liturgy of the Hours,* Antiphon of the *Magnificat,* Second Vespers
[7] *The Navarre Bible,* note to John 6:52
[8] John 6:52

original verb could be translated as 'chewing') which shows that Communion is a real meal. There is no room for saying that he was speaking only symbolically, which would mean the Communion was only a metaphor and not really eating and drinking the Body and the Blood of Christ.[9]

When we have received Communion Christ is not just spiritually present in us. He is *truly, really, and substantially* present in us. We shall never be able to appreciate sufficiently the intimacy with God himself – Father, Son and Holy Spirit – that we are offered in the eucharistic banquet.

When we say: Father, *give us this day our daily bread,* we should rejoice that it is possible for us to receive the *Bread of Life* every day. We should be filled with thanksgiving. We should be moved to frequent and, if possible, daily Communion. *If this is daily bread, why do you receive it only once a year? Receive each and every day what will be of such benefit to you. And be sure to live each day in a manner that makes you worthy to receive him.*[10]

40.3 The faith we need to eat the bread from Heaven. Holy Communion.

The Holy Eucharist acts in the same way as natural food – by conserving, nourishing, restoring and fortifying our spiritual life.[11] The Blessed Sacrament imparts the peace and joy of Christ to the soul as a *foretaste of eternal bliss.*[12] It erases venial sins from the soul and strengthens our ability to do good. By stimulating our supernatural life

---

[9] *The Navarre Bible,* note to John 6:54
[10] St Ambrose, *On the Sacraments,* V, 4
[11] cf Council of Florence, Decree *Pro armeniis, Dz* 698
[12] cf John 6:58; Dz 875

it serves as *the remedy for our daily needs.*[13]

Jesus is hidden in the appearance of the bread. He hopes that we will receive him often. *Come, for all is now ready.*[14] Many people have not come when invited, and Jesus is waiting for us. Let us pray to Jesus with words taken from today's *Liturgy of the Hours*: *Stay with us, Lord Jesus, for it is getting late. Be our companion along our journey. Lift up our hearts and inspire our feeble hope.*[15]

Faith is indispensable if we are to eat this bread. Our faith is manifested in the proper preparation of our soul. Those disciples who abandoned Our Lord because of this clear teaching of his rested their faith on their own judgment.

What of us? We can say with St Peter: *Lord, to whom shall we go? You have the words of eternal life.*[16] Let us resolve to improve our preparation for Communion by having more faith and love: *Adore him reverently, devoutly; renew in his presence the sincere offerings of your love. Don't be afraid to tell him that you love him. Thank him for giving you this daily proof of his tender mercy, and encourage yourself to go to communion in a spirit of trust. I am awed by this mystery of Love. Here is the Lord seeking to use my heart as a throne, committed never to leave me, provided I don't run away.*[17]

As we finish our prayer, let us echo those words spoken to Our Lord by the people in Capharnaum: *Lord, give us this bread always.*[18]

And when we pray the *Our Father,* let us reflect upon our needs and the needs of our brothers and sisters. We

---

[13] St Ambrose, *On the Sacraments*
[14] cf Luke 14:15 ff
[15] *Liturgy of the Hours,* Second Vespers prayer
[16] John 6:68
[17] St. J. Escrivá, *Christ is passing by,* 161
[18] John 6:34

have to pray with devotion: *Give us this day our daily bread*; give us what we require for our body and our spirit. Tomorrow we will have the blessed opportunity to have recourse once again to our Father God. He will reply to us: *Omnia mea tua sunt,*[19] everything I have is yours.

---

[19] cf Luke 15:31

TWENTY-EIGHTH WEEK: TUESDAY

41. FORGIVE US OUR TRESPASSES

41.1 We are sinners. Sin is always an offence against God.

Every day in the *Our Father* we pray: Father, *forgive us our trespasses.*

We are sinners. St John reminds us in his first epistle: *If we say that we have no sin, we deceive ourselves, and the truth is not in us.*[1] The universal contamination of sin is recognised in both the Old Testament[2] and the New Testament.[3] No day goes by without our having to seek pardon from the Lord for our faults and offences. We offend him in small ways, in more serious actions and omissions; in our thoughts, our words and our deeds. *What Revelation makes known to us is confirmed by our own experience. For when man looks into his own heart he finds that he is drawn towards what is wrong and sunk in many evils which cannot come from his good Creator ... Man therefore is divided in himself.*[4]

Today let us take those words of the publican in the Temple as our prayer: *God, be merciful to me a sinner!*[5] If we pray this prayer with true humility it will do us much good. The Lord gave us this parable for our benefit.

People frequently confuse sin and its consequences. Many become depressed by personal failure or humiliations.

---

[1] 1 John 1:8
[2] cf Job 9:2; 14:4; Prov 20:9; Ps 13:1-4; 50; 1 ff; etc.
[3] cf Rom 3:10-18
[4] Second Vatican Council, *Gaudium et spes,* 13
[5] Luke 18:13

They equate sin with their ruined ideals and ambitions, or with their negative effects on others. Yet sin is first and foremost an offence against God. It is only secondarily an offence against ourselves or our neighbours. The confession of King David is appropriate here: *I have sinned against the Lord.*[6] David had committed adultery and had arranged for the death of Uriah in battle. His fundamental offence, however, did not consist in the adultery, the evil plotting, the abuse of power or the scandal given to the people by his behaviour. The gravest evil had to do with the fact that he had offended God.

If we do not follow the law we will surely suffer serious consequences. But sin can only be committed against God. The prodigal son says to his father: *I have sinned against heaven and before you.*[7] *Without these words, 'Father I have sinned', man cannot really enter the Mystery of Christ's Death and Resurrection, to draw from it the fruits of Redemption and Grace. These are key words. They show particularly man's great interior opening to God: 'Father I have sinned before you' ...*

The Psalmist speaks even more clearly: 'Tibi soli peccavi' – 'Against thee, thee only have I sinned' (Ps 50:4).

That 'Against thee, thee only' does not diminish all the other dimensions of moral evil, such as sin with regard to other people, with regard to the human community. However, 'sin' is a moral evil mainly and definitively with regard to God himself, to the Father in the Son. Therefore 'the (contemporary) world' – and the prince of this world – work very hard indeed to dim and wipe out this aspect in man.

On the contrary, the Church ... works above all in order that every man may find himself again with his own sin before God only – and consequently that he may accept the salvific power of forgiveness contained in Christ's

---

[6] 2 Sam 12:13
[7] Luke 15:18

Passion and Resurrection.[8]

It is a great heavenly gift for us to be able to recognise our sins and draw near to the fountain of divine mercy. Father, *forgive us our trespasses!* The Lord will answer by bestowing on us a great peace.

41.2 The Lord is always ready to forgive us. Every sin can be forgiven as long as the sinner is repentant.

In making this necessary acknowledgment of our sins, it is not enough to call them to mind lightly; for it is necessary that the recollection of them be bitter, that it touch the heart, pierce the soul, and imprint sorrow. Wherefore, the pastor should treat this point diligently, that his pious hearers may not only recollect their sins, and iniquities, but recollect them with pain and sorrow; so that with true interior contrition they may betake themselves to God their Father, humbly imploring Him to pluck from the soul the piercing stings of sin.[9]

The Lord is ready to forgive everyone. *He who comes to me I will not cast out.*[10] *It is not the will of my Father who is in heaven that one of these little ones should perish.*[11] As St Thomas has taught us, the omnipotence of God is manifested above all in divine pardon and mercy. God shows in this fashion that He has the supreme power to forgive sins.[12] The Gospels record many occasions when Jesus demonstrates his mercy for sinners. He receives sinners. He attends to them. He beckons them. He understands them. He pardons them. The Pharisees were wont to criticise Jesus for his approach. He rebukes them with those immortal words: *Those who are well have no*

---

[8] St John Paul II, *Angelus,* 16 March 1980
[9] *Catechism of the Council of Trent,* IV, 14, 6
[10] John 6:37
[11] Matt 18:14
[12] St Thomas, *Summa Theologiae,* 1, q. 25, a. 3 ad 3

need of a physician, but those who are sick.[13] *For t.. of man came to seek and to save the lost.*[14]

Proper pardon for an offence can only be given by t.. one who is offended. Only God can forgive sins. As Jesus told the Pharisees: *Who can forgive sins but God only?*[15] Jesus brings these words to fulfilment before their eyes. After the Resurrection He confers upon his Church and her ministers the power to forgive sins. He tells the Apostles: *Receive the Holy Spirit. If you forgive the sins of any, they are forgiven; if you retain the sins of any, they are retained.*[16]

The Lord is always willing to grant pardon through the Sacrament of Penance. The Catechism of the Council of Trent states: *Wherefore we ought to be firmly convinced, that since He commands us in this petition to implore his paternal mercy, He will not fail to bestow it on us. For this petition assuredly implies that God is so disposed towards us, as willingly to pardon those who are truly penitent. God it is against whom, having cast off obedience, we sin ... But it is also God, our most beneficent Father, who, having it in his willingness to do so, has also obliged men to ask him for pardon, and has taught them the words in which to ask. To no one, therefore, can it be a matter of doubt that under his guidance it is in our power to be reconciled to God.*[17]

41.3 The one condition for forgiveness: that we forgive others. What our pardon should be like.

Forgive us our trespasses as we forgive those who trespass against us. We pray these words many times each day. The Lord asks us to imitate God's paternal mercy. *Be*

---

[13] Matt 5:31
[14] Luke 19:10
[15] Luke 5:21
[16] John 20:22-23
[17] *Catechism of the Council of Trent,* IV, 24, 11

s your heavenly Father is merciful.[18] The
e of repeating this counsel: Forgive, and
en ... For the measure you give will be the
ack.[19]

Son

245

...has forgiven us for many offences. We have no
right to harbour resentment against anyone. We have to
learn to forgive with all our heart. Our pardon should be
sincere, profound and prompt. Sometimes we feel hurt for
no objective reason, but only because our self-love has
been bruised. If perhaps we have indeed been seriously
offended we must necessarily remember our own serious
transgressions against the Lord. Christ *does not accept the
offering of those who foster division. He sends them away
from the altar to make peace and achieve reconciliation.
God wants to be given prayers of peace. His greatest
objective is our peace, social harmony, and the unity of the
faithful in the Father, the Son and the Holy Spirit.*[20]

Let us examine our reaction when people 'rub us the
wrong way'. To follow Christ in ordinary life is to find in
this very area a royal road to serenity. We should take care
to avoid even the most minute fault against charity. The
small contradictions of social life should not detract from
our happiness. If there comes a time when we have to
forgive someone as the result of a serious offence, it is then
we will do well to recall the behaviour of Jesus who asked
pardon for those who crucified him. We will thus savour
the true love of God. Our heart will be enriched and
expanded in its capacity to love. We cannot forget that
*nothing makes us more like unto God than to be ever ready
to pardon others.*[21] Our generosity towards others will win
for us the divine pardon.

---

[18] Luke 6:36
[19] Luke 6:37-38
[20] St Cyprian, *Treatise on the 'Our Father',* 23
[21] St John Chrysostom, *Homilies on St Matthew's Gospel,* 19, 7

42. TEMPTATION AND EVIL

42.1 Jesus Christ allowed himself to be tempted. We too suffer temptations and trials. These are opportunities to prove our love for God.

Lead us not into temptation but deliver us from evil. This is the final petition in the *Our Father*.

After having sought God's pardon for our sins, we immediately pray for the grace not to offend him again. We ask his help that we be strengthened in time of trial. *For life in this world is a trial ... We ask God that we be not left to our own devices. We ask for his constant paternal guidance. 'Deliver us from evil'. From what evil? From the malice of the devil, the source of everything bad.*[1] The devil exists. He never tires of sowing anxiety in God's creatures and at the same time fomenting their alienation from him. St John Paul II stated: *There are times when the existence of evil among people is particularly apparent. Then it becomes even clearer that the powers of darkness that reside in and operate through man are larger than him.*

It seems that people today almost do not want to see this problem. They do everything to put the existence of those 'rulers of this world of darkness', those 'tactics of the devil' referred to in the Epistle to the Ephesians, from their minds. Yet there are times in history when this reluctantly accepted truth of revelation and of Christian faith is completely manifest, almost tangible.[2]

Jesus, who is our model, wanted to be tempted so that

---

[1] St Peter Chrysologos, *Sermon 67*
[2] St John Paul II, *Address,* 3 May 1987

we might learn how to endure like him and overcome such trials. *For we have not a high priest who is unable to sympathise with our weaknesses, but one who in every respect has been tempted as we are, yet without sinning.*[3] We will experience temptation in one guise or another throughout the course of our life. Perhaps we will suffer even more temptation when we are trying to follow Christ closely. The grace we have received at Baptism and through our pursuit of sanctity will be at risk until the moment we die. It follows that we must be on the look-out, alert like a sentry on watch. And it will be necessary for us to keep in mind the firm assurance that we will never be tempted beyond our strength.[4] We can overcome temptation if we flee from occasions of sin and if we rely on divine assistance. *But should anyone plead human infirmity to excuse himself for not loving God, it should be explained that He who demands our love pours into our hearts by the action of the Holy Spirit the fervour of his love (Rom 5:5); and this good Spirit our heavenly Father gives to those that ask him (Luke 9:13). With reason, therefore, did St Augustine pray: 'Give what thou commandest, and command what thou pleasest'. As, then, God is ever ready to help us, especially since the death of Christ the Lord by which the prince of this world was cast out, there is no reason why anyone should be disheartened by the difficulty of the undertaking. To him who loves, nothing is difficult.*[5]

Temptation in and of itself is not evil. It provides, in fact, an opportunity for us to show the Lord that we love him more than anything else. Temptation can serve as a means for our growth in virtue and sanctifying grace. *Blessed is the man who endures trial, for when he has stood the test he will receive the crown of life which God*

---

[3] Heb 4:15
[4] cf 1 Cor 10:13
[5] *Catechism of the Council of Trent*, III, 1, 7

has promised to those who love him.[6] Of course, it would nevertheless be most recklessly foolish for us to desire or provoke temptation in any way. Conversely, it would be a mistake for us to surrender to excessive fears regarding temptation, as if God were not present by our side. *Don't be troubled if, as you consider the marvels of the supernatural world, you hear that other voice – the intimate, insinuating voice of the 'old man'. It's 'the body of death' that cries out for its lost privileges. God's grace is sufficient for you: be faithful and you will conquer.*[7]

42.2 What temptation is. Good effects that our struggle against it may produce.

St Thomas gives us this definition of temptation: *Temptation is nothing more than to be put to the test. When a person is tempted, it is his virtue that is tried.*[8] Temptation is whatever may separate us from the faithful fulfilment of the Will of God. We may experience temptations that spring from our human nature, which has been wounded by original sin and is prone to evil from our very childhood. Concupiscence is in our make-up. Furthermore, the devil incites us to evil. He takes advantage of our weakness and promises us a happiness with him that he can in no way give. His promises are empty. St Peter warned the early Christians: *Be sober, be watchful. Your adversary the devil prowls around like a roaring lion, seeking some one to devour.*[9] Tertullian gives us the remedy: *Only he who trusts in God has nothing to fear from the devil.*[10]

The devil is allied with *the world* and with our passions. *The world* is here intended to mean whatever in

---

[6] Jas 1:12
[7] St. J. Escrivá, *The Way,* 707
[8] cf St Thomas, *Commentary on the Lord's prayer*
[9] 1 Pet 5:8
[10] Tertullian, *Treatise on prayer,* 8

our existence separates us from God. This includes those we come in contact with who live solely for self-love and sensuality, those who have their gaze fixed entirely on temporal worldly affairs. Such people consider Christian detachment and chastity to be absurd remnants of days gone by ... They hold voluntary mortification in contempt, even though it is absolutely indispensable for following Christ. These souls have become incapable of understanding the things of God. It suits them better to introduce and persuade others to their way of life, from which God is absent or, so they think, largely under control. With their words and behaviour try to lead everyone else along this broad highway of pride. They will even seek to discourage people who are endeavouring to live their Christian vocation seriously, by mounting and sustaining a campaign of ridicule against them.

God allows us to undergo temptation so that we may obtain a greater good. His Providence has so arranged things that trials and contradictions may yield good fruits. At times these tests may turn out to be the best means of bringing us closer to him.

Temptation frequently acts as a kind of barometer of our spiritual life. It is precisely in difficulty and in temptation that we discover our true capacity for generosity, sacrifice and detachment ... We will in similar circumstances also encounter our own hidden envy, greed, sensuality and pride, as well as our astonishing capacity to do evil. These are good moments for us to grow in self-knowledge and humility. We will see how weak we are, how much help we need from the Lord. As a result, we will find it easier to ask for the Lord's assistance. How often we should pray those words to our Father God: *Lead us not into temptation but deliver us from evil!* Our experience of trial will help us to understand the defects of others. We will better appreciate their struggle, and we will be of greater service to those among whom we live a...

The experience of temptation can inspire us...
virtue. In order to overcome a doubt against faith...
an earnest act of faith. Whenever we cut short a ... ...ative
thought or purely critical comment we are simultaneously
improving our relationship with the Lord. We should
approach difficult periods in our life as opportunities in
which to deepen our love for the Virgin, to grow in
humility, to be more docile and sincere in spiritual
direction ... We cannot allow ourselves to be alarmed or
discouraged by temptation. Nothing can separate us from
God without our consent. No one can sin if he or she
withholds consent to sinning. If the Lord permits us to
suffer a time of trial it is because He wants us to become
more united to him.

Temptation, then, can be a source of the grace and
merit that leads to eternal life. *And because thou wast
acceptable to God, it was necessary that temptation should
prove thee.*[11] With these words the Angel Raphael
explained the logic of God to Tobias. Many Christians
have found great comfort at the hour of trial from this
passage of the Old Testament.

42.3 The means to overcome temptation.

If we are to overcome temptation, we must have
recourse to God's help. He can do all things: *In the world
you have tribulation; but be of good cheer, I have
overcome the world.*[12] With Christ by our side, we can say:
'Omnia possum in eo qui me confortat', I can do all things
in him who strengthens me.[13] *'Dominus illuminatio mea et
salus mea, quem timebo?'* The Lord is my light and my

---

[11] Tob 12:13
[12] John 16:23
[13] Phil 4:13

salvation; whom shall I fear?[14]

God has given us the Guardian Angels to help us in times of trial and danger. *For he will give his angels charge of you to guard you in all your ways. On their hands they will bear you up, lest you dash your foot against a stone.*[15] We should seek the help of the Guardian Angels at all times, but especially when we are experiencing temptation. Our Guardian Angel is a very powerful ally and friend who is ready to assist us when we are in trouble.

We will be best prepared against temptation when we are faithful to our personal prayer, when we avoid lukewarmness, when we keep in mind the need to practice mortification. We are strong when we flee from occasions of sin. *Keep your heart with all vigilance; for from it flow the springs of life.*[16] When we work well with intensity and order we will avoid laziness and vice. We should always keep in mind that it is easier to resist temptation at the beginning. *This is the moment when the enemy is at the door of the soul. That is why people say: 'attend to the first signs; it is hard to cure an old wound'.*[17] Even when the wound is 'old', however, we can always have recourse to a remedy in the Sacrament of Penance.

We can do effective combat against temptation in the setting of spiritual direction. When we reveal our temptations, we are well along the road to overcoming them. Let us ask the help of Our Lady that we may be victorious in the trials of our interior life.

---

[14] Ps 26:1
[15] Ps 90:11-12
[16] Prov 4:23
[17] Thomas á Kempis, *The Imitation of Christ*, 1, 13, 5

43. CHOSEN FROM ALL ETERNITY

43.1 A unique and unrepeatable vocation.

From the loneliness of his prison cell St Paul writes a letter to the first Christians in Ephesus. He begins with a paean of thanksgiving for all the gifts he has received from the Lord, especially the gift of his vocation. God has likewise chosen each one of us to be his disciples, to extend his Kingdom on earth. The Apostle emphasises the radical equality that characterizes the universal call to holiness. *Before the world was made, He chose us, chose us in Christ, to be holy and spotless, and to live through love in his presence, determining that we should become his adopted sons, through Jesus Christ for his own kind purposes, to make us praise the glory of his grace, his free gift to us in the Beloved, in whom, through his blood, we gain our freedom, the forgiveness of our sins.*[1]

Each one of us has been called from all eternity to fulfil a divine vocation. God the Father brought us into life (no one has been born by accident). He created our soul. He drew us into his intimate life through the Sacrament of Baptism. By means of this sacrament God *has commissioned us; He has put his seal upon us and given us his Spirit in our hearts as a guarantee.*[2] He has given us a specific work to accomplish in this life and has prepared a place for us in Heaven.

Within the universal call to holiness God also has a specific vocation in mind for each of his children. He calls

---

[1] *First Reading*, Year II, Eph 1:4-6
[2] 2 Cor 1:21-22

the great majority of the faithful to live in the middle of the world so as to sanctify temporal realities. God calls a small number of his children to withdraw from the world and live a consecrated life, thereby giving a public testimony for the glory of God. The Lord helps us to become aware of and understand our vocation in a mysterious and delicate fashion. Even within the vocation of married couples, single people and priests, God points out a personal path to his Love. *In fact, from eternity God has thought of us and has loved us as unique individuals. Every one of us he called by name, as the Good Shepherd 'calls his sheep by name' (John 10:3). However, only in the unfolding of the history of our lives and its events is the eternal plan of God revealed to each of us. Therefore, it is a gradual process; in a certain sense, one that happens day by day.*

To be able to discover the actual will of the Lord in our lives always involves the following: a receptive listening to the Word of God and the Church, fervent and constant prayer, recourse to a wise and loving spiritual guide, and a faithful discernment of the gifts and talents given by God, as well as the diverse social and historic situations in which one lives.[3]

As time goes on, God leads us by the hand to higher and higher degrees of sanctity. If we are faithful, if we are listening carefully, the Holy Spirit will guide us through the normal events and circumstances of our life to a deeper love for God.

43.2 God grants us the illuminations and the graces necessary for us to undertake the divine call.

Our vocation is a tremendous gift. We should thank God incessantly for this blessing. This is the light that illuminates our path. Without the knowledge of God's Will

---

[3] St John Paul II, Apostolic Exhortation, *Christifideles laici*, 30 December 1988, 58

for us, we would be at the mercy of our own will, a most unreliable and flickering candle indeed. When God gives us our vocation He grants us the lights and the graces we shall need in order to undertake the divine call. *Through the knowledge of his vocation, man comes to a definitive knowledge of himself, the world and God. This is the point of reference from which each person is enabled to judge past and present circumstances.*[4] To grow in understanding of the divine Will for us is always a reason for hope and joy.

Through the vocation God has given us, He invites us to enter into his intimate life, into a life of prayer. Christ asks us to make him the centre of our existence, to follow him right in the thick of daily realities: the home, the office, the world of work ... Christ calls us to see other people as children of God, as beings of great value who are the subject of divine predilection. We should help others in their material and spiritual necessities. We are talking here about our approach to the people who in one way or another share with us our daily lives, with all their strengths and weaknesses.

We may come to a realisation of the divine Will in a flash, as was the case with Paul on the road to Damascus. God may prefer, on the other hand, to disclose his Will to us little by little over time, as was the case with St Joseph. *It is not a question of simply knowing what God wants from each of us in the various situations of life. The individual must do what God wants, as we are reminded in the words that Mary, the Mother of Jesus, addressed to the servants at Cana: 'Do whatever he tells you' (John 2:5). However, to act in fidelity to God's will requires a capability for acting and the developing of that capability. We can rest assured that this is possible through the free and*

---

[4] J. L. Illanes, *Holiness and the World*, Madrid 1984, p. 109

responsible collaboration of each of us with the grace of the Lord which is never lacking. St Leo the Great says: 'The one who confers the dignity will give the strength!' This then is the marvellous yet demanding task awaiting all the lay faithful and all Christians at every moment: to grow always in the knowledge of the richness of Baptism and faith as well as to live it more fully.[5] This fullness is realised each day when we are faithful in little things, when we correspond with divine grace in the exercise of our normal responsibilities. This is true on days when we find the struggle not too arduous and on those inevitable occasions when we find it more difficult.

43.3 Perseverance in our specific vocation.

Elegit nos in ipso ante mundi constitutionem ... The Lord chose us before the creation of the world. And God does not regret the choices He has made. This truth should be the basis of our hope and our confidence that we will persevere in our vocation, no matter what obstacles we come up against, or what temptations we may experience. The Lord is always faithful. He gives us the graces necessary each day for our fidelity. St Francis de Sales has written: *Our Lord is constantly following the progress of his children, of those who possess his charity. He sees that they walk towards him. He extends his hand in difficulties. For these were the words of Isaiah: 'For I, the Lord your God, hold your right hand; it is I who say to you, Fear not, I will help you' (Is 41:13). As a consequence, we should have complete confidence in God and his assistance. Since we are not lacking in grace, He will conclude in us the good work of our salvation, which is already under way.*[6]

Combined with this trust in the divine help, we need to make a personal effort to live up to the Lord's calls during

---

[5] St John Paul II, *loc cit*
[6] St Francis de Sales, *Treatise on the Love of God*, III, 4

our entire life, for the gift of self to God is not accomplished in a single moment, or at a certain stage of one's life. God keeps calling us until the last minute ... At times we may find it irksome to remain faithful to the Lord, but we have to remember then that his yoke is sweet and his burden light.[7] We will then find happiness in the renewed struggle. God never asks of us more than we can handle. He knows us well and takes into account our human weaknesses and defects. He also counts on our sincerity and on the humility with which we begin again.

When we find ourselves fallen on hard times, Our Mother Mary should be our hope that we will move ahead once more. In Mary we will find the fortitude we so badly need. *Love Our Lady. And she will obtain abundant grace to help you conquer in your daily struggle. And the enemy will gain nothing by those perversities that seem to boil up continually within you, trying to engulf in their fragrant corruption the high ideals, those sublime commands that Christ himself has placed in your heart. 'Serviam!' I will serve!*[8]

---

[7] cf Matt 11:30
[8] St. J. Escrivá, *The Way*, 493

44. THE LEAVEN OF THE PHARISEES

44.1 The Pharisees as hypocrites.

So great were the crowds flocking to see Jesus that they were elbowing and trampling one another. Even in the midst of this crush, the Lord had words intended just for his disciples: *Beware of the leaven of the Pharisees, which is hypocrisy. Nothing is covered up that will not be revealed, or hidden that will not be known. Whatever you have said in the dark shall be heard in the light, and what you have whispered in private rooms shall be proclaimed upon the housetops.*[1]

The word *hypocrite* comes to us from ancient Greece. It signified an actor who put on a mask and costume in order to assume the personality of a particular character in a drama. He would thus pretend for the sake of the audience to be someone else, often someone very different from his real self. He would play the part of a king, a beggar or a general, say. It was sufficient for him to 'impersonate' someone else, to let the mask and the costume create his assumed identity. His performance was invariably a public theatrical one, and its success was always measured by the applause of the crowd.

The leaven, the prime influential characteristic, of many of the Pharisees was *hypocrisy*. They lived for the approval of men rather than of God. Their lives were as false and hollow as an actor's mask, as his performance on stage. The Pharisees had succumbed to the temptation of giving undue importance to the opinions of men at the

---

[1] Luke 12:1-3

expense of obedience to God. On a different occasion the Lord criticized them for being *whited sepulchres*: outside, they seem beautiful, but inside they are filled with decaying bones.[2] The Pharisees in fact led a double life – one life of masks, appearances, falsehood, which depended on the opinion of men; the other life, a careless and selfish relationship with God.

The Lord wants his disciples to be *leaven,* but good, wholesome *leaven.* He wants them to live a unity of life without masks, double-talk and lies. Jesus wants men and women who lead coherent and sincere lives of faith.

44.2 The Christian, a person with no guile.

Jesus himself taught us the way to behave: *Let what you say be simply 'Yes' or 'No'; anything more than this comes from evil.*[3] In dealings with other people, a man's word should be sufficient. One's 'yes' should be a 'yes', one's 'no' should be a 'no'. Jesus here underlines the value of one's promise to fulfil one's commitments.

As Christians, our word and our behaviour should be held in esteem by other people. We should seek in everything the truth, fleeing from hypocrisy and duplicity. In normal situations the word of a Christian should be sufficient guarantee of a promise's fulfilment. The truth should always be respected since it is a reflection of God himself. If we are in the habit of telling the truth, even in the least important matters, our word will come to have great reliability and strength. It will be worth its weight in gold. We will in this respect be imitating the life of the Lord.

At the opposite pole to this Christian behaviour is the *double-minded man, unstable in all his ways.*[4] This is the

---

[2] cf Matt 23:27
[3] Matt 5:37
[4] Jas 1:8

person who adopts a 'persona' like an actor, ready to do anything to please the crowd. St Bede observes that *the double-minded person wants to celebrate with the world, and there reign with God.*[5]

In our day there is a special need for men and women who are true to their word, who live a *unity of life,* who refuse to hide from the consequences of their beliefs, who will not be conditioned to fall in with the opinions or ways of other people. St Thomas Aquinas teaches[6] that truthfulness is the virtue that inclines us to speak the truth always and to manifest outwardly what we think inwardly. There are, of course, times when we are under no obligation to speak the truth, where we are, in fact, bound not to reveal it. Such cases may involve professional matters, national security or other serious issues. An important area where the same principle applies has to do with the sacramental seal of Confession and whatever relates to spiritual direction. There are various ways of withholding the truth without having to lie. Situations arise also in which information is being sought about a matter the enquirer has no business asking about. There may even be the extreme case of the aggressive inquisitor. *Let us remember, moreover, that often it is our own fault if we are asked indiscreet questions. If we were more recollected and silent, people would not ask them of us, or at least they would do so only rarely.*[7]

Let us imitate the Lord in his love for the truth. Let us resolve to shun falsehood and whatever smells of hypocrisy. *You were reading in that dictionary the synonyms for 'insincere': 'two-faced, surreptitious, evasive, disingenuous, sly'. As you closed the book, you asked the Lord that nobody would ever be able to apply those*

[5] St Bede, *Commentary on the Epistle of St James,* 1, 8
[6] cf St Thomas, *Summa Theologiae,* 2-2, q. 109, a. 3 ad 3
[7] R. Garrigou-Lagrange, *The Three Ages of the Interior Life,* II, p. 160

adjectives to you, and you resolved to improve much more in this supernatural and human virtue of sincerity.[8]

44.3 To love the truth and love having it be known.

Jesus says: *I am the Truth.*[9] The Lord has the truth in all its fulness. The truth comes to us from him.[10] Christ's teaching, his life and his death, all constitute a testimonial to the Truth.[11] Whoever has the truth is of God and hears the word of God.[12]

Truth has its origin in God. Falsehood has its source in opposition to God. This is why Jesus calls the devil *the father of lies,* since he was the first liar. As a result, he who lies has the devil for his father.[13] The Church reproves not only the liar who by his lie hurts another. She also disapproves of those who *lie for recreation or entertainment, as well as of those who lie for the sake of worldly interests,*[14] and this even if no one appears to suffer harm thereby.

The lack of honesty to be found in lying or hypocrisy, or in leading such a *double life* as insincerity involves, is a manifestation of interior discord. A man or a woman who lives like this is like a broken bell, discordant and out of tune. The Lord showed his appreciation for this virtue when He said of Nathaniel: *Behold, an Israelite indeed, in whom there is no guile!*[15] Jesus wants to be able to say this of every Christian.

We live in an epoch which puts a premium on

---

[8] St. J. Escrivá, *Furrow,* 337
[9] John 14:6
[10] cf John 1:14; 17
[11] cf John 18:37
[12] cf John 8:44
[13] cf John 8:42 ff
[14] *Catechism of the Council of Trent,* III, 37
[15] John 1:47

sincerity. And yet, our era has become known as the *time of the imposters, of falsehood and lying*.[16] *Among others, the list of imposters includes those members of the press who, spreading scandalous indiscretions and slanderous insinuations, appeal to people's lowest instincts, gradually corrupting their moral sense. To the press (one) could add movies, radio, television. These instruments, useful in themselves, when handled by shrewd operators bombard people with sounds and colours and hidden persuasion, which is all the more effective because of being hidden. Such media are capable, little by little, of making the best fathers hated by their children, of making white seem black, and vice versa.*[17] This is how the habits of thought and the customs of people are being transformed today.

Whenever possible, we should use the means of communication to give sound doctrine to society as a whole. We should stress those ideas which have a transcendental importance for social progress – the defence of life from its conception; the dignity of the family and of the person; social justice; the right to work; due concern for the weakest members of society ... In many cases we can communicate these ideas without difficulty – by writing a 'Letter to the Editor', by making telephone calls, by participating in opinion polls or on radio programmes. These are means available to us for showing our approval or disapproval of a programme or an article that either reinforces fundamental human morality or fails to do so. Admittedly, these are small measures, but many small measures can add up to a considerable impact on the media.

As we conclude our meditation, let us go to Our Lady for her help so that we may live the truth at every moment. She will teach us how to let the truth be known by others.

---

[16] cf A. Luciani, *Illustrissimi*, p. 115

[17] *ibid*, p. 117

Under her guidance we shall invite others to live a *unity of life* which is free from guile and hypocrisy.

The liturgy rejoices with the song: 'Tota pulchra es Maria, et macula originalis non est in te!' You are all fair, O Mary, without original sin! In Her there is not the slightest shadow of duplicity. I pray daily to our Mother that we may be able to open our souls in spiritual direction and the light of grace may shine in all our behaviour.

Mary will obtain for us the courage to be sincere, if we ask her for it, so that we may come closer to the Most Blessed Trinity.[18]

---

[18] St. J. Escrivá, *op cit,* 339

TWENTY-EIGHTH WEEK: SATURDAY

45. THE SIN AGAINST THE HOLY SPIRIT

45.1 Being open to divine mercy.

Today's Gospel passage from St Luke brings to our attention some remarkably strong words of Our Lord: *And every one who speaks a word against the Son of man will be forgiven; but he who blasphemes against the Holy Spirit will not be forgiven.*[1] St Mark, too, reports the Lord as saying that this blasphemy *never has forgiveness* and that one who offends in this way is *guilty of an eternal sin.*[2]

St Matthew in his turn quotes these solemn words of Christ in a context that allows for a better understanding of their import.[3] He relates that the people were astonished at Christ's miracles, so much so that they wondered: *Can this be the Son of David?*[4] Yet the Pharisees would not submit to the evidence of the many miracles performed before their very eyes. Their only explanation was to attribute Christ's amazing signs, his divine works, to the agency of the devil. Such was the hardness of their hearts that they would not accept the obvious. *It is only by Beelzebub, the prince of demons,* they said, *that this man casts out demons.* Precisely here do we find the unpardonable nature of the blasphemy against the Holy Spirit. They exclude the sources of pardon itself.[5] All sins can be forgiven, no matter how grave they might be. This is because God's

---

[1] Luke 12:10
[2] cf Mark 3:29
[3] cf Matt 12:32
[4] Matt 12:13
[5] cf St Thomas, *Summa Theologiae,* 2-2, q. 14, a. 3

mercy is infinite. What is required that they be forgiven, of course, is that the sinner recognise his sin as sin and believe in the mercy of the Lord. The hardness of the Pharisee's hearts would certainly impede the powerful effect of divine grace.

Jesus designates this attitude as *sin against the Holy Spirit.* It is unpardonable not because of its gravity and malice but for the closed disposition of the will against God. He who sins in this way deliberately places himself outside the scope of divine pardon.

St John Paul II warned of the seriousness of this attitude towards grace. *Blasphemy against the Holy Spirit, then, is the sin committed by the person who claims to have a 'right' to persist in evil – in any sin at all – and who thus rejects Redemption. One closes oneself up in sin, thus making impossible one's conversion, and consequently the remission of sins, which one considers not essential or not important for one's life.*[6]

Today let us ask the Lord for a radical sincerity and true humility so that we may face up to our faults and sins. We pray that we may not become accustomed to our failings, even in the area of venial sin. We should go to Jesus right away for pardon and for the life-giving action of the Holy Spirit. We should ask Our Lady for that *holy fear of God* so that we never lose our sense of sin and the necessary awareness of our weaknesses. *When our vision is clouded, when our eyes have lost their clarity, we need to go to the light. And Jesus Christ has told us that he is the Light of the world and that he has come to heal the sick.*[7]

45.2 The loss of the sense of sin.

Jesus revealed to mankind the Holy Spirit as a Person distinct from the Father and the Son. The Holy Spirit is the

---

[6] St John Paul II, Encyclical, *Dominum et vivificantem*, 18 May 1986
[7] St. J. Escrivá, *The Forge*, 158

Love that exists between the Persons of the Holy Trinity. He is the source and model of all created love.[8]

The Holy Spirit is present in all the actions of Jesus. It was during the Last Supper that Jesus spoke of the Spirit with the greatest clarity. There He revealed this Person to be distinct from the Father and the Son. The Holy Spirit is very much involved in the Redemption. Jesus refers to the Holy Spirit as the *paraclete* or *counsellor,* as one who acts as solicitor and advocate. The Greek world understood the word *paraclete* to mean a pleader who would speak on behalf of another in legal processes. The Holy Spirit also has a special mission with regard to the exercise of conscience in addition to the power of absolution found in sacramental Confession. Through absolution the sinner is absolved forever from his sins and filled with new life.

The Roman Pontiff has written about people today who resist the action of the Paraclete: *The action of the Spirit of truth, which works toward the salvific 'convincing concerning sin', encounters in a person in this condition an interior resistance, as it were an impenetrability of conscience, a state of mind which could be described as fixed by reason of a free choice. This is what Sacred Scripture usually calls 'hardness of heart' (cf Ps 81:13; Jer 7:24; Mark 3:5). In our own time this attitude of mind and heart is perhaps reflected in the loss of the sense of sin.*[9]

The opposite of hardness of heart is delicacy of conscience. This refinement of perception operates when the soul abhors all sin, including venial sin. The soul seeks to be docile to the inspirations of the Holy Spirit throughout the course of the day. St Augustine has taught: *When the sense of smell in one's soul is healthy, then we can immediately perceive the stench from our sins.*[10] Are

---

[8] cf Second Vatican Council, *Gaudium et spes,* 24
[9] St John Paul II, *loc cit,* 47
[10] St Augustine, *Commentary on the Psalms,* 37, 9

we as sensitive as this to the offences we commit against God? Do we react promptly against our faults and sins?

45.3 United to Christ, we will grasp the horror of sin. Discrimination and sensitivity of conscience.

Today many have lost or are losing their sense of sin. Consequently, they are losing their sense of God. Unnatural behaviour contrary to divine law is now treated as the normal course of things in films, on television, in the press ... Occasionally people deplore the visible sad consequences of this behaviour as it affects individuals and society, but without reference being made to the Creator. At other times, such 'lifestyles' are 'aired out' to attract public curiosity though without any attempt to treat the subject on a moral plane. Marital infidelity, scandal, defamation, divorce, lying, cheating ... There is no shortage of those, including many so-called Christians, who enjoy the drama of such highly-publicised situations, examining them with care, interviewing the protagonists, avidly following their adventures ... It seems as if people will do anything but call these actions by their name. In any event, what is wholly forgotten here is the most important factor: what it means to God, to him who gives true meaning to everything human. Some people choose to judge according to principles which leave no room for God, as if He never existed at all or doesn't play any role in our lives. Ours is by now a truly paganized environment. It has a lot in common with the world of the first Christians, which they transformed just as we have to transform ours.

We will feel the weight of our sins when we see them as offences against God. Sin separates us from God. It makes our soul incapable of listening to the Paraclete, the Holy Spirit. We may even reach that point of insensitivity described by St Augustine: There are those who have committed certain kinds of sins, sins without human victims, which they say are no sins at all.[11] What a gift it is to know the weight of our sins! This knowledge leads us to make many acts of contrition, to desire frequent Confession, to pray for union with God. St John of Avila taught: *If you are not feeling dejected because of your sin, then you still don't realize what it is you have done. Sin weighs on us: 'sicut onus grave gravatae sunt super me' (Ps 37:5). Sin weighs far more than I can imagine. What, then, is sin? It is an unresolvable debt, an unbearable burden which weighs more than anything.*[12] The Saint later reiterates: *If there can be no heavier burden than this, why don't we feel the weight of it? It is because we have no appreciation of the goodness of God.*[13] It was in the miraculous catch of fish that St Peter discovered the divinity of Christ and his own smallness. Look at his response: *He fell down at Jesus' knees, saying, 'Depart from me, for I am a sinful man, O Lord'.*[14] He besought the Lord to leave him because of his sinfulness. At the same time his eyes and his whole attitude implored the Lord to stay with him forever.

The filthiness of sins requires a point of reference. That standard is the holiness of God. The Christian can perceive a lack of love in himself once he becomes fully aware of the love of Christ. Otherwise, it will be an easy matter for him to justify his weaknesses. Peter had a profound love for Jesus. He knew how to repent for his denials. He would do it making an act of love: *Domine, tu omnia nosti, tu scis quia amo te.*[15] Perhaps we have used this prayer to express our own contrition. *Lord, you know*

---

[11] cf *idem, Sermon 278,* 7
[12] St John of Avila, *Sermon 25, for the Twenty-first Sunday after Pentecost*
[13] *ibid*, p. 355
[14] Luke 5:8-9
[15] John 21:17

all things, you know that I love you. We will appeal to the Lord with this act of love whenever we have been unfaithful. Contrition gives strength to the soul. It also imparts hope and a better sensitivity to God.

Let us ask Our Mother Mary, herself so docile to the motions of the Holy Spirit, to teach us to develop a delicate and discriminating conscience. Let us resolve not to become complacently accustomed to the wrong we do. We have to react promptly against even the smallest deliberate venial sin.

TWENTY-NINTH SUNDAY: YEAR A

46. GIVING TO GOD WHAT IS GOD'S

46.1 Loyal collaborators in fostering the common good.

The *First Reading* of today's Mass shows us how God chooses his instruments of salvation wherever He pleases.[1] To bring his People out of exile the Lord takes hold of Cyrus, a pagan king. The Lord uses political authority to do good. There is nothing in the universe that lies outside his paternal dominion.

In the Gospel for today[2] Jesus reaffirms the duty of all of us to obey civil authority. The Pharisees and the Herodians had attempted to lay a trap with their question: Was it licit to pay tribute to Caesar? There were those among the Jews who argued that such payments simply reinforced the tyranny of foreign domination over the Chosen People. If the Master were to acquiesce in this payment, the Pharisees would be able to accuse him of collaboration with the Romans. He would thus be discredited before a good part of the people. But if He were to oppose the tax, the Herodians, who were in league with the (occupying) civil power, would then have grounds for a denunciation to the Romans.

Jesus gives his enemies a profound response, which went far beyond their twisted expectations. He does not limit himself to a 'yes' or 'no'. The Master speaks: *Render therefore to Caesar the things that are Caesar's,* he says, *and to God the things that are God's.* Give to Caesar what rightfully belongs to him: tribute, obedience to just laws ...

---

[1] *First Reading,* Is 45:1; 4-6
[2] Matt 22:15-21

but nothing more. The State does not enjoy absolute power and dominion. As ordinary citizens, Christians have *the obligation of rendering to the state whatever material and personal services are required for the common good.*[3] For their part, civil authorities are obligated to act with equity and justice in the distribution of their goods and services. They have to serve the common good without looking for any personal gain. They have to legislate and govern with the greatest respect for the natural law and the rights of people. This includes the protection of life from the moment of conception, defence of the family, religious liberty, the rights of parents regarding the education of their children. The Lord speaks through the Prophet Isaiah: *Woe to those who decree iniquitous decrees!*[4]

Christians are obliged to pray for those who exercise civil authority. Rulers and governments have a great responsibility to carry out. Christians should fulfil their duties to society with virtually scrupulous exactitude. There should be no more loyal collaborators for the common good than the Christian faithful. This fidelity will spring naturally from well-formed consciences. Their relations with civil authority should become, in fact, a path to sanctity: the payment of taxes, the power to vote, our involvement in associations for public welfare, active participation in political life should that be our calling ... Let us examine ourselves today to see if we are truly being good examples to others of fostering the common good.

46.2 The religious dimension of man.

The Lord recognized the civil power and its rights, but He also stated quite clearly that we have to respect the rights of God.[5] Human activity cannot be reduced to

---

[3] Second Vatican Council, *Gaudium et spes,* 75
[4] Is 10:1
[5] cf Second Vatican Council, *Dignitatis humanae,* 11

strictly social and political spheres of action. Every individual has a profound religious dimension to his being. It informs all of his works and gives them tremendous dignity. This explains why the Lord adds those important words: Give ... *to God the things that are God's.*

Whenever a Christian plays a part in public affairs, in education, say, or in cultural life, he or she cannot behave as if to reserve the faith for some better occasion in the future. *The distinction which Christ made was not intended to relegate religion to the temple – to the sacristy – so that temporal realities would develop apart from divine and Christian law.*[6] Quite the contrary; Christians are challenged to be *light* and *salt* in the middle of the world. We are called to transform the environments in which we live and work, so as to make them more human. We should strive to make the path to God accessible for as many of our fellow men as possible. In the words of the Second Vatican Council: *The laity accomplish the Church's mission in the world principally by that blending of conduct and faith which makes them the light of the world; by that uprightness in all their dealings which is for every man such an incentive to love the true and the good and which is capable of inducing him at last to go to Christ and the Church; by that fraternal charity that makes them share the living conditions and labours, the sufferings and yearnings of their brothers, and thereby prepare all hearts, gently, imperceptibly, for the action of saving grace; by that full awareness of their personal responsibility in the development of society, which drives them on to perform their family, social and professional duties with Christian generosity.*[7]

---

[6] St. J. Escrivá, *Letter,* 9 January 1959
[7] Second Vatican Council, *Apostolicam actuositatem,* 13

46.3 The Faith, a powerful light.

When it comes to fundamental questions of social morality, Christians should be fully aware of the fact that their religious faith serves as a powerful light illuminating the whole area of the common good. The teachings of God and his Church are not an obstacle to human welfare or scientific progress. They are rather a sure guide for the realization of those worthy goals. When, for example, a Christian maintains the indissolubility of marriage, he is showing the way to guaranteeing the health of society.[8] He thus provides huge benefit to all. It is not a question of safeguarding our own special privileges. We have so much to give for the good of society! This is what we can learn from the example of the first Christians. A person with a well-formed conscience can make an enormous contribution to the real welfare of his or her fellow citizens. The Christian has a most precious light to offer amidst so much darkness!

What has come to pass in our society is most lamentable, as was pointed out by Cardinal Luciani, later Pope John Paul I: *In this same society there is a terrible moral and religious void,* he wrote, *Today all seem frantically directed toward material conquests: make money, invest, surround oneself with new comforts, live the 'good life'. Few think also of 'doing good'.*

God – who should fill our life – has, on the contrary, become a very distant star, to which people look only at certain moments. People believe they are religious because they go to church; but outside of church they want to lead the same life as many others, marked by small or big deceits, acts of injustice, sins against charity; and thus they totally lack coherence.[9] This is not the way to *render to God the things that are God's.* The proper path lies in

---

[8] cf J. M. Pero-Sanz, *Believers in Society,* Madrid 1981, p. 30
[9] A. Luciani, *Illustrissimi,* p. 179

living a coherent life of faith. We should act as children of God in the halls of government as well as in the living-rooms of our friends. We should have the firm conviction that the Church is an unquenchable source of truth, the only source capable of filling our modern age's *terrible moral and religious void.* A society without these values is at the mercy of aggressive elements and prey to a gradual dehumanization. God is not a *distant star* out of touch with mankind. He is a most powerful light who gives meaning and significance to all human affairs. We Christians, then, are the ones who have to transform the world we live in, in alliance with all people of good will. How can we stand idly by in the defence of human life from its beginnings? Shall we be silent in the face of genetic manipulations that degrade the subject and at the same time every other human person? In another area, what is to be done about the right of parents to educate their children?

Render to God the things of God. The Lord is the life of every person from the moment of conception. The Lord sanctified family life in Nazareth and later taught us to respect the indissolubility of marriage. The Lord revealed these truths even though many of his hearers were scandalized at his message. Despite all social pressures and propaganda to the contrary, married Christians should take care not to block the wellsprings of life. Truly, all men and women should make a serious effort to receive good formation for their consciences.

Our entire life is for the Lord, and everything in it. How is it possible that we could reserve some area of it for our sole personal domain? Let us ask Our Lady to give us the joy of knowing that we are children of God. She will help us to realise our personal responsibilities in society at large.

TWENTY-NINTH SUNDAY: YEAR B

47. *TO SERVE*

47.1 Christian life consists in imitating Christ.

As a disciple before his master, as a child before his mother, so should the Christian be oriented in all his or her activities before Christ. The child learns to speak by listening to the mother. He makes an effort to copy her words and mannerisms. This should be the pattern of our behaviour with respect to Jesus. We should imitate his every word and deed. Christian life consists in the imitation of Christ. St Peter wrote: *For to this you have been called, because Christ also suffered for you, leaving you an example, that you should follow in his steps.*[1] St Paul encouraged the first Christians with similar words: *Have this mind among yourselves, which was in Christ Jesus.*[2] Jesus is the exemplary cause of all holiness, of all love for God the Father. This is not only because of his deeds, but because of his very being. Christ's way of acting was an external manifestation of his love for and union with the Father.

We grow in holiness not so much by an external imitation of Jesus as by an internal imitation. St Paul taught the Colossians: *... you have put off the old nature with its practices and have put on the new nature ...* [3]Through the workings of this daily renewal in our life we should weed out whatever does not conform to Christ's teachings. We want our feelings and attitudes to resemble more and more what those of Jesus would be in similar circumstances. In

---

[1] 1 Pet 2:21
[2] Phil 2:5
[3] Col 3:9

this way, our life will become a prolongation of Christ's life. *For those whom He foreknew He also predestined to be conformed to the image of his Son.*[4] Divine grace acts in concert with our free will to make us like to God. We will be saints if God the Father can say these words of us: *This is my beloved Son, with whom I am well pleased.*[5] Our sanctity, therefore, lies in becoming through grace what Christ is by nature: sons of God.

The Lord is our all in all. *This tree is for me a plant of eternal salvation. I am fed by it. It satiates me. Through its roots I am deepened and through its branches I am extended. I rejoice at its dew. Its spirit is like a welcome wind that fertilizes me. I have pitched my tent in its shadow. There I have escaped the heat of the day and find cool comfort. Its leaves are my covering. Its fruits are my delight. I freely enjoy these fruits which have been reserved for me from the beginning of time. This tree is my food when I am hungry. It provides my clothing when I am naked. Its leaves are the spirit of life. They have nothing to do with the leaves of the fig tree. When I fear the Lord, He is my protection. In my weakness, He is my strength. When I do battle, He is my prize. When I triumph, He is my trophy. He is for me the straight and narrow path.*[6] I do not want anything apart from him.

47.2 Jesus teaches us that He has come not to be served but to serve. How to put this maxim into practice.

Today's Gospel recounts the memorable request which James and John made to Jesus. They wanted to hold places of honour in his kingdom. Their petition provoked a storm of indignation among the Apostles. Jesus took this opportunity to teach the Twelve: *You know that those who*

---

[4] Rom 8:29
[5] Matt 3:17
[6] St Hippolytus, *Easter Homily*

*are supposed to rule over the Gentiles lord it over them,
and their great men exercise authority over them. But it
shall not be so among you; but whoever would be great
among you must be your servant, and whoever would be
first among you must be slave of all.*[7] Finally, Jesus gives
them the greatest reason by far: *For the Son of man also
came not to be served but to serve, and to give his life as a
ransom for many.*

The Lord repeated this idea on any number of
occasions *Non veni ministrari sed ministrare.*[8] His whole
life was a service to others. His doctrine is a constant
appeal to mankind to forget self and live for others. He
went throughout Palestine serving each person He met
along the way: *singulis manus imponens.*[9] Christ's life and
teaching are with us to the present day in the Church and in
a special way in the Holy Eucharist. Jesus is ready to serve
us, to keep us company with his humility and grace. On the
night before his Passion and Death Jesus emphasised the
importance of this message when he washed the feet of his
disciples. He urged his closest followers to do the same for
their brethren.[10]

The Church is the continuation of the salvific mission
of Christ in the world. Her very reason for being lies in
serving mankind through the preaching of the Word and
the celebration of the sacraments. *Sharing the noblest
aspirations of men and suffering when she sees them not
satisfied, she wishes to help them attain their full
flowering, and that is why she offers men what she
possesses as her characteristic attribute – a global vision
of man and of the human race.*[11]

---

[7] Mark 10:35-45
[8] Matt 20:8
[9] Luke 4:40
[10] cf John 13:4 ff
[11] Bl. Paul VI, Encyclical, *Populorum progressio,* 26 March 1967, 13

As we seek to imitate the Lord we Christians should be ready to give cheerful service to God and other people without expecting anything in return. We should serve even those who do not appreciate our help. Many will not understand our cheerful attitude of self-denial. We should be content in the knowledge that Christ knows full well the efforts we are making on his behalf. The *pride* of a Christian is precisely in this dimension: to serve as the Master served. Yet we learn how to serve only when we are close to Jesus.

When you start out each day to work by Christ's side and to look after all those souls who seek him, remember that there is only one way of doing it: we must turn to the Lord. Only in prayer, and through prayer, do we learn to serve others.[12] Prayer will give us all the strength and humility we require to serve others.

47.3 Serving with joy.

Our service to God and others should be characterized by our humility. We can think of ourselves as the little donkey that had the honour of carrying Jesus through the streets of Jerusalem in triumph.[13] We always have to keep in mind the importance of rectitude of intention. In the words of Cardinal Luciani, later Pope John Paul I: *When I am paid a compliment, I must compare myself with the little donkey that carried Christ on Palm Sunday. And I say to myself: If that little creature, hearing the applause of the crowd, had become proud and had begun – jackass that he was – to bow his thanks left and right like a prima donna, how much hilarity he would have aroused! Don't act the same!*[14] We should help others in such a way that they do not even take note of our attentions, if that is possible. Our

---

[12] St. J. Escrivá, *The Forge,* 72
[13] cf Luke 19:35
[14] A. Luciani, *Illustrissimi,* p. 50

only compensation will then be the loving glance of Christ. Surely that is the highest payment possible!

The Psalmist encourages us in this regard: *Serve the Lord with gladness!*[15] This ideal should be our guide even in the more unpleasant aspects of daily life. Such sacrifices make social and family life much more pleasant. We should resolve to really excel in our spirit of service to others, always with a cheerful disposition. We will find abundant opportunities to live out our resolution in family life, at the office, among our neighbours ... This spirit also includes people we may meet only once in our life. When we behave in this manner we will come to understand that *to serve is to reign.*[16]

We can learn from Our Lady how to be helpful to others, how to have an eye for their needs, how to make their lives pleasant on earth, how to gently point their sights towards Heaven. She gives us the best example: *In the middle of the rejoicing at the feast in Cana, only Mary notices that they are short of wine. A soul will notice even the smallest details of service if, like her, it is alive with a passion for helping its neighbour, for God.*[17] When we practise this life of service we will be blessed to find Jesus in our midst. He will tell us: *Truly, I say to you, as you did it to one of the least of these my brethren, you did it to me.*[18]

---

[15] Ps 99:2
[16] cf St John Paul II, Encyclical, *Redemptor hominis,* 4 March 1979, 21
[17] St. J. Escrivá, *Furrow,* 631
[18] Matt 25:40

TWENTY-NINTH SUNDAY: YEAR C

48. THE POWER OF PRAYER

48.1 Trusting and persevering prayer.

To you I call; for you will surely heed me, O God; turn your ear to me; hear my words. Guard me as the apple of your eye; in the shadow of your wings protect me.[1] This is the Entrance Antiphon for today's Mass.

The texts of today's liturgy focus our attention on the power of trusting and persevering prayer to reach the mind of God. In the Gospel passage St Luke prefaces the parable with an explanation of Christ's intent: *Jesus told his disciples a parable about the need to pray continually and never lose heart.*[2] In the supernatural life there are actions which are performed once and for all, such as Baptism and Holy Orders. Other actions are repeated many, many times, such as pardoning, understanding, smiling cheerfully ...

There are other actions and attitudes which we should practice continually. Among these we find the spirit of prayer, which is the manifestation of a living faith in our Father God. St Augustine commented on this Gospel passage by emphasising the close connexion between faith and trusting prayer: *If one's faith weakens, prayer withers ... Faith is the fountain of prayer ... A river cannot flow if its source is dried up.*[3] Our prayer needs to be continuous and confident like the prayer of Jesus, our model: *Father, I thank thee that thou hast heard me. I knew that thou*

---

[1] *Entrance Antiphon*, Ps 16:6-8
[2] Luke 18:1-8
[3] cf St Augustine, *Sermon 115*, 1

hearest me always.[4] God is always listening to our prayers.

The *First Reading* from the book of Exodus presents us with the scene of the Chosen People in battle with the Amalekites at Rephidim.[5] Moses decides to pray to God on a hilltop while Joshua and his forces take on the enemy assault. *As long as Moses kept his arms raised, Israel had the advantage; when he let his arms fall, the advantage went to Amalek.* To keep Moses praying, Aaron and Hur supported his arms, one on each side. They were thus able to keep Moses praying until sunset. *With the edge of the sword Joshua cut down Amalek and his people.*

We cannot grow weary of praying. If we should ever become tired of praying, let us ask our friends to shore us up. The Lord sends us many graces in times of trial. These graces are more necessary and more important than the gifts we ask for. St Alphonsus Liguori has taught: *The Lord wants to grant us his graces, but He also wants us to ask for them. One day he said to his disciples: 'Hitherto you have asked nothing in my name; ask and you will receive, that your joy may be full' (John 16:24). It was as if he were saying: Do not complain to me if you are not filled with blessings. Complain to yourselves for not having sought from me what you need. From now on, ask of me and your prayers will be answered.*[6] St Bernard has commented that many people complain like this, saying that the Lord has forsaken them. But Jesus himself laments that these same complainers have not really asked for his assistance.[7] Let us resolve to pray as Moses did: with perseverance that nothing could shake, and at times with the help of his friends as was necessary. A great deal depends on our devotion.

---

[4] John 11:42

[5] Ex 17:8-13

[6] St Alphonsus Liguori, *Sermon 46 for the Tenth Sunday after Pentecost*

[7] cf St Bernard, *Sermon 17 on various themes*

Let us examine the quality of our prayer today. Is it persevering, trusting, insistent, tireless? *Persevere in prayer, as the Master told us. This point of departure will be your source of peace, of cheerfulness, of serenity, and so it will make you humanly and supernaturally effective.*[8] There is nothing more powerfully effective than steadfast prayer.

48.2 Perseverance in prayer. The parable of the unjust judge.

We pray in the *Responsorial Psalm*: *I lift up my eyes to the mountains: from where shall come my help? My help shall come from the Lord, who made heaven and earth.*[9]

The parable in today's Gospel presents us with a marked contrast of personalities. On the one hand there is the unjust judge, *who had neither fear of God nor respect for man.* He does not practise the two essential components of the virtue of justice. The Prophet Isaiah had already spoken of this kind of person in the Old Testament: *They do not defend the fatherless, and the widow's cause does not come to them.*[10] They *acquit the guilty for a bribe, and deprive the innocent of his right.*[11] Jeremiah also makes reference to such people: *They know no bounds in deeds of wickedness,* he says, *they judge not with justice the cause of the fatherless, to make it prosper, and they do not defend the rights of the needy.*[12]

The Lord sets in contrast to the unjust judge the figure of the widow, the ancient symbol for the defenceless person. More specifically, the tireless perseverance of the widow is juxtaposed to the firm resistance of the unjust

---

[8] St. J. Escrivá, *The Forge,* 536
[9] *Responsorial Psalm,* Ps 120:1-2
[10] Is 1:23
[11] Is 5:23
[12] Jer 5:28

judge. The unexpected conclusion to the parable is the result of the ceaseless petitions of the poor widow. After many refusals to hear her case, the judge finally relents. And so, the weaker party has triumphed. The reason for her victory lies not in any conversion on the judge's part. The widow has simply worn down the defences of the judge to the point of his capitulation by not giving up. The Lord concludes the parable with this query: *Now, will not God see justice done to his chosen who cry to him day and night even when he delays to help them?* Jesus wants us to see the main message of the parable: God, who is full of mercy, awaits our steadfast prayer.

Until the end of time the Church will offer up constant supplication to God the Father through Jesus Christ in the unity of the Holy Spirit. The Church prays for all the needs of her sons and daughters. This is the primary responsibility of the Church, the first duty of her priests. This is the most important thing that we, the faithful, can accomplish since we too are defenceless like the widow of the parable.

At the conclusion of the parable, Jesus adds: *But when the Son of Man comes, will He find any faith on earth?* Will the Lord find faith as unswerving as that of the widow? This is the faith of the children of God who believe in the goodness and power of their Father in Heaven. Man may come to shut God out of his life. He may not feel any need for God. He may seek reasons and solutions for those problems in life to which only the Lord can provide satisfactory answers. Such as these will never find the good things, the truths, which are indispensable. As the Virgin Mary announced in the *Magnificat*: *He has filled the hungry with good things, and the rich He has sent empty away.*[13] We have to go to God like needy children.

---

[13] Luke 1:53

Of course, we also have to employ whatever human means are required, given the circumstances. For many goods, however, we will find that only the divine mercy is efficacious. The Holy Curé d'Ars would tell the story of a founder of an orphanage who was considering the use of advertisements to attract donations. The Saint advised the founder: *Rather than making noise in the papers, why don't you make a fuss before the Tabernacle?* The Lord wants us to bring our concerns before him right there. There is nothing to prevent us from putting ads in the paper too, if that will help.

Down through the centuries Christian people have been moved to present their petitions to God through their Mother Mary. St Bernard teaches that *our advocate was assumed into Heaven so that she could act as Mother of the Judge and Mother of Mercy. There she will work on behalf of our salvation.*[14] Let us not fail to go to her with our many needs each day.

48.3 Prayer as the direct consequence of faith.

Prayer is the direct consequence of a living faith. At the same time we find in prayer greater *firmness in our faith.*[15] Both enjoy a unity of purpose. As a result, everything we ask for should help to make us better. If this were not to be the case, *we would not become more pious, but greedy and ambitious.*[16] When we pray to God for a new home, for help in an important examination, we should consider whether that request will fulfil the Will of God or not. We can pray for certain goods, for our health, for the health of a friend, for a way out of a tight spot ... Yet if we live by faith, if we have unity of life, then we will have a deeper understanding of the relative importance

---

[14] St Bernard, *Sermon I on the Assumption of the Blessed Virgin Mary,* 1
[15] St Augustine, *The City of God,* 1, 8, 1
[16] *ibid*

of material goods and human wants. After all, what we really want is God himself. He is the ultimate end of our prayers. When we pray for things here on earth we should only desire what will bring us closer to him.

God is especially pleased with our prayers for spiritual benefits, for ourselves as well as for our relatives, friends and acquaintances. We should pray for the people around us that they may come closer to the Lord. How much we owe our families and friends! *I happened to hurt the hand of a friend. When I saw that his look was so sad and reproachful, I feared that you were not in his heart. And I felt dismayed as if I were standing before an empty tabernacle.*

O my God, if you were not in him, my friend and I would be so far apart. His hand in mine would be nothing more than the meeting of flesh, his heart only the heart of a man.

I firmly desire that your Life be in him and in me. This is because I want my friend to be my brother, thanks to you.[17]

Let us take advantage of this month of the Holy Rosary to pray to Our Lady for all our needs, and for the needs of our friends and acquaintances.

---

[17] M. Quoist, *Prayers to be said in the street,* Salamanca 1962

49. THE HOPE OF OUR LIFE

49.1 Temporal goods and supernatural hope.

A man approached the Lord and asked him to settle the question of a disputed inheritance.[1] Judging from the reaction of Jesus it seems that this man was more concerned about his financial problem than he was about the preaching of the Lord. The Messiah had been preaching about the Kingdom of God. The timing and nature of the petition seem, to say the least, somewhat inopportune. Jesus responds: *Man, who made me a judge or an arbiter over you?* Then Jesus turned to everyone present and said: *Take heed, and beware of all covetousness; for a man's life does not consist in the abundance of his possessions.* To underscore his teaching, the Lord tells them a parable. There was a rich man whose lands yielded an immense harvest. It was such a bumper crop that his barns could not accommodate it. He rashly concluded that his bad times were gone forever. His livelihood was now completely guaranteed. He decided to tear down his old barns and have big new ones thrown up to hold his vast stocks of grain. Regrettably, this was where his plans came unstuck. He resolved to eat, drink and be merry since life had been so good to him. But the rich man had forgotten one basic fact – the insecurity of our existence on this earth. He had chosen to put his hope in passing things. It did not cross his mind that everyone is called to a life-long struggle.

God entered by surprise into the life of this prosperous and self-confident landowner. *'Fool! This night your soul*

---

[1] Luke 12:13-21

is required of you; and the things you have prepared, whose will they be?' So is he who lays up treasure for himself, and is not rich toward God.

The man was foolish because he staked his future on the things of earth, things which are by nature transient and corruptible. We should not confuse the legitimate desire to acquire the necessities of life for one's family with the mistaken drive to possess as much as one can, no matter what the cost. Our heart has to be set on Heaven. If the Lord is truly our hope, we will be happy with many goods or with few goods. *Increased possession is not the ultimate goal of nations nor of individuals. All growth is ambivalent. It is essential if man is to develop as a man, but in a way it imprisons man if he considers it the supreme good, and it restricts his vision. Then we see hearts harden and minds close, and men no longer gather together in friendship but out of self-interest, which soon leads to oppositions and disunity. The exclusive pursuit of possessions thus become an obstacle to individual fulfilment and to man's true greatness. Both for nations and for individual men, avarice is the most evident form of moral underdevelopment.*[2] Our hope in God will be extinguished if we give in to a disordered love for possessions. Let us resolve not to fall into this foolish error. There is no greater treasure than to live in Christ.

49.2 Christian detachment.

Holy Scripture repeatedly warns us to focus our hearts on God. St Peter wrote to the first Christians: *Therefore gird up your minds, be sober, set your hope fully upon the grace that is coming to you at the revelation of Jesus Christ.*[3] St Paul advised Timothy: *As for the rich in this world, charge them not to be haughty, nor to set their*

---

[2] Bl. Paul VI, Encyclical, *Populorum progressio*, 26 March 1967, 19
[3] 1 Pet 1:13

hopes on uncertain riches, but on God, who richly furnishes us with everything to enjoy.[4] St Paul points out that *the love of money is the root of all evils; it is through this craving that some have wandered away from the Faith and pierced their hearts with many pangs.*[5] The Church continues to remind us of this truth in our own times: *Therefore all the faithful are invited and obliged to holiness and the perfection of their own state of life. Accordingly, let all of them see that they direct their affections rightly, lest they be hindered in their pursuit of perfect love by the use of worldly things, and by an adherence to riches which is contrary to the spirit of evangelical poverty, following the apostle's advice: 'Let those who use this world not fix their abode in it, for the form of this world is passing away' (cf 1 Cor 7:31).*[6]

Our disordered attachment to the use of material goods may spring from our *intention*. This is when we desire things for their own sake, as if they were an ultimate end. Our attachment may also be related to the *manner* in which we go about acquiring goods. This fault may be evidenced by an attitude of anxiety in our pursuit of wealth, in a disregard for our health, in lack of attention to the education and formation of our children, in our preoccupied absence from family life ... Another expression of this problem lies in *the way we use things* – whether we use them simply for our personal benefit, whether we give alms or not ...

The disordered love for material goods presents a grave obstacle to following the Lord. Seen in a positive light, the exercise of detachment and right intention serves to prepare the soul for receiving spiritual goods. *If you want to be your own masters at all times, I advise you to*

---

[4] 1 Tim 6:17
[5] 1 Tim 6:10
[6] Second Vatican Council, *Lumen gentium*, 42

make a very real effort to be detached from everything, and to do so without fear or hesitation. Then, when you go about your various duties, whether personal, family or otherwise, make honest use of upright human means with a view to serving God, his Church, your family, your profession, your country, and the whole of mankind. Remember that what really matters is not whether you have this or lack that, but whether you are living according to the truth taught us by our Christian faith, which tells us that created goods are only a means, nothing more. So, do not be beguiled into imagining that they are in any way definitive.[7]

If we live with Christ close by our side we will need few possessions in order to be happy as children of God. If we are not close to Christ we will find that no accumulation of possessions will ever satisfy us.

49.3 Our hope is in the Lord.

A priest friend tells the following story: *Many years ago, I was doing my term of military service in the region of Navarre, in Spain. We would do our military service during our vacations from the university. I was stationed at a little town called Abaurrea. I well remember the day when a brand-new second lieutenant showed up at the post to receive his orders. The commander told him to report to the town of Jaurrieta and, almost as an afterthought, told him to make his way there on horseback ... The new subaltern was in a dither about the prospect since he had never ridden a horse before. All during dinner he was asking about horses and looking for suggestions. Finally, someone said to him: 'Listen, all you have to do is mount the horse with confidence. Don't let your mount suspect that this is your first time, that you have never ridden*

---

[7] St. J. Escrivá, *Friends of God*, 118

before. This is absolutely critical ...'

Early the next morning a soldier brought a horse for the new officer along with another mount for his gear. The officer climbed onto his horse but in such a way that the animal knew immediately who was in charge. It took off at a trot and the second lieutenant was clearly alarmed. The horse eventually stopped when it felt like it. It began to graze, paying no attention to the officer pulling on its reins. Then, again when the horse felt like it, it would break into a trot along the highway. Every once in a while it would begin to canter. The sorry officer was totally distraught. Then he came up with a team of army engineers laying some electrical cables. One of the engineers called out: 'Hey, you! Where are you heading for?' And the young officer replied with an air of resignation, 'Who, me? I'm going to Jaurrieta, but what I don't know is where my horse is going ... '

Perhaps we have also been asked the question: 'Hey, you! Where are you going?' We may have had occasion to answer: 'Who, me? I'm headed for Love; I'm headed for Truth; I'm headed for Joy. What I don't know is where life is taking me! [8]

How marvellous it would be if we could answer to this question: *I am going to God through my work, via my difficulties, perhaps by way of my ill-health ... This is where the goods of the earth should be leading us!* What a shame if we have converted something that is only a means into an absolute end! Let us consider in our prayer today whether our profession is a means to finding God, of arriving at our desired destination. Does the possession of material goods serve to make us better souls?

Jesus Christ teaches us over and over again that the Christian's hope does not lie in treasures on earth, where

---

[8] A. G. Dorronsoro, *Time to Believe*, pp. 111-112

moth and rust consume and where thieves break in and steal.[9] Christ offers us an *incorruptible inheritance*. Christ himself is *our hope*.[10] Nothing else can fill our heart. In Christ we will find the everlasting goods of the spirit. Material things can be a means to the achievement of our human and supernatural end. But they are just that: means. We must not convert them into ends.

Holy Mary, *our hope,* will help us to put our hearts in the right place – which is in her Son. We go to her with confidence. *Sancta Maria, Spes nostra, ora pro nobis.*

---

[9] Matt 6:19
[10] 1 Tim 1:1

50. WITH THE READINESS OF LOVE

50.1 Having one's lamps burning.

Let your loins be girded, and your lamps burning, and be like men who are waiting for their master to come home from the marriage feast, so that they may open to him at once when he comes and knocks.[1] These words the Lord addresses to us in today's Gospel. The phrase *to gird one's loins* is a metaphor derived from the customs of the Hebrews and from the peoples of the Middle East in general. A person would hitch his long, voluminous garment up before setting off on a journey so as to travel the more smoothly on the dusty roads. We read in the book of Exodus how God instructed the Israelites in the rite of the Passover sacrifice: *In this manner you shall eat it: your loins girded, your sandals on your feet, and your staff in your hand.*[2] The Israelites were to dress in readiness for their desert-passage to the Promised Land. In the same way, *having one's lamps burning* is a symbol of the kind of expectant readiness appropriate for someone awaiting the arrival of another.

Once again the Lord reminds us that our attitude ought to be that of one about to start out on an important journey, or of one who is all prepared for the coming of an important guest. Christian life cannot be characterized by drowsiness and neglect. For this there are two reasons. First of all, the enemy does not take vacations. He is constantly at work against us. *Your adversary the devil*

---

[1] Luke 12:35-38
[2] Ex 12:11

prowls around like a roaring lion, seeking someone to devour.[3] Secondly, no one in love is lethargic and sleepy-headed.[4] *Vigilance is proper to love. When one loves another, the heart is always alert, eagerly expectant. Not a minute passes without the loved-one's being on our mind ... Jesus asks for our love. That is why He calls us to be vigilant.*[5] Near the papal summer residence in Italy there is an image of Our Lady at the roadside, with an inscription that reads: *Cor meum vigilat.* The heart of the Virgin is ever vigilant for Love. We should make this inscription our own. We should be vigilant *for love,* to *discover that Love* who passes so close to us. St Ambrose teaches that if the soul is asleep Jesus will pass by without even knocking. But if the heart is attentive he will knock and ask to come in.[6] Jesus passes by throughout the course of the day. What a pity if through our being half-asleep we were to fail to greet him!

'I love thee, O Lord, my strength. The Lord is my rock, and my fortress, and my deliverer' (Ps 17:2-3). The most precious and most lovable thing I can imagine is You. Help me, my God! I love you with all the ardour of the nature you have given me. This is much less than I ought to love you, but it is no less than I am able to love you ... I can love you more if you increase my ability to love, though I certainly will never love you as you deserve.[7] Let us not allow, because of a lack of vigilance on our part, other things to occupy the place in our heart reserved for the Lord. Jesus, teach me to keep my heart free for you. I want my heart to be ready for you when you come.

---

[3] 1 Pet 5:8
[4] cf Song 2:5
[5] Ch. Lubich, *Meditations,* p. 33
[6] cf St Ambrose, *Commentary on Psalm 18*
[7] St Bernard, *Treatise on the love of God,* VI, 16

50.2 The value of being vigilant in matters of apparently little moment.

I will take my stand to watch, and station myself on the tower, and look forth to see what He will say to me, and what I will answer concerning my complaint.[8] St Bernard comments on these words of the Prophet Habakkuk: *This attitude of watchfulness applies to us as well, my brothers, because now is the hour of combat.*[9] We have to be prepared to fight every day, often in little things, because of the many obstacles that can separate us from God. Our determination to be vigilant can become practical in the faithful fulfilment of our norms of piety. Those encounters with the Lord fill us with strength and peace. We need to be on the look-out for any weakening of our resolve as a result of fluctuations of mood or mere transient feelings.

Our struggle may also be centred on the practice of charity towards others, on the formation of our character, on the effort to be more cordial, to live a constant spirit of service, to be cheerful ... Perhaps we need to put more effort into doing a better job at work, into being punctual, into keeping up our human, professional and spiritual formation ... This attitude of vigilance does not guarantee that we shall always be victorious. We shall inevitably know both victories and defeats (goals we have failed to achieve, resolutions carried out in a half-hearted manner ...). Many of our defeats, however, will be of relative importance. For those that prove more serious we should make reparation and be contrite before the Lord. He will give us the strength to carry on. St John Chrysostom once wrote to someone who had fallen away from the Faith: *The worse thing is not that the warrior has fallen in battle. The worse thing would be that he remain down. It is not the end when someone falls wounded in the fray. What is*

---

[8] Hab 2:1
[9] St Bernard, *Sermon 5:4*

lamentable is when the wounded person does not go to get proper treatment for his wound.[10]

Let us not forget that our 'struggle in little things' serves to strengthen the soul and enhance its docility to the action of the Holy Spirit. The other side of the coin is that our neglect of little things provides the breach in our defences where the enemy frequently has us at a disadvantage: we may be neglectful or careless in matters of punctuality, in the quality of our prayer, in remembering the value of little mortifications at meals, in the guarding of our senses ... *We must convince ourselves that the worst enemy of a rock is not a pickaxe or any other such implement, no matter how sharp it is. No, its worst enemy is the constant flow of water which drop by drop enters the crevices until it ruins the rock's structure. The greatest danger for a Christian is to underestimate the importance of fighting skirmishes. The refusal to fight the little battles can, little by little, leave him soft, weak and indifferent, insensitive to the accents of God's voice.*[11]

50.3 Being alert to the threat of lukewarmness.

God is very pleased at the sight of a soul that is attentive to his coming, day in and day out. Jesus says in today's parable: *Blessed are those servants whom the master finds awake when he comes; truly, I say to you, he will gird himself and have them sit at table, and he will come and serve them.* God is ready to do wonderful things for us. It is worth while to be vigilant. Our souls should be filled with hope, listening for the footsteps of the Lord.

A heart in love is always alert like the sentry on guard duty. The soul sunk in lukewarmness is, by contrast, fast asleep. Lukewarmness may be thought of as a downward-sloping plane leading one further and further away from

---

[10] St John Chrysostom, *Epistle 2 to Theodore*, 1
[11] St. J. Escrivá, *Christ is passing by*, 77

God. Gradually, the one who is 'neither hot nor cold' becomes interested in the advantages of not over-doing things, about merely avoiding mortal sin, about not over-reacting to or making a big issue of venial sin. This attitude of half-hearted struggle is easily justified by reasons of naturalness, of expediency, of health, of empathy with others. The lukewarm person becomes increasingly sympathetic towards his own failings, caprices and love of comfort. Human weaknesses assume a subjective necessity. The soul's powers of resistance become weaker and weaker and almost guarantee the eventual collapse into serious sin.

When the soul is steeped in lukewarmness, it lives without concrete goals in the interior struggle. It travels on a descending spiral. The effort to become better is shrugged aside. The heart experiences a feeling of empti-ness concerning the things of God, concerning God him-self. The lukewarm person tries to fill that void with worldly things, but his striving is in vain. His dealings with God become cold and lifeless. Before the onset of lukewarmness, there has always been a history of small infidelities which bit by bit contribute to the soul's sense of alienation.

Let your loins be girded and your lamps burning ... We must have a keen ear for the footsteps of the Lord. This is a daily challenge, and concerns specific points of concrete struggle. No one was more watchfully prepared for the coming of Christ than his Mother Mary. She will teach us how to be vigilant if we should ever find ourselves threatened by lukewarmness.

My Lord, how good you are to those who seek you! Imagine how good you will be to those who find you![12] We have found the Lord. Let us resolve never to lose him.

---

[12] St Bernard, *Treatise on the love of God*, VII, 22

TWENTY-NINTH WEEK: WEDNESDAY

51. MUCH WILL BE ASKED

51.1 Our responsibility for the graces we have received.

After Jesus had warned his disciples of the need to be vigilant, Peter asked if this teaching applied to them as his closest followers or to everyone.[1] Jesus then proceeded to emphasise the unpredictability of the time when God will finally call us to give an account of our stewardship. Christ could come *in the second watch, or in the third ...,* indeed at any hour. Jesus answers Peter's main question by making it clear that his teaching applies to all without exception. God will judge each one of us personally according to our circumstances and according to the graces we have received. Each of us has a mission to fulfil on this earth. We have to be faithful to this vocation to the end of our lives. We will be judged according to the fruits our efforts have borne. St Paul explained this idea to the early Christians in this way: *For we must appear before the judgment seat of Christ, so that each one may receive good or evil, according to what he has done in the body.*[2]

The Lord concludes his teaching with this consideration: *Everyone to whom much is given, of him will much be required; and of him to whom men commit much they will demand the more.* How much has the Lord entrusted to us? How many graces has He conferred on others as a result of our lives? How many people are depending on my own correspondence with grace? Today's Gospel passage is a clarion call reminding us of our responsibility with

---

[1] Luke 12:39-48
[2] 2 Cor 5:10

regard to our proper vocation. Each person serves as a soldier commissioned by God to guard a part of his fortress of the Universe. Some soldiers are stationed on the walls, others in the interior of the castle. Everyone needs to be faithful to his duty and assignment. No one can abandon their post. If this were to happen, then the fortress would be exposed to the assaults of hell.

A responsible Christian cannot allow his dedication to be diminished through a false sense of humility. While the believer is generally reassured by the knowledge of God's almighty power, he may become unduly discouraged at the evidences of the weakness of human nature. Yet God will repeatedly grant the grace to make even defeat turn into victory. In sum, God will never give up on us.

Among those around you, apostolic soul, you are the stone fallen into the lake. With your word and example produce a first ripple ... and it will produce another ... and then another, and another ... each time wider. Now do you understand the greatness of your mission?[3]

51.2 Our responsibility at work. Professional prestige.

Our ability to respond to God is a sign of our human dignity. Only a free agent can choose to be responsible and elect to do what conforms to the Will of God and to his own perfection.[4]

For the Christian living in the middle of the world, he or she must choose to act responsibly in daily work. Work should be ordered to the glory of God, to the service of society, to the fulfilment of family obligations. It also provides a vital area for personal apostolate. Pope John Paul I once spoke of the obligations of teachers: *Italian teachers have behind them classic examples of exemplary attachment and dedication to the school. Giosué Carducci*

---

[3] St. J. Escrivá, *The Way*, 831
[4] St Thomas, *Commentary on the Epistle to the Romans*, II, 3

was a professor at Bologna University. He went to Florence to attend certain celebrations. One evening he was taking leave of the Minister of Education. 'No', the Minister said, 'stay tomorrow, too'. 'I can't, Your Excellency. Tomorrow I have a lecture at the university and the students are waiting for me'. 'I dispense you'. 'You may dispense me, but I don't'. Professor Carducci had really a high sense both of the school and of the pupils. He was of the race of those who say: 'To teach John Latin, it is not enough to know Latin – one must also know and love John'. And again: 'The value of the lesson depends on the preparation'.[5] This was a man deeply in love with his work. How many times ought we to say: *I don't dispense myself,* even when the circumstances may offer us a way out.

A Christian with this sense of responsibility will endeavour to study as well as he possibly can and then perform to high standards in his place of work. This approach to work will yield as bonus the valuable asset of professional prestige. The goal holds true for all kinds of professions: for the mother of a family, for the university professor, for the office worker, for the businessman. *Whenever your will weakens in your ordinary work, you must recall these thoughts: 'Study, work, is an essential part of my way. If I were discredited professionally as a consequence of my laziness it would make my work as a Christian useless or impossible. To attract and to help others, I need the influence of my professional reputation, and that is what God wants'. Never doubt that if you abandon your task, you are going away from God's plans and leading others away from them.*[6]

51.3 Our sense of responsibility in the apostolate.

Every one to whom much is given, of him will much be

---

[5] John Paul I, *Angelus,* 17 September 1978
[6] St. J. Escrivá, *Furrow,* 781

required. Let us think for a moment of the countless graces we have received during our life. Many we know quite well. Many, many others are unknown to us. Each one of us has his hands full of graces: happiness, friendships, small but continual acts of service done for our benefit ... Let us meditate today on the question whether our life is a generous response to all the good things God has granted us.

In the parable we read in today's Gospel the Lord speaks of an irresponsible servant. He excuses his bad behaviour with this specious explanation: *My master is delayed in coming.* But the Lord has already arrived. He is in our midst every single day. We should look to him as a son in the presence of his Father, as a friend who stands facing his greatest Friend. And when, sooner or later, we are called to give an account of our stewardship in this life, we will see our Friend smile. We will join that long line of those who are drawing near to him. We will understand that our actions were like *a stone fallen into the lake.* Our dedication to our daily duties, to prayer and apostolate all have a wonderful and incalculable impact on our surroundings.

Jesus declares to his disciples: *Truly, truly, I say to you, he who believes in me will also do the works that I do; and greater works than these will he do, because I go to the Father.*[7] St Augustine has commented on these words: *He who believes in me will not be greater than I am. Rather, I will do great things through him. I will do even more by means of those who believe in me than I am doing now by myself.*[8] How many marvels has the Lord worked through the medium of our lives, when we have let him! His greatest works *consist in giving divine life to men through the action of the Holy Spirit. Then they will realize*

---

[7] John 14:12
[8] St Augustine, *Commentary on St John's Gospel,* 72, 1

their adoption as children of God ... Jesus indeed said: 'I am going to the Father'. But the departure of Jesus does not interrupt the salvation of the world. It actually serves to insure the growth and expansion of the Church. It does not lead to separation from his disciples, but to a different kind of presence among them. Their unity with Christ glorified enabled the disciples to do the kind of great works that reunite all men with the Father ... Jesus counts on us to help him complete his work. He works through us if we will only let him do so.

Similarly, when God was to come to earth for the first time, He sent to ask permission of Mary, a creature like us. Mary believed. She gave her complete assent to the plans of the Father. And what was the fruit of her faith? Through her 'yes' 'the Word was made flesh' (John 1:14) in her womb. She therefore made possible the salvation of all mankind.[9] We ask Our Lady to help us complete and fulfil the work entrusted to us by her Son – a vibrant apostolate wherever we are working.

---

[9] Ch. Lubich, *Words which give life*

52. *I CAME TO CAST FIRE UPON THE EARTH*

52.1 The divine zeal of Christ for all souls.

Just like any true friend the Lord reveals to his disciples his most intimate thoughts. He tells them of his zeal for the salvation of all souls: *I came to cast fire upon the earth; and would that it were already kindled!*[1] He has a holy impatience to ignite and offer his holocaust to the Father on Calvary for the sake of mankind: *I have a baptism to be baptized with; and how I am constrained until it is accomplished!* There on the Cross the fullness of God's love for his creatures was made manifest: *Greater love has no man than this, that a man lay down his life for his friends.*[2] We prove we are Christ's friends if we struggle to follow him.

St Augustine commented on this, today's Gospel passage: *People who believe in him are enkindled. They receive the flame of charity. That is why the Holy Spirit appeared in this form at Pentecost: 'And there appeared to them tongues as of fire, distributed and resting on each one of them' (Acts 2:3). Set aflame by this fire the Apostles set out across the entire world to inflame others, including their enemies. What enemies? Those who had forsaken God their Creator for the worship of man-made idols ... The faith of such as these has been smothered to ashes. It is good for them that they be set alight by this holy flame so that they may once again shine forth in Christ's glory.*[3]

---

[1] Luke 12:49
[2] John 15:13
[3] St Augustine, *Commentary on Psalm 96*, 6

This crucial task of setting the world on fire has been passed on to today's Christians. This fire of love and peace will strengthen and purify souls.

So let us go to the university, to the factories, into public life, to our own homes ... *If one were to set fires at different locations throughout a city, even if they were modest fires they would quickly consume the whole metropolis. Likewise, if in a city, at the most disparate points, one were to ignite the hearts of the inhabitants with the fire that Jesus brought to the world, then the good-will of those people would quickly over-run the city, lighting it up with love for God.*

The fire Jesus has brought to the world is himself. It is the fire of Love. This is the love which not only unites souls to God but unites souls to one another ... In each city these souls shall emerge from families: father and mother, son and father, mother and mother-in-law. This phenomenon can take place in parish life, in organisations, in schools, in offices, anywhere ... Each small flame for God necessarily kindles other flames. Divine Providence takes care to distribute these souls on fire where they can best serve the process. Through their action, many places in the world will be restored to the warmth of the love of God and renewed hope.[4]

52.2 Our apostolate in the middle of the world should spread like a flame of peace.

Apostolate in the middle of the world should spread like wildfire. Each Christian who lives the Faith seriously becomes a *point of ignition* at his or her place of work, among friends and acquaintances ... But this phenomenon will occur only when we make concrete the advice St Paul gave to the Philippians: *Have this mind among yourselves,*

---

[4] Ch. Lubich, *Meditations*, pp. 59-60

which was in Christ Jesus ...[5] The Apostle *challenges all Christians to live out in their lives, as much as possible, those sentiments which filled the Divine Redeemer when he offered himself up as a Sacrifice. Imitate his humility and present to God Almighty all the adoration, honour, praise and thanksgiving.*[6] This oblation is realized primarily in the Holy Mass, the unbloody renewal of the Sacrifice of the Cross. The Second Vatican Council teaches concerning the contribution of the laity: *For all their works, prayers and apostolic endeavours, their ordinary married and family life, their daily occupations, their physical and mental relaxation, if carried out in the Spirit, and even the hardships of life, if patiently borne – all these become 'spiritual sacrifices acceptable to God through Jesus Christ' (1 Pet 1:1). Together with the offering of the Lord's body, they are most fittingly offered in the celebration of the Eucharist. Thus, as those everywhere who adore in holy activity, the laity consecrate the world itself to God.*[7]

Christian life ought to be an imitation of the life of Christ, a participation in his divine Sonship. Through this way of life we will learn from Jesus how to relate to other people. When Jesus saw the multitude He had compassion on them, for they were *like sheep without a shepherd.*[8] Life held no meaning for them. Jesus had compassion on these people. His love was so great that He went to the extent of giving up his life for them and us on the Cross. This is the divine love which should fill our hearts. Then we too will have compassion on the people around us, who perhaps have strayed from the Lord. With the help of God's grace and our genuine friendship, hopefully we will bring these souls back to the Master.

---

[5] Phil 2:5
[6] Pius XII, Encyclical, *Mediator Dei,* 20 November 1947, 22
[7] Second Vatican Council, *Lumen gentium,* 34
[8] Matt 9:36

In the Holy Mass a surging current of divine love is transmitted from the Son to the Father through the Holy Spirit. The follower of the Lord participates in this love since he or she is incorporated in Christ. The Christian then extends this love to other people and to all earthly realities, which are thereby sanctified and made into a fitting offering to God. Our apostolate should have its roots in the Mass and should from there draw its efficacy. For the Mass is nothing less than the realization of the Redemption in our time by means of apostolic Christians. Jesus *came on earth to redeem everyone, because 'He wished all men to be saved' (1 Tim 2:4). There is not a single soul in whom Christ is not interested. Each soul has cost him the price of his Blood (cf 1 Pet 1:18-19).*[9] If we truly imitate Our Lord's example we can never be indifferent towards any soul.

52.3 Holy Mass and the apostolate.

When a Christian participates in the Holy Mass, his prayers should be concerned first of all with his brothers and sisters in the Faith. The Christian should feel more and more closely united to them in the *bread of life* and in *the cup of eternal salvation.* This is the time to pray for everyone, and especially for those who are most in need. We should grow in the spirit of charity and fraternity *because the Eucharist makes us all one. As a consequence, we therefore treat one another as family. The Eucharist unites the children of God into one family closely related to Christ and to one another.*[10]

Following this unique encounter with the Lord we will experience the same joy as was felt by the sick in Palestine once they had been cured by Jesus. They were so overjoyed at this manifestation of God's mercy that they went about the towns and villages of Palestine singing the

---

[9] St. J. Escrivá, *Friends of God,* 256
[10] Ch. Lubich, *The Eucharist,* Madrid 1977, p. 78

Lord's praises. When the Christian receives Communion at Holy Mass he should be moved to share this wonderful grace with others. Each encounter with the Lord brings with it this joy as well as the need to communicate it to other people. This was how Christianity grew so quickly in its early years. It spread like a conflagration of peace and love which no one could extinguish.

Let us resolve to centre our life upon the Holy Mass. Then we will find peace and serenity throughout the course of the day. We will want to let our friends know about the treasure of this sacrament. *If we attend Mass well, surely we are likely to think about our Lord during the rest of the day, wanting to be always in his presence, ready to work as He worked and to love as He loved. And so we learn to thank our Lord for his kindness in not limiting his presence to the time of the sacrifice of the altar. He has decided to stay with us in the Host which is reserved in the tabernacle.*[11]

The tabernacle should be a Bethany for us, *a quiet and pleasant place where Christ resides. A place where we can tell him about our worries, our sufferings, our desires, our joys, with the same sort of simplicity and naturalness as Martha, Mary and Lazarus.*[12] We will find in the Tabernacle the strength we need to do the Lord's work. In union with many other Christians[13] let us repeat the Lord's cry: *I came to cast fire upon the earth; and would that it were already kindled!*. This is the fire of divine love which will bring peace and joy to souls, to families and to society as a whole.

---

[11] St. J. Escrivá, *Christ is passing by,* 154
[12] *ibid*
[13] cf A. Vazquez de Prada, *The Founder of Opus Dei,* pp. 17, 110, 115

Twenty-Ninth Week: Friday

53. THE SIGNS OF THE TIMES

53.1 Realising that Christ is passing by.

Men have always been interested in the changing of the seasons and the climate. Sailors have an understandable concern for weather conditions, for the direction and force of the winds, for cloud formations. They analyse this information so as to forecast conditions in their work environment. In the Gospel for today's Mass the Lord addresses fishermen and farm-workers with this concern in mind: *When you see a cloud rising in the west, you say at once, 'A shower is coming'; and so it happens. And when you see the south wind blowing, you say, 'There will be scorching heat'; and it happens.*[1] Jesus gives his hearers something to think about – they can read the signs of the weather with very little evidence to go on, but they seem unable to read the abundant signs of the times regarding the Messiah! He asks them: *Why do you not know how to interpret the present time?* Many of them lacked good will and a right intention. Their eyes were closed to the light of the Gospel. The signs of the arrival of the Kingdom were evident in the Word of God, in the miracles worked by the Lord and in the very Person of Christ, right before their eyes.[2] Despite all of these signs, many of them predicted by the Prophets, they did not draw the appropriate conclusion. God was in their midst and they did not recognise him.

The Lord continues to pass by in our life. He tells us of his presence by a variety of signs, but we often do not

---

[1] Luke 12:54-59
[2] cf Second Vatican Council, *Lumen gentium,* 5

recognise him. Christ is present in sickness and tribulation which, if we accept God's Will, can serve to purify us. He exists in the people we work with, in those who need our help, in the members of our family, in the acquaintances of everyday life ... Jesus is behind that piece of good news. He is waiting for us to give him due thanks. He is ready to provide us with more blessings. Unfortunately, there are many occasions when we fail to thank him. What a shame that we should slight God because we are inordinately preoccupied with our own affairs!

What would our life be like if we really lived the presence of God? Wouldn't we find that much of our ill-humour and many of our personal problems would vanish into thin air? *If only we could live with more trust in divine Providence, strong in faith, in the certainty of God's daily protection, which never fails, how many worries and anxieties we would be spared! Then that fretfulness which, as Jesus said, is typical of pagans, of the 'heathen world' (Luke 12:30), that is, of people who lack a supernatural outlook on life, would disappear.*[3] This is the perspective of those who live as if the Master never came among us.

53.2 Faith and purity of soul.

The strength of our faith depends to a great extent on the disposition of our will. The Lord taught the listening crowds: *My teaching is not mine, but his who sent me; if any man's will is to do his Will, he shall know whether the teaching is from God or whether I am speaking on my own authority. He who speaks on his own authority seeks his own glory; but he who seeks the glory of him who sent him is true, and in him there is no falsehood.*[4] When one is unwilling to break off a dangerous relationship, when one works without rectitude of intention for the glory of God,

---

[3] St. J. Escrivá, *Friends of God,* 116
[4] John 7:16-18

then the conscience can easily be clouded, and impervious to the most obvious truths. *But a man may be so blinded by prejudice, so much at the mercy of his passions and his animosity that he can shake his head and remain unmoved; not only the evidence of external proofs, which is plain to the view, but even the heavenly inspirations which God conveys to our minds can go for nothing.*[5] If *good will* is lacking, if a person is not genuinely oriented towards God, the mind will encounter innumerable obstacles on the road to faith, to obedience and commitment to the Lord.[6] How many cases have we witnessed of someone's problems with the Faith being resolved by means of a good Confession! *God gives sight to those who are capable of seeing him. This is because the eyes of their mind are open to him. Everyone has eyes, but some people keep them screened from the light of the sun. They cannot see the sun at all. But even though the blind cannot see the sun, it continues to shine. So the people who can't see ought to blame their inability to see on their own defective vision.*[7]

To receive the Faith in all its fullness *we must have the humble attitude of a Christian soul. Let us not try to reduce the greatness of God to our own poor ideas and human explanations ... If we have this reverence, we will be able to understand and to love. The mystery will be a splendid lesson for us, much more convincing than any human reasoning.*[8]

Our moral disposition is very important for our friendship with God, especially with regard to humility and cleanness of heart. It may be that the cause of doubts and hesitation in the spiritual life can be traced to an opposition

---

[5] Pius XII, Encyclical, *Humani generis,* 12 August 1950
[6] cf J. Pieper, *The Faith Today,* Madrid 1968
[7] St Theophilus of Antioch, *Book 1,* 2, 7
[8] St. J. Escrivá, *Christ is passing by,* 13

to or a rejection of the divine Will.[9] St Augustine recounts his personal experience before his conversion: *For there was a hunger within me from a lack of that inner food, which is yourself, my God. Yet by that hunger I did not hunger, but was without desire for incorruptible food, not because I was already filled with it, but because the more empty I was, the more distaste I had for it.*[10] Let us purify our intention by a habitual turning to God in little things. *All the glory to God!* We will thus find ourselves in his presence.

53.3 Meeting Jesus and introducing him to others.

Today's Gospel ends with these words of the Lord: *As you go with your accuser before the magistrate, make an effort to settle with him on the way, lest he drag you to the judge, and the judge hand you over to the officer, and the officer put you in prison.* Everyone travels along the road that leads to judgment. Let us resolve to put aside petty complaints and resentments while we still have time. Let us now discover the signs of the times as they appear in our life. Once we reach the end of the road, it will be too late to remedy those faults. Now is the time for us to rectify the situation, to love, to make reparation. The Lord invites us to rediscover the true meaning of time. Perhaps we still have some debts outstanding – debts of gratitude, of pardon, even of justice ...

Naturally, we must also help others who travel with us on the road to understand the signs of the times, to recognise the footsteps of the Lord ... Maybe some people will not follow the Master because they have myopic vision. That was the problem with many of those in Palestine who heard Jesus preach. *The one that many are fighting is not the true God, but the false idea of God that*

---

[9] cf J. Pieper, *loc cit*
[10] St Augustine, *Confessions,* 3, 1, 1

they have formed: a God who protects the rich, who only asks and demands, who is envious of our progress in well-being, who constantly observes our sins from above to enjoy the pleasure of punishing them! ... God is not like that, but is at once good and just; father also to prodigal sons; not wanting us poor and wretched, but great, free, creators of our own destiny. Our God is so far from being man's rival that He wanted man as a friend, calling him to share in His own divine nature and in His own eternal happiness. And it is not true that He makes excessive demands of us; on the contrary, He is satisfied with little, because He knows very well that we do not have much ... This God will become more and more known and loved, by everyone, including those who reject Him today, not because they are wicked (they may be better than either of us), but because they look at Him from a mistaken point of view! Do they continue not to believe in Him? Then He answers: I believe in you![11] God is a loving Father. He will not cast off his children. Let us never lose our hope in him. Let us help others to make out the signs of the times. Just as the farmer can predict tomorrow's weather, so should the Christian be able to discern the face of Jesus, the Lord of history, in the major and minor affairs of mankind. With that wonderful knowledge in hand, the Christian can lead others to the truth.

---

[11] A. Luciani, *Illustrissimi*, pp. 17-18

54. THE BARREN FIG TREE

54.1 Giving fruit. The patience of God.

The Lord tells a parable in today's Gospel using for its setting a situation which was very familiar to the inhabitants of Palestine: *A man had a fig tree planted in his vineyard; and he came seeking fruit on it and found none.*[1] The man then expressed his frustration to the vinedresser: *Lo, these three years I have come seeking fruit on this fig tree, and I find none. Cut it down; why should it use up the ground?*

The fig tree symbolizes Israel, the Chosen People who had failed to correspond to Yahweh's countless invitations.[2] Yahweh is the owner of the vineyard. The fig tree represents anyone who does not heed the Lord's call to bear fruit.[3] The Lord sites the tree in the best location for bearing fruit. He provides all the attention and graces required. We are the subject of God's assistance from the very moment of our conception. He gives us a Guardian Angel to protect us all our days. He gives us the immense grace of Baptism, perhaps a few days after our birth. He gives himself to us in Holy Communion and through the entire course of our Christian formation ... Then there are the innumerable gifts and graces of the Holy Spirit that we have received. Despite all this care and cultivation, it is possible that the Lord may find we have borne little fruit in our life. Maybe he will find only bitter fruit. It is possible

---

[1] Luke 13:6-9
[2] cf Hos 9:10
[3] cf Jer 8:13

that our personal situation may reflect that prophetic metaphor of Isaiah: *Let me sing for my beloved a love song concerning his vineyard: My beloved had a vineyard on a very fertile hill. He digged it and cleared it of stones, and planted it with choice vines; he built a watchtower in the midst of it, and hewed out a wine vat in it; and he looked for it to yield grapes, but it yielded wild grapes.*[4] It produced sour fruit. What was the reason for this bad harvest, when everything had been done to ensure that it would be a good one? St Ambrose has written that the cause of spiritual sterility can frequently be traced to pride and hardness of heart.[5]

In spite of these disappointments God returns with renewed generosity time and time again to look for results. This is the *patience of God*[6] towards souls. He does not become discouraged by our lack of correspondence. He knows how to wait. He sees our faults and failings but he also sees our capacity for doing good. The Lord never gives up on any soul. He trusts us through thick and thin.

God himself has promised through the prophet Isaiah: *a bruised reed He will not break, and a dimly burning wick He will not quench.*[7] The pages of the Gospel are a continuous testimony to this consoling truth: the parable of the prodigal son, that of the lost sheep ..., the meeting with the Samaritan woman, with Zacchaeus ...

54.2 What God expects of us.

Let it alone, sir, this year also, till I dig about it and put on manure. And if it bears fruit next year, well and good; but if not, you can cut it down. It is Jesus who intercedes for us before God the Father, since *we are the*

---

[4] Is 5:1-2
[5] cf St Ambrose, *Commentary on St Luke's Gospel, in loc*
[6] cf 2 Pet 3:9
[7] Is 42:3

fig tree planted in the vineyard of the Lord.[8] St Augustine has commented: *The vinedresser intervenes. He steps in when the axe is about to fall upon the sterile root. He intercedes like Moses before God ... He who acts as mediator is full of mercy.*[9] *Let it alone, sir, this year also ...* How many times has this scene been repeated! Lord, give us another chance! *To realize that you love me so much, my God, and yet I haven't lost my mind!*[10]

Each and every person has a specific divine vocation. Every life that is lived without reference to the divine plan is wasted. The Lord awaits our correspondence with his many blessings. Of course we can never hope to give God as much as He gives us. *Man can never love God as much as He should be loved.*[11] Nevertheless, with the help of grace we can offer him many fruits of our love: acts of charity, deeds of apostolate, work well done ... When we examine our conscience at night we should be collecting those little fruits to put before the Lord. Then when we are called to depart from this world, *we will leave it a little bit better, a little more beautiful.*[12]

Let us examine our conduct in this time of prayer: if we were to go before the Lord this very day, would he find our arms full of good fruit? And what about our behaviour yesterday? And last week? Perhaps we shall find that our life is replete with good works done for the love of God. We may discover, on the other hand, that we have been thinking too much about our own concerns and that this has been a hindrance to the operation of divine grace. We know very well that when God does not receive all the glory life becomes sterile. Everything that is done without

---

[8] Theophylact, *Catena Aurea,* VI, p. 134
[9] St Augustine, *Sermon 254,* 3
[10] St. J. Escrivá, *The Way,* 425
[11] St Thomas, *Summa Theologiae,* 1-2, q. 6, a. 4
[12] G. Chevrot, *The Gospel in the open air,* Barcelona 1961

God will perish. Let us be sure to make some firm resolutions today. *God may have given us just one more year in which to serve him. Don't think of one, or even two. Just concentrate on this one year ...*[13]

54.3 With our hands full. Patience in the apostolate.

By this my Father is glorified, that you bear much fruit, and so prove to be my disciples.[14] This is what God wants from us: not the appearance of fruits but fruit that will last. This will include people who have returned to the sacrament of Confession, hours of work done well and with right intention, little mortifications at meals, the struggle to be on top of one's moods, living with a sense of order in the home and at work, the effort to arrive home with a cheerful disposition, little acts of service to people in need ... Let us not be content with mere appearances. Can I honestly say that my works correspond with the graces that God has granted me?

If St Luke is proceeding in chronological order in his Gospel, then *this parable follows the question about the Galileans whose blood Pilate had mingled with their sacrifices, and the tragedy of the eighteen men who died at the collapse of the tower in Siloam (Luke 13:4). Was it to be supposed that these men suffered because they were great sinners? The Lord denies this interpretation and says: 'Unless you repent you will all likewise perish'. It is not the death of the body that matters but the final disposition of the soul. The sinner who has 'all the time in the world' to repent and fails to do so will not come off a whit better than those who were taken by surprise. It is at this juncture that the Lord tells the parable of the barren fig tree. He warns us that even the patience of God has its limits. From the words of the vinedresser, though, it*

---

[13] St. J. Escrivá, *Friends of God*, 47
[14] John 15:8

appears that we can prolong the Lord's forbearance through our prayers. Without a doubt, this is very important. We can win some time for sinners to repent.[15]

Let us intercede before the Lord that he may extend his divine patience on behalf of those sinners with whom we can do apostolate. *We are in no hurry to have the tree cut down. We want it to grow through the Lord's forbearance, through his mercy. Let us not fell the tree when it can still give much fruit.*[16] Let us resolve to have patience in our own apostolates. Let us use all the human and supernatural means to bring people closer to Jesus.

Our Mother Mary will obtain the grace we need on this Saturday in the month of October. She will help us encourage souls to give abundant fruit, especially our friends and members of our family.

[15] R. A. Knox, *Pastoral Sermons,* pp. 188-189
[16] St Gregory Nazianzen, *Catena Aurea,* VI, p. 135

THIRTIETH SUNDAY: YEAR A

55. JOYFUL IN THE LORD

55.1 The Lord wants his disciples to be happy. We will find happiness when we fall in love with him.

The *Entrance Antiphon* for today's Mass reminds us how to be joyful: *Let the hearts that seek the Lord rejoice; turn to the Lord and his strength, constantly seek his face.*[1] When we don't seek the Lord, then we will find real happiness to be unattainable. Sadness springs from egoism, from the pursuit of comfort, from careless neglect in the things of God and of our fellow men ... In short, it springs from living for ourselves. But the Lord has made us to be happy. He wants us to be even more joyful when we follow his call. As it is written in the book of Joel: *Fear not, O land; be glad and rejoice, for the Lord has done great things! ... Be glad, O sons of Zion, and rejoice in the Lord, your God; for He has given the early rain for your vindication, He has poured down for you abundant rain, the early and the latter rain, as before.*[2]

Joy is indispensable to a Christian's life. When a soul is joyful, it has wings to fly towards God. A happy soul is closer to God and is able to undertake works of service for other people. In contrast, sadness paralyses one's desires for sanctity and apostolate. It is a great evil because it clouds our vision. This is why St Paul repeats his injunction to the early Christians: *Rejoice in the Lord always; again I will say, rejoice.*[3] Our Christian joy will prove to be

---

[1] *Entrance Antiphon,* Ps 104:34
[2] Joel 2:21-23
[3] Phil 4:4

a source of strength in time of trial. It will also serve to attract other people to the Faith.

Sadness does not come from suffering itself, but from the failure to look upon Jesus. St Thomas teaches that this infirmity of the soul is a vice provoked by disordered self-love. In addition, it can lead to many other problems.[4] It can be likened to a diseased root which will produce only bitter fruit. Sadness can be the cause of lack of charity, of a reckless love of comfort, of a surrender to temptations of the senses.

You need a heart which is in love, not an easy life, to achieve happiness.[5] Happiness is the first effect of love. Sadness is the sterile fruit of egoism, laziness and the absence of love. *Sadness moves the soul to anger and fury. Whenever we are sad, we know how easy it is for us to become upset at the slightest provocation. Sadness also inclines us to be suspicious and spiteful. Sometimes it may even lead a person to lose his senses.*[6] The sad soul falls into sin without a fight. Such gloominess is a sure road to destruction. *As a moth does by a garment, and a worm by the wood, so the sadness of a man consumes the heart.*[7]

If there should come a time when we experience this sickness of soul, let us examine our conscience with courage. Where have we placed our heart? *'Laetetur cor quaerentium Dominum'* – *'Let the hearts of them rejoice who seek the Lord'*. There you have light to help you discover the reasons for your sadness.[8]

How difficult it is to become sad when we walk in the presence of our Father God, when we are generous in the face of great sacrifice! Like St Paul, we can affirm: *I am*

---

[4] cf St Thomas, *Summa Theologiae*, 2-2, q. 28, a. 4

[5] St. J. Escrivá, *Furrow*, 795

[6] St Gregory the Great, *Morals*, 1, 31, 31

[7] Prov 25:20

[8] St. J. Escrivá, *The Way*, 666

filled with comfort. With all our affliction, I am overjoyed.[9]
If we are truly seeking the Lord in our life, nothing can
take away our peace and joy. Pain will act to purify the
soul. Suffering itself will be transformed to joy.

55.2 The greatest commandment and joy.

Laetetur cor quaerentium Dominum ... Let the hearts
of them rejoice who seek the Lord.

The Gospel for today's Mass is an invitation to joy
because it is an invitation to love.[10] The law of love is also
the law of joy. The virtue of joy is *not distinct from
charity, but a certain act and effect of it.*[11] Our joy and
good humour, whether in calm seas or in rough, constitute
a trusty barometer of our union with God.

The Pharisees approached Jesus to ask him which is
the greatest commandment of the Law. Jesus answered
them: *You must love the Lord your God with all your heart,
with all your soul, and with all your mind. This is the
greatest and the first commandment. The second resembles
it: You must love your neighbour as yourself.* This is what
we have to do – direct our entire being to God, serve our
neighbours, open ourselves to the Lord and forget about
ourselves. We have to put aside our longing for ease and
comfort, our vanity and our pride.

Many people labour under the delusion that they will
find greater happiness once they possess a 'sufficiency' of
things, once they achieve popularity or are more admired ...
They have forgotten that all they need is to have their heart
in love. No love can ever fill our heart like the love of God.
It is what our hearts were made for. All noble love acquires
its true meaning in the context of a radical love for the
Lord above all things. He who puts his heart in the things

---

[9] 2 Cor 7:4
[10] Matt 22:34-40
[11] St Thomas, *op cit,* 2-2, q. 28, a. 3

of this world will not find the love Jesus promised to his own.[12] This is because the worldly person does not know how to love in the deepest sense of the word. *Love has its greatest power when it is perfect. Then we forget our own feelings for the sake of the one we love. If this is really the case, if we seek only to please God, then even the greatest of trials will be made sweet.*[13] All trials and tribulations become easy to bear with the help of the Lord.

55.3 Bringing joy to those whom God has placed by our side.

In today's *Responsorial Psalm* we pray: *My God is the rock where I take refuge; my shield, my mighty help, my stronghold ... I love you, Lord, my strength.*[14]

We shall find our strength in God. We will also find our joy and peace there in the Lord. We should go to the Lord personally each day. Much, indeed everything, depends on our friendship with him.

We should bring this joy and peace to those whom God has placed by our side. Our homes should be *bright and cheerful,* like that of the Holy Family.[15] When people say that a home *seems like hell,* we immediately think of a home without love, without joy, without Christ. A Christian home should be cheerful because Christ is at its head. Being disciples of Christ means that we are living those human and supernatural virtues that are so intimately tied to joy: generosity, cordiality, the spirit of sacrifice, sympathy, concern for making life pleasant for others ...

We should bring our joy to the place where we work, to our business associates, to people we meet by chance on the street ... Many of these people are sad and troubled. We

---

[12] cf John 16:22
[13] St Teresa, *Foundations,* 5, 10
[14] *Responsorial Psalm,* Ps 17:2-4; 47; 51
[15] cf St. J. Escrivá, *Christ is passing by,* 22

should help them to see the joy of living in Christ. How many souls have found their way to God by means of this attractive virtue!

Christian joy is also necessary for the proper fulfilment of our ordinary obligations. The more important our duties, the more important is it that our attitude should be one of Christian joy.[16] When we have responsibility for others, then we have a duty to communicate this joy. Such is the case with parents, priests, spiritual directors, teachers ... The smiling face of the Lord should shine through our life and works. His perfect peace was shown during his Passion and Death. Precisely when we find our struggle the more taxing, then it is that we must turn to the poignant example of the Master.

Let us turn to Our Mother Mary, *'Causa nostrae laetitiae', Cause of our joy*. She will lead us to the path of true peace and joy if we should ever lose our way. We will then understand that the path to joy is the same as the path to God.

---

[16] cf P. A. Reggio, *Supernatural spirit and good humour,* p. 24

THIRTIETH SUNDAY: YEAR B

56. CHRIST IS PASSING BY

56.1 Going to Jesus whenever we are in need.

God passes alongside the lives of men giving his light and joy. In today's *First Reading*[1] the Lord rejoices at the salvation of the remnant of Israel on their return from exile to the Promised Land: *See, I will bring them back from the land of the North and gather them from the far ends of earth ... the blind and the lame ... a great company returning here.* After so much suffering, the Prophet announces the blessings of the Lord upon his People. *They had left in tears, I will comfort them as I lead them back; I will guide them to streams of water, by a smooth path where they will not stumble.*

Jesus fulfils all of these prophecies. He went about the world doing good,[2] even for those who did not ask his help. Christ is the revelation of the fullness of divine mercy to the most needy. No form of misery could separate men from Christ. He gave sight to the blind. He cured leprosy. He healed the lame and paralytics. He fed hungry multitudes. He expelled demons ... He approached people who had the greatest suffering in soul or body. *We are the ones who have to go to Jesus. Our eyes have been blind ... We have lain paralysed on our mats, incapable of reaching the grandeur of God. This is why our most lovable Saviour and Healer of souls has descended from on high.*[3]

We must have complete faith in the one who saves us,

---

[1] Jer 31:7-9
[2] cf Acts 10:38
[3] St Bernard, *Homily on the First Sunday of Advent*, 78

in this divine Doctor who was sent with the express purpose of curing us, and the more serious or hopeless our illness is the stronger our faith has to be.[4] There will be times in our lives when we experience more hardship than usual. We will have moments of greater temptation. We will grow weary of the struggle. We will have periods of interior darkness and trial. These are moments when we must turn to Jesus, who is always by our side. We must have a humble and sincere faith like the sick and the suffering people of the Gospels. Then we will cry out to the Master: *'Lord, put not your trust in me. But I, I put my trust in you'. Then, as we sense in our hearts the love, the compassion, the tenderness of Christ's gaze upon us, for he never abandons us, we shall come to understand the full meaning of those words of St Paul: 'virtus in infirmitate perficitur' (2 Cor 12:9). If we have faith in Our Lord, in spite of our failings – or, rather, with our failings – we shall be faithful to our Father, God; his divine power will shine forth in us, sustaining us in our weakness.*[5] What a great comfort it is for us to know that Christ is near us!

56.2 The mercy of the Lord. Bartimaeus.

The Gospel of today's Mass tells the story of Jesus curing the blind beggar called Bartimaeus.[6] The Master is leaving Jericho on his way to Jerusalem. This is when Bartimaeus makes his immortal appeal: *When he heard that it was Jesus of Nazareth, he began to shout and to say, 'Son of David, have pity on me'.* This man, who lived in complete darkness, had a tremendous desire for light, for clarity, for a cure. He sensed that this was his moment. How long he had been waiting for this opportunity! The Master had come within range of his voice! *Many of them*

---

[4] St. J. Escrivá, *Friends of God*, 193
[5] *ibid*, 194
[6] Mark 10:46-52

scolded him and told him to keep quiet, but he only shouted all the louder. He could not miss this chance. What a wonderful example for us to follow! For Christ is always within range of our voice, of our prayer. He is passing close by us so that we will not be afraid to call to him. St Augustine comments: *'Timeo Iesum transeuntem et non redeuntem'. He feared that Jesus would pass by and never return.*[7] We cannot neglect any opportunity for divine grace.

We should call to Jesus forcefully – even in the depths of our soul: *Iesu, Fili David, miserere mei! Jesus, Son of David, have pity on me!* Let us make the following words of St Bernard our very own: *My only merit is the mercy of the Lord. I will never lack any merit as long as He is merciful. And since the mercy of the Lord is super-abundant, then superabundant are my merits.*[8] We go to him with these merits: *Iesu, Fili David ...* St Augustine teaches that we should call out to Jesus with our prayer and good works.[9] These works include acts of charity, professional work well done, purity of soul after a contrite confession of our sins ...

The blind man overcame the obstacles of his environment and obtained his heart's desire. *Jesus stopped and said, 'Call him here'. So they called the blind man. 'Courage', they said, 'get up; he is calling you'. So throwing off his cloak he jumped up and went to Jesus.*

The Lord had heard the cries of Bartimaeus from the start. But He wanted the blind beggar to give us a graphic example of perseverance in prayer. Finally, he finds himself before the Lord. *And now begins a dialogue with God, a marvellous dialogue that moves us and sets our hearts on fire, for you and I are now Bartimaeus. Christ,*

---

[7] cf St Augustine, *Sermon 88*, 13
[8] St Bernard, *Homily on the 'Song of Songs'*, 61
[9] St Augustine, *Sermon 349*, 5

who is God, begins to speak and asks, 'Quid tibi vis faciam?' 'What do you want me to do for you?' The blind man answers, 'Lord, that I may see'. How utterly logical! And how about yourself? Can you really see? Haven't you too experienced at times what happened to the blind man of Jericho? I can never forget how, when meditating on this passage many years back, and realising that Jesus was expecting something of me, though I myself did not know what it was, I made up my own aspirations: 'Lord, what is it you want? What are you asking of me?' I had a feeling that he wanted me to take on something new and the cry 'Rabboni, ut videam', 'Master, that I may see', moved me to beseech Christ again and again, 'Lord, whatever it is that you wish, let it be done' ... It is now to you that Christ is speaking. He asks you, 'What is it you want of me?' 'That I may see, Lord, that I may see'. Then Jesus answers, 'Away home with you. Your faith has brought you recovery. And all at once he recovered his sight and followed Jesus on his way'. Following Jesus on his way. You have understood what Our Lord was asking from you and you have decided to accompany him on his way. You are trying to walk in his footsteps, to clothe yourself in Christ's clothing, to be Christ himself: well, your faith, your faith in the light Our Lord is giving you, must be both operative and full of sacrifice. Don't fool yourself. Don't think you are going to find new ways. The faith he demands of us is as I have said. We must keep in step with him, working generously and at the same time uprooting and getting rid of everything that gets in the way.[10]

56.3 The Messianic joy.

We read in today's *Responsorial Psalm*: *The Lord has done great things for us; we are filled with joy.* When the

---

[10] St. J. Escrivá, *op cit*, 197-198

Lord delivered Zion from bondage, it seemed like a dream. Then was our mouth filled with laughter, on our lips there were songs. Deliver us, O Lord, from our bondage as streams in dry land. Those who are sowing in tears will sing when they reap.[11]

This Psalm of jubilation records the good fortune of the Israelites who were allowed by Cyrus to return to the land of their fathers. The Chosen People were full of hope at the prospect of rebuilding the Temple and the Holy City. This Psalm was later chanted on pilgrimages to Jerusalem, particularly on the occasion of important Jewish feasts. This is why the Psalm has been called the *Pilgrimage Canticle*.

To the south of Palestine lies the Negev desert. During the rainy season this area would be converted into an oasis. As the captives from Babylon returned to Israel they asked the Lord to renew the earth, to establish a new period of blessings. Their tears were converted into the seeds of conversion and repentance for their past sins that had brought down divine punishment. The farmer who becomes wearied by sowing the field will one day return to reap the grain of his labours. So too the Chosen People sowed tears of reparation, the harvest from which they came to reap with joy and exaltation.[12]

This Psalm is a foretaste of the Messianic joy of which we also found an echo in the *First reading*. In today's Gospel, Bartimaeus partakes of this salvation which will have its fullness in the Passion, Death and Resurrection of Christ. Jesus was attracted to the total blindness and great poverty of Bartimaeus. The Lord more than compensated him for his hardships. After his cure, the life of Bartimaeus was utterly changed: *et sequebatur eum in via ...* He

---

[11] *Responsorial Psalm,* Ps 125:1-6
[12] cf D. de las Heras, *Ascetical and Theological commentary on the Psalms,* p. 325

followed him along the road. Bartimaeus had become a disciple of the Master. Our suffering, our blindness, can serve as the means for an encounter with Jesus. We can follow him with more humility, with greater purity. We can draw closer to him. *Courage! Get up; He is calling you. In those days, the Gospel tells us, the Lord was passing by; and they, the sick, called to him and sought him out. Now, too, Christ is passing by, in your Christian life. If you help him, many will come to know him, will call to him, will ask him for help: and their eyes will be opened to the marvellous light of grace.*[13]

Domine, ut videam: Lord, help me to see what it is you want of me. *Domina, ut videam*: My Lady, help me to see what my Lord wants me to do today. Help me to answer his call with generosity.

---

[13] St. J. Escrivá, *The Forge*, 665

Thirtieth Sunday: Year C

57. TRUE PRAYER

57.1 The need for prayer.

Once again we find that prayer is the theme of the Gospel of the day.[1] Here Jesus prefaces the parable of the Pharisee and the tax collector by insisting to his followers that *they ought always to pray and not lose heart.*[2] Taking into account all of his teachings, Jesus spoke more often about the need for prayer than about any other matter apart from faith and charity. The Master tells us in many different ways that prayer is absolutely necessary if we are to follow him. At the beginning of his Pontificate, St John Paul II declared: *For me, prayer is the first priority. Prayer is the basic prerequisite to service of the Church and the world ... Every believer should always think of prayer as an essential and indispensable component of one's vocation. It is the 'opus divinum' which precedes and overshadows every work. We well know that faithfulness to prayer, or its neglect, is a test of the vitality of religious life, apostolate and Christian fidelity.*[3] Without prayer, we cannot hope to follow Christ in the middle of the world. We need prayer as much as we need food to eat and air to breathe. This explains why the devil endeavours to keep Christians from praying with superficial excuses.

Some days before giving this address, the Pope had reminded a gathering of clergy and religious: *A constant danger with priests, even zealous priests, is that they*

---

[1] Luke 18:9-14
[2] cf Luke 18:1
[3] St John Paul II, *Address,* 7 October 1979

become so immersed in the work of the Lord that they neglect the Lord of the work.[4] This is certainly a danger that faces every Christian. For of what good is the most energetic apostolate if it is accomplished at the cost of one's friendship with the Lord? The achievement would end up worthless. This would have been a human endeavour where we sought only ourselves. The remedy for this malady is clear: *We must find time, we must make time, to be with the Lord in prayer.*[5] Prayer is *indispensable for you, today as yesterday.*[6]

Let us look and see whether our prayer, our friendship with Jesus, really influences our life of work, our family life, our friendships, our apostolate ... We know that everything is different once we have talked it over with Jesus. It is in our prayer that *the Lord gives light to understand his truths.*[7] Without the help of this light all would be darkness. This divine light will permit us to penetrate the mystery of God and of existence.

57.2 Humble and trusting prayer. The parable of the Pharisee and the tax collector.

The purpose of the parable in today's Gospel is to teach us the difference between true piety and false piety. As we hear in the *First Reading*: *The prayer of the humble pierces the clouds ...*[8] It always reaches God and attains its end.

St Luke points out that the Lord told this parable *to some who trusted in themselves that they were righteous and despised others.* The Lord uses two figures who were familiar to his audience: *Two men went up into the temple to pray, one a Pharisee and the other a tax collector.* Right

---

[4] *idem, Address in Maynooth,* 1 October 1979
[5] *ibid*
[6] *idem, Address in Guadalupe,* 27 January 1979
[7] St Teresa, *Foundations,* 10, 13
[8] Sir 35:17

from the start of the parable we can see that the men share an external purpose but have entirely different agendas. The Pharisee did not come to pray to God. He is really talking to himself instead. There is no love for God in his words, nor any vestige of humility for that matter. The Pharisee stands before God and gives thanks for his own rectitude. He compares his upright behaviour with that of other people and finds himself justified. It would appear that he does not really need God after all.

The tax collector *stood afar off.* Because he did not thrust himself forward, God was able to approach him the more easily. He who would not lift up his eyes to heaven now had the Lord of the Heavens within him ... Whether the Lord is near or far actually depends on you. Love, and He will approach.[9] God is very attentive to everything we say to him. The tax collector won God over through his humility and trust, because *God opposes the proud, but gives grace to the humble.*[10] The parable teaches us that our prayer should be full of humility, attentive and trusting. We should avoid acting like the 'praying' Pharisee with his self-centred monologue.

Jesus reminds us that humility has to be the foundation of our dealings with God. He wants us to pray like needy children desirous of his mercy. St Alphonsus Liguori advises us: *God wants us to go to him with confidence. Bring to him your work, your projects, your fears and whatever interests you. Act with a trusting and open heart. For God does not speak to those who never speak to him.*[11] Let us flee from the prayer of self-sufficiency, which is evidenced by complacency in our apostolate and pride in our interior struggle. Let us also avoid negative attitudes which reflect a lack of

---

[9] St Augustine, *Sermon 9,* 21

[10] Jas 4:6

[11] St Alphonsus Liguori, *How to converse continually and familiarly with God*

trust in God's grace. Pessimism may be a manifestation of hidden pride. The time spent in true prayer should always be a time of joy, confidence and peace.

57.3 Perseverance in prayer. Difficulties.

Let us prepare well our time of prayer. St Teresa has written: *Mental prayer is nothing else, in my opinion, but being on terms of friendship with God, frequently conversing in secret with Him Who, we know, loves us.*[12] Let us draw strength from our prayer to sanctify our daily work, to convert our contradictions into blessings, to overcome all difficulties. We will be strong to the extent that our prayer is authentic. When we begin our prayer, *we need to ready our heart, like someone who is tuning a guitar.*[13] We can offer up all of our day's work to the Lord, along with small mortifications, our interior recollection ... When we make our *act of the presence of God,* we have begun our special time of conversation with him. A short prayer may help to begin our dialogue. We should pray with devotion and attention: *I firmly believe that you are here, that you see me, that you hear me ...* God sees us. Our recognition of this reality is itself prayer, even though we may not say a word. He understands us and we understand him. We ask many things of him and He asks of us more generosity, more love, more struggle ...

We may not experience any special feelings in our prayer. This should not bother us. *For the person who makes a serious effort there will, however, be moments in which he seems to be wandering in a desert and, in spite of all his efforts, he 'feels' nothing of God. He should know that these trials are not spared anyone who takes prayer seriously ... In these moments, his prayer, which he will resolutely strive to keep to, could give him the impression*

---

[12] St Teresa, *Life,* 8, 7
[13] St Peter of Alcantara, *Treatise on Prayer and Meditation,* 1, 3

of a certain 'artificiality', although really it is something totally different: in fact it is at that very moment an expression of his fidelity to God, in whose presence he wishes to remain even when he receives no subjective consolation in return.[14]

We may think that our struggle in prayer is not bearing fruit, while God himself is immensely happy at our progress. The Lord will always give us his peace and his strength so that we may accomplish his work. We should never abandon our prayer. St Teresa of Avila has advised that *to lose one's way is – so it seems to me – nothing else but the giving up of prayer.*[15] Perhaps this is one of the more serious temptations which can afflict souls committed to the Lord's service: to abandon this daily conversation with God for apparent lack of fruit, for the sake of 'more important' things, even for apostolic activities ...

Nothing is more important than our daily appointment with Jesus. He is waiting for us. *At all costs, the decision to persevere in devoting a set time to private prayer daily must be made and carried out inflexibly. It does not matter if one can do no more than remain on one's knees for the period and only battle with complete lack of success against distractions; one is not wasting time.*[16] When we spend time with the Lord, we will always in the end be the richer for it.

Let us ask Our Lady that she teach us how to deal with her Son. We will follow her example in Nazareth and the years of Christ's public life. Let us firmly resolve never to neglect our prayer, and simply do our best to overcome distractions in this time of personal conversation with the Lord.

---

[14] S.C.D.F., *Letter on some aspects of Christian meditation,* 15 October 1989, 30

[15] St Teresa, *Life,* 19, 19

[16] E. Boylan, *This Tremendous Lover,* p. 283

58. LOOKING UP TO HEAVEN

58.1 A sick woman and the mercy of Jesus.

In today's Gospel St Luke recounts an incident that happened when Jesus was teaching in a synagogue on the sabbath.[1] *And there was a woman who had had a spirit of infirmity for eighteen years; she was bent over and could not fully straighten herself.* Without a word being spoken, Jesus is moved with compassion for her: *He called her and said to her, 'Woman, you are freed from your infirmity'. And He laid his hands upon her, and immediately she was made straight, and she praised God.*

But the ruler of the synagogue became indignant because Jesus had cured on the sabbath. With his shrivelled heart he could not comprehend the majesty of the divine mercy that had freed this woman from so much anguish. He was zealous for the observance of the letter of the Law,[2] but he was unable to grasp that God was well pleased with this miraculous healing. His heart was cold and his mind closed. He could not appreciate the true meaning of what had happened. The Messiah foretold by the Scriptures was standing right in front of him. And yet he had no hesitation in rebuking Jesus and the people around him: *There are six days on which work ought to be done; come on those days and be healed, and not on the sabbath day.* As on other similar occasions the Lord does not remain silent. *Then the Lord answered him, 'You hypocrites!' Does not each of you on the sabbath untie his ox or his ass from the manger,*

---

[1] Luke 13:10-17
[2] cf Ex 20:8

and lead it away to water it? And ought not this woman, a daughter of Abraham whom Satan bound for eighteen years, be loosed from this bond on the sabbath day? This woman, this *daughter of Abraham,* has far greater value in the Lord's eyes than does a beast of burden. *As he said this, all his adversaries were put to shame; and all the people rejoiced at all the glorious things that were done by him.*

The woman was freed from the spirit of infirmity that had enslaved her. Now she could stand up straight and look at Christ. She could look up to Heaven. She could see the world and everyone around her. We should meditate frequently on these passages that reveal the Lord's great mercy. *Jesus shows this refinement and affection not only to a small group of disciples, but to everyone: to the holy women, to representatives of the Sanhedrin, like Nicodemus, to tax collectors like Zacchaeus; He shows it to sick and healthy people, to teachers of the law and pagans, to individuals and to crowds.*

The Gospels tell us that Jesus had no place to rest his head, but they also tell us that he had many good, close friends, eager to have him stay in their homes when he was in the vicinity. They tell us of his compassion for the sick, of his sorrow for those who were ignorant or in error, his anger at the money changers who profaned the temple.[3]

The prayerful consideration of these scenes in the Gospel should lead us to have greater confidence in Jesus, especially when we ourselves are in need. May we struggle hard to lift up our hearts from the material world. We can never pass by pain or misery with indifference. We should react with the heart of the Master and have compassion on our neighbours.

---

[3] St. J. Escrivá, *Christ is passing by,* 108

58.2 What keeps us from seeing Heaven.

St Augustine comments upon this passage: *This was how the Lord found her after eighteen years: 'She was bent over and could not fully straighten herself' (Luke 13:11). She is a symbol of those who have their hearts set on the things of this world.*[4] Eventually, these souls lose the capacity to look up to Heaven, to contemplate God and to see him in the wonders of creation. *The person who is bent over is only able to see the ground at his feet. Whoever seeks what is of here below does not recall at what great a price he was redeemed.*[5] In this situation one forgets that created goods exist to serve us on our way to Heaven. In the end, the worldly soul is left with a thoroughly impoverished universe.

The devil prevented the woman of the Gospel passage from looking up to Heaven for eighteen years. Unfortunately, some people spend their entire lives just looking at the earth. They have become bound down by *the lust of the flesh and the lust of the eyes and the pride of life.*[6] The concupiscence of the flesh prevents the soul from seeing God. As Jesus taught, only the pure in heart will see God.[7] *Lust of the flesh is not limited to disordered sensuality. It also means softness, laziness bent on the easiest, most pleasurable way, any apparent shortcut, even at the expense of infidelity to God ...*

St John tells us that the other enemy is the lust of the eyes, a deep-seated avariciousness that leads us to appreciate only what we can touch. Such eyes are glued to earthly things and, consequently, they are blind to supernatural realities. We can, then, use this expression of sacred Scripture to indicate that disordered desire for material things, as well as that deformation which views

---

[4] St Augustine, *Commentary on Psalm 37,* 10
[5] St Gregory the Great, *Homilies on the Gospels,* 31, 8
[6] 1 John 2:16
[7] cf Matt 5:8

everything around us – other people, the circumstances of our life and of our age – with just human vision.

Then the eyes of our soul grow dull. Reason proclaims itself sufficient to understand everything, without the aid of God ... In this way does our existence fall prey unconditionally to the third enemy: pride of life. It's not merely a question of passing thoughts of vanity or self-love, it's a state of general conceit. Let's not deceive ourselves, for this is the worst of all evils, the root of every false step.[8] These enemies of our soul will never triumph if we struggle to be sincere and if we place our hope in the Lord. He will lift up our eyes to Heaven.

58.3 The full meaning of life and creation can only be found in God.

Our faith in Christ should be shown in the little details of our everyday life. In the course of our daily lives, we must *look up at the sky, at God, the supreme and final aim of all our desires and strivings.*[9]

When we look at God with eyes of faith, then we will be able to understand the eternal truths: historical events and events in our lives will take on a new meaning; pain and suffering will become comprehensible; our work will acquire a transcendental significance as an offering made to God.

The Christian should not run away from earthly realities. *He can receive them from God, and respect and reverence them as flowing constantly from the hand of God.*[10] The behaviour of the Christian will be animated by this new attitude: *Grateful to his benefactor for these creatures, using and enjoying them in detachment and liberty of spirit, man is led forward into true possession of them, as having nothing, yet possessing all things. 'All are*

---

[8] St. J. Escrivá, *op cit*, 5-6
[9] St John Paul II, *Angelus*, 8 September 1979
[10] Second Vatican Council, *Gaudium et spes*, 37

yours, and you are Christ's, and Christ [
3:22-23).[11] St Paul recommended to the [
Philippi: *Finally, brethren, whatever is t*
honourable, whatever is just, whatever is [
lovely, whatever is gracious, if there is a
there is anything worthy of praise, think about these things.[12]

The Christian acquires a true grandeur of soul when he becomes accustomed to referring temporal realities to God. He takes advantage of the circumstances and events of his life to give thanks to God, to ask for help, to seek pardon for sins and failings ... Since he never forgets that he is a son of God twenty-four hours a day, he never gets overly wrapped up in problems. He sees with supernatural vision the real value of things. *Rush, rush, rush! Hustle and bustle! Feverish activity! The mad urge to dash about. Amazing material structures ...*

On the spiritual level ... shams, illusions: flimsy backdrops, cheesecloth scenery, painted cardboard ... Hustle and bustle! And a lot of people running. It is because they work thinking only of 'today'; their vision is limited to 'the present'. But you must see things with the eyes of eternity, 'keeping in the present' what has passed and what has yet to come.

Calmness. Peace. Intense life within you. Without that wild hurry. Without that mad urge for change. From your own place in life, like a powerful generator of spiritual energy, you will give light and vigour to ever so many without losing your own vitality and your own light.[13]

Let us cast ourselves upon the mercy of the Lord so that He will grant us this gift, the ability to live by faith. Then we will walk on the earth with our eyes fixed on Jesus.

---

[11] *ibid*
[12] Phil 4:8
[13] St. J. Escrivá, *The Way,* 837

59. THE GLORY OF THE CHILDREN OF GOD

59.1 Our sense of divine filiation.

Whenever we read *Psalm 2* we come across this messianic reference: *I will tell of the decree of the Lord: He said to me, 'You are my son, today I have begotten you'.*[1] *The adverb 'today' speaks of eternity. It is the 'today' of the intimate life of God, the 'today' of eternity, the 'today' of the Most Holy and ineffable Trinity: Father, Son and Holy Spirit, who is eternal Love and eternally consubstantial with the Father and the Son.*[2]

According to its definition, *filiation* requires an equality of nature.[3] This is why Jesus is the only-begotten Son of the Father. We may say in a broader sense that all creatures, especially spiritual beings, are 'children of God'. But this filiation is inherently imperfect. Creatures cannot be equated with their Creator according to nature.

Of course, it is true that Baptism acts to regenerate the soul. This new birth into the supernatural order allows us to participate in the divine nature. This supernatural elevation to divine filiation represents an immense improvement on our natural filiation as creatures. St John teaches us in the Prologue to his Gospel: *But to all who received him, who believed in his name, He gave power to become children of God; who were born, not of blood nor of the will of the flesh nor of the will of man, but of God.*[4] As St Athanasius

---

[1] Ps 2:7
[2] St John Paul II, *Address,* 16 October 1985
[3] cf St Thomas, *Summa Theologiae,* 3, q. 32, a. 3 c.
[4] John 1:12-13

explains: *The Son of God became man so that the sons of men, the sons of Adam, might become sons of God ... He is the Son of God by his nature. We are sons of God by grace.*[5]

The concept of divine filiation holds a key place in the message of Jesus Christ. The Good News is an eloquent testimony to the overwhelming fact of God's love for mankind. St John wrote: See what love the Father has given us, that we should be called children of God; and so we are.[6] Our condition of being children of God fills our earthly existence with joy and hope. As St Paul tells us in one of the readings for today's Mass: *For the creation waits with eager longing for the revealing of the sons of God ... We know that the whole creation has been groaning in travail together until now; and not only the creation, but we ourselves, who have the first fruits of the Spirit, groan inwardly as we wait for adoption as sons ...*[7] The Apostle speaks of the fulness of this adoption since here on earth we have been made *sons of God,* the greatest of titles: *So through God you are no longer a slave but a son, and if a son then an heir.*[8]

The words spoken by the Father to his only begotten Son can be applied to each one of us: *You are my son, today I have begotten you. Today* means our life here on earth. *He says to us: 'You are my son'. Not a stranger, not a well-treated servant, not a friend – that would be a lot already. A son! He gives us free access to treat him as sons, with a son's piety and I would even say with the boldness and daring of a son whose Father cannot deny him anything.*[9]

---

[5] St Athanasius, *De Incarnatione contra arrianos,* 8
[6] 1 John 3:1
[7] Rom 8:19-23
[8] Gal 4:7
[9] St. J. Escrivá, *Christ is passing by,* 185

59.2 Sons of the Son.

You are my son ... The Lord spoke continually about this astounding reality to his disciples. Some times He would deal with the subject directly, as when He taught them to pray to God as a Father.[10] Similarly, He showed them that holiness consisted in filial imitation of the Father.[11] Jesus also communicated this idea through the various parables in which God is represented as a father.[12]

Divine filiation has to be understood as more than a symbolic relationship between ourselves and God. God did not want to treat us *like* his sons. He wanted to treat us *as* his sons. Clearly, our filiation can hardly be compared to that of Jesus. Yet our filiation is still something highly remarkable. It is a gift whose significance we can barely hope to grasp.[13]

Our filiation is a participation in the fulness of filiation enjoyed by the Second Person of the Holy Trinity. St Thomas explains: *From this filiation by nature we derive a certain likeness and participation.*[14] Through this filiation we are enabled to enter into the intimate life of the Holy Trinity. This is an authentic participation in the life of the Father, the Son and the Holy Spirit. We may understand our relationship as being sons of the Father in the Son through the Holy Spirit.[15] *Through the grace received in Baptism, man participate in the eternal birth of the Son from the Father because he is an adopted son of God: son of the Son.*[16] *Rising from the waters of the baptismal font,*

---

[10] cf Matt 6:9
[11] cf Matt 5:48
[12] cf J. Bauer, *Dictionary of Biblical Theology,* Barcelona 1967
[13] cf Maria C. Calzona, *Divine and Christian filiation in the world,* Pamplona 1987
[14] St Thomas, *Commentary on St John,* 1, 8
[15] cf F. Ocariz, *Children of God in Christ,* Pamplona 1972
[16] St John Paul II, *Address,* 23 March 1980

*every Christian hears again the voice that was o̶̶
on the banks of the Jordan River: 'You are my
Son; with you I am well pleased' (Luke 3:22). ᴵ̶ ̶ ̶ ̶
comes the understanding that one has been brought into
association with the beloved Son, becoming a child of
adoption (cf Gal 4:4-7) and a brother or sister of Christ.*[17]

Our sense of divine filiation should be present
throughout the course of the day. We can have recourse to
it especially in moments of trial. *It looks as if the whole
world is coming down on top of you. Whichever way you
turn you find no way out. This time, it is impossible to
overcome the difficulties.*

*But, have you again forgotten that God is your
Father? All-powerful, infinitely wise, full of mercy. He
would never send you anything that is evil. That thing that
is worrying you, it's good for you, even though those
earthbound eyes of yours may not be able to see it now.*

*'Omnia in bonum!' Lord, once again and always, may
your most wise Will be done!*[18]

59.3 Consequences of divine filiation.

Divine filiation is not simply one part of being a
Christian among others. In a certain sense it relates to
every aspect of our life of faith. Divine filiation is not,
strictly speaking, a virtue with its own attributes. It is,
rather, the frame of mind which exists in a baptized person
who is serious about his vocation. *The piety which is born
of divine filiation is a profound attitude of the soul which
eventually permeates one's entire existence. It is there in
every thought, every desire, every affection.*[19] We can come
to understand that God has given us his gifts so that we

---

[17] *idem*, Apostolic Exhortation, *Christifideles laici*, 30 December
1988, 11
[18] St. J. Escrivá, *The Way of the Cross*, Ninth Station, 4
[19] *idem, Friends of God*, 146

might become his sons, imitators of the Son to the extent of being *alter Christus, ipse Christus.*[20] We have to become more and more like Christ. Our life should be a reflection of his life. Divine filiation should be a frequent theme in our prayer. In this way our soul will be filled with peace despite the greatest temptations and contradictions. We will abandon ourselves into the hands of God's Providence. Naturally, we will continue our struggle to improve. We will use the human means available to us in the face of sickness, economic hardship, loneliness ... We will remember that even when they were enduring the worst of trials, the lives of the saints were always filled with joy.

Divine filiation is also the foundation of Christian fraternity. We have to get into the habit of seeing other people as sons and daughters of God, as brothers and sisters of Jesus Christ. We are all called to a supernatural destiny. Based on this realization, we will find it easier to offer assistance to all the people we find in need. We will help each one to find the path that leads to our common Father.

Our Mother Mary will teach us to savour those words of *Psalm 2* which we read at the start of today's meditation. These words are directed to each one of us: *You are my son, today I have begotten you.*

---

[20] cf *idem, Christ is passing by,* 96

THIRTIETH WEEK: WEDNESDAY

60. *AFTERWARDS YOU WILL UNDERSTAND*

60.1 We are in the hands of God. Everything that happens to us in some way comes from him. Consequently, everything is ultimately ordered to our benefit.

On that last night Jesus spent with his disciples He *rose from supper, laid aside his garments, and girded himself with a towel.*[1] St John is the Evangelist who has left us the most detailed description of what happened at the Last Supper. Clearly, the events of that night made a deep impression on John. The focus is Christ: *Then He poured water into a basin, and began to wash the disciples' feet, and to wipe them with the towel with which He was girded.* The Apostles are dumbfounded at the self-abasement of the Lord. Then Jesus comes to Peter who is not disposed to be cooperative: *Lord,* he says, *do you wash my feet?* Jesus answers him: *What I am doing you do not know now, but afterward you will understand.* Peter soon submits to the Lord's ministrations, as do the rest of the Apostles. Later, with the coming of the Holy Spirit, Simon will begin to fathom the meaning of that gesture of the Master. He had wanted to teach the pillars of his Church that their mission was one of service.

What I am doing you do not know now ... The same thing that befell Peter may happen to us. We can find it difficult to understand many of the things the Lord permits in our life – pain, sickness, economic ruin, unemployment, the death of a loved one ... Yet God's plans are ordered to our eternal happiness. Our mind can barely make out the

---

[1] John 13:4 ff

most immediate of realities. Shouldn't we put our trust in the Lord, in his loving Providence? Are we to trust the Lord only when things are going our way? We are in God's hands. We could never find a safer refuge. The day will come at the end of our life when the Lord will explain his ways to us, down to even the most insignificant occurrences.

In the face of every setback, of every failure, of every incomprehensible event and blatant injustice, we should reflect on those consoling words of the Lord: *What I am doing you do not know now, but afterward you will understand.* Then there will be no resentment or sorrow. Everything *that happens to us is foreseen by God, and is ordained to his glory and to the salvation of man. If what happens to us is good, God wants it for us. If it is bad, He does not want it for us, but allows it to happen because He respects man's freedom and the order of nature; in such unlikely circumstances it is nonetheless in God's power to obtain good and advantage for the soul – even bringing it out of evil itself.*[2] Whenever we find ourselves beset by difficulties let us say this simple and humble prayer: *Lord, you know better. I abandon myself into your hands. You'll explain it to me later on.*

60.2 Our sense of divine filiation. Omnia in bonum! Everything works towards the good.

In the reading for today's Mass, St Paul writes to the first Christians in Rome: *'Diligentibus Deum omnia cooperantur in bonum ...'* We know that in everything God works for good with those who love him.[3] Woes? Setbacks deriving from one thing or another? Can't you see that this is the Will of your Father God, who is good and who loves you – loves you personally – more than all the mothers in

---

[2] F. Suarez, *The Afterlife,* p. 158
[3] *First Reading,* Year I, Rom 8:28

the world can possibly love their children?[4] Our sense of divine filiation should lead us to discover that we are in the hands of a Father who knows the past, the present and the future. He has ordered everything for our good, even though his plans may not coincide with our plans of the moment. This realization should help us to be serene, even in times of grave crisis. Let us resolve to follow the advice of St Peter: *Cast all your anxieties on him, for He cares about you.*[5] No one could do a better job of watching out for us: God never makes mistakes. The people we know and love do let us down from time to time. This will never happen with the Lord, who is infinitely wise and all-powerful. Ever mindful of our freedom, he leads us on *suaviter et fortiter,*[6] with gentleness and the firm hand of a father, to our eternal happiness. This is what really matters. Our very faults and sins can be made to contribute to our welfare, since *God endures absolutely everything for the benefit of his children. Even those who err and fall by the wayside can receive grace to get it again and make progress in virtue. They will return to the fold humbler and more fitted and ready for the struggle.*[7] Contrition helps the soul to have a more profound and trusting love for God.

Insofar as we know ourselves to be children of God, life becomes a continual act of thanksgiving. The Holy Spirit will teach us to see even human catastrophe as a *divine caress* which should move us to gratitude. Thank you, Lord! This is our message to Jesus in moments of illness or bad news. This is how the saints of the Church have always reacted to contradiction. This has to be our attitude as well. *God is very pleased with those who recognise his goodness by reciting the 'Te Deum' in*

---

[4] St. J. Escrivá, *The Forge,* 929

[5] 1 Pet 5:7

[6] Wis 8:1

[7] St Augustine, *On conversion and grace,* 30

thanksgiving whenever something out of the ordinary happens, without caring whether it may have been good or bad, as the world reckons these things. For everything comes from the hands of our Father: so though the blow of the chisel may hurt our flesh, it is a sign of Love, as He smooths off our rough edges and brings us closer to perfection.[8]

60.3 Confidence in God will not make us passive creatures. We will always use the means that are available to us.

Increased confidence in and dependence on God will not diminish our personal responsibility. God does not want us to be lazy or negligent in our duties. We have to do battle with physical or moral evil, using the means available to us. We well know that our struggle itself is pleasing to God, and that it can be the source of many supernatural and human fruits. In the event of sickness, we should accept it and offer it up to God. We should at the same time pursue whatever medical remedy is required: going to see the doctor, resting, taking the appropriate medicines ... In the case of injustice, social inequalities and widespread poverty we ought to join together with other people of good will in order to find practical solutions. We should react in the same way to ignorance and to obvious lack of formation ... There could be nothing further from our Christian spirit than passivity in the face of deprivation, suffering and need.

God is our loving Father. He looks after us. He counts on our using our intelligence and common sense. He wants to work through the agency of our fraternal love. He has given us any number of talents which we should not allow to rust in disuse. We can be sanctified even when we

---

[8] St. J. Escrivá, *op cit,* 609

apparently meet failure in our life. It may be that in a particular instance we could not have tried any harder. The Lord will readily sanctify these so-called *failures,* but cannot be expected to bless acts of omission or irresponsibility.

Let us resolve to do whatever we see to be necessary in each situation and then pray: *omnia in bonum!* Whatsoever the results may be, they should help us to love God more, to reinforce our union with him. Through our divine filiation, we will encounter the protection and the paternal affection which everyone needs and treasures. St Teresa gives us this advice distilled from her lifelong experience: *Have confidence in him. Be of good heart because His Majesty is very solicitous to what you need. Have no fear that you will be lacking anything.*[9] When we draw close to the Lord, we can win every battle, even those that appear to have been defeats.

---

[9] St Teresa, *Foundations,* 27, 12

61. THE LOVE OF JESUS

61.1 Our refuge and our strength lie in the love of God. Going to the Tabernacle.

On his way to the Holy City, Jesus stops for a moment to express his disappointment at its rejection of his message: *O Jerusalem, Jerusalem ... How often would I have gathered your children together as a hen gathers her brood under her wings ...*[1] The Lord describes how He protects his own: *as a hen gathers her brood.* Jesus watches over us from the Tabernacle. He is alert to the dangers that threaten us. He is ever ready to cure our wounds. He continually shares with us his Life. This has been our prayer to him on many occasions: *'Pie pellicane, Iesu Domine, me immundum munda tuo Sanguine ...'*

O loving Pelican! O Jesu Lord!
Unclean I am but cleanse me in Thy Blood;
Of which a single drop, for sinners spilt,
Can purge the entire world from all its guilt.[2]

The Lord is our refuge and our strength. The image of his just ones seeking protection from the Lord *as a hen gathers her brood* is to be found repeatedly in Sacred Scripture. The Psalmist prays: *Keep me as the apple of thine eye; hide me in the shadow of thy wings.*[3] *For thou art my refuge, a strong tower against the enemy. Let me dwell in thy tent for ever! Oh to be safe under the shelter of thy wings!*[4]

---

[1] Luke 13:34
[2] Hymn, *Adoro te devote*
[3] Ps 17:8
[4] Ps 61:3-4

The Prophet Isaiah employs this image to reassure the Chosen People of God's protection against the Egyptians: *Like birds hovering, so the Lord of hosts will protect Jerusalem.*[5]

At the close of our earthly life Jesus will be our Judge and Friend. While we live on earth his mission is to save us, to give us all the help we need. From the Tabernacle, Jesus protects in a thousand ways. How can we imagine that He is indifferent towards our problems and our worries?

Jesus has wanted to remain present throughout the world so that we might seek him more readily for friendship and assistance. *If we are suffering pain and discomfort, He will lighten our burden and comfort us. If we succumb to illness, either He will provide a remedy or He will give us the strength to suffer it for the sake of eternal life. If we find ourselves at war with the devil and our passions, He will supply us with arms for the battle so that we can resist and ultimately be victorious. If we are poor, He will enrich us with all kinds of good things in this life and in eternity.*[6] Let us resolve to seek his company every single day without fail. Those few minutes spent in our *Visit* will be among the most productive moments of the day. *And what are we to do in the presence of the Blessed Sacrament? Love him. Praise him. Thank him. Ask of him. What does a poor man do in the presence of a wealthy man? What does a sick person do in the presence of a doctor? What does a thirsty person do at the sight of a fountain of sparkling water?*[7]

---

[5] Is 31:5
[6] St Jean Vianney, (The Curé d'Ars), *Sermon on Maundy Thursday*
[7] St Alphonsus Liguori, *Visits to the Blessed Sacrament,* 1

61.2 Jesus in the Blessed Sacrament will grant us all the assistance we require.

Our confidence that we will be victorious in trial and tribulation is not founded on our own limited resources but on the protection of the Lord. He has loved us from all eternity to the point of sacrificing his Son for our salvation. Jesus remains present among us in the Tabernacle. As a consequence, He may be very close to the place where we live or work. He is ready to help us, to heal us, to give us energy for our earthly sojourn. All we have to do is draw close to him. He is waiting for us. Nothing should separate us from God, for as St Paul teaches in today's Mass: *If God is for us, who is against us? He who did not spare his own Son but gave him up for us all, will He not also give us all things with him? ... Who shall separate us from the love of Christ? Shall tribulation, or distress, or persecution, or famine, or nakedness, or peril, or sword?*[8] Nothing can separate us from God, if we are determined to abide with him.

Clothed in grace, we can cross mountains (cf Ps 103:10), and climb the hill of our Christian duty without halting on the way. If we use these resources with a firm purpose and beg Our Lord to grant us an ever-increasing hope, we will possess the infectious joy of those who know they are children of God: 'If God is for us, who is against us?' (Rom 8:31).[9]

Even though the Lord permits us to experience strong temptations, family difficulties, sickness or reverses of any kind – no trial, no matter how fierce, can separate us from Jesus. By making a devout visit to the Tabernacle nearest to us we will reach out to the powerful hand of God. We will then be able to say: *Omnia possum in eo qui me*

---

[8] *First Reading,* Year I, Rom 8:31-39
[9] St. J. Escrivá, *Friends of God,* 219

confortat.[10] I can do all things in him who strengthens me. As St Paul tells us in today's reading: *For I am sure that neither death, nor life, nor angels, nor principalities, nor things present, nor things to come, nor powers, nor height, nor depth, nor anything else in all creation, will be able to separate us from the love of God in Christ Jesus our Lord.* This is a song of trust and optimism which we should make our own.

St John Chrysostom reminds us that *Paul himself had to fight against numerous adversaries. He was attacked by barbarians. His guards laid traps for him. There were times when he was opposed by his own faithful in great numbers. Yet Paul was triumphant. Let us not forget that the Christian who is faithful to the laws of God will win out over those who oppose him and even over Satan himself.*[11] If we stay close to Jesus in the Eucharist we will be victorious in every engagement, though sometimes we may appear to have been overcome ... The Tabernacle will be our strength. That is why Jesus wanted to remain with us in a tangible way, so that we could seek his help. *Come to me* ... He invites us, and beckons to us every day.

61.3 United to the Tabernacle, we will win every battle. Eucharistic souls.

Our serenity is rooted in the Lord. We do not close our eyes to reality. We look at the present and to the future with optimism because the Lord is by our side.

Life's difficulties can in the end yield for us great good. We are never alone in even the most overwhelming circumstances. Just as we appreciate the company of a friend when things are going badly, so should we be grateful for the company of our Friend in the nearest Tabernacle. We should go to him for consolation, peace

---

[10] Phil 4:13
[11] St John Chrysostom, *Homilies on the Epistle to the Romans,* 15

and strength. *What more can we want,* wrote St Teresa, *than so good a Friend at our side, Who will not forsake us when we are in trouble and distress, as they do who belong to the world!*[12]

St Thomas More realized that his doom was sealed when he was called to testify before the Lambeth tribunal. He bade farewell at home to the people of his household because he did not want them to follow him to the wharf as was their custom. Only his son-in-law William Roper and his favourite daughter Margaret accompanied him on this final short journey, together with a few servants. Everyone aboard the upstream ferry was silent. After a while, More whispered into the ear of Roper: *Son Roper, I thank our Lord the field is won.* Roper later wrote that he did not comprehend the meaning of these words. With the passing of time he came to understand that More's faith had given him the confidence of victory over any obstacle.[13] He knew without a shadow of a doubt that the Lord would be with him in his ultimate battle. If we seek to be close to Jesus, to be *eucharistic souls,* the Lord will watch over us *as a hen gathers her brood.* We too can be strengthened in the knowledge that *the field is won.*

Be a eucharistic soul! If the centre around which your thoughts and hopes turn is the Tabernacle, then, my child, how abundant the fruits of your sanctity and apostolate will be![14] The Mother of God contemplates her Son in Heaven. She will put the right words on our lips if we don't know what to say. She will provide a prompt response to make up for our tongue-tied clumsiness.

---

[12] St Teresa, *Life,* 22, 10
[13] cf St Thomas More, *The Agony of Christ*
[14] St. J. Escrivá, *The Forge,* 835

62. WITHOUT HUMAN RESPECTS

62.1 The clear example of Jesus.

If someone had been asked to speak at the synagogue, the Jews had the custom of inviting him to dinner. It so happened that one day after Jesus had been preaching in a certain town he was invited to dine with the leading Pharisees of the community.[1] Unfortunately, their intentions were far from praiseworthy. They wanted to entrap Jesus and, if possible, catch him out in something He would say or do. St Cyril comments on this situation: *The Lord accepts their invitation so that he may reach out to those who are present through his words and miracles.*[2] The Master took advantage of every conceivable opportunity to redeem souls. These banquets were ideal occasions on which to speak of the Kingdom of Heaven.

Once everyone had been seated, an unexpected visitor arrived: *And behold, there was a man before him who had dropsy.* It is likely that these receptions were to some extent 'open' to the public, and that more or less anyone could wander in. The sick man says nothing. He asks for nothing. He simply stands before the divine Physician: *This too should be our posture and interior attitude. We need to place ourselves before Jesus. We should stand in front of him with our dropsy, with our miseries and sins ... God will look on us with infinite compassion. We can have absolute confidence that he will take us by the hand and cure us.*[3]

---

[1] Luke 14:1-6
[2] St Cyril of Alexandria, in *Catena Aurea,* VI, p. 160
[3] I. Dominguez, *The Third Gospel,* Madrid 1989

At the sight of the sick man who stands before him, Jesus is filled with compassion. He cures the affliction even though He knows that there are those who will criticize him for curing on the Sabbath. Jesus acts in a forthright manner. He pays no heed to human respect, to what others will say. His critics consider themselves to be the authentic interpreters of the Law. Later on, the Lord will show them that mercy should be exercised even on the Sabbath. He provides an example gleaned from the common sense of the countryside: *'Which of you, having an ass or an ox that has fallen into a well, will not immediately pull him out on a Sabbath day?' And they could not reply to this.*

We may find obstacles to our faith in the environment around us, such as envy, prejudice and misunderstandings due to ignorance. Our response should be the same as that of Jesus. We should not be afraid to give clear testimony to our beliefs. This type of behaviour can be of great apostolic value. On the other hand, *it is terrible how much harm we can do if we allow ourselves to be carried away by the fear or the shame of being seen as Christians in ordinary life.*[4] Let us not fail to make manifest our Christian faith, always with humility and naturalness, whenever the situation requires it. We will never regret having acted in a manner so consistent with our deepest beliefs. The Lord will be filled with joy at such evidence of our fidelity.

62.2 A Christian with a strong faith will not be moved by human respect.

The entire life of Jesus is filled with unity and strength. We never see him vacillating. *His very turn of phrase, with its ever-recurring 'I am come,' 'I am not come,' gives expression to the stern, determined Yea and*

---

[4] St. J. Escrivá, *Furrow,* 36

Nay of his life and the inflexibility of his purpose ... In the whole of his public ministry not one single instance can be found where He had to reflect on an answer, or when he hesitated in indecision, or when he reversed a statement or an action.[5] Jesus asks his followers for this same firm response. People who are unduly concerned with human respect manifest a superficial formation and an over-all weakness of character. To succumb to human respect is to give more weight to someone else's opinion than to the teachings of Christ. The warning of Jesus is unequivocal: *For whoever is ashamed of me and of my words ..., of him will the Son of man also be ashamed, when He comes in the glory of his Father with the holy angels.*[6]

Our giving in to human respect may be the result of comfort-seeking, of a desire to 'swim with the current.' This attitude can also spring from the fear of endangering one's public standing or one's professional position. We may want to be the same as everyone else, remaining inconspicuous and therefore undisturbed. Yet whoever wants to follow the Lord ought to keep in mind the example of so many faithful Christians who have been totally committed to Christ and his teachings. St John Chrysostom has written: *Our lives as Christians shine out before others. We should pay no heed to criticisms. It is more than likely that the person who seeks sanctity will encounter some hostility. This opposition should not hinder us, for it can only enhance our glory in heaven. But one thing is needful and that is to order our conduct towards perfection. If we attend to this path, we will lead other souls out of the shadows and into the light of faith.*[7] We will be a strong support for those who weaken. A coherent life of faith has a profound attraction for others. It merits

---

[5] K. Adam, *Son of God,* pp. 78-80
[6] Mark 8:38
[7] St John Chrysostom, *Homilies on St Matthew's Gospel,* 15, 9

the respect of everyone. In many cases, God uses this conduct to bring others to the Faith. Good example always sows good seed that will, sooner or later, bear fruit. St Teresa points out: *The habit of performing some conspicuously virtuous action through seeing it performed by another is one which very easily takes root. This is good advice: do not forget it.*[8]

Undoubtedly, people have a natural tendency to protect their reputations from ridicule. They normally do not want to stand out from the crowd and go against the mainstream of contemporary opinion. The love of Christ will help us to overcome these tendencies, to exercise *the freedom of the children of God.* We can then act with courage and humility in even the most adverse of circumstances.

62.3 The example of the first Christians.

The first Christians had their faith grounded on a firm foundation. They were able to act heroically in times of trial. Joseph of Arimathea and Nicodemus, for example, were not known publicly as disciples when Jesus worked his miracles. Yet they were not afraid to go to the Roman Procurator to ask for the body of the Lord: *They are courageous in the face of authority, declaring their love for Christ 'audacter' – 'boldly' – in the time of cowardice.*[9] The Apostles behaved with similar courage under the pressure tactics of the Sanhedrin and in the face of the later persecutions. St Paul summarizes their attitude: *For the word of the cross is folly to those who are perishing, but to us who are being saved it is the power of God.*[10] For many of our friends and neighbours it may appear like *folly* to honour the bonds of matrimony, to avoid participation in

---

[8] St Teresa, *The Way of Perfection*, 7, 8
[9] St. J. Escrivá, *The Way*, 841
[10] 1 Cor 1:18-19

dishonest business ventures, to obey the Church's teachings on birth control, to be detached from material goods, to practice corporal mortification ... St Paul declares that he was never ashamed of the Gospel.[11] This was his advice to Timothy: *for God did not give us a spirit of timidity, but a spirit of power and love and self-control. Do not be ashamed then of testifying to our Lord, nor of me his prisoner, but take your share of suffering for the gospel in the power of God.*[12]

Let us return to our Gospel passage. Even though the Lord found himself in a hostile environment, he went ahead and cured the man with dropsy. Surely he could have waited for a more opportune time and place? But the Lord wanted to teach us to fulfil our obligations regardless of what people may say. Only one thing should matter to us – it is what God wants us to do in any given situation. What other people may think is of only secondary importance. If we should ever restrain ourselves it should be out of prudence rather than out of cowardice. Can we do any less for the One who suffered death for our sake, even death on a cross?

Through our life of coherent faith we can provide others with an immense good. What a joy it is for the Lord to see us living as his faithful disciples without fear of contradictions! Our Lady showed great courage in standing at the foot of the Cross, amidst tremendous hostility and pain. Let us ask her for the gift of such strength.

---

[11] cf Rom 1:16
[12] 2 Tim 1:7-8

THIRTIETH WEEK: SATURDAY

63. THE SEAT OF HONOUR

63.1 The best seats.

Every day provides a wonderful chance to grow in love for the Blessed Virgin. Many Christians all over the world have the custom of honouring Our Lady on Saturdays. She will teach us to foster our humility, which is fundamental to our growth in virtue. Mary *is the gate through which all God's graces pass. She seasons our good actions, imparting an enhanced value to them. She makes our offering even more acceptable to God. Finally, she grants us the title of possessors of the divine Heart. It might even be said that she induces God to be our servant. This is because God has never been able to resist the supplication of a humble heart.*[1] She is so necessary to our salvation that Jesus takes advantage of every opportunity to confer praise and blessings on her.

The Gospel of today's Mass relates that Jesus was invited to a banquet.[2] At the table there were places of greater and lesser honour. The invited guests were no doubt over-anxious as to who would get the better seats. Jesus took notice of their concern. Perhaps He waited for the conclusion of the meal before leading the conversation to a higher plane: *When you are invited by any one to a marriage feast, do not sit down in a place of honour ... But when you are invited, go and sit in the lowest place, so that when your host comes he may say to you, 'Friend, go up*

---

[1] St Jean Vianney, (The Curé d'Ars), *Sermon on the Tenth Sunday after Pentecost*
[2] Luke 14:1; 7-11

*higher'; then you will be honoured in the presence of all
who sit at table with you. For everyone who exalts himself
shall be humbled, and he who humbles himself shall be
exalted.*

Jesus had probably taken a lesser seat at the suggestion
of the host. He lived humility. He also noticed the bad
manners of the other guests. They were totally mistaken in
not giving the best seat to the Lord. The guests should have
been overwhelmed by the presence of Jesus right there in
the room with them. In the course of our lives, how often
do we observe a similar phenomenon? What an enormous
effort people make to be noticed and remembered and
admired! What little effort is put into being close to God!
Today in our time of prayer let us ask the Blessed Virgin to
teach us humility. This is the only way to grow in love for
her Son, to be close to him. Humility always wins the
divine Heart.

*'Quia respexit humilitatem ancillae suae' – because
He has looked graciously upon the lowliness of his
handmaid ... I am more convinced every day that authentic
humility is the supernatural basis for all virtues! Talk to
Our Lady, so that she may train us to walk along that
path.*[3]

63.2 Mary's humility.

Our Lady teaches us the way of humility. This virtue
should not be thought of as an essentially negative
exercise, even though it does involve a denial of one's
pride, a tempering of our ambition and the extinction of our
egotism and vanity. Our Lady did not experience any of
these temptations and yet was blessed with the highest
degree of humility. If we examine the word *humility* we
find it to be derived from the Latin *humus*, which means

---

[3] St. J. Escrivá, *Furrow*, 289

earth, soil, or dirt. *Humility* signifies a recognition of our human origin in the dust of which Adam was made. The virtue of humility, therefore, consists in the living out of a realistic appraisal of our comparative insignificance as creatures who are totally dependent on God.[4] *Humility, by inclining us toward the earth, recognizes our littleness, our poverty, and in its way glorifies the majesty of God ... The interior soul experiences a holy joy in annihilating itself, as it were, before God to recognize practically that He alone is great and that, in comparison with His, all human greatness is empty of truth like a lie.*[5] This self-abnegation in no way impoverishes the soul. It does not limit the legitimate aspirations of the creature. On the contrary, this virtue works to ennoble the soul, giving it wings on which to explore wider horizons.

At the very moment when God chose Our Lady to be his Mother she proclaimed herself to be his handmaiden.[6] When Mary hears those words of praise from Elizabeth, *Blessed art thou amongst women,*[7] she is actually beginning a time where she will put herself at the service of her cousin. Even though she is *full of grace,*[8] Mary keeps the secret to herself. Not even Joseph is told of the mystery. Mary leaves it to divine Providence to find the opportune moment to enlighten him. She sings, for joy, of her wondrous blessings. She gives all the glory to God. For her part, she offers up her littleness and her entire consent.[9] *She knew nothing of her own dignity. Because of this, in her own eyes, she had not the slightest importance. She never depended on herself; she depended entirely on God,*

---

[4] cf R. Garrigou-Lagrange, *The Three Ages of the Interior Life*, II, p. 118

[5] *ibid*

[6] cf Luke 1:38

[7] Luke 1:42

[8] Luke 1:28

[9] cf Luke 1:47-49

on his Will. Thus she was able to judge the extent of her own lowliness, and to understand her own helpless, but, nevertheless, secure condition as a creature: feeling herself incapable of anything and sustained only by the goodness of God. As a result of this selflessness she surrendered herself completely to God and lived solely for him.[10] Mary never sought her own glory, never longed for the best seat at banquets. She never looked for praise on account of her divine Motherhood. She lived solely for the glory of God.

Humility is grounded in the truth, in reality. It is based on the certitude that creature and Creator are separated by an infinite distance. Once it recognizes how God crosses that gulf for the sake of his beloved creatures, the soul grows in humility and gratitude. The more it is elevated before God, the more does the soul understand and appreciate the vastness of this distance. That is why the Virgin was so humble. The *Handmaid of the Lord* is the *Queen of the Universe.* She is the fulfilment of those words of Jesus at the close of today's parable: *He who humbles himself shall be exalted.* The humble person will hear the invitation of the Lord: *Friend, go up higher. Let us learn how to put ourselves at the service of God without condition. Then we will be elevated to undeserved but incredible heights. We shall be participating in the intimate life of God. We shall be 'like Gods'! Yet our progress will have been along the way of humility and docility to the Will of God.*[11]

63.3 Fruits of humility.

Humility leads us to discover that everything we have that is good comes from God, both in the order of nature and in the order of grace. The Psalmist prays: *Behold, thou hast made my days a few handbreadths, and my lifetime is*

---

[10] F. Suarez, *Mary of Nazareth*, pp. 105-106
[11] A. Orozco, *Looking to Mary*, Madrid 1981

as nothing in thy sight. Surely every man stands as a mere breath! Surely man goes about as a shadow! Surely for nought are they in turmoil; man heaps up, and knows not who will gather![12] Our contribution is beset by weakness and error. At the same time, humility has nothing at all to do with timidity. The humble soul rests in the hands of God and is filled with joy and thanksgiving as a result. The saints have been magnanimous people; they have undertaken impressive tasks for God's glory. The humble person is daring because he counts upon the grace of Almighty God. He prays all the time because he is convinced of his radical dependence on God. He lives in constant gratitude for this help. He seems to have a gift for making friends and doing apostolate ... Inasmuch as humility is the foundation for all the virtues, it is especially the foundation for the virtue of charity. To the extent that we forget about ourselves we will be concerned with the welfare of others. St Francis de Sales has written: *Humility and charity are the principal virtues. They act as mother hens while the other virtues follow them like little chicks.*[13] Conversely, pride is the *mother and root* of every sin, including mortal sin.[14] Pride is the greatest single obstacle to the action of divine grace.

Pride and sadness often walk hand-in-hand.[15] Joy is part of the patrimony of the humble soul. *Let us turn our eyes towards Mary. No creature ever surrendered herself to the plans of God more humbly than she. The humility of the 'ancilla Domini' (Luke 1:38), the handmaid of the Lord, is the reason we invoke her as 'causa nostrae laetitiae,' cause of our joy. After Eve had sinned through her foolish desire to be equal to God, she hid herself from*

---

[12] Ps 38:5-6
[13] St Francis de Sales, *Letters,* fragment 17
[14] St Thomas, *Summa Theologiae,* 2-2, q. 162, a. 7-8
[15] cf Cassian, *Conferences,* 16

the Lord and was ashamed: she was sad. Mary, in confessing herself the handmaid of the Lord, becomes the Mother of the divine Word, and is filled with joy. May the rejoicing that is hers, the joy of our good Mother, spread to all of us, so that with it we may go out to greet her, our Holy Mother Mary, and thus become more like Christ, her Son.[16]

---

[16] St. J. Escrivá, *Friends of God,* 109

THIRTY-FIRST SUNDAY: YEAR A

64. YOUR ONE AND ONLY FATHER

64.1 The paternity of God.

Jesus spoke to the crowds and to his disciples about the vanity of the Pharisees: *They do all their deeds to be seen by men ... they love the place of honour at feasts and the best seats in the synagogues, and salutations in the market places, and being called rabbi by men.* But there is only one Teacher and Doctor who is Christ. And there is only one Father, *who is in heaven.*[1] All wisdom springs from Christ. He is *the Teacher who saves, sanctifies and guides, who lives, who speaks, rouses, moves, redresses, judges, forgives, and goes with us day by day on the path of history, the Teacher who comes and will come in glory.*[2] The teaching of the Church is the teaching of Christ. Her teachers are to be measured according to the standard of the Lord.

In like manner, we say that there is one heavenly Father who is the source of all paternity in heaven and on earth: *ex quo omnis paternitas in caelis et in terra nominatur.*[3] God enjoys the fulness of paternity. Earthly fathers participate in this paternity when they contribute to new life. Those people who foster faith in others also partake in this paternity. St Paul writes to the first Christians at Corinth *as my beloved children. For though you have countless guides in Christ, you do not have many*

---

[1] Matt 23:1-12
[2] St John Paul II, Apostolic Exhortation, *Catechesis tradendae,* 16 October 1979, 9
[3] Eph 3:15

fathers. For I became your father in Christ Jesus through the gospel. I urge you, then, to be imitators of me.[4] Those believers knew quite well that in their emulation of Paul they would be imitators of Christ. The Apostle was a faithful reflection of the spirit of the Master and of God's loving concern for them.

The word 'Father' can be used in a meaningful way not only to signify physical paternity but also spiritual paternity. Therefore the Roman Pontiff is justly known as 'the common Father of all Christians'.[5] Whenever we honour our physical parents or our spiritual parents, then we are giving honour and glory to God. Earthly fathers can reflect the divine paternity. So one very good way to live divine filiation is to honour our earthly parents.

64.2 Participation in the divine paternity.

St Paul wrote to the Christians of Galatia with all the tenderness of a father and a mother. He knew of the difficulties they were experiencing in their new-found faith. Paul suffered at his inability to look after these believers who lived so far away: *My little children, with whom I am again in travail until Christ be formed in you!*[6] He compares them to the child in a mother's womb. The Apostle felt a paternal responsibility for his children in need. The Church teaches us that the people who foster our faith through preaching and Baptism should also be seen as parents.[7] We participate in the spiritual paternity of the many Christians whom we have helped to find Christ. Sometimes this formation entails suffering and fatigue. This paternity increases to the degree of one's generosity. God manifests his fatherhood to Christians *like a teacher*

---

[4] 1 Cor 4:14-16
[5] *The Navarre Bible,* note to Eph 3:15
[6] Gal 4:19
[7] cf *Catechism of the Council of Trent,* III, 5, 8

*who instructs not only his disciples but whoever is capable
of understanding him.*[8] This spiritual paternity is an
important part of the earthly reward which God grants to
those who respond to a divine vocation. *He is generous. He
returns a hundredfold; and this is true even of children.
Many deprive themselves of children for the sake of his
glory, and they have thousands of children of their spirit –
children, as we are children of our Father in heaven.*[9]

The Blessed Virgin exercises her maternity over
Christians and over all mankind.[10] Mary will teach us how
to have a magnanimous soul, large enough for the many
people we want to bring to her Son. *Let us remember,
furthermore, that merciful love also means the cordial
tenderness and sensitivity so eloquently spoken of in the
parable of the prodigal son (cf Luke 15:11-32), and also in
the parables of the lost sheep and the lost coin (cf Luke
15:1-10). Consequently, merciful love is supremely indispensable between those who are closest to one another:
between husbands and wives, between parents and
children, between friends; and it is indispensable in
education and in pastoral work.*[11] St Ambrose has written
these bold words which should not fail to make a real
impression on us: *According to the flesh, there is only one
Mother of Christ; according to the faith, Christ is the fruit
of all of us.*[12]

*If we become identified with Mary and imitate her
virtues, we will be able to bring Christ to life, through
grace, in the souls of many who will in turn become
identified with him through the action of the Holy Spirit. If*

---

[8] St Thomas, *Summa Theologiae,* 1, q. 103, a. 6
[9] St. J. Escrivá, *The Way,* 779
[10] cf Second Vatican Council, *Lumen gentium,* 61
[11] St John Paul II, Encyclical, *Dives in misericordia,* 30 November
1980, 14
[12] St Ambrose, *Commentary on St Luke's Gospel,* 2, 26

we imitate Mary, we will share in some way in her spiritual motherhood. And all this silently, like Our Lady; without being noticed, almost without words, through the true and genuine witness of our lives as Christians, and the generosity of ceaselessly repeating her 'fiat,' which we renew as an intimate link between ourselves and God.[13]

64.3 Apostolate and spiritual paternity.

St Paul identified himself with Christ and his teaching: *I am the good shepherd. The good shepherd lays down his life for his sheep.*[14] This explains his *anxiety for all the churches.*[15] He felt responsible for the many souls who had been converted through his preaching. He wanted to keep them on the right path. This was his constant pre-occupation. It was also the cause of his greatest suffering. *Who is weak, and I am not weak? Who is made to fall, and I am not indignant?*[16] St Paul is an exemplary model for every pastor in the Church. The Second Vatican Council has called on all pastors to behave *as fathers in Christ.*[17] They should *take care of the faithful whom they have begotten by baptism and their teaching.*

Our love for those we have brought closer to God is not a mere superficial affection. It is the same love that the Incarnate Son has for us. The Son has given it to us so that we might give it to others. *What does the child's love for others generate in him? The same desire as that of the Son: their sanctification and salvation.*[18] This love will make us more concerned for others in their pursuit of sanctity: good example, fraternal correction when necessary, a word of

---

[13] St. J. Escrivá, *Friends of God*, 281
[14] John 10:11
[15] 2 Cor 11:28
[16] *ibid*, 29
[17] Second Vatican Council, *loc cit*, 28
[18] B. Perquin, *Abba, Father*, p. 278

encouragement, joy, optimism, good advice. Our friends should be able to count on our daily prayer and mortification.

This paternal love *always involves a special readiness to expend oneself and be poured out for the sake of those who come within one's range of activity. In marriage, this readiness, even though open to all, consists mainly in the love that parents give to their children. In virginity this readiness is open to all, who are embraced by the love of Christ the Spouse.*[19] In the case of virginity or apostolic celibacy, the Lord expands the heart of his disciple to a more profound capacity. For generosity to God does not put restrictions on the human heart. Quite the contrary; this disposition enriches and ennobles the potential of our human nature.

As we care for those around us we will come to understand the tender mercy which our Father God has for us. This realization will help us to persevere in our struggle for holiness. We will find new strength to forge ahead.

St Joseph can teach us a great deal about how to look after others. St John Paul II asked: *Why should the 'fatherly' love of Joseph not have had an influence upon the 'filial' love of Jesus? And vice versa, why should the 'filial' love of Jesus not have had an influence upon the 'fatherly' love of Joseph, thus leading to a further deepening of their unique relationship? Those most sensitive to the impulses of divine love have rightly seen in Joseph a brilliant example of the interior life.*[20] Let us learn from the Holy Patriarch and how to grow in love for our neighbour.

---

[19] St John Paul II, Apostolic Letter, *Mulieris dignitatem,* 15 August 1988, 21

[20] *idem,* Apostolic Exhortation, *Redemptoris custos,* 15 August 1989, 27

THIRTY-FIRST SUNDAY: YEAR B

65. TO LOVE WITH DEEDS

65.1 The First Commandment.

The texts of today's Mass show us the continuity between the Old Testament and the New Testament, as well as the perfection of divine Revelation. In the *First Reading* we hear the First Commandment stated in no uncertain terms: *Listen, Israel: The Lord our God is the one Lord. You shall love the Lord your God with all your heart, with all your soul, with all your strength.*[1] This passage was well known to all the Jews. They repeated it twice each day, in their morning and evening prayers.

In the Gospel we read of a scribe's encounter with the Lord.[2] He had been listening to the dialogue between Jesus and the Sadducees. The scribe was impressed by the Lord's response to their questions. He was moved to inquire personally into the teaching of the Master. *Which is the first of all the commandments?* he asked. Jesus paused to give time to this apparently sincere individual, even though He had spoken so harshly of the scribes and the Pharisees in general. At the close of their conversation Jesus has some words of encouragement for the scribe: *You are not far from the kingdom of God.* Jesus is always ready to spend time with souls who express an interest in him. The Lord repeats those words from Holy Scripture: *Listen, Israel: The Lord our God is the one Lord. You shall love the Lord your God with all your heart ...*

This is the first of all the commandments. It is the

---

[1] Deut 6:2-6
[2] Mark 12:28-34

culmination of all the others. But what is
of this love that is insisted on? Cardinal
r Pope John Paul I – wrote the following
n imaginary letter to St Francis de Sales:
*According to you, the man who loves God must board the
ship of God, determined to accept the course set by his
commandments, by the guidance of those who represent
Him, and by the situations and circumstances of life that He
permits. You imagined an interview with Marguerite, when
she was about to embark for the Crusades with her husband,
St Louis IX, King of France: 'Where are you going,
Madame?' 'Where the King goes.' 'But do you know exactly
where the King is going?' 'He has told me in a general way.
I am not concerned to know precisely where he is going,
however: I care only about going with him.' ... That king is
God, and we are all Marguerites if we really love God ...*

*To feel, with God, like a child in its mother's arms;
whether He carries us in his right arm or in his left arm is all
the same: we leave it up to him.*[3] This is the only thing that
matters: to be with Jesus. The place where we are, the pain
that we may suffer, our success or our failure – these must be
accepted as having only a relative importance. If anything,
our circumstances should help us to love God more. We
would do well to follow the poetic counsel of St Teresa:

Let nothing disturb thee;
Let nothing dismay thee:
All things pass;
God never changes.
Patience attains
All that it strives for.
He who has God
Finds he lacks nothing:
God alone suffices.[4]

---

[3] A. Luciani, *Illustrissimi*, pp. 106-107
[4] St Teresa, *Complete Works*, III, Poem IX, p. 288

65.2 Corresponding to the love God has for us.

We pray in today's *Responsorial Psalm*:
I love you, Lord, my strength.
My God is the rock where I take refuge;
my shield, my mighty help, my stronghold.[5]

Psalm 17 can be thought of as a *Te Deum* which David directs to Yahweh. He wants to thank God for all the help he has received throughout his life.[6] The Lord had delivered David from his enemies. He had given him many victories over the Gentiles. After the rebellion of Absalom the Lord had returned Jerusalem to David. He had received assistance from God time after time. This explains David's thanksgiving and his love: *I love you, Lord, my strength.* God had forever been David's ally, his stronghold, his refuge, his shield ... Yahweh always supported him: *He delivered me, because he delighted in me.*[7] Each one of us might repeat these very same words. The determining factor in our lives is the fact that God loves us. This reality should fill the heart with hope and consolation: *In this the love of God was made manifest among us, that God sent his only Son into the world, so that we might live through him. In this is love, not that we loved God but that He loved us and sent his Son to be the expiation for our sins.*[8] The Incarnation is the supreme manifestation of the love of God for each one of his children. This love existed even before the Incarnation, for it springs from the divine nature: *I have loved you with an everlasting love.*[9] This love has preceded Creation itself. St Thomas teaches that this same love is the

---

[5] *Responsorial Psalm,* Ps 17:2-4; 47; 51
[6] cf D. de las Heras, *Ascetical and Theological Commentary on the Psalms,* Zamora 1988
[7] Ps 17:19
[8] 1 John 4:9-10
[9] Jer 31:3

source of every grace we receive.[10]

What is even more amazing is that *God's love has been poured into our hearts through the Holy Spirit, who has been given to us.*[11] St Augustine has written: *We have been loved even when we were most undesirable. God has wanted to grant us something to praise him with.*[12] This same saint has also said: *Listen! Think of the way you were loved when you were not lovable. Listen to how you were loved when you were clumsy and ugly, before there was anything in you that was worthy of love. Because you have been loved first, you have been made worthy of being loved.*[13]

Can we really fail to correspond to such a great love? The Lord asks us to love him with deeds and with the affections of the heart. Every day we should come to know more about the Sacred Humanity of Jesus, which is the best route to the Trinity. *The Father loves the Son.*[14] He loves us too: *Thou hast loved them even as thou hast loved me.*[15] He loves us even more when we love his Son: *He who loves me will be loved by my Father.*[16]

Love is shown in deeds. It is shown in the confidence of children who go to their Father whenever there is a problem. This should be a daily affair. We should have a joyful spirit of thanksgiving for the many blessings we have received. We should give him our loyalty as his sons and daughters, in the place where he has situated us. *In the castle of God we seek to accept any position: cook or scullion, waiter, groom, baker. If it please the King to call*

---

[10] St Thomas, *Summa Theologiae*, 1, q. 43, a. 5
[11] Rom 5:5
[12] cf St Augustine, *Commentary on St John's Gospel*, 102, 5
[13] *idem, Sermon 142*
[14] John 3:35
[15] John 17:23
[16] John 14:21

us to his privy council, we will go, without being too moved, knowing that the recompense does not depend on the position but on the loyalty with which we serve.[17] God wants us to be happy in the place where we are. How many times ought we to tell him: *Lord, I love you ..., but teach me how better, how best to love!*

65.3 Love shown with deeds.

A biographer of St Teresa of Avila provides this illustration of refined charity from the early days of the convent of St Joseph's: *When money ran very short the nuns contented themselves with dry bread, but there was never any lack of wax candles for the altar and everything connected with divine worship was as exquisitely perfect as possible. A visiting priest was scandalized: 'What! A scented towel to wipe one's hands before saying Mass?' Teresa, her fine face lighting up with fervour, took the blame on herself: 'It is from me my daughters get this imperfection. But when I remember the way Our Lord reproached the Pharisee for not receiving him with sufficient honour, I could wish that everything here in the church, from even its very threshold, were perfumed with sweet waters ...'*[18] The Lord greatly appreciates such signs of sincere affection.

We will show our love for the Lord by our faithful fulfilment of his commandments and by the way we carry out our duties in the middle of the world. Our love will be shown by our hatred of sin and of every occasion of sin, by our exercise of charity in little details like a genuflection well made, punctuality in our norms of piety, a loving glance at an image of Our Lady ... It is precisely in the context of these little offerings that we keep alive the flame of our love for the Lord.

---

[17] A. Luciani, *op cit,* p. 106
[18] M. Auclair, *Teresa of Avila,* p. 173

Everything we do for the Lord is of relative importance compared with God's initiative. *God loves me. And John the Apostle writes: 'Let us love God, then, since God loved us first.'* As if this were not enough, Jesus comes to each one of us, in spite of our patent wretchedness, to ask us, as he asked Peter: *'Simon, son of John, do you love me more than these others?'*

This is the moment to reply: *'Lord, you know all things, you know that I love you!'* adding, with humility, *'Help me to love you more. Increase my love!'*[19]

[19] St. J. Escrivá, *The Forge*, 497

THIRTY-FIRST SUNDAY: YEAR C

66. ZACCHAEUS

66.1 The desire to meet Christ. Employing the necessary means.

The readings for today's Mass focus our attention once more on God's infinite mercy. It is logical that the Church should give so much emphasis to this ineffable reality. What could be more important than the mercy of God? It is the fountain of our hope. We creatures are very much in need of divine pardon. We do well to remind ourselves frequently that the Lord is *full of mercy.*

In the *First Reading,* the book of Wisdom presents God's goodness and love for all creation and especially for his sons and daughters: *And how, had you not willed it, could a thing persist, how be conserved, if not called forth by you? You spare all things because all things are yours, Lord, lover of life, you whose imperishable spirit is in all. Little by little, therefore, you correct those who offend, you admonish and remind them of how they have sinned, so that they may abstain from evil and trust in you, Lord.*[1]

The Gospel relates the meeting between Jesus and Zacchaeus.[2] The Lord was passing through Jericho on his way to Jerusalem. At the entrance to the city Jesus had cured a blind beggar of his affliction. The beggar had won his cure because of his faithful, persevering prayer to Jesus, despite the admonitions of the crowd. Once Jesus had entered the city, the streets were thronged with people. There amidst the crowd was *one of the senior tax*

---

[1] Wis 11:25-26; 12:1-2
[2] Luke 19:1-10

collectors, a wealthy man who was well known in Jericho. *The Roman Empire had no officials of its own for the collection of taxes: in each country it used local people for this purpose. These were free to engage agents. The global amount of tax for each region was specified by the Roman authorities; the tax collectors levied more than this amount, keeping the surplus for themselves: this led them to act rather arbitrarily, which was why the people hated them. In the case of the Jews, insult was added to injury by the fact that the chosen people were being exploited by Gentiles.*[3]

St Luke tells us that Zacchaeus *was anxious to see what kind of man Jesus was, but he was too short and could not see him for the crowd.* Yet he eventually got his wish by putting to one side any concern he might have had for public opinion: *so he ran ahead and climbed a sycamore tree to catch a glimpse of Jesus, who was to pass that way.* Zacchaeus must have had a burning desire in his heart for him to put his reputation at risk by this kind of behaviour. What a wonderful example he gives to each one of us who share his longing to see Jesus, to remain with Jesus. Let us take advantage of today's prayer to examine the sincerity and vigour of our desires. St John Paul II commented on this passage: *Do I want 'to see Christ'? Do I do everything 'to see him'? This question, two thousand years later, is as relevant as it was then, when Jesus passed through the cities and villages of his land. It is a relevant question for each of us personally today: Do I want to? Do I really want to? Or do I perhaps rather avoid the encounter with him? Do I prefer not to see him and do I prefer him not to see me (at least in my way of thinking and feeling)? And if I already see him in some way, then do I prefer to see him from afar, not drawing too near, not*

---

[3] *The Navarre Bible,* note to Matt 5:46

venturing before his eyes so as not to perceive too much ...
so as not to have to accept the whole truth that is in him,
that comes from him – from Christ?[4]

66.2 The detachment and generosity of Zacchaeus.

Christ will reward our efforts to draw near to him. As
a matter of fact, He will more than reward us. *When Jesus*
reached the spot he looked up and spoke to him:
'Zacchaeus, come down. Hurry, because I must stay at
your house today'. What tremendous news! The man who
was content to see Jesus from his perch on a tree had been
called by his name. Jesus treated him as an old friend. With
great naturalness, Jesus invites himself to the home of
Zacchaeus. St Augustine has written: *Zacchaeus had given*
so much importance to seeing Jesus pass by that he earned
the pleasure of his company at home.[5] The Master read his
heart. He did not want to forego this unique opportunity.
When Zacchaeus discovers that he is personally loved by
the one who introduces himself as the awaited Messiah, he
is touched to the depth of his soul and opens his heart.[6]
Right away, he wants to be next to the Master: *he hurried*
down and welcomed him joyfully. He had found the
immense joy which accompanies every true encounter with
Jesus.

Zacchaeus received the Master. Now he had
everything. *He was not frightened by the fact that to*
receive Christ into his house might jeopardize, for
example, his professional career, or make difficult some
actions connected with his activity as chief tax collector.[7]
He shows by his actions that he has genuinely embarked on
a new life. He has become another disciple of the Master:

---

[4] St John Paul II, *Address*, 2 November 1980
[5] St Augustine, *Sermon 174*, 6
[6] St John Paul II, *Address*, 5 November 1989
[7] *idem, Address,* 2 November 1980

Look, sir, I am going to give half my property to the poor, and if I have cheated anybody I will pay him back four times the amount. Zacchaeus promised to make restitution beyond what was required by the Mosaic Law.[8] In addition, he gave away half of his fortune to the poor! Once we encounter Christ, He will inspire us to be generous with other people. He will move us to share whatever we have with the needy. Zacchaeus understood that his discipleship required a complete detachment from temporal goods.

My God, I see I shall never accept you as my Saviour unless I acknowledge you as my Model at the same time. Since you yourself chose to be poor, make me love holy poverty. I resolve, with your grace, to live and die in poverty, even though I may have millions at my disposal.[9]

66.3 Jesus is always seeking us out. The virtue of hope in our interior life and apostolate.

When Jesus went into the house of Zacchaeus many people complained at his association with a sinner. *He has gone to stay at a sinner's house.* Meanwhile, the Lord responded to the conversion of Zacchaeus with some of the most beautiful words of the Gospels: *Today salvation has come to this house, because this man too is a son of Abraham; for the Son of Man has come to seek out and save what was lost.* The Lord's call is full of hope. If God should ever permit us to experience difficulties or times of trial, we must trust in the sure knowledge that the Good Shepherd will always be watchful on our behalf. St Ambrose has written: *Of all people to choose from, He singled out the chief of the tax collectors. Who can lose hope for themselves when even such a man attained*

---

[8] Ex 21:37
[9] St. J. Escrivá, *The Forge*, 46

salvation?[10] The Lord never forgets his own.

The figure of Zacchaeus should teach us that no one is beyond the reach of God's grace. As far as the people of Jericho were concerned, Zacchaeus was an outcast from the chosen people. The Gospel even suggests that this was indeed the case.[11] Nevertheless, from the time of his arrival in Jericho, Jesus was thinking of this man. Despite all appearances to the contrary, Zacchaeus had had a great longing to see the Master. According to St Luke's account, he was also prepared to repent of his injustice and dishonesty and make reparation. There are many people not unlike Zacchaeus in our environment. They would like very much to see Jesus. They are waiting for some one to look upon them with compassion and invite them to a new life.

We should never abandon hope in anyone, even when all seems lost. God is omnipotent and his mercy is limitless. It exceeds all human judgment. The story is told of a holy woman who had a remarkable experience of the power of divine mercy. One of her relatives had committed suicide by jumping off a bridge. This woman was so distraught and depressed by the event that she was unable even to pray for her unfortunate kinsman. One day the Lord asked her why she did not pray for this relative as she did for other people. Somewhat taken aback by the words of Jesus, she answered: *You know very well that he jumped off a bridge and killed himself.* Then the Lord responded: *Don't forget that between the bridge and the water I was present.*

This woman had never doubted the divine mercy before. Yet from that day her confidence in the Lord knew no bounds. She prayed from then on for her poor relative with renewed intensity and faith. A similar event took

---

[10] St Ambrose, *Commentary on St Luke's Gospel, in loc*
[11] cf Luke 19:7-10

place in the life of the holy Curé d'Ars.[12] The moral of these accounts is the same: whenever we consider the goodness and compassion of God for his sons and daughters, we will be cured of our earth-bound pessimism.

Let us never doubt the goodness and mercy of God for his children. No matter how extreme the circumstances may be, let us firmly resolve to bring people to Jesus. His mercy will always be greater than our poor human limitations.

---

[12] F. Trochu, *The Curé d'Ars,* p. 180

67. WITHOUT WAITING FOR A REWARD

67.1 Being generous even when our efforts seem in vain.

Jesus had been invited to dine at the home of an important Pharisee.[1] The Master makes use of the image of a banquet to underline our social responsibilities. On this occasion Jesus said to his host: *When you give a lunch or a dinner, do not ask your friends, brothers, relations or rich neighbours, for fear they repay your courtesy by inviting you in return.* Jesus tells him who it is he should be inviting – the poor, the crippled, the lame, the blind ... This is the criteria for the Lord's guest list: *That they cannot pay you back means that you are fortunate, because repayment will be made to you when the virtuous rise again.*[2]

We well know that friends, relatives and wealthy acquaintances will respond to our invitations with invitations of their own. The investment bears immediate fruit. This can, of course, be an upright way of behaving, especially when our goal is to build friendships, increase our apostolate, strengthen family bonds and so on ... Yet in and of itself this is a purely human mode of behaviour. The pagans act in a manner not markedly different. The Lord taught on another occasion: *If you love those who love you, what credit is that to you? For even sinners love those who love them. And if you do good to those who do good to you, what credit is that to you? For even sinners do the same.*[3]

---

[1] cf Luke 14:1
[2] Luke 14:12-14
[3] Luke 6:32

Christian charity goes much further than mere human charity. The Christian gives for love of God without expecting anything in return. The poor and the infirm have nothing to pay you back with. This is the way to see Christ in others. The image of the banquet does not refer exclusively to material goods. It includes whatever one person can offer another: respect, joy, optimism, companionship, attention ...

The story is told that St Martin, before he was baptized a Christian, had a vision of Christ in his sleep. The Lord was wearing the cloak of a Roman official, a garment which Martin had recently given to a poor person. He recognized his old cloak and then heard Jesus saying to the angels round about him: *Martin is only a catechumen, and see how he has given me his cloak.* The saint also heard the Lord say: *Truly, I say to you, as you did it to one of the least of these my brethren, you did it to me.*[4] This dream filled Martin with hope and peace. He was baptized soon thereafter.[5]

We have to be generous without expecting any reward in return. We should give ourselves completely in the apostolate, in almsgiving, in works of mercy, without looking for compensation. Charity does not seek for repayment. *Love does not insist on its own way; it is not irritable or resentful.*[6] We have to sow without yearning for immediate fruits. The Lord teaches us through this parable to give without measure, without any calculation of reward. Then we will receive in abundance.

67.2 The reward for generosity. Giving with joy.

It is better to give than to receive. Generosity expands and rejuvenates the heart. It increases our capacity to love.

---

[4] Matt 25:40
[5] cf P. Croiset, *The Christian Year,* Madrid 1846, IV
[6] 1 Cor 13:5

Egotism has exactly the opposite effect. It impoverishes the heart and limits one's horizons. The more we give, the richer we become. Many times we do not see the fruit of our labours, nor do we reap much in the way of gratitude. But it is sufficient for us to know that Christ is the reason for our generosity. And so, nothing is lost. Listen to this advice from St Augustine: *You do not realize the value of the good you are doing,* he writes, *Think of how the farmer sows without seeing his crop in front of him. He trusts in the land to deliver his harvest. So why don't you put your trust in God? The day of the harvest will surely come. Imagine yourself in the middle of the planting season. The more we sow today, the more we can reap tomorrow. Remember those words of Holy Scripture: 'He that goes forth weeping, bearing the seed for sowing, shall come home with shouts of joy, bringing his sheaves with him' (Ps 125:6).*[7] Charity does not lose heart in the absence of immediate results. Charity knows how to wait. Charity is patient.

Every person has a basic need to give. The person who does not know how to share with others has a handicapped heart. When we truly give to others, our heart is filled with joy. We are then in a better condition to understand the Lord who gave his life as a ransom for us.[8] When St Paul wrote to thank the Philippians for their assistance to him, he stated that their generosity would be richly rewarded: *Not that I seek the gift; but I seek the fruit which increases to your credit.*[9] St Leo the Great has recommended that *whoever gives alms should do so with tranquillity and joy. The less you hold back for yourself, the greater will be your final reward.*[10]

---

[7] St Augustine, *Sermon 102, 5*
[8] cf Matt 20:28
[9] Phil 4:17
[10] St Leo the Great, *Sermon 10 on Lent*

St Paul encouraged the first Christians to be generous in both action and spirit: *For God loves a cheerful giver.*[11] No one can be grateful for a gift or service done grudgingly or with a mean spirit, least of all the Lord. As St Augustine points out, *If you give the bread with a heavy heart, then both the bread and the reward have been lost.*[12] In contrast, the Lord is more than delighted by the person who gives with joy.

67.3 Putting one's talents at the service of others.

There is a tremendous amount of work to be done on behalf of people in need, whether their poverty is material, cultural or spiritual ... Our contribution might be in the form of money, time, companionship, kindness, good manners ... The basic idea is that we should put our God-given talents into the service of others. *Here is an urgent task: to stir up the consciences of believers and non-believers, to gather together men of good will, who are willing to help and to provide the material instruments which are needed for the work with souls.*[13]

Today's Gospel teaches us that it is better to give than to receive. We need to convince ourselves of this truth. We should not pester people to repay us for our 'generosity.' We should give without expecting anything in return. Ordinarily, it is advisable that parents do not remind their children of all that has been done for them. A wife should not prepare for her husband a detailed list of services rendered, nor should the husband imagine that the family is in his debt for his professional work. The total value of our labours is better left in the hands of our Father God. God prefers that we give without rendering a bill or insisting on a receipt, that we give whole-heartedly for his sake alone.

---

[11] 2 Cor 9:7
[12] St Augustine, *Commentary on the Psalms,* 42, 8
[13] St. J. Escrivá, *Furrow,* 24

This should be our attitude even when our good works are taken for granted or misinterpreted. *I saw a blush on the face of that simple man; he was almost in tears. He had contributed generously to good works, giving honest money which he himself had earned, and then he heard that 'good people' had called his actions dishonest.*

With the candidness of a beginner in these battles of God, he murmured: 'They see that I make a sacrifice ... and they still sacrifice me!' I talked to him slowly: he kissed my crucifix, and his natural indignation was changed into peace and joy.[14]

The Lord asks us to understand others, even though others may not understand or even try to understand us. Perhaps sometimes they are like the guests invited to the banquet who could not bring themselves to respond to the Lord's invitation. We have to care for other people despite the possibility that they may ignore us. We should be performing acts of service for people who very probably will not do the same for us. Let us make life pleasant for those around us, no matter how they or others treat us. Everything we do should spring from a largeness of heart. We cannot keep a running tally of credits and debits. People who complain about the ingratitude of others should take a close look at their own rectitude of intention. Generosity should not lead to recriminations and collapse. Selfless sacrifice should make the heart bigger. It should uplift it with the consoling thought that God is pleased with our efforts. *The more generous you are for God, the happier you will be.*[15]

With her *fiat*, Our Mother Mary gave her entire being to the Lord. She will help us to give without the slightest taint or vestige of self-seeking. Mary will show us how to be generous in the thousands of little details of ordinary life.

---

[14] *ibid*, 28
[15] *ibid*, 18

68. CHRISTIAN SOLIDARITY

68.1 Members of one Body.

The Lord has wanted us to be united to him as members of one living body. St Paul teaches us in the *First Reading*: *All of us, in union with Christ, form one body, and as parts of it we belong to each other.*[1] Every Christian is bonded to the Church by the most intimate of ties. The Mystical Body of Christ is much more united than any individual or social being. The very Life of Christ flows through the Body. Each part vitally depends on the others. The smallest injury or pain affects the entire organism. The whole Church labours to heal its every wound. *In the words of St Paul we find again the faithful echo of the teaching of Jesus himself, which reveals the mystical unity of Christ with his disciples and the disciples with each other, presenting it as an image and extension of that mystical communion that binds the Father to the Son and the Son to the Father in the bond of love, the Holy Spirit (cf John 17:21). Jesus refers to this same unity in the image of the vine and the branches: 'I am the vine, you the branches' (John 15:5), an image that sheds light not only on the deep intimacy of the disciples with Jesus but on the necessity of a vital communion of the disciples with each other: all are branches of a single vine.*[2]

Each and every faithful Christian enriches the entire Church through the practice of good works and the pursuit

---

[1] *First Reading,* Year I, Rom 12:5-16
[2] St John Paul II, Apostolic Exhortation, *Christifideles laici,* 30 December 1988, 12

of holiness. At the same time, the individual Christian is enriched in a personal way. *This is the 'Communion of Saints' which we profess in the Creed. The good of all becomes the good of each one and the good of each one becomes the good of all.*[3]

Through our pursuit of sanctity we contribute in a mysterious but real way to the supernatural life of all the members of the Church. We win a continuous stream of supernatural merit for others through our faithful fulfilment of daily duties, through our prayer, through sickness borne with a Christian spirit ... *If you pray for the entire community, then the prayer of the community will come back to you. This is because you form a part of the whole. So you can thus obtain great benefits. The prayer of each member of the People of God is enriched by the prayer of the rest.*[4] Does our meditation on this truth move us to be more generous today? Now?

68.2 Unity in charity.

Every single one of us should feel the duty to contribute to the building up of the Mystical Body of Christ and of human society, of all mankind. We can accomplish this by our determined effort to improve personally, by the active practice of the virtues. *Each one sustains the rest and the rest sustain each one.*[5] This explains why there really is a close connection between the so-called 'personal' and 'social' virtues. *No virtue worthy of its name can foster selfishness. Every virtue necessarily works to the good both of our own soul and to the good of those around us. We are all of us men and all likewise children of God, and we cannot think that life consists in building up a brilliant 'curriculum vitae' or an outstanding*

---

[3] *ibid*, 28
[4] St Ambrose, *Treatise on Cain and Abel*, 1
[5] St Gregory the Great, *Homilies on Ezekiel*, 2, 1, 5

career. Ties of solidarity should bind us all and, besides, in the order of grace we are united by the supernatural bond of the Communion of Saints.[6]

St Paul lists the different gifts and charisms that God has granted us for the service of others. The greatest gift of them all is charity. Through the exercise of charity we can sow good all around us. *Love each other as much as brothers should, and have a profound respect for each other. Work for the Lord with untiring effort and with great earnestness of spirit. If you have hope, this will make you cheerful. Do not give up if trials come; and keep on praying. If any of the saints are in need, you must share with them; and you should make hospitality your special care.*

We may wonder whether we have anything to offer our brothers and sisters in the Faith. Yet the practice of charity for the love of Christ is within reach for everyone who follows the Master. Every single day we give a great deal and we receive a great deal in return. Our life is a continual human and supernatural exchange, a process of giving and taking. How happy the Lord is to see us respond to difficulties in his Church by making acts of loving reparation! How pleased Jesus is to see us make the *needs of the saints* our own! There is no such thing as a weakness or strength in isolation. Both good and evil have important consequences. When we sow a grain of wheat in the earth, it will later bear its full-eared contribution to the crop. The crop will be good if the seed was good. The crop will be bad if the seed was bad. If we seek the Lord with confidence, then our friends too will draw close to him. If we weaken in our struggle, then our friends may fail to advance. The Catechism of the Council of Trent teaches us: *Whatever good and holy works are undertaken by an*

---

[6] St. J. Escrivá, *Friends of God,* 76

*individual benefit everyone. Charity is the virtue that
makes this possible, since it does not seek its own reward.*[7]
We cannot fail to sow good seed. Our life is a great act of
sowing where nothing is lost. We have before us countless
opportunities to do good, to enrich others, to build up the
Mystical Body of Christ. Let us not let slip these
opportunities. We cannot wait for better opportunities
which may never materialize.

68.3 Unity in the Faith. Apostolate.

When God created us, He made us brothers and sisters
of one another. We were created with both familial and
social needs. God also ordered the supernatural world in a
complementary fashion. The Holy Trinity has desired to
save all men by means of human instruments. The divine
plan is accomplished when we carry on a lively personal
apostolate in the middle of the world, in the course of our
normal occupations – in the home, the barber shop, the
office, the bank, the Parliament ... *In the apostolate
exercised by the individual, great riches are waiting to be
discovered through an intensification of the missionary
effort of each of the lay faithful. Such an individual form of
apostolate can contribute greatly to a more extensive
spreading of the Gospel, indeed it can reach as many
places as there are daily lives of individual members of the
lay faithful. Furthermore, the spread of the Gospel will be
continual, since a person's life and faith will be one.
Likewise the spread of the Gospel will be particularly
incisive, because in sharing fully in the unique conditions
of the life, work, difficulties and hopes of their sisters and
brothers, the lay faithful will be able to reach the hearts of
their neighbours, friends, and colleagues, opening them to
a full sense of human existence, that is, to communion with*

---

[7] *Catechism of the Council of Trent*, I, 10, 23

God and with all people.[8] Each member of the body works for the good of the rest of the body. We should seek to keep alive the light of faith in others. This is the greatest good we can offer. St Teresa of Avila has written: *Whenever I read in the lives of saints of how they converted souls, I seem to feel much more devout, more tender, and more envious of them than when I read of all the martyrdoms that they suffered. This is an inclination given me by Our Lord; and I think He prizes one soul, which by his mercy, and through our diligence and prayer, we may have gained for him, more than all the other services we can render him.*[9]

In the course of our apostolate of bringing people to Christ we will surely develop a sincere concern for their temporal needs. How much ignorance, misery and loneliness there is in the world! Our persevering friendship with the Lord will serve to fill our hearts with his mercy. We will be inspired to share whatever we have – talents, time, material goods, joy ... If certain problems are beyond our power to change, at least we can contribute the warmth of our friendship. Let us not abandon the sick, the handicapped, the downhearted, the overwhelmed ... Let us join together with other Christians and people of good will for the sake of the common good. We have to put aside any causes of separation or conflict, thereby imitating the first Christians. They astounded the pagan world with the testimony of their mutual love and solidarity. Even in the face of stark poverty, they practised the *New Commandment*: *A new commandment I give to you, that you love one another; even as I have loved you, that you also love one another. By this all men will know that you are my disciples, if you have love for one another.*[10] True love can overcome any obstacle.

---

[8] St John Paul II, *loc cit,* 28
[9] St Teresa, *Foundations,* 1, 7
[10] John 13:34-35

69. THE FRUITS OF THE CROSS

69.1 Understanding suffering.

The Cross is the essential mark of a Christian because it was the vehicle for the world's Redemption. The Lord frequently used the expression *bear the cross* to summarize in this figure the Christian meaning of pain and contradiction. In today's Gospel Jesus emphasizes this truth: *Whoever does not bear his own cross and come after me, cannot be my disciple.*[1] On another occasion the Lord said to the crowd: *If any man would come after me, let him deny himself and take up his cross daily and follow me.*[2] (Under the Roman occupation crucifixion and its preliminaries were a fairly common occurrence, and the people of Palestine knew exactly what this figure of speech meant.)

Suffering is a universal reality that has many manifestations. St Paul compared suffering to the pains of a woman in childbirth: *We know that the whole creation has been groaning in travail together until now.*[3] We know from experience that all creatures suffer in one form or another, both rich and poor, young and old, men and women. It is for this reason that St Peter warns the first Christians: *Beloved, do not be surprised at the fiery ordeal which comes upon you to prove you, as though something strange were happening to you.*[4] It almost seems as if pain is an integral part of human nature. Nevertheless, the Faith teaches us that suffering first came into the world as a result of sin. In his

---

[1] Luke 14:27
[2] Luke 9:23
[3] Rom 8:22
[4] 1 Pet 4:12

infinite goodness, God created man to live in his presence free from sin. God intended man to move immediately from a temporal paradise to the ultimate joy of eternal bliss.

The sin of Adam wrecked this wonderful scheme of things that had been promised. This sin has been transmitted from one generation to another. It brought pain and death into world. Yet the Lord became man and experienced both these evils, as well as human limitations such as hunger, thirst and exhaustion. Jesus accepted suffering to the greatest degree possible in his Passion and Death. He thereby converted human suffering and pain into an immense good. What is more, we Christians are invited to participate in the Passion of Jesus through our experience of suffering and through voluntary mortification.[5]

Faith in sharing in the suffering of Christ brings with it the interior certainty that the suffering person 'completes what is lacking in Christ's afflictions'; the certainty that in the spiritual dimension of the work of Redemption he is serving, like Christ, the salvation of his brothers and sisters. Therefore, he is carrying out an irreplaceable service. In the Body of Christ, which is ceaselessly born of the cross of the Redeemer, it is precisely suffering permeated by the spirit of Christ's sacrifice that is the irreplaceable mediator and author of the good things which are indispensable for the world's salvation. It is suffering, more than anything else, which clears the way for the grace which transforms human souls. Suffering, more than anything else, makes present in the history of humanity the powers of the Redemption.[6]

We can collaborate with Christ's salvific mission by accepting the pains, contradictions and difficulties of ordinary life. The Lord permits suffering in our life for the purpose of our sanctification and that of the entire Church. Pain has thus acquired a deeper meaning. We can become

---

[5] cf Col 1:24
[6] St John Paul II, Apostolic Letter, *Salvifici doloris,* 11 February 1984, 27

active participants in the Lord's work of salvation. By
sanctifying our suffering here on earth, we will win for
ourselves the glory of Heaven.[7]

69.2 The fruits of the Cross in Christian life.

The tree of the Cross is replete with fruits. Suffering
can help us become more detached from the things of the
earth, such as physical health. *Deus meus et omnia! My
God and my all!*[8] This was the exclamation of St Francis of
Assisi. When we have the Lord in our lives, we can
weather any storm. *Blessed is he who can say whole-
heartedly: My Jesus, You are everything to me!*[9]

Trials and tribulations offer us a chance to make
reparation for our past faults and sins. St Augustine teaches
that on such occasions the Lord comes to us like a
physician to heal the wounds left by our sins. Tribulation is
the divine medicine.[10] Suffering moves us to have recourse
to the divine mercy. As the Lord said through the lips of
the Prophet Hosea: *Come, let us return to the Lord; for He
has torn, that He may heal us.*[11] Jesus himself invites and
urges us to rely on him in times of trial: *Come to me, all
who labour and are heavy laden, and I will give you rest.*[12]
How many times have we experienced his consolation!
Truly Christ is *our refuge and our strength.*[13] In the midst
of life's many tempests, Christ is our one safe harbour.

Contradictions, sickness and pain challenge us to
acquire and live many virtues such as faith, fortitude, cheerfulness, humility, docility to the divine Will ... Countering

---

[7] cf A. Tanquerey, *The divinization of suffering*
[8] St Francis of Assisi, *Opusculi,* Pedeponti, 1739, I
[9] St Alphonsus Liguori, *Abbreviated sermons,* 43, 1
[10] cf St Augustine, *Commentary on the Psalms,* 21, 2, 4
[11] Hos 6:1
[12] Matt 11:28
[13] Ps 45:2

these problems also allows us to earn a great deal of super-natural merit. *When you think of all the things in your life which remain worthless for not having been offered to God, you should act like a miser, anxious to get hold of every opportunity you can and to make use of each and every suffering. For if suffering is always there for us poor creatures, what can it be but stupidity to waste it?*[14] Surely there are periods in our life when there is no shortage of such opportunities. Let us not fail to convert them into spiritual goods.

Sorrow that is borne with a Christian spirit is a wonderful road to holiness. Our interior life virtually needs contradictions and obstacles if it is to prosper. St Alphonsus Liguori has stated that just as a fire needs contact with air, so does the soul require tribulation if it is to be perfected.[15] Even temptations can serve to renew our love for the Lord. *No temptation has overtaken you that is not common to man. God is faithful, and He will not let you be tempted beyond your strength, but with the temptation will also provide the way of escape, that you may be able to endure it.*[16] Any trial that is borne with the Lord's help will bring us added blessings.

69.3 Going to Jesus and Mary in sickness and in times of trial.

Whenever we are beset by difficulties let us go to Jesus with confidence. In the words of the Psalmist, let us pray thus: *In my distress I cry to the Lord, that He may answer me.*[17] *For we are powerless against this great multitude that is coming against us. We do not know what to do, but our eyes are upon thee.*[18] We will always find

---

[14] St. J. Escrivá, *Furrow,* 997
[15] St Alphonsus Liguori, *op cit,* p. 823
[16] 1 Cor 10:13
[17] Ps 119:1
[18] 2 Chron 20:12

peace and strength in the merciful Heart of Jesus. Let us not be the ones to hear that tender rebuke of the Master: *O man of little faith, why did you doubt?*[19] St Teresa of Avila once exclaimed: *But oh, God! What little power has the strongest opposition when Thou, Lord, art pleased to bestow courage.*[20] Let us ask Jesus for this *courage* when we run up against suffering and trial.

With the Lord by our side, there is nothing we cannot do. Separated from him, we will collapse almost immediately. *With so good a Friend and Captain ever present, Himself the first to suffer, everything can be borne. He helps, He strengthens, He never fails, He is the true Friend.*[21] With Jesus, we will learn how to weather difficulty with joy and good humour. In this we shall be imitating the lives of the saints.

The Lord will also show us how to view our problems with objectivity . We should take care to see things as they really are. We should not invent problems because of a lack of humility or an over-active imagination. There are many times when a contradiction can be born quietly without making a big issue of it and allowing it to develop into some kind of Greek tragedy. As we finish our meditation today, let us go to the Blessed Virgin. She will teach us how to bring fruit from difficulty.

'Cor Mariae perdolentis, miserere nobis!' Invoke the Heart of Holy Mary, with the purpose and determination of uniting yourself to her sorrow, in reparation for your sins and the sins of men of all times. And pray to her – for every soul – that her sorrow may increase in us our aversion from sin, and that we may be able to love the physical or moral contradictions of each day as a means of expiation.[22]

---

[19] Matt 14:31
[20] St Teresa, *Foundations*, 3, 4
[21] *idem, Life*, 22, 9
[22] St. J. Escrivá, *op cit*, 258

70. THE FRIEND OF SINNERS

70.1 It is the sick who have need of healing. Jesus has come to cure them.

We read in the Gospel for today's Mass that the tax collectors and sinners were drawing near to Jesus to hear his teaching. *And the Pharisees and the scribes murmured, saying, 'This man receives sinners and eats with them'.*[1]

His whole life testifies to the fact that Jesus was without sin. He even challenges his adversaries: *Which of you convicts me of sin?*[2] *A man 'without sin', Jesus Christ during his whole life is engaged in a struggle against sin, and against all that gives rise to sin, beginning with Satan who is the 'father of lies' ... (cf John 8:44).*[3]

Even though fully engaged in this struggle against sin and its deepest causes, Jesus does not distance himself from sinners. On the contrary, He approaches each and every person. During his earthly life He was to be found habitually in the company of *sinners*. This is the frequently-repeated testimony of the Evangelists. It is confirmed by the conduct of the enemies of Christ, who went so far as to label him as one who was the *friend of tax collectors and sinners.*[4] The life of Christ is a continual reaching out to souls in need. We may recall the case of Zacchaeus. Jesus went over to him and announced: *Zacchaeus, make haste and come down; for I must stay at*

---

[1] Luke 15:1-10
[2] John 8:46
[3] St John Paul II, *Address*, 10 February 1988
[4] cf Matt 11:18-19

your house today.[5] In a similar way He accepted all kinds of social invitations so that he might reach out to his lost sheep. St Mark recalls the day Jesus called Matthew to follow him. He then went to eat at Matthew's house; there *many tax collectors and sinners were sitting with Jesus and his disciples.*[6] When the Pharisees expressed their indignation at this sight Jesus answered them: *Those who are well have no need of a physician, but those who are sick ...*[7] Jesus appears most appealing to us as He sits in the company of sinners and outcasts. He offers his joy and peace to every individual. The supreme manifestation of Christ's love for mankind is of course his sacrifice on Calvary. Yet even in the course of his going up to Jerusalem, Jesus showed an ongoing interest in the affairs of men. He gives life and meaning to that moving pledge: *For the Son of man also came not to be served but to serve ...*[8] Jesus intends to serve everyone, not only those who follow his call, but even those who seem completely hardened to the divine Word.

In today's meditation we should resolve to increase our confidence in Jesus. Our confidence should increase with the dimensions of our difficulties. This is especially true if we should happen to get a real sense of our own limitations. St Teresa has written: *Ah, how hard a thing am I asking of Thee, my true God! I ask Thee to love one who loves Thee not, to open to one who has not called upon Thee, to give health to one who prefers to be sick and who even goes about in search of sickness.*[9]

---

[5] cf Luke 19:1-10
[6] cf Mark 2:13-15
[7] cf Mark 2:17
[8] Mark 10:45
[9] St Teresa, *Exclamations of the Soul to God,* 8

70.2 The lost sheep. God's joy at the sight of our daily conversions.

Jesus was always with people, even after day was done.[10] There were many times when they would not let him rest.[11] His life was totally given over to his brothers and sisters.[12] He loved them with the greatest love that the world has ever seen.[13] He was *raised for our justification*[14] and ascended into Heaven to prepare a place for us.[15] He sent us the Holy Spirit to forestall our becoming orphans.[16] The more we have needed him, the more He has been among us. This divine mercy exceeds anything the human mind can imagine. This superabundant mercy *is proper to God and is the greatest manifestation of his omnipotence.*[17]

The Gospel for today's Mass continues with that most beautiful parable of God's solicitude for sinners: *What man among you with a hundred sheep, losing one, would not leave the ninety-nine in the wilderness and go after the missing one till he found it? And when he found it, would he not joyfully take it on his shoulders and then, when he got home, call together his friends and neighbours? 'Rejoice with me', he would say 'I have found my sheep that was lost'.* St Gregory the Great has commented: *Supreme Mercy will not abandon us even when we abandon him.*[18] The Good Shepherd never gives up on a single one of his sheep.

The Lord also wants to express heaven's joy at the conversion of a single sinner: *In the same way, I tell you,*

---

[10] cf Mark 3:20
[11] cf *ibid*
[12] cf Gal 2:20
[13] cf John 13:1
[14] cf Rom 4:25
[15] cf John 14:2
[16] cf John 14:18
[17] St Thomas, *Summa Theologiae*, 2-2, q. 30, a. 4
[18] St Gregory the Great, *Homily 36 on the Gospels*

there is rejoicing among the angels of God over one repentant sinner. St Gregory the Great would here compare the Lord to a commander engaged in battle. The commander values the repentant soldier who, having once fled from the field of battle, returns to the thick of the fray with renewed determination. This soldier is of more use to his General than his compatriot who never fled but never displayed any valour either. Similarly, the farmer prizes the land that produces thorns and wheat far higher than any barren ground.[19] God is delighted when we begin again after small defeats, when we struggle to correct defects in our character, when we fight to overcome any sense of discouragement. He values the way we pursue our studies, the effort we put into doing our work well, our striving to begin and end on time, our avoiding making unnecessary phone calls ... God sees our generosity in those small habitual mortifications which no one else notices. This daily struggle keeps us close to the Lord.

Whenever we begin again, each and every day, our heart is filled with joy – and so is the Master's. Every time we allow Jesus to enter into our life we please God immeasurably. The Sacred Heart of Jesus *overflows with joy whenever a lost soul has been recovered. Everyone has to join in the celebration – all the angels and the saints in Heaven as well as the just on earth, for this wonderful development.*[20] *Rejoice with me ...,* Jesus invites us. There is also a special joy whenever we bring a friend or relative back to the sacrament of pardon. Here Jesus awaits his brothers and sisters with open arms.

The Church sings in an ancient hymn: *Lord, you have worn yourself out looking for me: O that your labours will not have been in vain!*[21]

---

[19] cf *idem, Homily 34 on the Gospels,* 4

[20] G. Chevrot, *The Gospel in the open air*

[21] Hymn, *Dies irae*

70.3 Jesus Christ comes out to look for us.

Jesus Christ comes in search of us. He took upon himself all the evil of the world and yet He seeks us out. He knows better than anyone the foul nature of sin; nevertheless *He is not angry. The Just One presents to us the moving image of divine mercy ... To the Samaritan woman, the one who had six husbands, He says simply: 'Give me to drink' (John 3:4-7). Christ knows what the soul can become – it can be a reflection of God himself. What possibilities there are! God wants only good things for the soul.*[22]

Jesus draws near to the sinner with real respect. His words are always an expression of love for the individual. Let us meditate on the words He spoke to the woman caught in adultery: *Go, and do not sin again.*[23] Then we have the case of the paralytic who was brought to the Lord by his friends. Jesus tells him: *Take heart, my son; your sins are forgiven.*[24] In his dying hour, Jesus assures the Good Thief: *Truly, I say to you, today you will be with me in Paradise.*[25] These are words of pardon, of joy, of consolation. With what great love Christ awaits us in each Confession! If only we could realize how much He wants us to return to him!

The Good Shepherd has such a burning desire to reclaim his lost sheep that He goes out to find it himself. As soon as He finds his lost sheep, He showers it with affection. He carries it home upon his shoulders. Having returned safely to the flock, *the lost sheep brings a great peace to the fold, even to the watch dog.*[26] The divine attentions lavished upon the repentant sinner are truly

---

[22] F. Sopena, *Confession*

[23] John 8:11

[24] Matt 9:2

[25] Luke 23:43

[26] F. Sopena, *op cit*

overwhelming.

God's pardon does not consist only in forgiveness and in the blotting out and forgetting of our sins. This would certainly be a great deal. But along with the remission of our sins God infuses new life into the soul. He strengthens it and fortifies it. That which was dead is converted into being itself a source of life. Barren ground is made to bear abundant fruit.

In today's Gospel reading the Lord teaches us about the immense value of a single soul. He is ready to do anything for the sake of one conversion. How happy He is at the sight of a renewed friendship! We should share the Lord's concern that no one stray from his flock. If anyone has wandered away from the Lord's fold we must pray that he or she will return as soon as possible.

71. TO PRAY FOR THE DEAD

71.1 Praying for the souls in Purgatory, a time-honoured Christian custom.

During this month of November the Church acts like the good Mother she is by directing many suffrages to God for the souls in Purgatory. She invites us to pray about the meaning of our life in the light of eternity.

The liturgy reminds us that the souls in Purgatory eagerly await this work of charity engaged in by their brothers and sisters on earth. These prayers can help to shorten a soul's time of purification. We see, therefore, that death does not undo the bonds of Christian community. As a matter of fact, death can serve to perfect those bonds. Union with Christ is stronger than any physical separation. The Holy Spirit binds all Christians together. The love and fidelity of the Church on earth wins joy and relief for those souls who long to enter into eternal bliss. This stream of charity rises up to the benefit of the souls in Purgatory even when we are distracted. Yet when we make sure to direct these prayers for this intention, we can work an even greater good.[1]

The Second Book of the Maccabees recounts a great battle in which the Israelites were victorious over the Idumeans thanks to God's assistance. On the following day Judas Maccabeus ordered that his fallen soldiers were to be brought back to be buried with their kinsmen. It was thereupon discovered, however, that *under the tunic of every one of the dead they found sacred tokens of the idols*

---

[1] cf M. Schmaus, *Dogmatic Theology*, II, p. 503

of Jamnia, which the law forbids the Jews to wear. And it became clear to all that this was why these men had fallen. So they all blessed the ways of the Lord, the righteous Judge, who reveals the things that are hidden; and they turned to prayer.[2] Judas took up a collection and received two thousand drachmas of silver which he sent *to Jerusalem to provide for a sin offering.* The inspired author concludes: *In doing this he acted very well and honourably, taking account of the resurrection. For if he were not expecting that those who had fallen would rise again, it would have been superfluous and foolish to pray for the dead. But if he was looking to the splendid reward that is laid up for those who fall asleep in godliness, it was a holy and pious thought. Therefore he made atonement for the dead, that they might be delivered from their sin.*

The Second Vatican Council has declared: *Fully conscious of this communion of the whole Mystical Body of Jesus Christ, the pilgrim Church from the very first ages of the Christian religion has cultivated with great piety the memory of the dead, and because it is a holy and wholesome thought to pray for the dead that they may be loosed from their sins, also offers suffrages for them.*[3] As St Ephraim, an early Doctor of the Church, has observed: *If the army of Maccabeus was able to expiate the sins of their fallen comrades, imagine how much more supernatural good is done by the priests of the Son through their prayers and holy offerings!*[4]

The first Christians were so accustomed to praying for the dead that this feature was soon included in the Holy Mass. Accordingly, we read in the First Eucharist Prayer: *Remember also, Lord, your servants N. and N. who have gone before us with the sign of faith and rest in the sleep of*

[2] cf 2 Mac 12:39-46
[3] Second Vatican Council, *Lumen gentium,* 50
[4] St Ephraim, *Testamentum,* 78

peace. Grant them, O Lord, we pray, and all who sleep in Christ, a place of refreshment, light, and peace. In the Second Eucharistic Prayer we have this petition: *Remember also our brothers and sisters who have fallen asleep in the hope of the resurrection, and all who have died in your mercy: welcome them into the light of your face.*[5] *This prayer for the suffering Church in Purgatory seems to have come down to us from the Roman liturgy to judge by some of the expressions used in the Latin text. The opening words of some of these can be seen in inscriptions on tombs in the Catacombs – 'With the sign of the faith'; 'in the sleep of the just'; 'a place of refreshment'. These and similar expressions are found in the Catacombs of Priscilla and in the accounts of the martyrdom of Saints Perpetua and Felicity.*[6]

This teaching, that we the living have the power to intercede for the dead, has always been held by believers. It was solemnly declared a truth of the Faith by the Second General Council of Lyons in 1274.[7]

Let us take advantage of today's time of meditation to pray for the souls of the faithful departed, souls that continue to depend on our assistance. Let us examine the quality of our prayer for these souls. We should remember that this is a wonderful work of mercy that is most pleasing to the Lord.

71.2 Our prayers and good works can shorten the time souls spend in Purgatory.

O God, thou art my God, I seek thee, my soul thirsts for thee; my flesh faints for thee, as in a dry and weary land where no water is.[8] *My soul thirsts for God, for the*

---

[5] *Roman Missal,* Eucharistic Prayers I and II
[6] F. Suarez, *The Sacrifice of the Altar,* London 1990
[7] Second General Council of Lyons, Dz 464 (858)
[8] Ps 62:1

living God. When shall I come and behold the face of God?[9]
We can imagine that these inspired words summarize the
continual prayer of the holy souls in Purgatory.

Sins involve a double disorder. First of all, they are an
offence against God. They make the soul his enemy. In the
case of mortal sin the soul makes a radical choice contrary
to its final end. Mortal sin merits eternal separation from
God. For the forgiveness of mortal sins committed after
Baptism we must have recourse to the sacrament of
Confession.

In addition to the loss of friendship with God, sin also
damages the sinner himself. It hampers one's personal
growth and that of the community of the faithful. *For sin
has diminished man, blocking his path to fulfilment.*[10] *A
soul that lowers itself through sin drags down with itself
the Church and, in some way, the whole world.*[11] The soul
suffers from the consequences of sin even after receiving
sacramental absolution. Besides his particular penance, the
sinner needs to make reparation in this life through good
works and indulgences. The Church *believes in the
possibility of a purification for the elect before they see
God, a purification altogether different from the punishment of the damned. This is what the Church means when
speaking of Hell and Purgatory.*[12] In the Book of
Revelation Heaven is described in these terms: *But nothing
unclean shall enter it.*[13]

The holy souls in Purgatory experience a great sorrow
as well as a great joy. They know that they are confirmed

---

[9] Ps 41:2
[10] Second Vatican Council, *Gaudium et spes,* 13
[11] St John Paul II, Apostolic Exhortation, *Reconciliatio et paenitentia,*
2 December 1984, 16
[12] S.C.D.F., *Letter to Bishops on Certain Questions concerning
Eschatology,* 17 May 1979, 7
[13] Rev 21:27

in grace and are *en route* to Heaven. We can assist their progress by means of our prayers, especially in the Holy Mass, which is the supreme offering. The Church has established the Feast of All Souls as a means of encouraging the faithful to persevere in this regard. Throughout the month of November the Church reminds us of our responsibility to pray for the faithful departed. We are encouraged to seek indulgences on their behalf. The Lord has deigned that any good work which is performed by a person in the state of grace can benefit our deceased brothers and sisters. We apply these merits in the form of suffrages. Each day that passes offers many possibilities for this work of mercy: whenever we receive the sacraments, especially Holy Communion; when we pray the Holy Rosary; when we offer up physical suffering and the contradictions of daily life. Here we have a wonderful motive for doing our professional work or studies in the best manner possible.

71.3 Indulgences.

Indulgences are of special importance in our effort to assist the souls in Purgatory. The Church teaches that indulgences can be gained in two forms – plenary and partial. There are certain indulgences which are intended exclusively for the benefit of the faithful departed. The Church grants partial indulgences for many works of piety such as mental prayer, the reciting of the *Angelus* or *Regina Coeli,* the use of religious objects which have been blessed by a priest (i.e., a crucifix, a rosary, a scapular, a medal ...). If the object has been blessed by the Roman Pontiff or a prelate the owner may gain a plenary indulgence on the feast of Saints Peter and Paul by making an act of faith. Other opportunities for partial indulgences include the reading of Sacred Scripture, the praying of the *Memorare,* spiritual communions, the litanies, praying the

Adoro te devote, the *Salve,* prayers for the Pope, retreats ... Certain acts may earn us a plenary indulgence if we fulfil the ordinary requirements: these are normally Confession, Holy Communion and prayer for the Roman Pontiff. The plenary indulgence remits all the temporal pain caused by sin. Such an indulgence may be obtained by having the family pray the Rosary, by making *the Way of the Cross,* by praying for one half hour before the Blessed Sacrament, by visiting a cemetery to pray for the dead in the first eight days of November ...

According to the teachings of St Thomas Aquinas[14] and many other theologians, the holy souls in Purgatory are able to pray for their loved ones on earth. These souls do not know the concrete needs of the living, unless God wants them to, but they do pray for our intentions in general. They pray for us and we pray for them. We do this even though we do not know whether these souls remain in Purgatory or have ascended to Heaven. The holy souls in Purgatory can no longer merit graces, but can intercede for us before the Lord. They can help us a great deal in our daily lives, *providing special assistance to those who were their friends on earth.*[15] They certainly want their friends to attain salvation. During this month of November let us resolve to pray for the holy souls in Purgatory by offering up many suffrages on their behalf.

---

[14] cf St Thomas, *Summa Theologiae,* 1, q. 89
[15] M. Schmaus, *op cit,* p. 507

72. SERVING ONE MASTER

72.1 Being wholly committed to God.

It was the custom in ancient times that the servant belonged entirely to his master. This dedication would brook no other occupation or allegiance to any other lord. It is in this context that we may better understand the words of Jesus in today's Gospel: *No servant can serve two masters; for either he will hate the one and love the other, or he will be devoted to the one and despise the other. You cannot serve God and mammon.*[1]

Our commitment to follow Christ ought to encompass all our actions. We should not live a double life with one part of it allocated to God and another part to our own separate concerns. Everything in our life should be oriented to God – our studies, our professional work, our ordinary affairs ... This is because we belong wholly to God. It follows that we should direct all our activity and love to our heavenly Father. *Spirituality can never be understood as a collection of pious and ascetical practices set alongside a collection of rights and duties appropriate to one's circumstances; on the contrary, to the extent that they respond to God's will, these have to be taken up and vitalised supernaturally through some particular form of developing a spiritual life – this development has to be achieved precisely in and through those circumstances of life.*[2]

Our desire to love and serve the Lord should be a

---

[1] Luke 16:13-14
[2] Bl. A. del Portillo, *On Priesthood,* p. 68

unifying theme in everything we do. When we make our morning offering we give the Lord possession over all the joys and sorrows of the coming day. Nothing lies outside of this gift or should be held back from it. *In our ordinary behaviour we need a power far greater than that of the legendary King Midas, who changed all he touched to gold.*

We have to change, through love, the human work of our usual working day into the work of God: something that will last for ever.[3]

What is the material we are to offer up? It is the little concerns of daily life, the care we show for the implements and equipment we use at work, our serenity in the face of unexpected setbacks, our punctuality, the effort we put into fulfilling our duties ... All of this ought to be ordered to the Lord and offered to him. He will give these tiny offerings a great and lasting value.

72.2 Unity of life.

Our determination to live as children of God should be realized in ordinary life: at work, in the home and among our friends. At every hour of the day we should be striving to be men and women of faith, that is to say, to be full-time Christians. We cannot confine our relationship with God to those few moments we spend inside a church. We have to live out our friendship with God in the middle of the world, in our workplace, in our recreation, in social gatherings. We should reflect Christ's love in everything we do. This was St Paul's counsel to the first Christians: *So, whether you eat or drink, or whatever you do, do all to the glory of God.*[4] St Basil has commented on this passage: *When you sit down at table, pray. When you eat your bread, give thanks to God who is so generous. If you have some wine,*

---

[3] St. J. Escrivá, *The Forge*, 742
[4] 1 Cor 10:31

remember that he has created it to bring us merriment and comfort in affliction. When you are getting dressed, give thanks to the one who gave you these clothes. When you look up at the firmament and behold the beauty of the stars above, fall down at the feet of God and adore his infinite Wisdom that is manifest in all Creation. Do the same at sunrise and sunset, when you are asleep and when you are awake. Give thanks to the God who created all this wonder for your benefit, so that you might know, love and praise his name.[5] All noble realities should serve to bring us to the Lord.

When someone is in love he thinks of his beloved twenty-four hours a day. This is the kind of love we should have for Jesus Christ. It should constitute the essence of our being, the driving force behind all our actions. He is our one and only Lord. He is the one we want to glorify through our work well done. Jesus is our inspiration when we try to practise the social doctrine of the Church, when we strive to protect the environment ... This all-embracing outlook leads a Christian to make an effort to be cordial and optimistic, to be punctual at work, to make good use of time, to overcome temptations to laziness ...

If our love of God is authentic, it will shine out from and be appreciable in every aspect of our existence. We know and respect the legitimate autonomy of temporal affairs with respect to religion. There are no *Catholic answers* to society's problems *per se*. That having been said, we also recognise that Christians and Christianity belong in all facets of society as a leavening influence.[6] This explains why the apostolate is a spontaneous activity which emanates from Christians in every imaginable kind of circumstances. Apostolate is nothing more than the outpouring of one's love for God.

---

[5] St Basil, *Homilia in Julittam martirem*
[6] cf I. Celaya, *Unity of Life and Christian fullness,* Pamplona 1985

72.3 Rectitude of intention.

St Luke tells us that Jesus preached these words not only to his disciples but also to his bitterest critics: *The Pharisees, who were lovers of money, heard all this, and they scoffed at him.* We may observe this phenomenon even in our own day. *The Pharisees jeered at what Jesus was saying, in order to justify their own attachment to material things; sometimes people make fun of total commitment to God and detachment from material things because they themselves are not ready to practise virtue: they cannot even imagine other people really having this generosity: they think they must have ulterior motives.*[7]

Jesus does not hesitate to denounce the hypocrisy of the Pharisees: *You are those who justify yourselves before men, but God knows your hearts; for what is exalted among men is an abomination in the sight of God.* The Lord uses a very strong term to describe the conduct of the Pharisees: *abomination. The original Greek word means worship of idols, and, by derivation, the horror this provoked in a true worshipper of God. So the expression conveys God's disgust with the attitude of the Pharisees who, by wanting to be exalted, are putting themselves, like idols, in the place of God.*[8] Jesus warns his followers about 'false shepherds' *who like to go about in long robes, and love salutations in the market places and the best seats in the synagogues and the places of honour at feasts, who devour widow's houses and for a pretence make long prayers ...*[9] Such people have no love for God.

God can read men's hearts. We should strive to rectify our intention many times each day. We need to reject any temptation to vanity and vain-glory which might cheapen our total dedication to God's service. All our actions

---

[7] *The Navarre Bible,* note to Luke 16:13-14
[8] *ibid,* note to Luke 16:15
[9] Luke 20:45-47

should be oriented to the glory of God. To illustrate this idea, Pope John Paul I when he was still Patriarch of Venice recalled a little story about a cook (It was from Tolstoy): *Outside the kitchen door the dogs were lying. John (the cook) slaughtered a calf and threw the entrails into the yard. The dogs fell on them, ate them, and said: 'He's a good cook; he cooks well'. Some time after that, John was shelling peas, peeling onions; he threw the husks into the yard. The dogs rushed over, sniffing scornfully, they said: 'The cook is spoiled; he's worthless now'. John, however, was not upset by this opinion; he said, 'It is the master who must eat and enjoy my meals, not the dogs. The master's appreciation is enough for me'.*[10]

If we are completely dedicated to God's service we will not pay the slightest attention to idle criticism of what we do. We want to please God more than anyone else. With the passing of time we will see that this selfless behaviour is one of the best contributions we can make to the welfare of other people.

Our Mother Mary will teach us how to live entirely for God's glory. Don't ever lose the supernatural point of view. Correct your intention as the course of a ship is corrected on the high seas – by looking at the star, by looking at Mary. Then you will always be sure of reaching harbour.[11]

---

[10] A. Luciani, *Illustrissimi,* p. 12
[11] St. J. Escrivá, *The Forge,* 749

THIRTY-SECOND SUNDAY: YEAR A

73. THE PARABLE OF THE TEN VIRGINS

73.1 Christ is the bridegroom who is coming.

In today's Gospel, Jesus makes reference to social customs with which his listeners were perfectly familiar.[1] This is why the Lord does not spend time on general explanations. *Among the Jews,* for example, *it was common practice for women to be given in marriage at a very young age ... It was then the custom to celebrate the betrothal. After this first stage of the marriage the woman, who was quite often still an adolescent, would continue to reside with her parents for some further time. Then, after some months, say, had passed, the wedding ceremony itself would take place. It consisted of the solemn transfer of the betrothed from her parents' house to the residence of her spouse, to their new home, in order to initiate their life in common as husband and wife. This ceremony was frequently celebrated in the late afternoon. Such was the case of the wedding feast in Our Lord's parable.*

The transfer of the betrothed from her parents' home to her new abode always took on a specific character of solemnity, and would be conducted in a festive mood that in small villages would spread and reach out to all of its inhabitants. An entourage would then be organized to accompany the betrothed during the transfer. This escort was usually composed of the bride's friends. The transfer itself would begin the moment the spouse arrived to fetch his beloved. Upon arrival at her new house, those who had just escorted the betrothed couple would join the other

---

[1] Matt 25:1-13

invited guests in the bridegroom's house, and the festivities of the wedding would immediately commence once the gates had been shut.[2]

Today's parable concerns a bridegroom who happens to arrive unexpectedly in the middle of the night. The question is whether the escorting bridal party is ready to receive him. The bridegroom is Christ. He will come again in some future time. The virgins represent mankind. Some are vigilant while others have been careless. The time of waiting is a symbol of our life on earth. The arrival of the bridegroom and the wedding celebration signify the inauguration of the state of eternal bliss in the company of Christ.[3] The parable brings to our mind that fateful moment when God calls each and every soul to himself. This is the moment of death. Following God's judgment, some souls enter fully into God's presence while others find themselves excluded from the wedding feast forever.[4] The Old Testament teaches us about death: *If a tree falls to the south or to the north, in the place where the tree falls, there it will lie.*[5] At the time of death, the state of the soul is fixed for all eternity.

The ten virgins of the parable were entrusted with a serious responsibility. They were to await the coming of the bridegroom, who was expected at any moment. Five of the virgins took their assignment seriously. They did everything possible to be on guard: *The wise took flasks of oil with their lamps.* The other five virgins were foolish: *They took no oil with them.* They became caught up in other concerns and neglected their primary duty of welcoming the bridegroom. We cannot forget that God is our ultimate end. Everything else is of secondary

[2] F. Suarez, *The Afterlife*, p. 83
[3] cf F. Prat, *Jesus Christ*, Mexico 1946
[4] cf Luke 13:25; Matt 7:23
[5] Eccl 11:3

importance, whether it be success, fame, poverty or wealth, health or sickness ... These temporal concerns can be beneficial to us – but only if they help us to keep our lamps burning. We need to maintain a good supply of oil, of good works, especially works of charity.

Let us remember to keep our eyes fixed on the Lord and not become distracted by things of secondary importance. St Josemaria Escrivá had the habit of saying, *There are things we fail to remember, not because we have short memories but because we are short of love.*[6] We have to be careful not to fall into carelessness and lukewarmness in our spiritual life. We cannot allow ourselves to become attached to the things of this world to the detriment of the things of God. *When we arrive in the presence of God He will ask us two questions: if we are members of the Church and if we have laboured for the Church. Everything else is of little value, whether we have been rich or poor, famous or unknown, highly thought of or disgraced, whether we have been sick or healthy, whether we have a good or bad name.*[7] Let us examine the motivations for our conduct. Do we seek the Lord in what we do, or do we seek ourselves? If Christ were to call us to himself today, would he find us vigilant, our lives replete with good works?

73.2 The particular judgment.

But at midnight there was a cry, 'Behold, the bridegroom! Come out to meet him'.

In the immediate aftermath of our death we will encounter God in the *particular judgment.* At that time we will see before our eyes all the good works and sins of our past life. How delighted we will be to review those many acts of faith we have made to Jesus Christ present in the Tabernacle! We will take comfort in the countless

---

[6] Quoted by F. Suarez, *The Afterlife,* p. 89
[7] St J. H. Newman, *Sermon for Septuagesima Sunday: Judgment*

genuflections we have made with love, in the many hours of work we have offered to God, in the smile and good cheer we have brought to our workplace, in the efforts we have made to bring a friend to the sacrament of Confession. We will also contemplate with joy our participation in works of mercy, our prompt recourse to the sacrament of Confession whenever we have sinned ... And yet, how much sorrow we will have at the sight of those occasions when we have offended God, those hours of work or study which we failed to sanctify, those lost opportunities for apostolate with our friends ... What a shame to behold so little generosity and attention to God's grace! How grieved we will be by so much neglect!

It is Christ who will judge us. *He is the one ordained by God to be judge of the living and the dead.*[8] As St Paul reminded the first Christians at Corinth: *For we must all appear before the judgment seat of Christ, so that each one may receive good or evil, according to what he has done in the body.*[9] If we are faithful in the little things of each day, then we will have no fear in coming before Christ. On the contrary, we will feel an immense peace and joy at the prospect of this encounter. St Teresa of Avila provides this moving description of that moment: *For it will be a great thing at the hour of death, when we are going we know not whither, to realize that we shall be judged by One whom we have loved above all things, and with a passion that makes us entirely forget ourselves. Once our debts have been paid we shall be able to walk in safety. We shall not be going into a foreign land, but into our own country, for it belongs to him whom we have loved so truly and who himself loves us.*[10]

Right after death the soul will find itself within the

---

[8] Acts 10:42
[9] 2 Cor 5:10
[10] St Teresa, *The Way of Perfection,* 40, 8

banqueting hall or outside the bolted doors forever. St Thomas Aquinas teaches that the soul is lifted up or brought down by its merits or the lack thereof (i.e., sins, omissions, failings ...).[11]

Let us meditate today on the condition of our soul. Are we making a sincere effort to rectify our intention, to sanctify our daily work? Let us take to heart those words of today's *Responsorial Psalm*: *O God, thou art my God, I seek thee, my soul thirsts for thee; my flesh faints for thee, as in a dry and weary land where no water is.*[12] My Lord, I am convinced that the things of this world have no meaning unless they lead me to you.

73.3 Preparing ourselves for judgment: the examination of conscience.

There are things we fail to remember, not because we have short memories but because we are short of love. The person in love does not forget. As long as the Lord is our highest priority, we will remain vigilant. We will not become distracted. We will heed the Lord's counsel at the conclusion of this parable: *Watch therefore, for you know neither the day nor the hour.*

To prepare ourselves for this encounter with the Lord we need to acquire a profound understanding of ourselves. We are now living in a time of testing. As St Paul warned the Corinthians: *If we judged ourselves truly, we should not be judged.*[13] Let us not be taken by surprise, then, by our past faults and failings. We need to make a daily *examination of conscience* so that we can identify our trouble spots and apply the necessary remedy. *So, to make sure that there are no surprises at the last moment, I often like to take this book in my own hands – this book that I'm*

---

[11] St Thomas, *Summa Theologiae,* Suppl., q. 69, a. 1
[12] *Responsorial Psalm,* Ps 62:1
[13] 1 Cor 11:31

*in the process of writing, whether I like it or not, as long as
I live. I like to take it up and open it and let my soul read it.
And that's very easy and very useful to do at the time of
prayer or of examining one's conscience. I like to think
that every day of my life is a page of this book; and when I
begin a day what I have in front of me is a blank sheet of
paper. And sometimes I run quickly through the pages
already written, and allow the blank pages to pass through
my fingers – the pages which are as yet unwritten because
the time hasn't yet come. And in a funny way some pages
always stay on my fingers: they are the days I don't know
whether I'll get to write, because I don't know when the
Lord will show me this book for the last time.*[14]

We do not know how much time is left to us to correct
and improve the manuscript of our book. The examination
of conscience helps us to ask pardon for our mistakes. This
exercise also gives us the time to rectify our behaviour. If
we examine our conscience each night we will be well
prepared to make a good Confession. It is through frequent
consideration of the eternal truths of death and judgment
that we prevent ourselves from being deceived by our pride
and by the attractions of this world.

*The 'name of the game' is examination of conscience.
You will gain a great deal of knowledge of yourself and of
your character and your life. You will teach yourself to
love God and to pin down your desire to make good use of
your days by making clear, effective resolutions ... Friend,
take up the book of your life and turn its pages every day,
so that you won't be surprised when it is read on the day of
your particular judgment, and won't be ashamed when it is
published on the day of the universal judgment.*[15] The Lord
calls those unprepared virgins *foolish*. There is no greater
act of stupidity than to put at risk one's eternal happiness.

---

[14] S. Canals, *Jesus as Friend*, p. 74
[15] *ibid*, p. 76

As we finish this time of prayer let us go to Our Lady, *Mother of mercy, our life, our sweetness and our hope.* She will help us to purify our life so that it may bear abundant fruit. We should pray to our Guardian Angel as well: *The Guardian Angel always accompanies us as our principal witness. It is he who, at your particular judgment, will remember the kind deeds you performed for Our Lord throughout your life. Furthermore, when you feel lost, before the terrible accusations of the enemy, your Angel will present those intimations of your heart – which perhaps you yourself might have forgotten – those proofs of love which you might have had for God the Father, God the Son, God the Holy Spirit.*

That is why you must never forget your Guardian Angel, and that Prince of Heaven shall not abandon you now, or at that decisive moment.[16]

---

[16] St. J. Escrivá, *Furrow,* 693

74. THE VALUE OF ALMSGIVING

74.1 To give with whole-hearted generosity.

The readings for this Sunday's Mass sing the praises of two holy women. In the *First Reading* the Lord sends Elijah to Zarephath in Sidon to be cared for by a widow.[1] Even though the region was suffering from a great famine, the widow gave food to the Prophet. She trusted in the promise of Elijah: *The jar of meal shall not be spent, and the cruse of oil shall not fail, until the day that the Lord sends rain upon the earth.* This is, in fact, what happened. Jesus would later recall this episode in his preaching.[2]

In today's Gospel we find Jesus seated in the Temple watching the people put money into the treasury.[3] *Many rich people put in large sums. And a poor widow came, and put in two copper coins, which make a penny.* From a purely human point of view the widow's gift was of minute importance. Yet as far as Jesus was concerned this gift had an enormous significance. As the poor widow was leaving the Temple, Jesus pointed her out to his disciples: *Truly, I say to you, this poor widow has put in more than all those who are contributing to the treasury. For they all contributed out of their abundance; but she out of her poverty has put in everything she had, her whole living.* The Lord praises acts of generosity for the sake of divine cult as well as all gifts made with a pure heart. Jesus values the disposition of the giver more than the gift received. He

---

[1] 1 Kings 17:10-16
[2] cf Luke 4:25 ff
[3] Mark 12:41-44

looks not only *on the amount given, but into the very heart of the donor.*[4]

Almsgiving is a work of mercy that is most pleasing to the Lord. Jesus will reward our generosity far more than we can imagine. The holy Curé d'Ars would often say: *A house of charity will never be poor.* The habitual practice of giving alms summarizes a good many of the virtues and draws down divine favour. Holy Scripture frequently encourages this expression of generosity as in the Book of Tobias: *Do not turn your face away from any poor man, and the face of God will not be turned away from you. If you have many possessions, make your gift from them in proportion; if few, do not be afraid to give according to the little you have. So you will be laying up a good treasure for yourself against the day of necessity. For charity delivers from death and keeps you from entering the darkness; for all who practice it, charity is an excellent offering in the presence of the Most High.*[5] Should anyone ignore this teaching they will most certainly experience the fate of that selfish rich man who was sent to Hell for his cold indifference to Lazarus.[6]

As the poor widow returned to her home she must have been filled with a great joy. What a surprise must have lain in store for her at the end of her life! She would finally see the look of love which Jesus had cast upon her that ordinary morning in the Temple. God watches all of our actions with interest and affection.

74.2 Almsgiving manifests our love and generosity towards the Lord.

Authentic almsgiving springs from a merciful heart. We feel moved to provide some relief for those in need, to

---

[4] St John Chrysostom, *Homilies on the Epistle to the Hebrews,* 1
[5] Tob 4:7-11
[6] cf Luke 16:19 ff

contribute to the upkeep and expansion of the Church, to support whatever good works benefit the common good. By giving alms we can become detached from the things of this world. Almsgiving can dispose the heart to be more attentive to the Will of God. *True detachment leads us to be very generous with God and with our fellow men. It makes us actively resourceful and ready to spend ourselves in helping the needy. A Christian cannot be content with a job that only allows him to earn enough for himself and his family. He will be big-hearted enough to give others a helping hand both out of charity and as a matter of justice.*[7]

The first Christians showed their fraternal love in an exemplary way. They assumed responsibility for the material needs of all the members of the community of believers. This explains why there are so many references to generosity in the *Acts of the Apostles* and the Epistles of St Paul. The Apostle gave the Christians at Corinth specific guidelines to follow: *On the first day of every week, each of you is to put something aside and store it up, as he may prosper ...*[8] It was not a matter of simply giving what was left over, what was extra. The idea was to give even in spite of grave economic difficulties. This was the situation of the churches in Macedonia. St Paul lauds the heroic spirit of generosity of these believers: *for in a severe test of affliction, their abundance of joy and their extreme poverty have overflowed in a wealth of liberality on their part. For they gave according to their means, as I can testify, and beyond their means, of their own free will, begging us earnestly for the favour of taking part in the relief of the saints.*[9] These Christians not only gave donations to the Church in Jerusalem, but also *gave themselves to the Lord*

---

[7] St. J. Escrivá, *Friends of God*, 126
[8] 1 Cor 16:2
[9] 2 Cor 8:2-4

and to us by the will of God.[10] Perhaps St Paul is here referring to their contribution to the work of evangelization. St Thomas has commented on this passage: *This indeed should be the order of charity: first of all, man must be acceptable to God. If a person is not living so as to please God, then his gifts will not be acceptable to the Lord.*[11] Almsgiving, in whatever form it may take, is an expression of our love and generosity to the Lord. Our charity does not consist principally in the value of our gifts but, rather, in the love for God we bear in our soul. *Our humble offering may be insignificant in itself, like the oil of the widow of Zarephath or the coins of the poor widow in the Temple. Yet our offering becomes pleasing in the eyes of God thanks to our union with Jesus.*[12]

74.3 God rewards our generosity beyond all telling.

Almsgiving attracts the blessing of God and produces abundant fruits. It can heal the wounds of sin.[13] Almsgiving is *the shield of hope, the teacher of faith, the medicine for sin. It lies within the reach of every person who wants to practise it. Charity has its own grandeur, while at the same time being easy to accomplish. It brings no risk of persecution. It is the crown of peace and truth, the greatest gift from God. It is necessary for the weak and glorious for the strong. Through almsgiving the Christian attains grace, wins pardon from Christ our judge and makes God in some way a debtor.*[14]

We have to give alms with rectitude of intention. Our heart must be directed to God much as in the case of the

---

[10] 2 Cor 2:5
[11] St Thomas, *Commentary on the Second Letter of Paul to the Corinthians*, 2, 5
[12] St John Paul II, *Homily in Barcelona*, 7 November 1982
[13] cf *Catechism of the Council of Trent*, IV, 14, 23
[14] St Cyprian, *On good works and almsgiving*, 27

poor widow in the Temple. We ought to be generous, especially with those things which are most dear to us. It may just happen that someone has a greater need for them than we do. *Don't be mean and grudging with people who, without counting the cost, have given of their all, everything they have, for your sake. Just ask yourselves, how much does it cost you – in financial terms as well – to be Christians?*[15] Our gifts have to spring from a compassionate heart, one that is filled with love for God and other people. Over and above the material value of our gifts we need to keep in mind the importance of our interior disposition. The spirit of true charity is intimately interconnected with a joyful heart. Today's *Liturgy of the Hours* includes that homage of St Paul to the power of God: we are treated *as sorrowful, yet always rejoicing; as poor, yet making many rich; as having nothing, and yet possessing everything.*[16] Later in that same Epistle, St Paul makes sure to remind us: *For God loves a cheerful giver.*[17]

God will reward our generosity beyond all telling. Whatever we have given away in time, energy, resources..., the Lord will return to us a hundredfold. *The point is this: he who sows sparingly will also reap sparingly, and he who sows bountifully will also reap bountifully.*[18] This was how God multiplied the food which the widow of Zarephath put at the disposition of Elijah. In like manner Jesus multiplied the loaves and the fishes.[19] *Thus says the Lord: ... You gave me a little, I returned to you a great deal. You gave me temporal goods and I responded with celestial goods. You gave me things that will perish, I gave*

---

[15] St. J. Escrivá, *loc cit*

[16] *Liturgy of the Hours,* Antiphon of Lauds, 2 Cor 6:10

[17] 2 Cor 9:7

[18] 2 Cor 9:6

[19] cf John 6:9

you what is eternal ...[20] St Teresa has affirmed: *For I know now, by experience in many things, that if from the first I resolutely persevere in my purpose, even in this life His Majesty rewards it in a way which he only understands who has tried it.*[21]

Let us ask Our Lady to give us a generous heart. We have to give things, but we also have to give ourselves. Let us not be miserly with our time, our wealth, our energy. There are so many needy people and worthy apostolic ventures awaiting our assistance. The Lord beholds our compassion in much the same way that he observed the poor widow in the Temple. He has a look of love for both of us.

---

75. THE DIGNITY OF THE HUMAN BODY

75.1 The resurrection of the body as declared by Jesus.

The liturgy for this Sunday's Mass brings our attention to one of the truths of the Faith listed in the Creed: the resurrection of the body and the reality of life everlasting. In the *First Reading* we find the mother and seven sons who preferred death to betraying God's Law by eating swine's flesh.[1] After having been tortured by the king's servants, the fourth son declared: *One cannot but choose to die at the hands of men and to cherish the hope that God gives of being raised again by him.*

The Old Testament speaks in a number of places of the hope of resurrection. At the time of Our Lord's life most of the Jews believed in this truth except the Sadducees, who also denied the immortality of the soul, the existence of angels and the power of divine Providence.[2] In today's Gospel passage we read how some Sadducees approached Jesus with the intention of tripping him up.[3] According to the Levirate law, if a man were to die without issue, then his brother would be under obligation to marry the widow and provide him with descendants.[4] The Sadducees cunningly pose for Jesus a situation of this kind affecting a man with seven brothers: *In the resurrection, therefore, whose wife will the woman be? For the seven had her as wife.* By means of this far-fetched dilemma, the Sadducees attempt

---

[1] 2 Mac 7:1-2; 9-14
[2] cf J. Dheilly, *Biblical Dictionary,* 'Sadducees'
[3] Luke 20:27-38
[4] cf Deut 25:5 ff

to ridicule the doctrine of the resurrection of the body.

Ignoring the patent absurdity of this problem Jesus goes on to reaffirm the doctrine of the resurrection of the body. He reveals to us some of the characteristics of life after death: people *neither marry nor are given in marriage ... because they are equal to angels and are sons of God, being sons of the resurrection.* Jesus then argues from Sacred Scripture, using a quotation from Moses.[5] In conclusion, Our Lord tells the Sadducees: *Now, He is not God of the dead, but of the living; for all live to him.* Moses called the Lord the God of Abraham, the God of Isaac and the God of Jacob, all of whom were long dead by that time. The message is that these patriarchs were physically dead but not spiritually dead. They lived on in God because of their immortal souls. They only awaited the resurrection of their bodies.[6] The Sadducees were silenced. *They no longer dared to ask him any question.*

We Christians profess in the *Creed* our hope in the resurrection of the body and life everlasting. *The importance of this final article of the baptismal Creed is obvious: it expresses the goal and purpose of God's plan, the unfolding of which is described in the Creed. If there is no resurrection, the whole structure of faith collapses, as St Paul states so forcefully (cf 1 Cor 15). If the content of the words 'life everlasting' is uncertain for Christians, the promises contained in the Gospel and the meaning of creation and Redemption disappear, and even earthly life itself must be said to be deprived of all hope (cf Heb 11:1).*[7] We have to remind ourselves of the crucial fact that our soul is immortal, that it will be united to our physical body at the end of time, that the union of our body and soul

---

[5] Ex 3:2; 6

[6] cf *The Navarre Bible,* note to Luke 20:27-40

[7] S.C.D.F., *Letter to Bishops on Certain Questions concerning Eschatology,* 17 May 1979

has an eternal destiny. Everything which we undertake in this life ought to be oriented to this momentous truth: *We belong to God completely, soul and body, flesh and bones, all our senses and faculties.*[8]

75.2 Our body is destined to give glory to God once it is united with our soul.

Sacred Scripture teaches us that death was not part of God's original plan for mankind. It is a consequence of the sin of our first parents.[9] Through his resurrection Christ demonstrated his power over death: *Mortem nostram moriendo destruxit et vita resurgendo reparavit. God our Father, by raising Christ your Son you conquered the power of death and opened for us the way to eternal life.* So sings the Church in the *Opening Prayer* for Easter. With his resurrection Christ has robbed death of it's sting. He has made his death an act of redemption. It is through him and with him and in him that our bodies will rise again on the last day. They will be united with our souls, which if we have been faithful will have been giving glory to God since the time of our death if there was no need for purification.

To resurrect means to lift up something that has fallen down,[10] to bring again to life that which was dead, to restore to life that which has succumbed to dust. The Church has always taught that the resurrection of Christ is the foundation of our Faith. She has also consistently believed in the resurrection of our physical bodies *in which we live, subsist and move.*[11] The soul will then be re-united with its proper body. The Magisterium has stated quite

---

[8] St. J. Escrivá, *Friends of God,* 177

[9] cf Rom 5:12

[10] cf St John Damascene, *On the orthodox Faith,* 27

[11] cf J. Ibanez – F. Mendoza, *The divine and Catholic faith of the Church,* Madrid 1978

precisely that men and women *will be resurrected in their own physical bodies.*[12] Our meditation on these teachings may help us to grasp the great dignity of each person, a dignity which is distinct and superior to that of any other being in Creation. Man not only has free will, but *he is the divine masterpiece, made in the image and likeness of his Creator, gifted with an immortal soul by divine gift.*[13] Man is superior to all other creatures because he can be a temple of the Holy Spirit, as long, that is, as he is in the state of grace. St Paul insisted with the early Christians on the importance of this idea: *Do you not know that your body is a temple of the Holy Spirit within you, which you have from God?*[14]

Our bodies are anything but some kind of prison for our souls. *We look forward, as St Paul says, to the redemption of our bodies; they are not encumbrances which we drag about with us, they are first-fruits of eternity, entrusted to our keeping*[15] The soul and body belong to one another in a natural relationship. God made the one for the other. St Cyril of Jerusalem exhorts us: *Respect your body since it is your good fortune to be a temple of the Holy Spirit. Do not stain your body ..., and if perchance you have stained it, purify it right away through penance. Clean it while you still have time.*[16]

75.3 Our divine filiation, which has commenced in the soul through grace, will be consummated by the glorification of the body.

The exalted dignity of man was already present from the moment of Creation. It acquired its full expression with

---

[12] *ibid*
[13] St Cyril of Jerusalem, *Catechesis,* IV, 18
[14] 1 Cor 6:19
[15] R. A. Knox, *The Hidden Stream,* p. 196
[16] St Cyril of Jerusalem, *Catechesis,* IV, 25

the Incarnation of the Word.[17] Each and every man has been *included in the mystery of the Redemption, and with each one Christ has united himself for ever through this mystery. Every man comes into the world through being conceived in his mother's womb and being born of his mother, and precisely on account of the mystery of the Redemption is entrusted to the solicitude of the Church. Her solicitude is about the whole man and is focussed on him in an altogether special manner. The object of her care is man in his unique unrepeatable human reality, which keeps intact the image and likeness of God himself.*[18]

St Thomas teaches that our divine filiation, commenced in the soul through grace, will be consummated by the glorification of the body ...; just as our soul has been redeemed from sin, so too our body will be redeemed from the corruption of death.[19] The Angelic Doctor goes on to cite the words of St Paul to the Philippians: *Our commonwealth is in heaven, and from it we await a Saviour, the Lord Jesus Christ, who will change our lowly body to be like his glorious body, by the power which enables him even to subject all things to himself.*[20] The Lord will transform our weak and corruptible bodies into a glorious state. We must never be lacking in respect for our body. Neither should we worship it as if it were our final abode. We have to exercise control over our body through mortification and penance, otherwise it will *turn traitor.*[21]

Once again, we turn to St Paul for guidance: *You are not your own; you were bought with a price. So glorify God in your body.*[22] St John Paul II preached on this topic:

---

[17] Tertullian, *On the Resurrection,* 63

[18] St John Paul II, Encyclical, *Redemptor hominis,* 4 March 1979, 13

[19] St Thomas, *Commentary on the Epistle to the Romans,* 8, 5

[20] Phil 3:20-21

[21] cf St. J. Escrivá, *The Way,* 196

[22] Cor 6:19-20

Purity, as the virtue, that is, the capacity of 'controlling one's body in holiness and honour' (cf 1 Thess 4:4), together with the gift of piety, as the fruit of the dwelling of the Holy Spirit in the 'temple' of the body, brings about in the body such a fulness of dignity in interpersonal relations that God himself is thereby glorified. Purity is the glory of the human body before God. It is God's glory in the human body, through which masculinity and femininity are manifested.[23]

Our Mother Mary was assumed body and soul into Heaven. She will remind us at every opportunity that our body has been created to give glory to God, both now here on earth and for evermore in Heaven.

---

[23] St John Paul II, *Address,* 18 March 1981

76. THE IMPORTANCE OF GIVING GOOD EXAMPLE

76.1 People who are susceptible to bad example. Scandal.

Today's Gospel contains some of the strongest words ever uttered by Our Lord: *Temptations to sin are sure to come; but woe to him by whom they come! It would be better for him if a millstone were hung round his neck and he were cast into the sea, than that he should cause one of these little ones to sin.*[1] He concludes with this warning: *Take heed to yourselves.* St Matthew provides the setting for these words.[2] The Apostles had been importuning Our Lord to say who would be the greatest in the Kingdom of Heaven. Jesus called a child to his side so as to emphasize his teaching: *Unless you turn and become like children, you will never enter the Kingdom of Heaven. Whoever humbles himself like this child, he is the greatest in the Kingdom of Heaven.* As Jesus looked upon this little one, He must have had in mind many others who would lose their innocence as a result of scandal. It seems as if Our Lord was revealing the burden of this weight to his disciples in those words: *Take heed to yourselves.*

To give scandal is to be responsible for another's failure or spiritual ruin because of one's words, acts or omissions.[3] When Jesus speaks of *these little ones,* he has in mind all children. In their innocence they reflect the

---

[1] Luke 17:1-3
[2] cf Matt 18:1-6
[3] St Thomas, *Summa Theologiae,* 2-2, q. 43, a. 1

image and likeness of God. Yet Jesus was also thinking of the many, many people who, for one reason or another, are especially liable to be affected by bad example. Few sins are as serious as these since *they tend to undermine the greatest work of God which is the Redemption of souls. They kill the soul by alienating it from the life of grace, something which is more valuable than physical life. Scandal provokes a multitude of sins.*[4] How precious must man be in the eyes of the Creator, if he 'gained so great a Redeemer' (Hymn 'Exultet' from the Easter Vigil), and if God 'gave his only Son' in order that man 'should not perish but have eternal life' (cf John 3:16).[5] We can never lose sight of the inestimable value of each person: Christ has died for each and every one. *For every soul is a wonderful treasure; every man is unique and irreplaceable. Every single person is worth all the blood of Christ.*[6]

76.2 We have to give good example to the people around us.

Following the Master's lead, St Paul asked the first Christians to avoid giving scandal particularly to those who will have had little formation: *Only take care lest this liberty of yours somehow become a stumbling block to the weak.*[7] We exercise a great influence on those among whom we live. We have to give good example to the people around us.

The Lord preached his doctrine fearlessly, even though he knew the Pharisees would take offence.[8] This was a case of false scandal. It arises when people are not willing to accept the truth and look for contradictions or excuses

---

[4] *Catechism of St Pius X,* 418
[5] St John Paul II, Encyclical, *Redemptor hominis,* 4 March 1979, 10
[6] St. J. Escrivá, *Christ is passing by,* 80
[7] 1 Cor 8:9
[8] cf Matt 15:12-14

instead. We are familiar with this behaviour in our own
day. People pretend to be *scandalized* because a couple has
many children, because they are happy with what God has
given them, because they have chosen to live their
Christian vocation to the full. A faithful Christian will find
that his behaviour is frequently at odds with a pagan
environment. He or she will *scandalize* many people. St
Peter recognized this clash of values when he described
Christ using words from the Prophet Isaiah: *A stone that
will make men stumble, a rock that will make them fall (Is
8:14-15).*[9] This was also Simeon's prophecy to the Blessed
Virgin.[10] We should not be surprised if the same thing
happens to us. Nevertheless we should try as much as
possible to practice charity with other people. We should
not seek out confrontation. Let us remember that the Lord
sent Peter to pay the Temple tribute, even though he was
not obliged to do so. Jesus did not want to shock the tax
collectors who considered the Lord an exemplary Jew.[11]
We will never be lacking in opportunities to imitate the
Master in this regard. *I don't doubt your good intentions. I
know you act in the presence of God. But – and there is a
'but'! – your actions are witnessed or may be witnessed by
men who judge by human standards ... And you must set a
good example for them.*[12]

Scandal becomes especially deleterious when it
emanates from people who enjoy a certain measure of
public authority or prestige: parents, teachers, government
officials, writers, artists ... and from anyone who has
responsibility for forming others. St John of Avila has
commented on this sad state of affairs: *If the simple folk
live in a lukewarm state, the situation is regrettable. They*

---

[9] cf 1 Pet 2:8
[10] cf Luke 2:34
[11] cf Matt 17:21
[12] St. J. Escrivá, *The Way*, 275

hurt themselves, but a remedy is possible. If, however, it is the teachers who are lukewarm, then the Lord's warning must needs be considered: 'Woe to him by whom they come!' Great harm can come from their lukewarmness, because it will easily spread to others and dampen their spiritual fervour.[13]

The Lord wants us to be aware of the good and the evil we can do by the words we speak. *Can you know what damage you do throwing stones with your eyes blind-folded?*

Neither do you know – because you're blinded by thoughtlessness or passion – the harm you produce, at times very great, dropping uncharitable comments that to you seem trifling.[14] The person who is responsible for scandal has the obligation to repair the damage he has done. This obligation is one of charity and, at times, one of justice. Public scandal calls for public reparation. And because it is typically impossible to make sufficient reparation, there remains the obligation of further prayer and penance. A contrite soul will always find the most charitable way to repair the damage done.

This Gospel passage should move us to say to the Lord: Forgive me, Jesus, if I have ever given scandal to your *little ones,* even without knowing it. We can ask for pardon for these hidden sins in Confession. Then we must resolve to be more prudent in response to the Lord's warning: *Take heed to yourselves.*

76.3 Our obligation to make reparation for the many offences against God.

Our conduct should lead people to say what was said of Our Lord: *He went about doing good ...*[15] Let us fill our

---

[13] St John of Avila, *Sermon 55*
[14] St. J. Escrivá, *The Way,* 455
[15] Acts 10:38

life with works of charity and mercy. Normally, these works will consist of very tiny details: making an effort to smile, to give encouragement, cheerfully assisting our colleagues at work, forgiving and forgetting the mistakes of our neighbours ... This behaviour is a real testimony we can give to the world. It is by our charity that people will recognise us as disciples of Christ.[16] We may also see this charity as a measure of our union with God.

Scandal damages and destroys. Charity, on the other hand, builds up and heals. Charity is the path that leads to the Lord. Our good example provides a worthy antidote to the evil that many people disseminate in this life, sometimes without even being aware of it. Our good example will prepare the ground for a most fertile apostolate. *Let us never lose sight of the fact that Our Lord has promised his effectiveness to friendly faces, to cordiality, to good manners, and to clear, persuasive words which direct and form without wounding: 'Blessed are the meek, for they shall inherit the earth'. We should never forget that we are men and women relating to other men and women, even when we want to do good to souls. We are not angels: therefore our appearance, our smile, our manners, are factors which condition the effectiveness of our apostolate.*[17]

While scandal tends to alienate souls from God, charity inspires souls to seek the gates of Heaven. St Teresa has observed: *I think He (God) prizes one soul which by his mercy, and through our diligence and prayer, we may have gained for him, more than all the other services we can render him.*[18] Let us never be indifferent in the face of evil. We have to respond to moral sickness with a spiritual remedy: with many acts of reparation to the

[16] cf John 13:35
[17] S. Canals, *Jesus as Friend,* p. 41
[18] St Teresa, *Foundations,* 1, 7

Lord and a renewed dedication in the apostolate. The greater the evil may be, the greater should be our desire to sow good seed. Let us never forget to pray for those poor souls who exercise a bad influence on others. We should also pray for the many souls who become alienated from God as a result of a negative conversation, a certain book or article, or a bad television programme ... The Lord will hear our prayer and our Blessed Lady will obtain special graces for these intentions. When we meet Our Lord at the end of our life we will find that these acts of reparation have built up a great treasure for us in Heaven.

77. UNPROFITABLE SERVANTS

77.1 Without sanctifying grace, all of our activity is worthless.

In today's Gospel passage Our Lord takes a situation from ordinary life to teach us a divine truth.[1] Jesus asks: *Will any one of you, who has a servant ploughing or keeping sheep, say to him when he has come in from the field, 'Come at once and sit down at table'? Will he not rather say to him, 'Prepare supper for me, and gird yourself and serve me, till I eat and drink; and afterward you shall eat and drink'?* Given the social conditions of that age, the servant would hardly expect praise for carrying out orders. The Lord applies this reality to the supernatural life: *So you also, when you have done all that is commanded you, say, 'We are unworthy servants; we have only done what was our duty'.*

It would be a mistake to think that Jesus approves of the arbitrary manner of the master in the illustration. Yet Jesus has no hesitation in using a fairly commonplace circumstance to communicate the more effectively with his audience about the relationship between a creature and the Creator. From the very beginning to the very end of our days everything has come to us as a gift from Our Father God. In the words of St Ambrose, *You cannot think yourself greater than you are simply because you are a child of God. You ought to recognize the effect of grace, yes, but you cannot forget the lowliness of your nature. Nor would I have you become vain simply because you fulfil your duty. Remember that, in like manner, the sun and the*

---

[1] Luke 17:7-10

moon and the angels do exactly what they are supposed to do.[2] Do we see our service to God in the same light?

Let us not forget that it is only because of God's generosity that we have been elevated to the dignity of sons of God. We have in no way earned such a status or such a title. As a matter of fact, it would be more appropriate for us to consider ourselves *unprofitable servants.* We are absolutely incapable of doing God's Will without the assistance of his grace. Divine grace is what enables us to work for Christ. Our natural powers are wholly inadequate to the challenges of the supernatural struggle. We are merely *the brush in the hand of the artist.*[3] God's masterpieces are always the product of the divine Artist. No praise is given to the artist's tools – and with good reason. It is our good fortune to know that we are contributing in some small way to God's salvific plan. It would be ridiculous if we were to pretend to claim credit for what God has done.

If we are humble, we will *walk in the truth.* We will keep in mind our condition of being *unprofitable servants.* As a consequence, we will ask God to give us more grace. Another practical effect of this teaching is that whenever we are praised we will quietly give Jesus all the glory. Whatever good we do or receive has to be attributed, first and foremost, to God. The Lord is able *to use a stick to bring forth water from a rock. He has the power to make a little bit of mud bring sight to the blind.*[4] Do we serve as the Lord's mud, as his rod to bring forth water in the middle of the desert? Christ is the true author of these marvels. What would the mud or the stick accomplish by itself?

---

[2] St Ambrose, *Commentary on St Luke's Gospel, in loc*
[3] cf St. J. Escrivá, *The Way,* 612
[4] J. Pecci (Leo XIII), *Guidebook for humility,* 45

77.2 The Lord never withholds his assistance.

The Lord emphasizes the paramount importance of divine grace in his parable of the vine and the branches.[5] *Christ, sent by the Father, is the source of the Church's whole apostolate. Clearly then, the fruitfulness of the apostolate of lay people depends on their living union with Christ.*[6] Jesus makes sure He leaves no room for doubt: *I am the vine, you are the branches. He who abides in me, and I in him, he it is that bears much fruit, for apart from me you can do nothing.*[7]

As St Paul wrote to the Philippians: *God is at work in you, both to will and to work for his good pleasure.*[8] God's grace is indispensable if we are *to will and to work* meritorious deeds. It is essential for us to keep in mind, however, this vital distinction: grace builds on nature; it does not replace our nature. We have to do our part. St Augustine has likened our need for divine assistance to our need for light by which to see.[9] It is the eye that sees. The light allows the eye to fulfil its nature. Similarly, divine grace allows us *to will and to work,* but it never overrides our freedom. The awesome reality of our dependence on God should inspire us to a constant prayer of thanksgiving. God is always disposed to send us the necessary graces.

Through the liturgy the Church continually asks us to pray for divine help. If we ask with humility and faith the Lord will always heed our request. St Francis de Sales illustrated God's generosity with these words: *A tender mother leads along her little child, helps him and holds him up as long as she sees need for it, and lets him take a few steps by himself in places that are very level and not*

---

[5] cf John 15:1 ff
[6] Second Vatican Council, *Apostolicam actuositatem*, 4
[7] John 15:5
[8] Phil 2:13
[9] St Augustine, *On nature and grace*, 26, 29

too difficult. Now she takes him by the hand and holds him steady; now she takes him up in her arms and carries him. It is thus too that Our Lord himself takes constant care to lead forward his children, that is, those who possess charity.[10]

This divine solicitude should never be a motive for passivity. On the contrary, we should find God's grace a steadfast source of strength in our ascetical struggle and apostolate. We have to work as if everything depended on us. At the same time we cannot forget that everything depends on Jesus. This is the royal road to sanctity.

77.3 Co-workers with God.

St Paul makes use of an image from the farm to teach about our participation in apostolic work: *I planted, Apollos watered, but God gave the growth. So neither he who plants nor he who waters is anything, but only God who gives the growth ... For we are God's fellow workers.*[11] What a wonderful thing it is to know that we are collaborators with God in his work of Redemption! In some mysterious way the Lord has need of us. We have to remember always that it is God who plants the seed of faith and helps it to grow and bear fruit. Pope St Pius X touched upon this question in an encyclical about the priesthood: *It may be that weeping as they go they (priests) scatter the seed; it may be that with anxious care they nourish it; but to make it sprout and bring forth the cherished fruit, this is the work of God alone and his powerful assistance. This, also, is to be well considered, that men are nothing more than instruments which God uses for the saving of souls, and that these instruments must be fit, therefore, to be handled by God.*[12] Man is capable of undertaking great

---

[10] St Francis de Sales, *Treatise on the Love of God,* III, 4
[11] 1 Cor 3:6-9
[12] St Pius X, Encyclical, *Haerent animo,* 4 August 1908

things when he is humble. This is when he protects his union with Christ through prayer.

For the brush to be useful it has to transmit the colours and tones desired by the artist. The brush has to subordinate its own qualities and characteristics to the plan and intention of the painter. It is the painter who composes the painting. He creates the effects of light and shadow. He employs the vivid and subdued tones. He imparts the harmony, meaning and profundity. It would also be good to note that the brush has to be firmly united to the hand of the artist. It is like an extension of his arm. If there is no such union, then the intention of the artist may be jeopardized.

We want to be in the hands of the Lord. Yet we know that there are many times when this is not the case. Let us tell Jesus in the intimacy of our prayer: *I think of my wretchedness, which seems to be on the increase despite the graces you give me. It must be due to my failure to correspond. I know that I am completely unprepared for the enterprise you are asking of me. And when I read in the newspapers of so very many highly qualified and respected men, with formidable talents, and no lack of financial resources, speaking, writing, organizing in defence of your kingdom ... I look at myself, and see that I'm a nobody: ignorant, poor: so little, in a word. This would fill me with shame if I did not know that you want me to be so. But Lord Jesus, you know how gladly I have put my ambition at your feet ... To have Faith and Love, to be loving, believing, suffering. In these things I do want to be rich and learned: but no more rich and learned than you, in your limitless Mercy, have wanted me to be. I desire to put all my prestige and honour into fulfilling your most just and most lovable Will.*[13]

---

[13] St. J. Escrivá, *The Forge*, 822

Our Mother Mary was the most faithful collaborator with the Holy Spirit in the work of Redemption. She will teach us how to be good instruments in the hands of the Lord. Our Guardian Angel will second this intention by reminding us that we are only *unprofitable servants* doing the Lord's bidding.

78. THE IMPORTANCE OF THE SOCIAL VIRTUES

78.1 Jesus cultivated the social virtues.

Today's Gospel recounts Our Lord's healing of ten lepers.[1] We are shown how disappointed Jesus was that only one of the lepers, the Samaritan, returned to give thanks. *Was no one found to return and give praise to God except this foreigner?* There is no mistaking that the Lord was perturbed. A simple display of gratitude was the least those nine men could have done to show their appreciation for their miraculous cure. Jesus appreciates the gratitude of the humble and is hurt by the coldness of the egoist. It so happens that gratitude is a mark of nobility and a strong bond of social harmony. Giving thanks should be second nature to us since we receive countless gifts from other people, just as we provide countless favours in return. St Bede has written[2] that the Samaritan in this Gospel account was saved by his sense of gratitude.

Jesus was in no way indifferent to the practice of the social virtues. The social virtues are a means by which people demonstrate their respect for one another. They are thus a manifestation of interior refinement. When Simon the Pharisee neglected to give Jesus the customary forms of welcome, Our Lord did not hesitate to complain publicly of this lack of good manners. Throughout the course of his life and preaching, Jesus taught us the real importance of friendship, cordiality, temperance, love for the truth,

---

[1] Luke 17:11-19
[2] cf St Bede, in *Catena Aurea,* VI, p. 278

understanding, loyalty, industriousness, sincerity ... He emphasized the value of the human virtues by the use of examples and parables from everyday life. He took care to form the Apostles in the theological virtues as well as in human virtues such as sincerity[3] and magnanimity.[4] Jesus thought so highly of these human virtues that he was moved to say: *If I have told you earthly things and you do not believe, how can you believe if I tell you heavenly things?*[5] Christ is *perfect God and perfect Man.*[6] He exemplifies all of the virtues. Jesus is our exemplar extra-ordinary when it comes to dealing with God and dealing with other people. The life of Christ was aptly summarized by his contemporaries: *'Bene omnia fecit', he has done all things well.*[7] These words apply not only to his miracles, but also to his participation in ordinary affairs. It would be wonderful if people were to say the same thing about us, his followers in the middle of the world.

78.2 Gratitude. Our capacity for friendship. Mutual respect.

In today's *First Reading* St Paul writes to Titus and the church at Crete about the importance of living the social virtues: *Remind them to be submissive to rulers and authorities, to be obedient, to be ready for any honest work, to speak evil of no one, to avoid quarreling, to be gentle, and to show perfect courtesy toward all men.*[8]

The social virtues make daily life more pleasant. They dispose the soul to a closer union with God and to a conscientious pursuit of the supernatural virtues. The

---

[3] cf Matt 5:37

[4] cf John 9:1-3

[5] John 3:12

[6] *Athanasian Creed*

[7] Mark 7:37

[8] *First Reading,* Year II, Titus 3:1-7

Christian knows how to transform the practice of the social virtues into so many acts of love for God. Charity ennobles, and elevates these actions to a higher plane.

Gratitude is a human virtue that adds a great deal to social life. It consists of the affectionate recognition of a favour received. We manifest our desire to reciprocate in some fashion. Sometimes it is only possible to say *thank you* or respond with some similar expression. Our gratitude is shown by the cheerfulness we impart to the words. St Thomas has taught that *according to the natural order of things, it is fitting that the recipient of a favour should respond with due gratitude to his benefactor.*[9] It certainly costs us very little to show our gratitude. The effects of the virtue are manifold, and it contributes remarkably to a more friendly environment. As we become more sensitive and grateful to other people we find ourselves acting almost instinctively for the general welfare: that our house be clean and orderly, that our workplace be attractive and agreeable, that our appearance is neat ... If at any time we should find things a little out of order we will make an effort to forgive and forget. We should do our best to make life pleasant for others without giving in to a self-centred obsession with geometric neatness or absolute efficiency. We should also try to be thankful for those services which we pay for as well as those services which are our due: by giving thanks to the attendant who waits on us, by showing appreciation to the bus-driver who waits patiently while we get on board ...

The social virtues find their culmination in our increased capacity for friendship with a wide variety of people. Wouldn't it be wonderful if we could call everyone in our workaday world *friends*! Not just neighbours, colleagues or acquaintances, but *friends*. This would entail

---

[9] St Thomas, *Summa Theologiae*, 2-2, q. 106, a. 3 c.

a genuine struggle on our part to be unselfish, understanding, optimistic, loyal and eager to serve ... We need to live friendship within the family: among our brothers and sisters, with our children, with our parents. True friendship is not prevented by difference in age. Friendliness and true friendship are indispensable to apostolate.

The story is told that when Alexander the Great was on his deathbed his relatives were persistently asking him: *Alexander, where are your treasures?* He responded: *My treasures? They are in the pockets of my friends.* When we die, our friends should be able to say that we shared with them everything we possessed.

Mutual respect is also indispensable to social harmony. The Faith teaches us that we must respect other people because they are made in the image and likeness of God. Each person has been redeemed at the cost of the Most Precious Blood of Our Lord.[10] This includes those we may find a bit annoying for one reason or another. This virtue would also have us respect all created things, since they have come to us from the hand of God. Everything as well as everyone can and should be treated in such a way as to give glory to God the Creator.

78.3 Affability. Optimism and cheerfulness.

Another virtue which makes social life more pleasant is *affability*. It may express itself in the form of a friendly greeting, a small compliment, a cordial gesture of encouragement. This virtue leads us to overcome our inclination to irritability, rash judgments and actions ... , basically, to live as though other people didn't matter. *Elizabeth's start of joy at the Visitation emphasizes the gift that can be contained in a mere greeting, when it comes from a heart full of God. How often can the darkness of*

---

[10] 1 Pet 1:18

loneliness, oppressing a soul, be dispelled by the shining ray of a smile and a kind word! A good word is soon said; yet sometimes we find it difficult to utter. We are restrained by fatigue, we are distracted by worries, we are checked by a feeling of coldness or selfish indifference. Thus it happens that we may pass by persons, although we know them, without looking at their faces and without realizing how often they are suffering from that subtle, wearing sorrow which comes from feeling ignored. A cordial word, an affectionate gesture would be enough, and something would at once awaken in them: a sign of attention and courtesy can be a breath of fresh air in the stuffiness of an existence oppressed by sadness and dejection. Mary's greeting filled with joy the heart of her elderly cousin Elizabeth (cf Luke 1:44).[11] This is how we can lighten the load of the people around us.

Another aspect of affability lies in the practice of *kindness,* in *understanding* towards the defects and mistakes of other people (we don't have to be constantly correcting others), in *good manners* evinced by our words and behaviour, in *sympathy, cordiality* and *words of praise* at an opportune moment ... *The spirit of sweetness is truly the spirit of God ... It makes the truth understandable and acceptable. We have to be intransigent towards every form of evil; nevertheless, we have to deal kindly with our neighbour.*[12]

A truck-driver once pulled over at a highway rest stop for a cup of coffee. He needed a break because he had many miles ahead of him. He sat at the counter and a young boy came to wait on him. The truck-driver asked with a smile, *Busy day?* The young fellow looked up and smiled back. Some months later, the truck-driver returned to the same stop. Much to his surprise, the young fellow

---

[11] St John Paul II, *Address,* 11 February 1981
[12] St Francis de Sales, *Letters,* Fragment 110

remembered him as if they were old friends. The truth is that people have a great thirst for smiles. They have an enormous longing for cheerfulness and encouragement. Every day we encounter a good number of people who await that momentary gift of our joy.

Through the practice of the social virtues we can open up many doors. We cannot allow ourselves to be cut off from any of our neighbours or colleagues. The Lord wants us to do an effective apostolate of friendship and confidence. We need to introduce other people to that greatest of all gifts which is friendship with Jesus.

THIRTY-SECOND WEEK: THURSDAY

79. LIKE A WALLED CITY

79.1 The charity lived by the first Christians.

One of the readings for today's Mass is a passage from St Paul's Letter to Philemon. It is the briefest and perhaps most heartfelt epistle written by the Apostle. Philemon was a Christian of Colossae. He had a runaway slave by the name of Onesimus, whom Paul had met and converted in a Roman prison. Here we have one more palpable demonstration of the universal scope of primitive Christianity. The Faith won over wealthy people like Philemon and slaves like Onesimus. St John Chrysostom surveys the variegated scene in one of his homilies: *Aquila had a business selling dyed cloth in front of a workshop; another worked as a prison guard; another, Cornelius, was a centurion; Timothy was a sick man; Onesimus was a slave and a fugitive. And all of these different sorts of people had converted to the Faith. Their worldly occupations and conditions did not pose any obstacle. Every one of them became a saint – men and women, young and old, slave and free, soldiers and countryfolk.*[1]

We may wonder about what plans St Paul had for Onesimus. Perhaps at first he wanted his assistance in Rome.[2] Yet soon he changed his mind. He gave Onesimus back to Philemon with only one request: that Philemon treat Onesimus as a brother in the Faith. The Apostle does not make this request in the form of a command, even though he surely could have done: *Though I am bold*

---

[1] St John Chrysostom, *Homilies on St Matthew's Gospel,* 43
[2] cf Philem 13-14

enough in Christ to command you to do what is required, yet for love's sake I prefer to appeal to you – I, Paul, an ambassador and now a prisoner also for Christ Jesus – I appeal to you for my child, Onesimus, whose father I have become in my imprisonment. (Formerly he was useless to you, but now he is indeed useful to you and to me.) I am sending him back to you, sending my very heart. I would have been glad to keep him with me, in order that he might serve me on your behalf during my imprisonment for the gospel.[3]

For a time this slave was *useless* to his master since he had run away. Now he had become *useful*. St Paul is here playing on the meaning of the name Onesimus, which indeed happens to mean *useful*. If previously he was of little use, now he is of use both to the Apostle and to Philemon. Paul instructs Philemon to receive Onesimus as if he were Paul himself: *So if you consider me your partner, receive him as you would receive me.*[4] St John Chrysostom points out: *See how St Paul had no shame in defending a fugitive slave. He refers to Onesimus as his child, his very heart, his beloved brother. How would I have reacted in this situation? Jesus Christ became Man to the point of making slaves his blood brothers. If slaves are the brothers of Christ, then they are our brothers as well.*[5] These words of the Apostle assume even greater weight if we consider the circumstances of slavery in the ancient world. Slaves had no rights and no dignity whatsoever. The fact that Christians showed this kind of interest in slaves truly stunned the people of that time. And what about ourselves in today's world? Do we exclude anyone from our dealings or our affection for reasons of social class, of race or level of education?

---

[3] Philem 9-13
[4] cf *The Navarre Bible,* note to Philem 6
[5] St John Chrysostom, *Homilies on the Epistle to Philemon,* 2, 15-16

St Paul closes this short letter with some levity: *If he has wronged you at all, or owes you anything, charge that to my account. I, Paul, write this with my own hand, I will repay it – to say nothing of your owing me even your own self.* Surely if they were to total up the balance sheet, Philemon would find that he owed Paul the most valuable thing he possessed – his Christian faith.

Let us resolve to take a lesson from these first Christians on how to live charity in a practical and profound manner. Our first apostolate should always be with those who are closest to us. We should do our best to see that they persevere in the Faith. We should also be attentive to those people we know who live apart from Christ. Let us try to win them back to the Lord through our friendship and esteem.

79.2 The fortitude that comes from charity.

'Frater qui adiuvatur a fratre quasi civitas firma'. A brother who is helped by his brother is like a walled city.[6] So says the Book of Proverbs. We may well imagine the tremendous external difficulties which threatened believers in the earliest days of Christianity. Probably one of their strongest modes of defence was the charity they practiced towards one another. Charity makes us as solid as a fortress wall, able to sustain any assault. The New Testament is replete with encouragement in this regard. For example, St Paul wrote to the Galatians: *Bear one another's burdens, and so fulfil the law of Christ.*[7] When we see that our brothers and sisters are weighed down by difficulties, we have to be ready to share the load, no matter how heavy it turns out to be. This is the sentiment to be found in a letter from St Ignatius of Antioch to his disciple, St Polycarp: *Bear the infirmities of all, like a master athlete. The*

---

[6] Prov 18:19
[7] Gal 6:2

greater the toil, the greater the reward.[8]

This responsibility is shared by all Christians. Each believer has to be on the watch for the welfare of others of the faithful, especially those in his or her immediate circle. St Augustine has written: *They are your servants, my brothers, whom you will to be your sons; they are my masters, whom you have commanded me to serve if I would live by you.*[9] Our earnest determination to help others will bring us out of ourselves. It will expand our heart. We cannot excuse ourselves from serving others for lack of time, through fear of becoming involved, or because of worries of one kind or another. We have to be concerned about the health of others, about their rest, about their peace of mind, about their spiritual life. Sick people deserve even more attention than almost anyone else. Let us give them extra moments of our company. Let us show a real interest in their speedy recovery. We should encourage people to sanctify their suffering by helping them to pray as much as they are able.

The practice of charity can give us a fortitude like that manifested by the first Christians. This can be of great consolation when we encounter obstacles to the Faith in our own day. We need to look out for one another in such a way that no one feels lonely in time of trial. This is supernatural common sense. *If a city is to be defended, then the people throw up a great wall of fortification. A constant guard is mounted. But, if any tiny area is left unprotected, without a doubt that is where the enemy will strike.*[10]

With the support of fellow Christians we will make of ourselves *a walled city, a strong fortress.*[11] Together we

---

[8] St Ignatius of Antioch, *Epistle to St Polycarp,* 1, 3
[9] St Augustine, *Confessions,* 10, 4, 6
[10] St Gregory the Great, *Morals,* 19, 21, 33
[11] cf *The Liturgy of the Hours,* Fourth Sunday of Lent, Evening Prayer

will find the strength and energy to surmount any difficulty
that arises on our path to God. If we were acting alone this
kind of security would be nearly impossible. Yet Sacred
Scripture tells us: *A threefold cord is not quickly broken.*[12]
Charity gives us strength. *'Frater qui adiuvatur fratre
quasi civitas firma'* – *'A brother who is helped by his
brother is like a walled city'. Think for a moment and make
up your mind to live that brotherhood I've always
recommended to you.*[13]

79.3 Virtues related to charity.

St Paul does not make a direct appeal to Philemon for
the freedom of Onesimus. He expresses this desire in a
refined manner without forcing Philemon's hand. *Refresh
my heart in Christ. Confident of your obedience, I write to
you, knowing that you will do even more than I say. This is
an echo of the gracious sentiments expressed at the
beginning of the letter,* observes St John Chrysostom,
*'knowing that you will do even more than I say'. Can we
imagine any more persuasive words? What could be more
convincing than this gentle esteem shown by Paul to
Philemon? How can he fail to respond to this type of
request?*[14] This is the delicacy of one who knows himself
to be addressing a brother in the Faith.

The practice of charity involves a whole series of
virtues. These virtues support and defend charity. They
include loyalty, gratitude, mutual respect, friendship,
deference, affability, refinement ... If we are to live the
Lord's New Commandment, we will often need to be on
top of our moods. We will have to make an effort to be
cordial, to spread good cheer, to be optimistic. It may be
more natural for us to act in just the opposite way, to give

---

[12] Eccles 4:12
[13] St. J. Escrivá, *The Way,* 460
[14] St John Chrysostom, *Homilies on the Epistle to Philemon,* 21

in to critical spirit, to let slip harsh words, to use bad language, to become easily annoyed ... These are signs of a lack of supernatural struggle.

St John has left us this concise summary of Christianity: *By this we know love, that He laid down his life for us; and we ought to lay down our lives for the brethren.*[15] We must firmly resolve to give of ourselves day after day, in the midst of our work, in the context of the home, with our friends, relatives and acquaintances. Then we will be fulfilling the New Commandment of the Lord: *A new commandment I give to you, that you love one another; even as I have loved you, that you also love one another. By this all men will know that you are my disciples, if you have love for one another.*[16]

Jesus has set the standard which the Christians of every age must strive to follow. This is how Christians will be distinguishable from those who have still not entered the Church. What a shame if we were not to live up to that standard! We would thereby confuse everyone, and at the same time would lose the honour of being known as children of God. It is in these very sad circumstances that we foolishly neglect divine assistance, that aid which is so necessary if we are to give witness to a paganized and indifferent environment.

Let us rather do our best that the world may be amazed at the wondrous spectacle of our fraternal charity. Then they will say of us what was said in earlier times: 'See how they love one another!'.[17]

---

[15] 1 John 3:16
[16] John 13:34-35
[17] Ch. Lubich, *Meditations*, p. 46

THIRTY-SECOND WEEK: FRIDAY

80. A CHRISTIAN OUTLOOK ON DEATH

80.1 We cannot be blind to our final moment on earth. Preparing for death on a daily basis.

In the Gospel for today's Mass Jesus predicts that his coming in glory will take people unawares.[1] *For as the lightning flashes and lights up the sky from one side to the other, so will the Son of man be in his day.* The Lord tells us that nothing can block his Second Coming at the end of time.

The disciples had a natural curiosity about when and where this would happen. *Where, Lord?* they asked him. *Where the body is,* He replied, *there the eagles will be gathered together.* Jesus teaches us that everyone will be drawn to the Son of God at the end of time just as eagles converge on their prey. The same may be said about each individual person's moment of death. St Paul with this in mind sent these words of warning to the first Christians at Thessalonica: *For you yourselves know well that the day of the Lord will come like a thief in the night.*[2] It is one more call to vigilance. We cannot be blind to our final moment on earth, *the day of the Lord,* when we will meet God face to face. St Augustine has written that the Lord keeps the circumstances of his coming hidden so that we may be always on the alert.[3]

There are certain environments today where it is not so easy to speak about death and dying. The very mention of

---

[1] Luke 17:26-37
[2] 1 Thess 5:2
[3] cf St Augustine, *Commentary on Psalm 120,* 3

the subject is regarded by some as a s
Nonetheless, it is the certainty of death th
life. The Church invites us to meditate
inevitability of our death so that we will
surprise when our time comes. Pagan cultu
live as though death were a distant mirage
only affects other people. Regrettably, many who consider
themselves good Christians can be unduly influenced by
such a seductive approach to life. They are led astray
because they have failed to come to terms with the real
meaning of death. Rather than see death as a *friend,* or even
as a *sister,*[4] they view it as an enormous catastrophe, as
something that will undermine all their worldly hopes and
accomplishments. This earthbound approach explains why
death has to be put in the closet, as it were. It is too
uncomfortable a subject to deal with. Instead of looking
upon death as the *key* to the fullness of joy, the tendency is
to see it as the *end of the road,* the check-out counter on
what is for them a kind of terrestrial shopping spree. These
misguided people have lost sight of the fact that every man is
in possession of an eternal soul. Death is nothing more than
a *change of lodging.*[5] The liturgy often reminds us of this
truth: *vita mutatur, non tollitur.*[6] Life changes, it is not
something we are deprived of. Christians believe that death
represents the end of an earthly pilgrimage. Believers
prepare for death on a daily basis.[7] It is through the
sanctification of ordinary realities that we will win Heaven
as an eternal reward. The Christian who behaves accordingly
will not be alarmed by death's arrival. He will have been
patiently readying himself for this definitive encounter with
the Lord. In the words of St Cyprian, death *is a stepping up*

---

[4] cf St. J. Escrivá, *The Way,* 735 and 739

[5] cf *ibid,* 744

[6] *Roman Missal,* Preface for the dead

[7] cf C. Pozo, *Theology of the afterlife,* Madrid 1980

...rnity after we have run in this earthly race.[8]

If at any time you feel uneasy at the thought of our ...ster death because you see yourself to be such a poor creature, take heart. Heaven awaits us and consider: what will it be like when all the infinite beauty and greatness, and happiness and Love of God will be poured into the poor clay vessel that the human being is, to satisfy it eternally with the freshness of an ever new joy?[9]

80.2 Death acquires a new meaning with the Death and Resurrection of Christ.

Sacred Scripture expressly teaches us: *God did not make death, and He does not delight in the death of the living.*[10] There was no such thing as death, with all its pain and suffering, before our first parents committed the Original Sin. The rebellion of our first parents led to the loss of this praeternatural gift. By his disobedience, Adam lost his friendship with God and the gift of immortal life. Since that time, our passage to *the house of the Father,* our final resting place, takes us to this fateful gateway – the moment when we *depart out of this world to the Father.*[11]

Jesus Christ *abolished death and brought life.*[12] He removed the essential evil from death and gave it a new meaning, making death into a stepping stone to Life. His victory is shared by all who believe in him and participate in his Life. The Master has told us: *I am the resurrection and the life; he who believes in me, though he die, yet shall he live, and whoever lives and believes in me shall never die.*[13] Death is the enemy of the natural life of man. Christ has

---

[8] St Cyprian, *Treatise on mortality,* 22
[9] St. J. Escrivá, *Furrow,* 891
[10] Wis 1:13
[11] John 13:1
[12] 2 Tim 1:10
[13] John 11:25

converted it into our *friend* and *sister,* Though the human person suffer defeat at the hands of this foe, he or she can in the end be triumphant thanks to Christ's immortal sacrifice. For a materialistic society in which pleasure and comfort reign supreme, death and even life itself are devoid of lasting value. Those who adopt a pagan life-style behave as if suffering, failure and death were curses to be avoided at any cost. Such people act as if Christ never achieved the Redemption.

The Psalmist says in his prayer to God: *Those who hate the righteous will be condemned.*[14] But *precious in the sight of the Lord is the death of his saints.*[15] From her earliest days the Church has celebrated the anniversaries of the death by martyrdom of her saints. The Church says that these are *dies natalis,* birth-days to that new Life which entails joy without end. St John tells us in the Book of Revelation: *I heard a voice from heaven saying: 'Write this: Blessed are the dead who die in the Lord henceforth'. 'Blessed indeed', says the Spirit, 'that they may rest from their labours, for their deeds follow them!'*[16] We will be rewarded for even the smallest service we have done for the Lord, such as the gift of a glass of water.[17] The Second Vatican Council has declared: *For after we have obeyed the Lord, and in his Spirit nurtured on earth the values of human dignity, brotherhood and freedom, and indeed all the good fruits of our nature and enterprise, we will find them again, but freed of stain, burnished and transfigured, when Christ hands over to the Father: 'a kingdom eternal and universal ...'*[18] All the things of the world will perish and be forgotten, but *their good deeds will follow them.*

---

[14] Ps 33:21

[15] Ps 115:15

[16] Rev 14:13

[17] Matt 10:42

[18] Second Vatican Council, *Gaudium et spes,* 39

80.3 What we can learn from the reality of death.

Death can teach us many things about life. The consideration of death will inspire us to live with only what we need, to be detached from the things we own and use, to respect the lasting merit of our good works.

Death also teaches us to make good use of each and every day. As the ancients would say, *Carpe diem,*[19] make the most of the present moment. It is a pagan maxim, but we can impart a Christian meaning to it by living each day with joy as if it were our whole life. It is a chance that will never be repeated. During our examination of conscience we can please Almighty God with the quantity of our acts of love, aspirations, dealings with our Guardian Angel, favours on behalf of others, the quiet fulfilment of our duties, our struggle to be patient, perhaps ... The Lord will convert these deeds into splendid jewels of eternal worth. Death ends our time of meriting.[20] Let us not waste the days that remain to us in our life.

We do not know when we will die. The very uncertainty helps us to be watchful, like the doorkeeper awaiting the arrival of his Master.[21] We have to be alert in our examination of conscience to discover and recognise our failings during the course of the day. Let us have recourse to frequent Confession in order to cleanse our soul from venial sin and from any omissions that would indicate a lack of love. Our meditation on death will move us to work more earnestly on the great project of our own sanctification. *Look carefully then how you walk, not as unwise men but as wise, making the most of the time.*[22] We need to make up for lost time. Let us take to heart the wise observation of Seneca, written almost twenty centuries

---

[19] Horace, *Odes,* 1, 11, 7
[20] cf Leo X, Bull, *Exsurge Domine,* 15 June 1520, prop. 38
[21] cf Luke 12:35-42
[22] Eph 5:15-16

ago: *It is not that we have so little time, but that we have wasted so much of it.*[23]

We should certainly want to have a long life so that we can give God abundant service. We ought to go before the Lord with our arms full. It is so right for us to love life, since it is a gift from God. If we are faithful to our Christian vocation, when the time comes for our encounter with the Lord we will be prepared to make a tremendous act of Love for our Father God. St Ignatius of Loyola has written these words to encourage us: *As in one's whole life, so also in one's death, each one should struggle to give glory to the Lord our God. May He be honoured and glorified. May other people be edified by the example of our patience and fortitude, by the testimony of our living faith, our hope and our love for the eternal goods ...*[24] Our last moment on earth should be spent for the glory of God. What great joy we will give to the Lord when we present to him our professional work, our apostolate, those many, many details of our service to our neighbours, the joy we contributed to family life, the effort we made to overcome our defects ...

We will leave behind us works that will endure. We will take our departure from this world in a way described by a poet: *I left my love the shore and the singing current. I did not return to the bank for his love was the water.*[25]

---

[23] Seneca, *De brevitate vitae,* 1, 3
[24] St Ignatius of Loyola, *Constitutions S. I.,* p. 6, c. 4, n. 1
[25] B. Llorens, *A secret spring,* Madrid 1949

THIRTY-SECOND WEEK: SATURDAY

81. THE PRAYER OF PETITION AND DIVINE MERCY

81.1 We put all our confidence in the infinite goodness of God.

The Lord has taught us about our need for prayer in many different ways. God is always pleased to receive our petitions. Jesus himself prayed to the Father so as to give us a lasting example. God and his goodness are the source of each and every moment of life. We are wholly dependent on him and He is completely in love with us. This explains why He wants us to recognise our total dependence on him, and why this recognition is of such great benefit to us. As a consequence of this awareness we will struggle so much the harder to live in his love and protection.

Jesus wanted to encourage us to offer prayers of petition. He went so far as to give us a guarantee of divine attention when we pray in this way. At the same time He pointed out the fundamental aspects of any request we make to God. In the Gospel for today's Mass Jesus tells the parable of the widow whose persistence eventually prevails upon the wicked judge.[1] In his closing words on this parable Jesus presents God the Father's reaction as being exactly the opposite of the judge's: *And will not God vindicate his elect, who cry to him day and night? Will He delay long over them?* If even the wicked judge could be made to react with justice, how much more readily will a just and merciful God respond to our pleas? In contrast to

---

[1] Luke 18:1-8

the obduracy of the judge, God is always attentive to our needs and solicitous for us. This is the basic meaning of the parable – it stresses the difference between God's mercy and human selfishness.

The judge attempts to put the widow off by making some weak excuses. In the end, however, *he said to himself, 'Though I neither fear God nor regard man, yet because this widow bothers me, I will vindicate her, or she will wear me out by her continual coming'.* God responds to our petitions in an entirely different way. *Hear what the unrighteous judge says. And will not God vindicate his elect, who cry to him day and night? Will he delay long over them?* St Augustine has commented on this passage: *Those who make persevering prayer to God should take heart, for God is the fountain of all justice and mercy.*[2] If unfailing prayer could assuage the hard-heartedness of a judge *who was capable of every foul deed, what effect will it have on the Father of all mercy, who is God?*[3]

The children of God should express their love in their trusting and persevering prayer. *If God seems at times to be slow in responding, it is because He is preparing a better gift. He will not deny us. We well know that the long-awaited gift is all the more precious for the delay in its being granted ... Ask, seek, insist. Through this asking and seeking you will be better prepared to receive God's gift when it comes. God withholds what you are not yet ready for. He wants you to have a lively desire for his greatest gifts. All of which is to say, pray always and do not lose heart.*[4] We must never become discouraged in our petitions to God. *My God, teach me how to love. My God, teach me how to pray.*[5] Love and prayer are inseparably connected.

---

[2] St Augustine, in *Catena Aurea,* VI, p. 295
[3] Theophylact, in *Catena Aurea,* VI, p. 296
[4] St Augustine, *Sermon 61,* 6-7
[5] St. J. Escrivá, *The Forge,* 66

81.2 To have recourse always to divine mercy.

The prayer of a righteous man has great power in its effects.[6] This power derives from the fact that we pray in the name of Jesus.[7] Jesus is our Mediator with God the Father.[8] The Holy Spirit moves our soul to make supplication, even when we do not know what it is we want. He who gives us everything asks that we ask. What greater security could we want? The only limiting factor is our own capacity to receive God's gifts. It is like filling a small cup from a gushing fountain.

The Lord is compassionate and merciful.[9] He knows very well our defects and our errors. Sacred Scripture frequently portrays the Lord as a God of mercy. He is *abounding in steadfast love and faithfulness.*[10] St Thomas Aquinas wrote that divine omnipotence shows itself especially resplendent in the exercise of divine mercy.[11] God's mercy is abundant and infinite. The Angelic Doctor states: *To say that someone is full of mercy is like saying his heart is full of woe. He experiences the miseries of another with the same force and sadness as if they were his own. He makes his best effort to remedy the problem because it has become his problem. This is the effect of mercy. Of course, God does not become saddened by thus making his own the miseries of his creatures. Yet He does work to remedy those problems, those defects, because to act in this way does correspond to his divine nature.*[12]

St John Paul II taught us: *Christ confers on the whole of the Old Testament tradition about God's mercy a*

---

[6] Jas 5:16

[7] cf John 15:16; 16:26

[8] cf St Cyril of Jerusalem, *Commentary on St John's Gospel,* 16, 23-24

[9] Jas 5:11

[10] cf Ex 34:6; Joel 2:13; Luke 1:4

[11] cf St Thomas, *Summa Theologiae,* 1, q. 21, a. 4; 2-2, q. 30, a. 4

[12] *idem, op cit,* 1, q. 21, a. 3

definitive meaning. Not only does He speak of it and explain it by the use of comparisons and parables, but, above all, He himself makes it incarnate and personifies it. He himself, in a certain sense, is mercy.[13] He knows us through and through. He sympathises with our infirmities, with our financial difficulties, with all the burdens we carry about in this life. *It is true that each of us is very much out for himself; but God our Lord does not mind if we lay all our needs before him at Mass. Who doesn't have things to ask for? Lord, this illness ... Lord, this sorrow ... Lord, that humiliation which I don't seem to be able to bear out of love for you ... We desire the welfare, joy and happiness of the people in our own home; we are saddened by the condition of those who hunger and thirst for bread and for justice, of those who experience the bitterness of loneliness and of those who end their days without an affectionate smile or a helping hand.*

But what really makes us suffer, the greatest human failure we want to remedy, is *sin, separation from God, the danger that souls may be lost for all eternity.*[14] Our most urgent petition to the Lord should be for the spiritual well-being of our neighbours, those people we deal with every day.

81.3 The intercession of Our Blessed Mother.

From the earliest times Christians have been inspired to pray to God through the intercession of Mary, his Mother, who is also our Mother. The Blessed Virgin demonstrated the power of her intercession at Cana of Galilee. She asked her Son to work his first miracle on behalf of a pair of newlyweds and their family. The Lord says that his hour has not yet come, but proceeds to obey

---

[13] St John Paul II, Encyclical, *Dives in misericordia,* 30 November 1980, 2

[14] St. J. Escrivá, *In Love with the Church,* 47

his mother. The Second Vatican Council has stated: *In the public life of Jesus, Mary makes significant appearances. This is so even at the very beginning, when at the marriage feast of Cana, moved with pity, she brought about by her intercession the beginning of miracles of Jesus the Messiah.*[15] Mary is always present in the salvific work of Jesus. On that specific occasion she not only resolved the immediate crisis concerning the wine, which Jesus provided in great measure, but she also confirmed the faith of the disciples. *This, the first of his signs, Jesus did at Cana in Galilee, and manifested his glory; and his disciples believed in him.*[16]

Our Blessed Mother is always attentive to the needs and problems of her children. She is a wonderful intercessor on our behalf. She will speed our petitions to the Lord, and put them better than we could if they so require. St Alphonsus Liguori once preached about this topic: *Why are the prayers of Mary so highly regarded by God? Let us remember that the prayers of the saints are the prayers of his servants. But the prayers of Mary are the prayers of his Mother. This is the reason for their efficacy and authority. Since Jesus has an incredible love for his Mother, He responds to her every request ...*

To go deeper in our understanding of Mary's importance we need only turn to the Gospel text ... The wine failed at the marriage feast of Cana. The bridal party was at risk of great embarrassment. No one asked Mary to become involved, to seek her Son's assistance. Here we see the heart of Mary quick to respond with sympathy for the family ... She takes the task of intercession upon herself. Acting on her own initiative she asks Jesus for a miracle ... If this was her way of acting when no one had asked for help, what will be her response to those who pray for her

---

[15] Second Vatican Council, *Lumen gentium,* 58
[16] John 2:11

intercession?[17]

We customarily dedicate our Saturdays to Mary. Today is a good opportunity to go to her more frequently and with greater love. *Ask your Mother Mary, ask St Joseph and your Guardian Angel to speak to the Lord and tell him the things you can't manage to put into words because you are so dull.*[18]

---

[17] St Alphonsus Liguori, *Abbreviated sermons,* 48
[18] St. J. Escrivá, *The Forge,* 272

THIRTY-THIRD SUNDAY: YEAR A

82. GENEROSITY TOWARDS GOD

82.1 We are stewards of God's gifts.

During these final weeks of the liturgical year, the Church calls us to consider the eternal truths. These truths are of immediate relevance to our souls. As we read in the *Second Reading* of today's Mass, our encounter with the Lord will arrive without warning, *like a thief in the night.*[1] No matter how prepared we think we are for its arrival, death always takes us by surprise.

In today's Gospel the Lord teaches us that we must spend our earthly life in such as way as to win Heaven.[2] Jesus compares our time on earth to a long-term leasing arrangement. *For it will be as when a man going on a journey called his servants and entrusted to them his property; to one he gave five talents, to another two, to another one, to each according to his ability. Then he went away.* The owner knew the capacity of each of his servants. He did not want to burden every one of them with the same responsibility. That would have been unjust. He therefore gave according to each one's capability to receive. Despite the different amounts allotted to them, each servant had been entrusted with a considerable sum. After some time had passed, the master returned from his travels and came to settle accounts with his men. The servant with five talents produced five talents more. In like manner, the servant with two talents had doubled his share. These servants had made good use of their time to yield

---

[1] 1 Thess 5:1-6
[2] Matt 25:14-30

additional earnings. Consequently, each one thoroughly deserved these wonderful words of praise and blessing from their lord: *Well done, good and faithful servant; you have been faithful over a little, I will set you over much; enter into the joy of your master.*

The meaning of the parable is crystal clear. We are the servants. The talents are the qualities God has bestowed on us – our intelligence, our ability to love, our power to make others happy, temporal goods ... The journey of the master signifies the duration of our life. His unexpected return signifies our death. The settling of accounts is our judgment. The banquet is Heaven. The Lord frequently reminds us in the Gospels that we do not own what we have. We are stewards entrusted with God's property. A day will come when we shall have to give an account of our behaviour. Let us examine our whole approach to the gifts we have received from God. Do we think of ourselves as stewards, or do we live under the illusion that we are the true owners of what we possess?

We might want to reflect on our attitude towards our body and senses. Do we really use them so as to give glory to God? Do we contribute to the common good with our belongings, our professional work, our friendships? The Lord wants to see that his gifts have been well administered. His reward is in direct proportion to what he has already granted us. *Every one to whom much is given, of him will much be required; and of him to whom men commit much they will demand the more.*[3]

Well done, good and faithful servant; you have been faithful over a little. This is what the lord said to the man who received five talents. What men may see as *much*, God views as *little. Enter into the joy of your master* – this outcome is what God sees as valuable. *What no eye has*

---

[3] Luke 12:48

seen, nor ear heard, nor the heart of man conceived, (is) what God has prepared for those who love him.[4] We surely want to be found vigilant when the Lord arrives. Nothing could be more important. Let us make use of the time we have to make ready. How happy He will be to find us alert and on the watch! My Lord, we will tell him, I have lived my life for your glory and nothing else.

82.2 Life is a time to serve God enthusiastically.

But he who had received the one talent went and dug in the ground and hid his master's money. When the lord asked this servant to give an accounting, all he could offer were excuses. He said: *Master, I knew you to be a hard man, reaping where you did not sow, and gathering where you did not winnow; so I was afraid, and I went and hid your talent in the ground. Here you have what is yours.* This last servant *represents man when he is not faithful to God. This person is overcome with fear and self-love. He attempts to justify his behaviour by alluding to the purportedly unjust expectations of the lord who reaps where he has not sown.*[5] The master angrily responds to this lazy fellow: *You wicked and slothful servant!* He had disregarded an essential truth – that *man was created to know, love and serve God in this life. Then he is to see him and possess him in Heaven. When God is known well, it is not hard to love him. And when God is truly loved, it is not difficult to serve him. Nor is it humiliating. In fact, it even becomes a pleasure to serve him. A person who truly loves does not even think that it is degrading and dishonourable to serve his beloved. He never feels humiliated while serving the one he loves. Now then, the third servant knew his master well. At least he had had as many opportunities to know him as the other two servants had. And in spite of*

---

[4] 1 Cor 2:9
[5] St John Paul II, *Address*, 18 November 1984

that it is obvious that he did not love him. And when love is missing, serving becomes very difficult.[6] We can see into this servant's heart from his cold description of the master as a *hard man.*

This lazy servant did not serve his master because of an absence of love. It is interesting to note that the opposite of laziness is *diligence.* The Latin root of *diligence* is *diligere,* to love, to choose after careful study. Love motivates a person to give true service. Laziness is the result of a failure to love. The Lord uses this parable to reprove those who either fail to develop their gifts, or pervert their use for the sake of self-love. Let us examine our conduct today. How do we use our time? Are we punctual and orderly in our work? When we are at home, do we give our full attention to family matters? Do we practice a lively apostolate of friendship and confidence? Are we seriously striving to extend the Kingdom of Christ to all souls?

82.3 Using our time well.

Life is short. That is why we have to make good use of the life we have remaining to us. Sacred Scripture reminds us over and over again about the fleeting nature of our earthly existence. *The breath in our nostrils is smoke ... Our life will pass away like the traces of a cloud and be scattered like mist that is chased by the rays of the sun and overcome by its heat.*[7] *Man is like a breath, his days are like passing shadow.*[8] *He comes forth like a flower, and withers; he flees like a shadow, and continues not.*[9] *Let the lowly brother boast in his exaltation, and the rich in his humiliation, because like the flower of the grass he will*

---

[6] F. Suarez, *The Afterlife,* p. 106
[7] Wis 2:2-4
[8] Ps 143:4
[9] Job 14:2

pass away.[10] *What a shame it would be to have as one's occupation in life that of killing time which is a God-given treasure! ... How sad not to turn to good account and obtain a real profit from the few or many talents that God has given to each man so that he may dedicate himself to the task of serving other souls and the whole of society!*

When a Christian kills time on this earth, he is putting himself in danger of 'killing Heaven' for himself, that is, if through selfishness, he backs out of things and hides away and doesn't care.[11]

If we are to make good use of our time, we need to fulfil our duties in an exemplary fashion. Making good use of our time could involve spending an afternoon caring for a sick person. It could mean helping a friend prepare for a difficult exam. A selfish person would look down on such activities as a *waste of time,* but we know that selfless acts of charity can win us entry to Heaven. Making good use of our time also involves putting our head and our heart into whatever we are doing, no matter how trivial or important our activity might appear to be. We should resolve not to spend time frivolously, for example by worrying about our past life. Nor should we fret unduly about the future. The Lord wants us to live in the present moment, to sanctify the only bit of time that truly exists, for the past and the future exist only in the imagination. Our Father God will grant us the grace to handle whatever trials may come our way. Jesus himself has given us this tender assurance: *Do not be anxious about tomorrow, for tomorrow will be anxious for itself. Let the day's own trouble be sufficient for the day.*[12] When we conscientiously struggle to live the present moment to the full, then we will find ourselves both more productive and less harried.

---

[10] Jas 1:9-10

[11] St. J. Escrivá, *Friends of God,* 46

[12] Matt 6:34

St Teresa of Avila once recalled the circumstances of her arrival in Salamanca to found a new convent. In the company of another nun named María del Sacramento, Teresa took possession of a house which had only just been vacated by some students and was a shambles. The two nuns entered the house by night and were exhausted from their journey and the cold weather. The church bells were ringing because it was the night of All Souls. A flickering candle was their only source of light in the dark and dingy building. The nuns gathered some straw and lay down to rest using two blankets they had borrowed. Once retired in these spartan conditions, María del Sacramento, who was overwrought with anxiety, asked Teresa: *Mother, if I died suddenly, what would you do here all alone?*

She was so much in earnest that her terror communicated itself to me, recalled the Mother Foundress, *I have always been afraid of dead bodies, even when there was someone else with me. All this time the bells were tolling without interruption for, as I have said, it was the night of All Souls, and it was only too easy for the demon to scare us by childish fancies ... Fortunately, I was dropping with sleep.*

Then Teresa said to the other nun: *Sister, if that should happen, I should have to think what to do. Just now, all I want to do is to sleep ...*[13]

We too can become overanxious about our worries and fears. We should do our best not to be troubled by future concerns which may be completely beyond our control. The same counsel applies to our approach to present-day difficulties. They should not rob us of our peace. Let us heed the advice of St Teresa: *If that should happen, I should have to think what to do.* We can always count on God's grace to help us on our way. Let us resolve to

---

[13] M. Auclair, *Teresa of Avila*, pp. 224-225

sanctify everything that awaits us in his loving Providence.

When a life comes to an end, perhaps we may think something like a candle has gone out. But we should also see death as the time when something like a tapestry has been completed. We have watched this tapestry being made from the reverse side where the design of the artwork is blurred and the knots and twisted loops of the needlework are prominent. Our Father God contemplates the tapestry from the good side. He is pleased to behold a finished work that manifests a life-long effort to make good use of time.

THIRTY-THIRD SUNDAY: YEAR B

83. THE SECOND COMING OF CHRIST

83.1 Our desire to see the face of Christ.

The Lord said: I think thoughts of peace and not of affliction. You will call upon me, and I will answer you, and I will lead back your captives from every place.[1] So does God speak through the Prophet Jeremiah in today's *Entrance Antiphon.*

Jesus Christ fulfilled the mission that the Father had entrusted to him. There is a certain sense, however, in which his work has yet to be completed. Jesus will come at the end of time to finish what He began. From her earliest days the Church has professed her belief in the Second Coming of Christ in glory, *to judge the living and the dead.*[2] The Catechism of the Council of Trent states: *The Sacred Scriptures inform us that there are two comings of the Son of God: the one when He assumed human flesh for our salvation in the womb of a virgin; the other when He shall come at the end of the world to judge all mankind. This latter coming is called in Scripture the day of the Lord.*[3]

As we enter the final days of the liturgical year the Church reminds us once more of this truth of faith. In the *First Reading,* the Prophet Daniel declares: *At that time shall arise Michael, the great prince who has charge of your people. And there shall be a time of trouble.*[4] The reference is to *the fulness of time,* and to the resurrection of

---

[1] *Entrance Antiphon,* Jer 29:11-12; 14
[2] *The Nicene-Constantinopolitan Creed*
[3] *Catechism of the Council of Trent,* I, 8, 2
[4] Dan 12:1-3

the body: *but at that time your people shall be delivered, every one whose name shall be found written in the book. And many of those who sleep in the dust of the earth shall awake, some to everlasting life, and some to shame and everlasting contempt.* The Prophet speaks of the special glory awaiting those who have contributed to the salvation of others: *And those who are wise shall shine like the brightness of the firmament; and those who turn many to righteousness, like the stars for ever and ever.*

Christians of every age have repeated that wonderful invocation: *Come, Lord Jesus!*[5] This prayer was so widely used that the early Church has passed it down to us in the original Aramaic.[6] This prayer has been translated into all modern languages and is one of the acclamations which may be used in Holy Mass following the Consecration. In that moment when Christ becomes truly present on the altar, the Church expresses her earnest desire to behold his coming in glory. In this way, *the liturgy on earth is harmonized with that of Heaven. Now, as in each and every Mass, there comes to us that consoling reply: 'He who gives testimony to these things says: Yes, I am coming right away'.*[7] Even though the moment has not arrived for us to be with Jesus in Heaven, we have a foretaste of this glory at the moment of Communion. St John Paul II made this plea: *Let us pray that the heartfelt prayer of the Church, 'Come, Lord Jesus', will become the spontaneous plea of every human heart. We can never be satisfied by the things of the world. Our hearts yearn for the promised blessings still to come.*[8] Then shall our glorified bodies be in the presence of God. Let us pray to Jesus with renewed

---

[5] Rev 22:20
[6] cf 1 Cor 16:22; *The Didache* 10:6
[7] St John Paul II, *Address*, 18 May 1980
[8] *ibid*

vigour: *Vultum tuum, Domine, requiram.*[9] Lord, I long to see your face.

83.2 His coming in glory.

The Lord is my chosen portion and my cup; thou holdest my lot. I keep the Lord always before me; because he is at my right hand, I shall not be moved. Therefore my heart is glad, and my soul rejoices; my body also dwells secure. For thou dost not give me up to Sheol, or let thy godly one see the Pit.[10] In the *Acts of the Apostles*[11]St Luke interprets today's *Responsorial Psalm* as referring to Christ and the events of his Second Coming. *The Lord is my chosen portion and my cup.* He has taken my side. *Therefore my heart is glad, and my soul rejoices; my body also dwells secure,* now and till the end of time. Then Christ will be seated *at the right hand of God.*[12]

Our Lord describes the last days in today's Gospel: *And then they will see the Son of man coming in the clouds with great power and glory. And then he will send out the angels, and gather his elect from the four winds, from the ends of the earth to the ends of heaven.*[13] Though his Incarnation and Passion took place in historical time without any great splendour, his Second Coming will astound the heavens and the earth. As has been earlier foretold by the Prophet Daniel, Jesus states: *The sun will be darkened, and the moon will not give its light, and the stars will be falling from heaven, and the powers in the heavens will be shaken.* He will come as the Redeemer of the world, as King, Judge and Lord of the Universe. The Fathers of the Church have taught us that he will not make a new

---

[9] Ps 26:8
[10] *Responsorial Psalm,* Ps 15:5; 8-10
[11] cf Acts 2:25-32; 13:35
[12] *Second Reading,* Heb 10:11-14; 18
[13] Mark 13:24-32

judgment. *He will summon to his tribunal those who judged him on earth. He who remained silent at that time will refresh the memories of his persecutors who deigned to insult Christ on the Cross. He will say to them: 'You did this to me yet I held my peace'.*

There on Calvary, Christ taught mankind the meaning of mercy. At his Second Coming all men will be obliged to submit to his reign, whether they want to or not ... This is why we pray in the Creed that we believe in him who *'ascended into Heaven and is seated at the right hand of the Father. He will come again in glory to judge the living and the dead, and his kingdom will have no end'.*[14] He will manifest his glory to his faithful servants and also to those who have denied him or persecuted his followers. All humanity will be there to see the Lord as He is: *Therefore God has highly exalted him and bestowed on him the name which is above every name, that at the name of Jesus every knee should bow, in heaven and on earth and under the earth, and every tongue confess that Jesus Christ is Lord, to the glory of God the Father.*[15]

Then we shall fully understand the transcendental importance of our daily struggle to follow Christ. What a treasure lies in those small details of service that we perform day after day for God and our neighbour! Jesus will reward those who prove faithful to the end. *Therefore my heart is glad, and my soul rejoices; my body also dwells secure.*

83.3 Waiting for the day of the Lord.

Today's *Responsorial Psalm* continues: *Thou dost show me the path of life; in thy presence there is fulness of joy, in thy right hand are pleasures for evermore.*[16]

---

[14] St Cyril of Jerusalem, *Catechesis 15 on the two comings of Christ*
[15] Phil 2:9-11
[16] *Responsorial Psalm*, Ps 15:11

The inspired writers of Holy Scripture often refer to the Second Coming with the Greek word *parousia*. This term was used to describe the solemn entry of the Emperor into a city or province. He would then be declared the saviour of that territory. These triumphal arrivals were usually the occasion for feasting and the beginning of a new calendar.[17] Everything combined to signify a new beginning. We ought to look forward to the Second Coming of Christ as to the occasion of a great celebration. The souls of the dead will then be reunited with their glorified bodies. A new calendar will then commence to inaugurate a new form of existence in the presence of God.

The first Christians were inspired by their longing for the *day of the Lord* to persevere in the face of every form of adversity. Over and over again St Paul invokes this future time of blessing. We should imitate the early Christians in this holy practice, especially when we encounter difficulties in our environment. As St Paul reminded the Christians at Thessalonica: *We are bound to give thanks to God always for you, brethren, as is fitting, because your faith is growing abundantly, and the love of every one of you for one another is increasing. Therefore we ourselves boast of you in the churches of God for your steadfastness and faith in all your persecutions and in the afflictions which you are enduring. This is evidence of the righteous judgment of God, that you may be made worthy of the kingdom of God, for which you are suffering.*[18]

From time to time the Lord may permit us to suffer for our beliefs. He allows us to experience sickness and pain. God wants us to put our trust in him. Then we will be more detached from our sense of personal importance, from the state of our health, from our possessions ... We will thus become better prepared for his second advent in glory. It is

---

[17] cf M. Schmaus, *Dogmatic Theology,* VII, p. 134
[18] 2 Thess 1:3-5

of vital importance that we who are living in the midst of the world maintain a lively remembrance that *the Kingdom of God, which had its beginnings here on earth in the Church of Christ, is not of this world, whose form is passing, and that its authentic development cannot be measured by the progress of civilization, of science or of technology. The true growth of the Kingdom of God consists in an ever-deepening knowledge of the unfathomable riches of Christ, in ever-stronger hope of eternal blessings, in an ever more fervent response to the love of God, and in an ever more generous acceptance of grace and holiness by men.*[19]

---

[19] Bl. Paul VI, *Credo of the People of God*, 27

THIRTY-THIRD SUNDAY: YEAR C

84. WORKING UNTIL THE LORD'S COMING

84.1 The prospect of eternal life inspires us to be diligent.

In these final Sundays of the liturgical year, the Church invites the faithful to meditate on *the last things*. In today's *First Reading* the Prophet Malachi speaks in the most graphic terms of the end of time: *For behold, the day comes, burning like an oven, when all the arrogant and all evildoers will be stubble; the day that comes shall burn them up, says the Lord of hosts, so that it will leave them neither root nor branch.*[1] Jesus warns us in today's Gospel that we must be alert for his coming again: *Take heed that you are not led astray ...*[2]

There were some Christians in the early Church who believed that the Second Coming was very imminent. They became so preoccupied about the approaching end of the world that they stopped bothering about practicalities, *living in idleness, mere busybodies, not doing any work.* St Paul laments this situation in his epistle to the Thessalonians which provides the *Second Reading* for today.[3] The Apostle alludes to his own life of constant work. He gives the faithful a memorable precept: *If any one will not work, let him not eat.* For those with nothing to do, says St Paul, *Such persons we command and exhort in the Lord Jesus Christ to do their work in quietness and to*

---

[1] Mal 4:1-2
[2] Luke 21:5-19
[3] 2 Thess 3:7-12

earn their own living.

Life is short, and our encounter with Jesus is near. Some time later He will come in glory, and there will be the resurrection of our bodies. These considerations should move us to become detached from earthly goods, to make good use of our time, to be doing a lively apostolate in the middle of the world. It is through these activities that we will win a place in Heaven. The Second Vatican Council was very insistent on the value of human work: *This council exhorts Christians, as citizens of two cities, to strive to discharge their earthly duties conscientiously and in response to the Gospel spirit. They are mistaken who, knowing that we have here no abiding city but seek one which is to come, think that they may therefore shirk their earthly responsibilities. For they are forgetting that by the faith itself they are more obliged than ever to measure up to these duties, each according to his proper vocation.*[4] These words summarize the imitation of Christ for the modern laity.

We must have our eyes set on Heaven, our ultimate and permanent homeland. At the same time, we need to have our feet firmly planted on the earth. We should work with intensity to give glory to God, to provide for the needs of our family, to improve our society. If we are not engaged in serious professional work, in some real job or other, how are we to sanctify ourselves in the middle of the world? It is only logical that for work to be acceptable to God it must first be acceptable to men. How well, then, am I doing my work in the factory, in business, in medicine, in the law firm ... Looking at things with complete impartiality, let me ask myself – Am I really earning my salary or my wage?

---

[4] Second Vatican Council, *Gaudium et spes,* 43

84.2 Work is one of the greatest goods of the person.

We must be convinced therefore that work is a magnificent reality, and that it has been imposed on us as an inexorable law which, one way or another, binds us all, even though some may try to seek exemption from it. Make no mistake about it. Man's duty to work is not a consequence of original sin, nor is it just a discovery of modern times. It is an indispensable means which God has entrusted to us here on this earth. It is meant to fill out our days and make us sharers in God's creative power. It enables us to earn our living and, at the same time, to reap 'the fruits of eternal life' (John 4:36).[5]

Human work is the ordinary means for our subsistence. It is a privileged setting for the development of the human virtues: manliness, constancy, tenacity, spirit of solidarity, order, optimism in the face of adversity ... *We have to behave as God's children toward all God's sons and daughters.*[6] We have to live *a spirit of charity, of harmony, of understanding.*[7] *We need to root out of our individual lives everything which is an obstacle to Christ's life in us: attachment to our own comfort, the temptation to selfishness, the tendency to be the centre of everything.*[8] *Through your work, through the whole network of human relations, you ought to show the charity of Christ and its concrete expression in friendship, understanding, human affection and peace.*[9] All noble work can be a means for bringing many souls to Christ. The opposite is also true. Laziness, sloth and slovenly ways can bring in their wake grave consequences. *For idleness teaches much evil.*[10]

---

[5] St. J. Escrivá, *Friends of God,* 57
[6] idem, *Christ is passing by,* 36
[7] *Conversations with Monsignor Escrivá,* 35
[8] St. J. Escrivá, *Christ is passing by,* 158
[9] ibid, 166
[10] Sir 33:27

Idleness undermines the possibility of one's human and supernatural perfection. Sloth leads to an erosion of character and opens the door to many temptations.

For much too long the idea of being a good Christian has been limited to the performance of pious practices without their having any integral connection with the world of work. What is worse, there are many religious authorities who mistakenly assert that it is basically impossible to be a full-fledged Christian in the middle of the world.[11] In the face of all this we must meditate seriously about the hidden life of Jesus. Through those silent years of professional work, the Lord teaches us the transcendental value of our daily toil. He proves that unity of life is possible. For it was in his workshop that the world's Redemption was taking place. Let us resolve to meet the Lord in every one of our working days. We ought to ask his help in whatever we are doing. We can offer up that work, no matter how trivial or how important it may appear to human eyes, and be God's partner, no less, in his Creation. Our work environment is a good place to exercise charity as well. We can cultivate the social virtues in our workplace by doing favours for our colleagues, by praying for their families, by being of assistance in their problems ... How important a role does the Lord play in my ordinary work?

84.3 Our professional work should not alienate us from God. On the contrary, it should bring us closer to him.

Our work should lead us to God. It should not become a cause of alienation from the Lord. We should be growing in our Christian vocation in our job, whatever it be. The dedicated Christian should keep in mind that he or she is a citizen of two cities: holding dual citizenship in the city of man and the city of God. Each Christian should strive to

---

[11] cf J. L. Illanes, *On the Theology of Work*, p. 57 ff

correspond to this great calling.[12] We should be cheerful, sincere and understanding with everyone at work.[13] We should be good workers and good friends to those we work with. St Paul exhorted the first Christians of Philippi with regard to this responsibility: *Finally, brethren, whatever is true, whatever is honourable, whatever is just, whatever is pure, whatever is lovely, whatever is gracious, if there is any excellence, if there is anything worthy of praise, think about these things.*[14]

The Christian will convert his work into prayer if he seeks only the glory of God and the good of others, if he offers up his work when beginning it, if he gives thanks to God when finishing it, if he asks God's help in time of trial ... *ut cuncta nostra oratio et operatio a te semper incipiat, et per te coepta finiatur* ... that our prayers and our work begin and end always with God. Work is our daily path to the Lord. *This is why man ought not to limit himself to material production. Work is born of love; it is a manifestation of love and is directed toward love. We see the hand of God, not only in the wonders of nature, but also in our experience of work and effort. Work thus becomes prayer and thanksgiving, because we know we are placed on earth by God, that we are loved by him and made heirs to his promises.*[15]

Work is the means to acquiring holiness for the Christian. It is also a source of grace for the whole Church, since *you are the body of Christ and individually members of it.*[16] When one believer is struggling to improve, then all the others move forward on their way to God. Work done to perfection is, of course, also of great benefit to mankind.

---

[12] cf Phil 1:27; 3:6
[13] cf Phil 2:3-4; 4:4; 2:15; 4:5
[14] Phil 4:8
[15] St. J. Escrivá, *Christ is passing by,* 48
[16] 1 Cor 12:27

Sweat and toil, which work necessarily involves in the present condition of the human race, present the Christian and everyone who is called to follow Christ with the possibility of sharing lovingly in the work that Christ came to do (cf John 17:4). This work of salvation came about through suffering and death on a Cross. By enduring the toil of work in union with Christ crucified for us, man in a way collaborates with the Son of God for the redemption of humanity. He shows himself a true disciple of Christ by carrying the cross in his turn every day (cf Luke 9:23) in the activity that he is called upon to perform.[17]

Through the practice of our profession we will find many opportunities to spread Christ's saving message – in a friendly conversation, in our reaction to setbacks, in our willingness to hear people out ... Our Guardian Angel will help us to say the right word at the right time.

We should prepare for the coming of the Lord by sanctifying our work. We should be helping others to think about their eternal destiny. Let us always make the best use of our time and resources for the greater glory of God. We cannot give in to laziness.

St Joseph is our Father and Lord. He will show us how to sanctify our daily work, just as he taught Jesus his trade. At the workbench where he plied his trade together with Jesus, Joseph brought human work closer to the mystery of the Redemption.[18] And close to Joseph we will always find Mary.

---

[17] St John Paul II, Encyclical, *Laborem exercens,* 14 September 1981, 27

[18] *idem,* Apostolic Exhortation, *Redemptoris custos,* 15 August 1989, 22

THIRTY-THIRD WEEK: MONDAY

85. THE LORD NEVER WITHHOLDS HIS GRACE

85.1 To pray more earnestly in moments of obscurity.

Today's Gospel relates an incident that happened as the Lord was going up to Jerusalem: *As he drew near to Jericho, a blind man was sitting by the roadside begging.*[1]

Several of the Fathers of the Church have held this blind man to be a symbol of *those who do not have a clear vision of eternal light.*[2] There are times when the soul can experience obscurity and even blindness. The path that once seemed so clearly defined can become more difficult to make out. What was light and joy can turn to shadows. Sadness can then overtake the soul. This situation may often be the consequence of personal sins or a failure to correspond to grace: *perhaps the dust we stir up as we walk – our miseries – forms an opaque cloud that cuts off the light from above.*[3] Another explanation is that the Lord may permit the onset of a period of obscurity as a means of purifying the soul, of increasing our humility and trust in him. When we experience this kind of trial everything demands more effort. That is only logical. These are times when the devil tries to plunge us more deeply into sadness and undermine our dedication.

No matter what its origin, what is a person to do in this quandary? The blind man of Jericho – *Bartimaeus, the son of Timaeus*[4] – has given us a wonderful lesson: we should

---

[1] Luke 18:35-43
[2] cf St Gregory the Great, *Homilies on the Gospels,* I, 2, 2
[3] St. J. Escrivá, *Christ is passing by,* 34
[4] Mark 10:46-52

...ord all the more earnestly. He is always near. He ... prayer. He will respond in his infinite mercy. ...gh it may seem as if He would pass us by, He is wholly conscious of our situation. Our prayers may be impeded by all kinds of difficulties. This is what happened to Bartimaeus: *And those who were in front rebuked him, telling him to be silent.* The blind man found his path to Jesus strewn with obstacles. We may experience the same phenomenon *when we want to return to God. Our past faults and failures seem to besiege our heart and becloud our understanding. Our spirits are thrown into confusion. It is as if our past sins wanted to silence our prayers.*[5] We feel the weight of our weakness and sins.

Let us take a lesson from the blind beggar: *But he cried out all the more, 'Son of David, have mercy on me!' The man whom the crowd wanted to silence raises his voice more and more. This is a model for us ... the greater our interior confusion, the more our difficulties on the way, so much the stronger should our prayers become.*[6]

It appeared as if Jesus would continue on his way to Jerusalem without halting. But he called the blind man to himself. Bartimaeus drew near and Jesus asked him: *'What do you want me to do for you?'* He said, *'Lord, let me receive my sight'. And Jesus said to him, 'Receive your sight; your faith has made you well'. And immediately he received his sight and followed him, glorifying God.*

At times it is very hard to figure out the causes for such trials. We may not know the reason, but we can be sure of the remedy. It is persevering prayer. *When darkness surrounds us and our soul is blind and restless, we have to go to the Light, like Bartimaeus. Repeat, shout, cry out ever more strongly, 'Domine, ut videam!' Lord, that I may see. And daylight will dawn upon you, and you will be able*

---

[5] St Gregory the Great, *op cit,* I, 2, 3
[6] cf *ibid,* I, 2, 4

to enjoy the brightness He grants you.[7]

85.2 Spiritual direction is the normal means by which God acts upon souls.

Jesus is the King of the Universe. He is able to cure any malady that He wants. He worked certain miracles with a word, a gesture, sometimes from a distance ... He also cured people in stages, as He did with the blind man in St John's Gospel.[8] In our day Jesus often gives his light to souls by means of his Church. When the Magi lost track of their star, they acted with common sense and asked the inhabitants of Jerusalem for help, eventually working their way up to Herod. *But we Christians have no need to go to Herod nor to the wise men of this world. Christ has given his Church sureness in doctrine and a flow of grace in the sacraments. He has arranged things so that there will always be people to guide and lead us, to remind us constantly of our way ... That is why, if the Lord allows us to be left in the dark even in little things, if we feel that our faith is not firm, we should go to the good shepherd ... He gives his life for others and wants to be in word and behaviour a soul in love. He may be a sinner too, but he trusts always in Christ's forgiveness and mercy.*[9]

No one can be his own spiritual director without an extraordinary grace from God. We know how little objectivity we have in looking at ourselves. The passions make it difficult, even impossible, for us to discern the right path we should be on. This is why holy Mother Church has always recommended that her children receive personal spiritual direction. If we do not take advantage of the means for guidance that the Lord puts within our reach, how can we be so bold as to expect extraordinary personal

---

[7] St. J. Escrivá, *Furrow,* 862
[8] cf John 9:1 ff
[9] St. J. Escrivá, *Christ is passing by,* 34

illuminations from Heaven? Jesus is ready to work miracles for souls, but He first wants to see sincerity and docility. The Lord will always give us his grace if we ask for it in humble petition.

St Teresa has written with her characteristic humility: *Our prayer must therefore be very earnest for those who give us light. What should we be without them in the midst of these violent storms which now disturb the Church?*[10] St John of the Cross has concurred: *He that desires to be alone, without the support of a master and guide, will be like the tree that is alone in the field and has no owner. However much fruit it bears, passers-by will pluck it all, and it will not mature.*

The tree that is cultivated and kept with the favour of its owner gives in due season the fruit that is expected of it.

The soul that is alone and without a master, and has virtue, is like the burning coal that is alone. It will grow colder rather than hotter.[11]

Let us never fail to have recourse to the Lord, especially when the going gets rough. If we take advantage of the means of spiritual direction, the Lord will be able to work miracles with us.

85.3 Having faith in the efficacy of spiritual direction.

Through our participation in spiritual direction we will learn how to identify our will with the divine Will. Let us consider the case of St Paul. Admittedly, he experienced a most unusual conversion, but afterwards God wanted him to be guided by other people. Ananias laid his hands on Paul and *immediately something like scales fell from his eyes and he regained his sight.*[12]

---

[10] St Teresa, *Life*, 13, 30
[11] St John of the Cross, *Complete Works*, III, *Spiritual Sentences and Maxims*, p. 219
[12] cf Acts 9:17-18

We have to see Christ in the person of our spiritual director. Like Christ, he will teach us, heal us and strengthen our soul for the rest of our journey. We will benefit from spiritual direction only if we approach it with *supernatural vision*. Without this lively sense of faith the exercise will be almost meaningless. At best it will be an exchange of opinions. If we have the proper attitude, spiritual direction can strengthen us in our effort to be identified with the Will of God. We should not expect our spiritual director to resolve our temporal problems. Our spiritual director will help us in our struggle for sanctity. Let us always remember that his mission is thoroughly supernatural in character.

We have to keep in mind that Christ and his Church want to reach us through other people. Let us resolve to have more and more faith and trust in this spiritual assistance. Bartimaeus drew near to Jesus who is the Way, the Truth and the Light. We too can approach Christ through the person who acts as his instrument in our formation. Spiritual direction may be likened to a grand construction project: *Have you seen how that imposing building was constructed? One brick after another. Thousands. But, one by one. And bags and bags of cement, one by one. And stone upon stone, each of them insignificant compared with the massive whole. And beams of steel, and men working, hour after hour, day after day ... Did you see how that imposing building was constructed? By dint of little things!*[13] A painting is composed of a series of brush strokes, one by one. A book is written page by page. A cable is strung wire by wire so that it may support an enormous weight.

If we make good use of spiritual direction, we will feel just like Bartimaeus after his cure. He followed Jesus with great joy, *glorifying God.*

---

[13] St. J. Escrivá, *The Way,* 823

86. THE FIDELITY OF ELEAZAR

86.1 Eleazar's exemplary faithfulness.

We have in today's *First Reading* an account of some events during the fierce persecution waged by King Antiochus against the Jewish people. The Temple was profaned and then sacrilegiously consecrated to Zeus. The Jews were not allowed to observe the Sabbath. During the monthly celebrations in honour of the king's birthday, the Jews were forced to take part in idolatrous sacrifices and eat ritually impure meat.

Today's *Reading* tells the story of a well respected Jewish scribe named Eleazar who was ninety years of age at the time of this persecution. He steadfastly refused to betray the faith of his fathers, preferring death to practising idolatry. It so happened that friends of Eleazar whom he had known for a long time had been persuaded to enforce Jewish compliance with pagan sacrifices. These men privately urged Eleazar to join in the sacrificial meal with meat of his own choosing, a compromise which, he was assured, would save him from execution. Yet Eleazar made a noble resolve to honour God and his holy law. This heroic decision was in accordance with his entire exemplary life. Eleazar realised that it would be beneath the dignity of a man of his years to engage in such dissimulation. He was also anxious not to give bad example to the young: *'Such pretence is not worthy of our time of life', he said, 'lest many of the young should suppose that Eleazar in his ninetieth year has gone over to an alien religion, and through my pretence, for the sake of living a brief moment longer, they should be led astray because of me, while I defile and disgrace my old age. For even if for the present I should avoid the punishment of men, yet whether I live or die I shall not escape the hands of the Almighty.*[1]

Eleazar refused to give in and so he was taken at once to be tortured. When he was about to die he groaned aloud: *It is clear to the Lord in his holy knowledge that, though I might have been saved from death, I am enduring terrible sufferings in my body under this beating, but in my soul I am glad to suffer these things because I fear him.* The inspired author relates that Eleazar's heroic death was *an example of nobility and a memorial of courage, not only to the young but to the great body of his nation.* We Christians should also be loyal to the Lord. No amount of 'peer pressure' or inconvenience should make us compromise our beliefs or our principles.

St John Chrysostom has called Eleazar the *proto-martyr of the Old Testament.*[2] Eleazar's serene composure in the face of martyrdom is in some way a foretaste of the joy in persecution that Jesus promised to his disciples.[3] The Lord also grants this joy to those who persevere in the faith and their vocation, despite every type of contradiction.

86.2 Obstacles that threaten fidelity.

The first Christians had the custom of speaking of their fellow Christians as *the faithful.*[4] This terminology came into common use during a period of harsh external difficulties, persecution, campaigns of slander and coercion. The pagan world of that time did its level best to impose its beliefs and practices on the Christian community, yet they remained *faithful* despite the most

---

[1] *First Reading,* Year I, 2 Mac 6:18-31
[2] St John Chrysostom, *Homily 3 about the holy Maccabees*
[3] cf Matt 5:12
[4] Acts 10:45; 2 Cor 6:15; Eph 1:1

grievous consequences. St John records these words in the Book of Revelation: *Be faithful unto death, and I will give you the crown of life.*[5] This is the challenge facing Christians of every age: *Be faithful unto death.* The Evangelist gives this warning from the same passage: *Do not fear what you are about to suffer. Behold, the devil is about to throw some of you into prison, that you may be tested, and for ten days.* These *ten days* may be understood to symbolize our time on earth. We do not have a lot of time. When we suffer some contradiction, even some discrimination because of our beliefs, how do we react? Do we firmly resolve to be faithful, no matter what people may say? St John Paul II stated: *It is easy to be consistent for a day or two. It is difficult and important to be consistent for one's whole life. It is easy to be consistent in the hour of enthusiasm; it is difficult to be so in the hour of tribulation. And only a consistency that lasts throughout the whole of life can be called faithfulness.*[6]

Sometimes the obstacles do not arise from our environment, but rather spring from within our being. Pride is the principal obstacle to fidelity. Next to pride there is lukewarmness, the spiritual disease that robs us of our joy in following Christ. Lukewarmness leads us to indulge in ridiculous fantasies. We may suffer from a period of spiritual obscurity or dryness. This problem may arise from our lack of struggle, or it may be God's way of purifying our intention. Whatever the cause may be, the solution will normally lie in humble recourse to spiritual direction and in persevering prayer to the Lord. If we are willing to be led, God will take us by the hand. St Josemaría Escrivá once recalled: *One of my most vivid childhood memories is of seeing, up in the mountains near my home, those signposts they planted alongside the hill paths. I was struck by those*

---

[5] Rev 2:10
[6] St John Paul II, *Address,* 26 January 1979

tall posts usually painted red. It was explained to me then that when the snow fell, covering up everything, paths, seeded fields and pastures, thickets, boulders and ravines, the poles stood out as sure reference points, so that everyone would always know where the road went.

Something similar happens in the interior life. There are times of spring and summer, but there are also winters, days without sun and nights bereft of moonlight. We can't afford to let our friendship with Jesus depend on our moods, on our ups and downs. To do so would imply selfishness and laziness, and is certainly incompatible with love.

Therefore, in times of wind and snow, a few solid practices of piety, which are not sentimental but firmly rooted and adjusted to one's special circumstances, will serve as the red posts always marking out the way for us, until the time comes when Our Lord decides to make the sun shine again. Then the snows melt and our hearts beat fast once more, burning with a fire that never really went out. It was merely hidden in the embers, beneath the ashes produced by a time of trial, or by our own poor efforts or lack of sacrifice.[7]

86.3 Being true to our promises and commitments.

Eleazar's heroic example was an inspiration to many of the Chosen People to remain true to the faith of their fathers. A person's fidelity has widespread consequences, even though one may not fully realize it. One of the great joys the Lord will give us in Heaven is the sight of how many have persevered in their faith and vocation thanks to our good example.

The human virtue which corresponds to *fidelity* is *loyalty*. Loyalty is essential for social harmony. Without

---

[7] St. J. Escrivá, *Friends of God*, 151

this virtue of loyalty all bonds and relations between peoples would degenerate into barbarism. *The faithful observance of contractual arrangements ensures tranquil relations between peoples.*[8] Social life is literally impossible in the absence of mutual trust, honour, loyalty. It may seem to us that these values are in short supply in today's business world and in the corridors of political power. Certain individuals are adept at and accustomed to using deception and manipulation to deform public opinion. A person's word of honour is frequently tossed aside in the face of more promising opportunities. People speak of the marital contract and other solemnly sworn commitments to God as if they had no lasting character. Some disobey their religious duties for the sake of pleasure, or wealth, or social advancement.

We Christians need to be the light and salt of the world. We have to give a heroic example of fidelity to our commitments, whether to God or to men. As St Augustine encouraged Christians of the Fourth Century: *The husband has to be faithful to his wife; the wife must be faithful to the husband. Both have to be faithful to God. Those of you who have committed yourselves to celibacy, be true to your promise. Remember that you are obliged to fulfil your commitments ... Make sure not to engage in any dishonest business dealings. Be vigilant against lying and perjury.*[9] St Augustine's counsel is just as valid today as it was then.

With all our trust in the Lord, let us persevere in the little things of each day. Then we will have the immense joy of hearing the Lord say to us in Heaven: *Well done, good and faithful servant; you have been faithful over a little, I will set you over much; enter into the joy of your master.*[10]

---

[8] Pius XII, *Address,* 24 December 1940, 26
[9] St Augustine, *Sermon 260*
[10] Matt 25:21-23

87. WE WANT CHRIST TO REIGN!

87.1 To re-establish all things in Christ.

As Jesus drew near to Jerusalem, many hoped that He would inaugurate the Kingdom of God on earth. They imagined that the Lord would make a triumphal entrance into the Holy City and that the Roman occupation would be overthrown. We know from the Gospels that the Apostles argued on several occasions about who would be the most powerful figure in the Messiah's government. These illusions were an extension of the hopes and fears of the Jewish people of that time. As part of his effort to correct these false expectations, Jesus told the parable recorded in today's Gospel.[1]

A nobleman went into a far country to receive kingly power. Many of the petty rulers of the Roman Empire had to go to Rome to receive investiture from the Senate and the Emperor. The nobleman in the parable leaves the administration of his territory in the hands of ten trusted associates. Before leaving, he gave them ten *pounds*. The *pound* was not negotiable currency, being used, rather, as a monetary unit for accounting purposes. It was equivalent to thirty-five grams of gold. The nobleman gave his deputies this charge: *Trade with these till I come.* They were to do their best to turn a profit. And this is what they did for days, weeks and months until the day of his return.

The Church has acted in a similar fashion since the day of Pentecost. At that time she received the immense Gift of the Holy Spirit, the infallible Word of God, the

---

[1] Luke 19:11-28

sacraments, indulgences ... St Josemaría Escrivá has commented: *In two thousand years a great task has been accomplished, and it has often been accomplished very well. On other occasions there have been mistakes, making the Church lose ground, just as today there is loss of ground, fear and a timid attitude on the part of some, and at the same time no lack of courage and generosity in others. But, whatever the situation, the human race is being continually renewed. In each generation it is necessary to go on with the effort to help men realize the greatness of their vocation as children of God, to teach them to carry out the commandment of love for God and neighbour.*[2] We have to make good use of these divine gifts.

Each and every Christian shares in this important responsibility. The Second Vatican Council has declared: *Enlivened and united in his Spirit, we journey towards the consummation of human history, one which fully accords with the counsel of God's love: 'To re-establish all things in Christ, both those in the heavens and those on the earth' (Eph 11:10).*[3] This is our charge until the Lord returns, until the moment of our death, which may not be so very far distant. We need to make the Lord present in all earthly realities. God has created all things and He maintains them in existence. Yet he wants us to offer them up to his glory. This is our task in business, politics, family life, sports, education ...

The Lord says to us in the Book of Revelation: *Behold, I am coming soon, bringing my recompense, to repay every one for what he has done. I am the Alpha and the Omega, the first and the last, the beginning and the end.*[4] We will find the meaning of our life in Christ and nowhere else. The entire Church and each of her members carry the

---

[2] St. J. Escrivá, *Christ is passing by,* 121
[3] Second Vatican Council, *Gaudium et spes,* 45
[4] Rev 22:12-13

treasure of Christ. We give glory to God whenever we struggle to be faithful to our duties as citizens and believers.

87.2 The rejection of Jesus.

While the ten trusted servants were busy with their trading, the other subjects of the absent nobleman had a different plan. *But his citizens hated him and sent an embassy after him, saying, 'We do not want this man to reign over us'.* The Lord must have felt considerable pain at the very thought of these words. Clearly, the parable was autobiographical in nature. Jesus is the nobleman who travels to a far-away land. The Lord was well aware of the rising hatred in the hearts of the Pharisees. Paradoxically, the more He manifested his goodness and mercy, the more his enemies hated him. How grieved the Master must have been in the face of this whole-hearted rejection! Their hatred would soon find its culmination during the Passion and Crucifixion.

The rejection in the parable is also meant to signify the treatment accorded to Our Lord in subsequent centuries. In our own time, there are abundant manifestations of this rebellious spirit. We find acts of hatred and indifference in literature, in the arts, in science, in family life ... One can almost hear the defiant shout: *Nolumus hunc regnare super nos!* We do not want this man to reign over us! *He is the author of the universe and of every creature, but He does not lord it over us. He begs us to give him a little love, as He silently shows us his wounds.*

Why then do so many people not know him? Why do we still hear that cruel protest: 'We do not want this man to reign over us'? (Luke 19:14) There are millions of people in this world who reject Jesus Christ in this way; or rather they reject his shadow, for they do not know Christ. They have not seen the beauty of his face, they do not realize how wonderful his teaching is. This sad state of affairs makes me want to atone to Our Lord. When I hear that endless clamour – expressed more in ignoble actions than in words – I feel the need to cry out, 'He must reign!' (1 Cor 15:25) ...

For many years now, Our Lord has urged me to repeat a silent cry, *'Serviam'* – *'I will serve!'* Let us ask him to strengthen our desire to give ourselves, to be faithful to his calling – with naturalness, without fuss or noise – in the middle of everyday life. Let us thank him from the depth of our heart. We will pray to him as his subjects, as his sons! And our mouth will be filled with milk and honey. We will find great pleasure in speaking of the kingdom of God, a kingdom of freedom, a freedom He has won for us (cf Gal 4:31).[5] Let us serve Jesus as our King and Lord, as the Saviour of all mankind and of each one of us. *Serviam!* I will serve you, Lord! This battle cry shall sound in the intimacy of our prayer.

87.3 Extending the Kingdom of Christ.

After a time, the nobleman, now vested with kingly authority, returned to his homeland. He generously rewarded those servants who had done as he had commanded. He castigated those who had wasted their time and his gifts. *The bad servant was not diligent, and he brought no return; he did not honour his master, and he was punished. Thus, then, to apply the faculties he has given me to know, to love, and to serve him, and by this diligence to refer my whole being to him, is for me to glorify God.*[6] This is the purpose of our life: to give glory to God now on earth and for evermore in heaven in the company of the Blessed Virgin, the angels and the saints. If we have this purpose well in mind, then we will be good

---

[5] St. J. Escrivá, *op cit,* 179
[6] J. Tissot, *The Interior Life,* p. 55

administrators of God's gifts.

St Augustine had the habit of saying, *Love is never burdensome.*[7] The Lord is eager to reward our fidelity in this life. What a treasure He has in store for us in Heaven! We have to use our time and resources to extend the reign of Christ on earth: in our home, among our neighbours, with our fellow students at the university, with our colleagues and clients at work ... We have to make a special effort to do apostolate with those who have in some way been entrusted to our care. St Augustine has left us this sage counsel: *Do not forsake the care of your little ones. Do everything you can for the salvation of your home.*[8]

In these days before the Feast of Christ the King, let us pray over and over again: *Regnare Christum volumus!* We want Christ to reign! First and foremost, we should be sure that Christ reigns in my mind, my will, my heart and my whole being.[9] *My Lord Jesus, grant that I may feel your grace and second it in such a way that I empty my heart, so that you, my Friend, my Brother, my King, my God, my Love ... may fill it!*[10]

---

[7] cf St Augustine, *Sermon 51,* 2
[8] *idem, Sermon 94*
[9] cf Pius XI, Encyclical, *Quas primas,* 11 December 1925, 21
[10] St. J. Escrivá, *The Forge,* 913

88. THE TEARS OF JESUS

88.1 Jesus is not indifferent to the fortunes of his children.

At the start of his triumphal march into Jerusalem Jesus began the descent along the western slope of the Mount of Olives. Jesus halted at a turn of the road where the Holy City suddenly came into view: *And when He drew near and saw the city He wept over it.*[1] All the joy and enthusiasm of his followers could not compensate for his tremendous sorrow. The Lord foresaw the wholesale destruction of this beloved city by Titus and his armies – *because you did not know the time of your visitation.* The Messiah had walked the streets of Jerusalem. He had taught the *Good News* in the Temple. His miracles had been witnessed by the inhabitants ... yet they did not respond. *Would that even today you knew the things that make for peace! But now they are hid from your eyes. For the days shall come upon you, when your enemies will cast up a bank about you and surround you, and hem you in on every side, and dash you to the ground, you and your children within you, and they will not leave one stone upon another in you; because you did not know the time of your visitation.*[2]

We can read between these lines the anguish that clutched the Saviour's loving heart.[3] Why had not Jerusalem responded to the repeated invitations of the

---

[1] Luke 19:41
[2] Luke 19:41-44
[3] L. C. Fillion, *The Life of Christ*, III, p. 246

Lord? Why were the Jewish leaders so obstinate in refusing to acknowledge the self-evident fulfilment of the Messianic prophecies? Jesus had given them many opportunities to change their hearts in the past. This was their last chance. With their steadfast refusal they brought down upon Jerusalem the terrible denouement of this awful prophecy. The Lord is overcome with sorrow at the thought of this catastrophe. Jesus is never indifferent to the fortunes of his children. His eyes are filled with tears. His words are halting and filled with grief.

St John has left us another account of the tears of Jesus. The Master had arrived in Bethany after the death of his dear friend Lazarus. He was approached by Mary, the sister of Lazarus, who was weeping inconsolably. *When Jesus saw her weeping, and the Jews who came with her also weeping, He was deeply moved in spirit and troubled; and He said, 'Where have you laid him?' They said to him, 'Lord, come and see'.* At this moment Jesus revealed his great sorrow at the death of his friend: *Jesus wept.* The Jews who were there present remarked: *See how He loved him!*[4]

Jesus is *perfect God and perfect man.*[5] He understood the meaning of friendship. He knew how to love. Whenever Jesus showed his feelings (as in these situations), He was expressing a true human love. Admittedly, this expression did not express the fulness of divine love, but it gives us some idea of God's attitude to his children. Let us meditate today on the Sacred Heart of Jesus. We should understand that God is very interested in our response to his grace and his friendship. He is moved by the sacrifices we make in order to visit him in the Blessed Sacrament every day. He is pleased by our sincere effort to grow in friendship with him. He follows our struggle to be

---

[4] John 11:33-36
[5] *Athanasian Creed*

charitable towards others, to serve him in the middle of the world ... He is very proud of our performance!

Man cannot live without love. He remains a being that is incomprehensible for himself, his life is senseless, if love is not revealed to him, if he does not encounter love, if he does not experience it and make it his own, if he does not participate intimately in it ... The man who wishes to understand himself thoroughly – and not just in accordance with immediate, partial, often superficial, and even illusory standards and measures of his being – he must with his unrest, uncertainty and even his weakness and sinfulness, with his life and death, draw near to Christ. He must, so to speak, enter into him with all his own self, he must 'appropriate' and assimilate the whole of the reality of the Incarnation and Redemption in order to find himself. If this profound process takes place within him, he then bears fruit not only of adoration of God but also of deep wonder at himself. How precious must man be in the eyes of the Creator, if he 'gained so great a Redeemer' (Hymn 'Exsultet' of the Easter Vigil), and if God 'gave his only Son' in order that man 'should not perish but have eternal life' (cf John 3:16).[6]

88.2 The Most Holy Humanity of Christ.

Authentic Christian life consists in an ever-deepening personal friendship with Christ. Our goal as Christians is to imitate the Master and incarnate his doctrine in our life. Following Jesus has nothing to do with esoteric theoretical speculation. Christianity is not just a battle against sin. Jesus wants us to love him with deeds. He wants us to recognize his love for us. *For Christ is alive. He is not someone who has gone, someone who existed for a time and then passed on, leaving us a wonderful example and a*

---

[6] St John Paul II, Encyclical, *Redemptor hominis*, 4 March 1979, 10

great memory.[7] Christ lives among us. We have to see him with the eyes of faith. We have to speak with him in our prayer. He hears us even before we say a word. Jesus is not indifferent to our successes and failures, to our joys and sorrows. *For by his incarnation the Son of God has united himself in some fashion with every man. He worked with human hands, He thought with a human mind, acted by human choice and loved with a human heart. Born of the Virgin Mary, He has truly been made one of us, like us in all things except sin.*

As an innocent lamb He merited for us life by the free shedding of his own blood. In him God reconciled us to himself and among ourselves; from bondage to the devil and sin He delivered us, so that each one of us can say with the Apostle: The Son of God 'loved me and gave himself up for me' (Gal 2:20).[8] His most holy Humanity is the bridge that leads us to our Father God.

Today we are considering the tears of Jesus for that city he loved so much. Jerusalem did not recognize the arrival of her Messiah, even though this arrival was the city's reason for being. We have to pray about those times when we have made the Lord weep by our sins and omissions. Have we ever left the Lord waiting expectantly for us like those nine lepers who failed to return and give thanks?

If we do not love Jesus, we will make no progress in the interior life. Our friendship with Christ must be nourished by the Gospels. There we will discover that Jesus is profoundly human and very close to us. At times we will see him wearied by the day's journey.[9] He is there seated beside Jacob's Well after a long, hot day. He is thirsty. Jesus turns his attention to a Samaritan woman. He converts her and then converts the whole town of Sychar.

---

[7] St. J. Escrivá, *Christ is passing by,* 102
[8] Second Vatican Council, *Gaudium et spes,* 22
[9] cf John 4:6

We see Jesus hungry. Once when he was travelling from Bethany to Jerusalem, he approached a fig tree that had only leaves on it.[10] We see Jesus worn out by an intense day of preaching to the crowds. He was so exhausted that He fell asleep aboard a boat in the middle of a serious storm.[11]

Christ had time for everyone he met along his way: *As he went ashore he saw a great throng; and he had compassion on them, and healed their sick.*[12] He cared for people's spiritual and physical needs. The life of Jesus is a marvellous fountain of love. If we contemplate his life we will find it so much easier to follow him whole-heartedly. *Whenever we get tired – in our work, in our studies, in our apostolic endeavours – when our horizon is darkened by lowering clouds, then let us turn our eyes to Jesus, to Jesus who is so good, and who also gets tired; to Jesus who is hungry and suffers thirst. Lord, how well you make yourself understood! How lovable you are! You show us that you are just like us, in everything but sin, so that we can feel utterly sure that, together with you, we can conquer all our evil inclinations, all our faults. For neither weariness nor hunger matter, nor thirst, nor tears ... since Christ also grew weary, knew hunger, was thirsty, and wept. What is important is that we struggle to fulfil the Will of our heavenly Father (cf John 4:34).*[13]

88.3 Having the same sentiments as Jesus.

The Lord's lament over Jerusalem contains a great mystery. Jesus had expelled demons, healed sick people, raised the dead, converted tax collectors and sinners. Yet all his efforts had come to naught as far as Jerusalem was concerned. Her people were too hard-hearted. We have

---

[10] cf Mark 11:12-13
[11] cf Mark 4:38
[12] Matt 14:14
[13] St. J. Escrivá, *Friends of God*, 201

here a glimpse of what effect this kind of rejection has on the Sacred Heart of Jesus. *At times, seeing those souls asleep, one feels an enormous desire to shout at them, to make them take notice, to wake them up from that terrible torpor they have fallen into. It is so sad to see them walk like a blind man hitting out with his stick, without finding the way! I can well understand how the tears of Jesus over Jerusalem sprang from his perfect charity.*[14]

The work of the Master is continued by his followers. We participate in the sentiments of the Sacred Heart. When we look at Jesus, we have to learn how to care for our fellow men. We have to treat each person with the respect he or she deserves. We should strive to understand our neighbour's defects and make allowance for them. Christ will teach us how to be authentically human. Every day we will seek to make life more pleasant for the people around us. We will give way in our likes and dislikes. We will show a sincere interest in the health of others. Above all, we will be concerned about the spiritual well-being of everyone we deal with in the course of the day. Let us bring them closer to Christ. St John Chrysostom has written: *There is no better sign by which a Christian may be identified, than the care he shows for his fellow man.*[15] Today we ask Our Mother Holy Mary to give us a heart like that of her Son. As a result, we will never be indifferent to the fortunes of our neighbours.

---

[14] *idem, Furrow,* 210
[15] St John Chrysostom, *Homily 6,* 3

THIRTY-THIRD WEEK: FRIDAY

89. A HOUSE OF PRAYER

89.1 Jesus expels the merchants from the Temple.

Today's *First Reading* from the *Book of Maccabees* recounts how Judas Maccabeus and his brothers defeated a superior Gentile army.[1] Following their victory in the field, Judas and his brothers decided to cleanse and re-dedicate the sanctuary of the Temple, which had been profaned by the Gentiles. *It was dedicated with songs and harps and lutes and cymbals. All the people fell on their faces and worshipped and blessed Heaven, who had prospered them. So they celebrated the dedication of the altar for eight days, and offered burnt offerings with gladness; they offered a sacrifice of deliverance and praise. They decorated the front of the Temple with golden crowns and small shields; they restored the gates and the chambers for the priests, and furnished them with doors. There was very great gladness among the people, and the reproach of the Gentiles was removed.* Judas, his brothers and the leaders of Israel declared that the dedication of the altar would be commemorated every year in that season. After so many years of humiliation, the Chosen People gave heartfelt thanks to God for their long-awaited deliverance.

The Gospel for today's Mass records the holy indignation of Jesus at the commercialisation of the Temple.[2] He expels the merchants from the sacred precincts which they have turned into a marketplace. *The Book of Exodus (23:15) commanded the Israelites not to*

---

[1] *First Reading,* Year I, 1 Mac 4:36-37; 52-59
[2] Luke 19:45-48

*enter the Temple empty-handed, but to bring some victim
to be sacrificed. To make this easier for people who had to
travel a certain distance, a veritable market developed in
the Temple courtyards, with animals being bought and sold
for sacrificial purposes. Originally this may have made
sense, but seemingly as time went on commercial gain
became the dominant purpose of this buying and selling of
victims; probably the priests themselves and Temple
servants benefited from this trade or even operated it. The
net result was that the Temple looked more like a livestock
mart than a place for meeting God.*[3]

Filled with a holy zeal for the house of his Father,
Jesus took action: *And making a whip of cords, He drove
them all, with the sheep and oxen, out of the Temple; and
He poured out the coins of the money-changers and
overturned their tables.*[4] The Lord proclaimed the true
purpose of the Temple, using a well-known verse from the
Prophet Isaiah: *My house shall be called a house of
prayer.*[5] Then Jesus added with some bitterness, *but you
have made it a den of robbers.* Our Lord wished to leave us
a lasting example of how we should respect sacred places.
We should enter the Christian temple – our churches – with
great respect for Jesus Christ who is truly present in the
Tabernacle. *Piety has its own good manners. Learn them.
It's a shame to see those 'pious' people who don't know
how to assist at Mass – even those who hear it daily – nor
how to bless themselves (they make some weird gestures
very hurriedly), nor how to bend their knee before the
Tabernacle (their ridiculous genuflections seem a
mockery), nor how to bow their heads reverently before an
image of Our Lady.*[6]

---

[3] *The Navarre Bible,* note to Matt 21:12-13
[4] John 2:15-17
[5] Is 56:7
[6] St. J. Escrivá, *The Way,* 541

89.2 The temple is a place of prayer.

My house shall be a house of prayer. What a wonderful clarity there is in this unforgettable expression! We have to honour God's intention. Let us go the Lord's house with love, joy and deep respect. God himself is waiting for us there.

We are all very familiar with the kind of ceremonial associated with state occasions, political life, academic convocations and sporting events such as the Olympics. We know that these functions have evolved a certain protocol which must be adhered to. This is something that is taken very seriously. These ceremonies are enriched by many details that have to do with dress, with order of precedence and manner of movement.

We find that similar traditional formalities apply to courtship and marriage. When people really care for one another, they show their love in little customary details of affection. Thus, the engagement ring is symbolic of the love between a man and a woman. When the man gives his fiancee the ring he uses a simple ritual act to express his most intimate feelings. The person, after all, is more than a composition of body and soul. He needs to manifest his emotions and beliefs in external actions. When we see someone make a reverent genuflection before the Tabernacle, for example, we sense that he or she believes in the presence of God there. The gesture springs from the innermost soul. It helps each and every one of us to have more faith and love. It is edifying to note something St John Paul II said in this regard. As a young man he was greatly impressed by the simple and sincere piety of his father: *The mere fact of seeing him on his knees had a decisive influence on my early years.*[7]

Christian people manifest their faith in a variety of

---

[7] A. Frossard, *Be Not Afraid!*, p. 14

signs and symbols: in their genuflections, in their tone of voice during the liturgy, in the use of incense, in the respect for sacred ornaments and objects, in the dignity of sacred music. The very splendour of the liturgical components facilitates our homage to God. When we study the artistic treasures of the sixteenth and seventeenth centuries we find that an object's value lies in direct proportion to its relation to the Holy Eucharist. In certain sacred vessels the artist's labours are evident only after close inspection, as if this art were intended for God alone. We should be moved by this kind of love for God towards a stronger faith.

The Lord appreciates our greeting whenever we enter his churches. We should greet him first before anyone else. We should also make the effort necessary to arrive for Holy Mass a few minutes before it begins. How much love do we put into our genuflections? Do we maintain a good posture in the presence of the Lord? Do we show by our actions and behaviour that we truly believe in the true presence of the Lord in the Tabernacle?

89.3 The meaning of authentic worship.

The Lord gave Moses very detailed instructions concerning the dignity to be accorded divine worship. He laid down specifications for the construction of the tabernacle, the ark of the Covenant and the altar. He gave Moses guidelines for sacred utensils and priestly vestments. He explained the rites of preparation for sacrificial victims. He listed the feasts to be celebrated. God named the tribe and the people who would exercise the priestly function.[8]

There on Mount Sinai God taught his Chosen People how to respect the objects used in his cult. The problem was that the Jews were continually being influenced by the

---

[8] cf Ex 25:1 ff

pagan religions all around them. God wanted to give his people a profound respect for the sacred. Jesus Christ underlined this teaching with a new spirit. His zeal for the house of God is fundamental to the Good News. By throwing the merchants out of the Temple, Jesus left no room for doubt about his meaning. He was willing to use strong words in his preaching on this subject: *Do not give dogs what is holy; and do not throw your pearls before swine.*[9]

It seems that there is an almost ubiquitous denial of anything sacred in our contemporary world. *In our day, a very false opinion is popularized which holds that the sense of religion implanted in men by nature is to be regarded as something adventitious or imaginary, and hence, is to be rooted completely from the mind as altogether inconsistent with the spirit of our age and the progress of civilization.*[10] How striking it is to note that the propagators of these ideas, who claim to be themselves so highly cultured, receive with such credulity the prognostications of computer programming. Everybody believes that there is 'Someone' ruling the universe, 'Someone' who is not bound by human knowledge or technology. *They have no faith, but they do have superstitions.*[11]

The Church teaches us that God is our one and only Lord. She has given us detailed instructions for the practice of divine cult. These guidelines are an expression of the Church's love and honour for God. Holy Mother Church wants each of its churches to be an authentic *house of prayer.* Holy Mass is to be the centre and root of Christian life. *Pastors should see to it that all churches and public oratories where the Blessed Sacrament is reserved remain open for at least several hours in the morning and evening*

---

[9] Matt 7:6
[10] St John XXIII, Encyclical, *Mater et Magistra,* 15 May 1961, 214
[11] St. J. Escrivá, *op cit,* 587

so that it may be easy for the faithful to pray before the Blessed Sacrament.[12] The presence of the Blessed Sacrament should be indicated according to traditional practices, such as by the use of a sanctuary lamp. The Blessed Sacrament should be reserved in a solid, inviolable tabernacle in the middle of the main altar or on a side altar, but in a truly prominent place. *It ought to be suitable for private prayer so that the faithful may easily and fruitfully, by private devotion also, continue to honour Our Lord in this sacrament.*[13] These practices are, first and foremost, manifestations of our love for Jesus Christ. They are secondarily intended to be indications of his Presence. *The pastor, therefore, should here teach that men should be so warmly interested in promoting the worship and honour of God as to be said rather to be jealous of him than to love him, in imitation of him who says ... 'Zeal for thy house has consumed me' (Ps 68:9).*[14]

---

[12] Sacred Congregation of Rites, Instruction, *Eucharisticum mysterium*, 25 May 1967, 51

[13] *ibid,* 53

[14] *Catechism of the Council of Trent,* III, 1, 29

90. LOVING THE VIRTUE OF CHASTITY

90.1 Without holy purity it is impossible to love.

The Sadducees came before Jesus to pose an absurd moral dilemma. Their intention was to ridicule the widely-held Jewish belief in the resurrection of the dead.[1] According to the Levite law, if a married man died without leaving issue, then his brother was under obligation to marry the widow so as to continue his brother's line.[2] The Sadducees twisted this precept into an argument intended to disprove the resurrection of the body. If each of a series of seven brothers had the same woman as his wife, they asked, at the time of the resurrection *whose wife will the woman be?*

The Lord answers this conundrum using texts from Sacred Scripture. He reaffirms the doctrine of the resurrection of the dead and then discusses certain qualities of those who will be in the glorified state. God has the power to raise up the dead. He will elevate men and women to equality with angels. Because they have immortal souls they will not marry, for there will be no need for reproduction of the species.[3] Procreation is necessary for the increase of the species here on earth. Yet life on earth is not definitive in nature. It is a time of testing for eternal life.

The Church teaches us that conjugal love belongs exclusively to the marital state, contributing both to

---

[1] Luke 20:27-40
[2] cf Deut 25:5 ff
[3] St Thomas, *Commentary on the Gospel of St Matthew,* 22, 30

procreation and mutual support. Christians are encouraged to practice the virtue of chastity or holy purity so that they may faithfully adhere to God's purpose with regard to the gift of sexual union. This virtue is very important because of the disorder found in human nature as a result of Original Sin and personal sins.

When we practice the virtue of chastity we seek not only purity of body but also purity of mind and heart. We should avoid those thoughts, affections and desires which separate us from the love of God and the demands of our vocation.[4] Without chastity, it is impossible to have true human love, much less true love for God. If a person were to abandon his struggle in the realm of holy purity, he would become subject to the tyranny of the senses. He would descend to an animal state: *It seems as if your spirit were growing smaller, shrinking to a little point. And your body seems to grow and become gigantic, until it gains control.*[5] The worldly person is incapable of having an authentic friendship with the Lord. In those early days when the Church was surrounded by a pagan and hedonistic environment she warned the faithful about *the pleasures of the flesh which act as cruel tyrants. Once they have enfeebled the soul through impurity, they render the soul incapable of doing good works.*[6] The practice of holy purity disposes the soul to the love of God and apostolate.

90.2 Marital chastity and virginity.

Chastity is by no means a negative virtue: *don't do this* and *don't do that*. Chastity has to do with giving one's heart to God. It is a *joyful affirmation*.[7] Chastity is a virtue for everyone. Each one should practice this virtue

---

[4] cf *Catechism of the Council of Trent*, III, 7, 6
[5] St. J. Escrivá, *Furrow*, 841
[6] St Ambrose, *Treatise on Virginity*, 1, 3
[7] cf St. J. Escrivá, *Christ is passing by*, 5

according to his or her own vocation in life. For those who are married, the practice of chastity leads to a stronger and more lasting love based on profound mutual respect. *This love transforms conjugal relations and uplifts them to the highest dignity of the person, while respecting all the while their physical nobility. When the husband and wife consider that their love can be the cause of new life, then they will find their physical union to be an authentic expression of love ...*

Yet, contrariwise, if this love is removed from sex, if the physical union is nothing more than selfishness, then the person loses his dignity while simultaneously profaning the dignity of the partner.

One of the surest guarantees of chastity in marriage is a strong and tender love for one another.

'But there is still a higher cause'. St Paul teaches us that chastity is a 'fruit of the Spirit' (cf Gal 5:23). In other words, it is a consequence of divine love. If we are to live holy purity in marriage we need a deep love and respect for our spouse, but we also need to have a great love for God. Anyone who wants to follow Jesus Christ will find that the practice of chastity is indispensable. When we live holy purity we become united in a special way with Jesus Christ. We draw near to God, just as Jesus promised to the pure of heart (cf Matt 5:8).[8]

Holy purity is neither the first nor the most important virtue. Christian life cannot be reduced to the pursuit of purity. But we well know that without holy purity there can be no love. Charity is the most important virtue. It is the fulfilment of all the virtues. Hence the crucial nature of holy purity. Without chastity, human love becomes corrupted. For those who have received the vocation to matrimony, their sanctification lies in the faithful

---

[8] J. M. Martinez Doral, *The holiness of conjugal life*, in *Scripta Theologica*, Pamplona 1989

fulfilment of their conjugal duties. This is how they are to encounter God. For those who have received the vocation to apostolic celibacy, their sanctification lies in a life of complete generosity to the Lord, *indiviso corde*,[9] without the mediation of an earthly love.

Let us meditate today on the example of Our Lady. Many Christians have the custom of doing so on this day of the week, on a Saturday. We know that Mary is the sublime model for both maternity and virginity. Many people like to call her *the Virgin* or the *Blessed Virgin Mary*. At the same time she is our Mother. It was God's wish that his Mother would also be a Virgin. Virginity is highly esteemed by God. This condition sends a message to the men and women of every age to the effect that the satisfaction of the sexual urge does not pertain to the perfection of the person. As Jesus says in today's Gospel: *Those who are accounted worthy to attain to that age and to the resurrection from the dead neither marry nor are given in marriage. There is a condition of life without marriage, in which man, male and female, finds at the same time the fulness of personal donation and of the intersubjective communion of persons, thanks to the glorification of his entire psychosomatic being in the eternal union with God. When the call to continence 'for the Kingdom of Heaven' finds an echo in the human soul ... it is not difficult to perceive there a particular sensitiveness of the human spirit, which already in the conditions of the present temporal life seems to anticipate what man will share in, in the future resurrection.*[10] Virginity and apostolic celibacy are an earthly foretaste or anticipation of Heaven.

In like manner the Church has always taught that *sex is not a shameful thing; it is a divine gift, ordained to life, to*

---

[9] cf 1 Cor 7:33
[10] St John Paul II, *Address*, 10 March 1982

love, to fruitfulness.

This is the context in which we must see the Christian doctrine on sex. Our faith does not ignore anything on this earth that is beautiful, noble and authentically human.[11] Those who choose to give themselves completely to God *do not do so because 'it is inexpedient to marry', or because of a supposed negative value of marriage, but in view of the particular value connected with this choice and which must be discovered and welcomed personally as one's own vocation. And for that reason Christ says: 'He who is able to receive this, let him receive it' (Matt 19:12).*[12] The Lord has given each one of us a specific mission to fulfil on this earth. He is immensely pleased whenever we fulfil our responsibilities with joy and generosity.

90.3 Doing apostolate concerning this virtue. Means for living holy purity.

The testimony given by Christians of lives ordered to God's love is a treasure the Church presents to the world. It is a proof of the reality of God's love. *Continence 'for the Kingdom of Heaven' bears, above all, the imprint of the likeness to Christ who, in the work of redemption, did himself make this choice 'for the Kingdom of Heaven'.*[13] The Apostles followed the example of Christ. As a result, they departed from the tradition of the Old Covenant where physical procreation was the only form of fecundity. The Apostles became convinced that celibacy allowed a person to follow Christ more closely and bring to fruition his apostolic charge. St John Paul II showed how the Apostles gradually came to the realization of *that spiritual and supernatural fruitfulness of man which comes from the*

---

[11] St. J. Escrivá, *Christ is passing by,* 24
[12] St John Paul II, *loc cit*
[13] *idem, Address,* 24 March 1982

Holy Spirit.[14]

In our times it may be that many, if not most people, find it very difficult to understand the virtue of chastity. They do not see the point of anybody's living apostolic celibacy or virginity in the middle of the world. The first Christians came up against the same kind of difficulties in a fiercely hostile environment. That is why our apostolate on behalf of chastity ought to include the practice of its related virtues. Through our cheerful and friendly behaviour we should make chastity attractive to others. We need to sow abundant doctrine about this virtue. Let us be sure to take care in the way we dress, in the way we exercise and pursue recreation. When a conversation takes a bad turn, we should not be afraid to cut short an impure discussion. We should also reject bad forms of entertainment. Above all, let us give a cheerful example with our own life. We should explain to our friends the beauty of this virtue, and how it is that many good fruits come from the practice of chastity – a greater capacity for love, generosity, joy, spiritual refinement ... We should proclaim loud and clear that purity is possible as long as we use the means that have been recommended by the Church for centuries: guarding the senses, avoiding occasions of sin, modesty, moderation in entertainment, temperance, frequent recourse to prayer and the sacraments – especially the Sacrament of Confession, sincerity, and last but not least, a tender love for the Blessed Virgin.[15] We will never, ever, be tempted beyond our strength.[16]

As we finish our prayer, let us go to Holy Mary, *Mater pulchrae dilectionis,* Mother of Fair Love. She will help us to increase our love in the face of the greatest temptations.

---

[14] *ibid*
[15] S.C.D.F., *Declaration on Certain Problems of Sexual Ethics,* 29 December 1975, 12
[16] cf 1 Cor 10:13

CHRIST THE KING

91. THE REIGN OF CHRIST

91.1 A reign of justice and love.

The Lord will reign for ever and will give his people the gift of peace.[1] These are the words of today's *Communion Antiphon*.

The Solemnity of Christ the King *is as it were a synthesis of the entire salvific mystery.*[2] This feast brings the liturgical year to a close. Over the past months we have celebrated the mysteries of the life of the Lord. Now we contemplate Christ in his glorified state as King of all Creation and of our souls. The feasts of the Epiphany, Easter and the Ascension also relate to Christ as King and Lord of the Universe, but the Church has wanted to have this feast as a special remembrance to modern man, who seems somewhat indifferent to his supernatural destiny.[3]

The texts for today's Mass emphasize the love of Christ the King. He did not come to establish his kingdom by force. His 'weapons' are goodness and a shepherd's solicitude: *I myself will search for my sheep, and will seek them out. As a shepherd seeks out his flock when some of his sheep have been scattered abroad, so will I seek out my sheep; and I will rescue them from all places where they have been scattered on a day of clouds and thick darkness.*[4] The Lord tends to his lost sheep, to those men and women who have gone astray through sin. He takes care to heal

---

[1] *Communion Antiphon*, Ps 28:10-11
[2] St St John Paul II, *Address*, 20 November 1983
[3] cf Pius XI, Encyclical, *Quas primas*, 11 December 1925
[4] *First Reading*, Year A, Ezek 34:11-12

their wounds. He goes so far as to die for his sheep. *As King, He came to reveal God's love, to be the Mediator of the new Covenant, the Redeemer of mankind. The kingdom which Jesus initiated works in its interior dynamism as 'leaven' and a 'sign of salvation' to build a more just, more fraternal world, one with more solidarity, inspired by the evangelic values of hope and of the future happiness to which all are called. Therefore, the Preface of today's Eucharistic celebration speaks of Jesus who has offered to the Father 'a kingdom of truth and life, of holiness and grace, of justice, love and peace'.*[5] This is what the Kingdom of Christ is all about. Each one of us is called to participate in this kingdom and expand it through our apostolate. The Lord should be present in our families, among our friends, neighbours and colleagues at work ... *Against those who reduce religion to a set of negative statements, or are happy to settle for a watered-down Catholicism; against those who wish to see the Lord with his face against the wall, or to put him in a corner of their souls, we have to affirm, with our words and with our deeds, that we aspire to make Christ the King reign indeed over all hearts, theirs included.*[6]

91.2 Christ must reign in our mind, our will and our actions.

Oportet autem illum regnare ... For he must reign ...[7]

St Paul teaches us that while Christ's Kingdom is achieved in time and space, it will attain its definitive fulness at the Last Judgment. The Apostle depicts this epochal event as a rite of homage to the Father: Christ will present all Creation to him as an offering. Then all things will be subjected to his rule.[8] His Second Coming will

---

[5] St John Paul II, *Address*, 26 November 1989
[6] St. J. Escrivá, *Furrow*, 608
[7] *Second Reading*, Year A, 1 Cor 15:25
[8] cf *ibid*, 1 Cor 15:23-28

establish *a new heaven and a new earth.*[9] He will thereupon vanquish the devil, sin, pain and death.[10]

Meanwhile, we Christians cannot be passively waiting for these momentous events to unfold. We have to desire ardently the establishment of his kingdom: *Oportet illum regnare!* First of all, the Lord must reign in our mind, in our will and in our actions. *He must reign in our minds, which should assent with perfect submission and firm belief to revealed truths and to the doctrines of Christ. He must reign in our wills, which should obey the laws and precepts of God. He must reign in our hearts, which should spurn natural desires and love God above all things, and cleave to him alone. He must reign in our bodies and in our members, which should serve as instruments for the interior sanctification of our souls.*[11] *Our Lord and our God: how great you are! It is you who give our life supernatural meaning and divine vitality. For love of your Son, you cause us to say with all our being, with our body and soul: 'He must reign!' And this we do against the background of our weakness, for you know that we are creatures made of clay.*[12]

Today's feast is an anticipation of the Second Coming of Christ in power and majesty. His glorious return will fill the hearts of his faithful with joy and wipe away every tear. This feast is also a summons for us to impregnate with the spirit of Christ all temporal realities. The Second Vatican Council has declared: *The expectation of a new earth must not weaken but rather stimulate our concern for cultivating this one. For here grows the body of a new human family, a body which even now is able to give some kind of foreshadowing of the new age.*

Hence, while earthly progress must be carefully distin-

---

[9] Rev 21:1-2
[10] cf *The Navarre Bible*, note to 1 Cor 15:23-28
[11] Pius XI, Encyclical, *Quas primas*, 11 December 1925, 21
[12] St. J. Escrivá, *Christ is passing by*, 181

*guished from the growth of Christ's kingdom, to the extent
that the former can contribute to the better ordering of
human society, it is of vital concern to the Kingdom of God.*

*For after we have obeyed the Lord, and in his Spirit
nurtured on earth the values of human dignity, brotherhood and freedom, and indeed all the good fruits of our
nature and enterprise, we will find them again, but freed
from stain, burnished and transfigured, when Christ hands
over to the Father: 'a kingdom eternal and universal ... '
On this earth that Kingdom is already present in mystery.
When the Lord returns it will be brought into full flower.*[13]
We collaborate in the expansion of this kingdom whenever
we make our ordinary world more human and more divine.

91.3 Extending the Reign of Christ.

Jesus replied to Pilate's questioning: *My kingship is
not of this world ...* At a later stage in the interview Jesus
tells the Roman Procurator: *I am a king. For this I was
born ...*[14] Although the Reign of Christ is not of this world,
it has its beginnings here. The Reign of Christ extends so
far as there are men and women who know themselves to
be children of God, who are nourished by him, who live for
him. Christ is a King who has been given all power in
Heaven and on earth, but He governs like one *gentle and
lowly of heart.*[15] His rule is to serve others. *The Son of man
came not to be served but to serve, and to give his life as a
ransom for many.*[16] His throne was a manger in Bethlehem
and then was a Cross on Calvary. He is *the ruler of kings
on earth*[17] whose tribute is the proof of our faith and love.

The first person formally to recognize Christ as king

---

[13] Second Vatican Council, *Gaudium et spes,* 39
[14] John 18:36-37
[15] cf Matt 11:29
[16] Matt 20:28
[17] *Second Reading,* Year B, Rev 1:5

was a condemned criminal. He captured the Lord's Heart with that humble request: *Jesus, remember me when you come in your kingly power.*[18] This man was able to grasp the real meaning of Christ's kingship even though it was the object of merciless ridicule from the clamouring throng. His faith deepened as Christ's divinity became increasingly obscured. *The Lord always grants us more than what we ask for. The thief merely asked to be remembered, but the Lord said: 'Truly, I say to you, today you will be with me in Paradise'. The essence of life is to live with Jesus Christ. And where Jesus Christ is, there is his Reign to be found.*[19]

Jesus speaks to us on the occasion of this solemn feast: *For I know the plans I have for you, says the Lord, plans for welfare and not for evil, to give you a future and a hope.*[20] Let us resolve to make our hearts conform to the Will of God. Let us ask his blessing on our efforts to extend his kingdom through our apostolate of friendship and confidence. *This is the calling of Christians, that is our apostolic task, the desire which should consume our soul: to make this kingdom of Christ a reality, to eliminate hatred and cruelty, to spread throughout the earth the strong and soothing balm of love.*[21]

If we are to make these ideals into reality we must turn once again to Our Lady. *Mary, the holy Mother of our king, the queen of our heart, looks after us as only she knows how. Mother of mercy, throne of grace: we ask you to help us compose, verse by verse, the simple poem of charity in our own life and the lives of the people around us; it is 'like a river of peace' (Is 66:12). For you are a sea of inexhaustible mercy.*[22]

---

[18] Luke 23:42
[19] St Ambrose, *Commentary on St Luke's Gospel, in loc*
[20] Jer 29:11
[21] St. J. Escrivá, *Christ is passing by,* 183
[22] *ibid,* 187

92. THE POOR WIDOW

92.1 We should not be afraid to be generous.

Each day the Jews would present all manner of offerings to the Lord in the Temple of Jerusalem. People would bring agricultural products such as flour and oil, wafers or toasted bread with a covering of oil and frankincense to make it pleasing to the Lord.[1] A portion of the offering would be burnt while the remainder would be eaten by the priests in the interior of the Temple.[2] The *holocaust* was that sacrifice whereby a previously sacrificed victim (a sheep or a bird) would be taken and then completely destroyed by fire. (*Holocaust* means wholly consumed by fire). In the times of Our Lord *perpetual sacrifice*[3] was offered in the Temple. This was a prefiguring of the immanent Eucharistic sacrifice.

The Jews also donated money as an offering to God and as a contribution to the Temple. The Temple treasury was situated in a highly visible location. One day Jesus sat near this spot and *watched the multitude putting money into the treasury. Many rich people put in large sums.*[4] Then he observed a poor widow pass by and donate two small coins.[5] St Mark has left us a record of their value: *which make up a penny.* It was an insignificant amount. Nevertheless, the Lord was moved by the widow's gift. He

---

[1] cf Lev 2:1-2; 14-15
[2] cf Lev 6:7-11
[3] cf Dan 8:11
[4] Mark 12:41
[5] cf Luke 21:1-4

knew that this was everything she owned. God valued her offering more highly than what the others had given. *For they all contributed out of their abundance; but she out of her poverty has put in everything she had, her whole living.* She made her offering with great confidence in divine Providence. God would reward her generosity even in her lifetime. St Augustine has commented: *The rich gave much because they had much to give away. She gave everything that she possessed. Yet she had a great deal because she had God in her heart. To possess God in the soul is worth all of the gold in Solomon's mines. Who has ever given more than this widow who left nothing for herself?*[6] We should not be afraid to be generous. Sometimes we may have to sacrifice things that seem to be necessary. But how few things are truly necessary! We have to offer to God everything we are and everything we have without saving anything for ourselves. There is an old saying that God is won over by the last coin. Is there anything in my heart that does not belong to the Lord? Time, belongings, friends ... ? What is Jesus asking from me right now? What does He want me to finish with or to relegate to secondary importance?

The Lord was so delighted by the generosity of this woman that He wanted to communicate his joy to his disciples.[7] The Sacred Heart will feel the same way when we give everything we have. *The Kingdom of God is priceless but at the same time it costs whatever you have down to the last penny ... Peter and Andrew had to abandon their boats and their nets. For the widow it was two copper coins (cf Luke 21:2). For someone else it was a cup of cold water (cf Matt 10:42) ...*[8]

---

[6] St Augustine, *Sermon 107 A*
[7] cf Mark 12:43
[8] St Gregory the Great, *Homily 5 on the Gospels*

92.2 Generosity without conditions. Saying 'yes' to the Lord.

Through his preaching and, most poignantly, through his Passion and Death, the Lord invites us to make a pleasing offering to God the Father. The sacrificial offering was no longer to be animals or food but an offering of one's self. St Paul expressed this idea to the first Christians in Rome in these terms: *I appeal to you therefore, brethren, by the mercies of God, to present your bodies as a living sacrifice, holy and acceptable to God, which is your spiritual worship.*[9] The Christian should unite himself with Christ in the Holy Mass. *In order that the oblation by which the faithful offer the divine Victim in this Sacrifice to the Heavenly Father may have its full effect, it is necessary that the people add something else, namely the offering of themselves as a victim ... Each should consecrate himself to the furthering of the divine glory, desiring to become as like as possible to Christ in his most grievous sufferings.*[10]

This offering of the self is often made in the little details of every day, from our morning offering to the sacrifices we make for the sake of social harmony. Our heart has to be open to the Lord's call. We should always say 'yes' to God. Our generosity needs to be complete, without any conditions. Let us consider this analogy from an early Christian text: *When a man has filled very suitable jars with good wine, and a few among those jars are left empty, then he comes to the jars, and does not look at the full jars, for he knows that they are full; but he looks at the empty, being afraid lest they have become sour. For empty jars quickly become sour, and the goodness of the wine is gone.*[11] The same thing happens with souls. They can go *sour.* If our friendship with God is half-hearted, it will not

---

[9] Rom 12:1

[10] Pius XII, Encyclical, *Mediator Dei,* 20 November 1947, 98-99

[11] The Pastor of Hermas, *Commandments,* 13, 5, 3

endure. We will find ourselves increasingly alienated from
Jesus. The Christian has to be coherent in his faith. He
must give himself to God without reserve. The Lord has to
occupy the centre of our thoughts and affections. We can
realize this total dedication by being faithful to God in the
day-to-day details of our vocation.

Let us not hesitate to give Jesus everything we have.
We must give ourselves completely. *Don't be taken in by
the hypocrites around you when they sow doubts as to
whether Our Lord has a right to ask so much of you.
Instead, put yourselves obediently and unconditionally in
the presence of God, like 'clay in the potter's hands' (Jer
18:6), and humbly confess to him: 'Deus meus et omnia!'
You are my God and my all.*[12]

92.3 The generosity of God.

An ancient legend from the East tells of a kingdom
where the subjects were obliged to present a gift to the
King whenever they would meet him. One day a humble
peasant found himself in the royal presence empty-handed.
So he cupped a little water in his hand and made this his
offering. The king was so pleased by the devotion of this
peasant that he bestowed upon him a bowl full of gold
coins.

The Lord is more generous than all the kings of the
earth. He has promised to reward us one-hundredfold in
this life and in the life to come.[13] God wants us to be happy
in this life. Those who follow the Lord with generosity will
experience his peace and joy. This gift is an anticipation of
Heaven. To have Jesus near us is, of course, the best
compensation possible. St Teresa has assured us: *If you but
lift your eyes to Heaven, thinking of him, He will repay*

---

[12] St. J. Escrivá, *Friends of God*, 167
[13] cf Luke 18:28-30

you, never fear.[14]

The Lord is waiting for us to offer our work, the difficulties of daily life, our deeds of service, the gift of our time and energy to others ... *It is necessary to go beyond the limits of strict justice, in imitation of the exemplary conduct of the widow, who teaches us to give with generosity even that which is meant for our own needs.*

Above all one must remember that God does not measure human actions by a standard which stops at the appearances of 'how much' is given. God measures according to the standard of the interior values of 'how' one places oneself at the disposal of one's neighbour: He measures according to the degree of love with which one freely dedicates oneself to the service of the brethren.[15]

Our offerings will be most pleasing to God if we make them through his Mother. St Bernard has recommended: *Entrust your small gift to the care of Mary. She will ensure that your offering is favourably received by the Lord.*[16]

---

[14] St Teresa, *The Way of Perfection,* 25, 5
[15] St John Paul II, *Address,* 10 November 1985
[16] St Bernard, *Homily on the Nativity of the Blessed Virgin Mary,* 18

93. OUR FEET OF CLAY

93.1 The statue with the feet of clay.

One of the readings for today's Mass comes from the *Book of Daniel.*[1] King Nebuchadnezzar had a dream which filled him with foreboding yet he seemed unable to remember its content. The Prophet Daniel describes the dream and then interprets its meaning: *You saw, O king, and behold, a great image. This image, mighty before you, and its appearance was frightening. The head of this image was of fine gold, its breast and arms of silver, its belly and thighs of bronze, its legs of iron, its feet partly of iron and partly of clay. As you looked, a stone was cut out by no human hand, and it smote the image on its feet of iron and clay, and broke them in pieces.* Everything came crashing down at once: the gold, the silver, the bronze, the iron and the clay *were broken in pieces, and became like the chaff of the summer threshing-floors; and the wind carried them away, so that not a trace of them could be found.*

Daniel shows that the dream represents the destruction of one kingdom after another. The chain of destruction was begun by Nebuchadnezzar himself, and would be climaxed by the arrival of a kingdom of the *God of heaven ... which shall never be destroyed.*[2] God's kingdom would overcome all other kingdoms and last to the end of time. This image may also be seen to represent every Christian: an intelligence of gold so as to know God, a heart of silver with a great capacity for love, an immense strength based

---

[1] Dan 2:31-35
[2] Dan 2:44

on the practice of the virtues ... All of which rests upon feet of clay.[3] The reality of our human nature is that we are essentially weak. We are liable to fall. This realization should lead us to be prudent and humble. The Christian has to be aware of his weakness and trust in the help of the Lord. This should be our constant prayer, and explains our practice of mortification and our dependence on spiritual direction. In this way our very weakness can become our pillar of strength. Surely we have all experienced the truth within this prayer of St Augustine: *Who is the man who will reflect on his weakness, and yet dare to credit his chastity and innocence to his own powers, so that he loves Thee the less, as if he had little need for that mercy by which Thou forgivest sins to those who turn to Thee.*[4]

It is the experience of our own sinfulness which convinces us of our frailty: *Those who seek to follow God taste many temptations and falls.*[5] God's grace and our good desires do not eliminate our proneness to sin. Our consciousness of this truth should make a big difference in our life. We have to depend on the strength of God rather than on our own unreliable resources. Again, let us learn from St Augustine's reflections on God's ways: *Amid the lower parts He has built for himself out of our clay a lowly dwelling, in which He would protect from themselves those ready to become submissive to him, and bring them to himself. He heals their injuries, and nourishes their love, so that they may not proceed further in self-confidence, but rather become weak.*[6] This is the way we Christians must travel. We have to cry out ceaselessly with a strong and humble faith, 'Lord, put not your trust in me. But I, I put my trust in you'. Then, as we sense in our hearts the love,

---

[3] cf St. J. Escrivá, *Christ is passing by*, 5; 181

[4] St Augustine, *Confessions*, 2, 7

[5] Origen, *Homily about the Exodus*, 5, 3

[6] St Augustine, *Confessions*, 7, 18

*the compassion, the tenderness of Christ's gaze upon us,
for he never abandons us, we shall come to understand the
full meaning of those words of St Paul, 'virtus in
infirmitate perficitur' (2 Cor 12:9). If we have faith in Our
Lord, in spite of our failings – or, rather, with our failings
– we shall be faithful to our Father, God; his divine power
will shine forth in us, sustaining us in our weakness.*[7]

93.2 The experience of personal weakness.

The Church teaches that a person who has been baptized
still suffers from concupiscence, the *fomes peccati* inherited
from our first parents.[8] The Second Vatican Council has
affirmed: *What Revelation makes known to us is confirmed
by our own experience. For when man looks into his own
heart he finds that he is drawn towards what is wrong and
sunk in many evils which cannot come from his good
Creator ... As a result, the whole life of men, both individual
and social, shows itself to be a struggle, and a dramatic one,
between light and darkness. Man finds that he is unable of
himself to overcome the assaults of evil successfully, so that
everyone feels as though bound by chains.*[9]

Like the statue in King Nebuchadnezzar's dream, we
too have feet of clay. We all have sinned. We know our
interior weakness. *No one is freed from sin by himself or by
his own efforts, no one is raised above himself or
completely delivered from his own weakness, solitude or
slavery; all have need of Christ who is the model, master,
liberator, saviour, and giver of life.*[10] Each Christian is like
an *earthen vessel* that contains a priceless treasure.[11] This
is why we must flee from occasions of sin, *for once placed*

---

[7] St. J. Escrivá, *Friends of God,* 194
[8] cf Council of Trent, Session 5, chap. 5
[9] Second Vatican Council, *Gaudium et spes,* 13
[10] *idem, Ad gentes,* 8
[11] 2 Cor 4:7

therein, we have no ground to rest on – so many enemies then assail us, and our own weakness is such, that we cannot defend ourselves.[12]

God in his infinite Wisdom has deigned that our very frailty may work to our benefit. *God wants your misery to be the throne of his mercy. He desires that your powerlessness be the seat of his omnipotence.*[13] God's power can shine forth from our weakness. Our experience of temptations and falls should inspire us to a closer union with Jesus. St Augustine renders this homage to God: *To your grace and to your mercy I ascribe it that you have dissolved my sins as if they were ice. To your grace I ascribe also whatsoever evils I have not done.*[14] In addition, these trials can school us in compassion for others.

Let us pray to Jesus with great confidence: *Lord, may neither our past wretchedness which has been forgiven us, nor the possibility of future wretchedness cause us any disquiet. May we abandon ourselves into your merciful hands. May we bring before you our desires for sanctity and apostolate, which are hidden like embers under the ashes of an apparent coldness. Lord, I know you are listening to us.*[15] Say this to him in the intimacy of your soul.

93.3 God shows his power and mercy through our weakness.

Pope John Paul I spoke at one of his General Audiences about the virtue of Christian hope and the human condition. *Someone will say: what if I am a poor sinner? I reply to him as I replied to an unknown lady, who had confessed to me many years ago. She was discouraged*

---

[12] St Teresa, *Life,* 8, 14
[13] St Francis de Sales, *Letters,* fragment 10
[14] St Augustine, *Confessions,* 2, 7
[15] St. J. Escrivá, *The Forge,* 426

because, she said, she had a stormy life morally. 'May I ask you', I said, 'how old you are?' 'Thirty-five'. 'Thirty-five! But you can live for another forty or fifty years and do a great deal of good. So, repentant as you are, instead of thinking of the past, project yourself into the future and renew your life, with God's help'.

On that occasion I quoted St Francis de Sales, who speaks of 'our dear imperfections'. I explained: God detests failings because they are failings. On the other hand, however, in a certain sense He loves failings since they give to him an opportunity to show his mercy, and to us an opportunity to remain humble and to understand and to sympathize with our neighbour's failings.[16]

If we should ever feel burdened by the knowledge of our weakness, if temptations should threaten to overwhelm us, let us remember what the Lord told St Paul during his time of trial: *My grace is sufficient for you, for my power is made perfect in weakness.* We will then echo that memorable prayer of the Apostle: *I will all the more gladly boast of my weaknesses, that the power of Christ may rest upon me. For the sake of Christ, then, I am content with weaknesses, insults, hardships, persecutions, and calamities; for when I am weak, then I am strong.*[17]

Even though we have feet of clay we can rest our confidence on the supernatural means that will make us ultimately victorious. God has remained with us in the Tabernacle. He has instituted the Sacrament of Confession to forgive us our sins and to give us renewed strength for the interior battle. He has put a Guardian Angel by our side to prepare a safe way. We can also depend on fraternal correction, on the good example of others, on the extraordinary assistance of the Communion of Saints. More important than anything else, however, is the protection we

---

[16] John Paul I, *Address*, 20 September 1978
[17] 2 Cor 12:9-10

receive from the Blessed Virgin Mary, Mother of God and our Mother. She is the *Refuge of sinners*; she will be our refuge. Today is a good opportunity for us to take her by the hand and never let go.

94. PATIENCE IN ADVERSITY

94.1 Patience, part of the virtue of fortitude.

Now that we have arrived at the close of the liturgical year it is fitting that the Lord should speak to us of the last days. Jesus predicts the destruction of Jerusalem which came to pass some forty years later. His Second Coming will be in *power and great glory.* Today's Gospel is the part of this discourse where Jesus warns his disciples of impending persecution.[1] The Lord exhorts his followers to persevere no matter what should happen. *'In patientia vestra possidebitis animas vestras'. By your endurance you will gain your lives.*

In the years that followed, the Apostles meditated on the Lord's warning: *A servant is not greater than his master. If they persecuted me, they will persecute you.*[2] Even the worst tribulation has a role to play in God's Providence. God permits contradictions because they can be the cause of greater goods. For example, the early Roman persecutions strengthened the primitive Church and deepened her supernatural spirit. This was to fulfil the Lord's prediction: *In the world you have tribulation; but be of good cheer, I have overcome the world.*[3]

Life presents us with all manner of problems and trials. Some are great and many are of little consequence. With the help of God's grace the soul can be strengthened by every trial. Certain contradictions emanate from other

---

[1] Luke 21:12-19
[2] John 15:20
[3] John 16:33

people, such as direct attacks or veiled threats from people who do not understand our vocation, or perhaps public opposition from a pagan culture or from declared enemies of the Church. Other contradictions have their origin in the limitations of our human nature. We may experience financial difficulties or grave family problems. At times we will become sick or exhausted or completely discouraged. If we are to persevere in adversity, we need to exercise patience. We should be cheerful no matter what develops, because we have our eyes fixed on Christ. He has encouraged us to move forward, to live in his peace. Our confidence should be anchored in the fact that Christ has been triumphant.

According to St Augustine, patience *is the virtue that allows us to bear adversity with a serene spirit ... We should prize this serenity of soul because it allows us to obtain greater goods.*[4] The Christian should learn how to endure physical and moral hardship without complaining. Usually we are presented with many different opportunities to practice this virtue in the ordinary circumstances of everyday life. The struggle may relate to the most mundane things – a character defect that keeps resurfacing, undertakings that don't go as we had planned, unexpected changes in schedule, the bad manners of a colleague at work, people who mean well but don't understand, traffic jams, delays in public transportation, too many phone calls, forgetfulness ... These are all occasions for us to grow in humility and become more refined in our charity.

94.2 Patience towards ourselves and others. Bearing well the contradictions of ordinary life.

Patience as a virtue should not be understood to mean passivity in the face of suffering. It is not a matter of

---

[4] St Augustine, *On patience, 2*

accepting the blows of outrageous fortune and ⌐ our fate. Patience belongs to the virtue of fortitude. When we practice patience, we strive to accept pain and trial as something coming from the hand of God. We therefore seek to identify our will with the Will of God. The virtue of patience enables us to endure persecution of every kind. Patience should be the foundation of our hope and joy.[5]

There are a great many ways in which a Christian can live this virtue. The first battleground should be in the area of one's own behaviour. It is so easy to become disheartened by our defects. We need to exercise patience in our interior struggle based on our unshakeable confidence in God's love for us. If we are to overcome a character defect, it will not happen overnight. Our victory will ultimately be won by the cultivation of humility, of trusting confidence in God, of greater docility. St Francis de Sales would remind people that we need to have patience with everyone, but first and foremost with ourselves.[6]

Whenever we have contact with other people we will encounter opportunities to exercise the virtue of patience. This is certainly the case when we help people to receive spiritual formation or when we tend to people who are sick. Let us always be understanding about the defects of others. So many of our neighbours are sincerely trying to improve. They may be trying to master an unfortunate temperament, a lack of education, mistaken notions ... If some of our friends habitually give in to their defects, this can have an upsetting effect on us. We may then give way to our impatience and thereby damage our friendship, perhaps irreparably. Charity will help us to be patient with others and to correct people when necessary. When we get

---

[5] cf St Thomas, *Commentary on the Epistle to the Hebrews,* 10, 35
[6] cf St Francis de Sales, *Letters,* fragment 139

flustered, though, let us not react right away. We should take a deep breath, smile, do whatever has to be done and take our concerns to the Sacred Heart. Jesus looks upon our struggle with great sympathy and compassion.

We have to exercise patience with regard to unexpected events that befall us and interfere with our plans: sickness, poverty, extreme heat or cold, the minor misfortunes of everyday existence such as crossed telephone lines, traffic jams, having forgotten something and left it at home, an unexpected visitor ... These little contradictions can cause us to lose our peace. Yet this is where the Lord is waiting for us, right there in the ups and downs of ordinary life. This is the raw material of our sanctity. This is precisely where we must struggle to sanctify ourselves and to sanctify others.

94.3 Patience and constancy in the apostolate.

Caritas patiens est.[7] Love is patient. The virtue of patience is an indispensable support for charity.[8] Our apostolate is a clear manifestation of charity. Here patience is essential. The Lord wants us to sow his seed with a great peace of mind. We should remember that He has prepared the field beforehand. Let us be mindful of the rhythm of the seasons. We should wait for the right time and place. Let us not give in to discouragement. Our hope should rest in the Lord. He will make a tiny shoot grow into a fine ear of wheat.

Jesus gives us many examples of how to live patience. The Lord was well aware that the crowds did not grasp the full import of his teaching: *Seeing they do not see, and hearing they do not hear, nor do they understand.*[9] Nevertheless, Jesus manifests a tireless devotion to these same people. He travels through the length and breadth of

---

[7] 1 Cor 13:4
[8] cf St Cyprian, *About the good of patience,* 15
[9] Matt 13:13

Palestine. It is clear that even the Twelve Apostles had their limitations. The Lord tells them on the eve of his Passion, *I have yet many things to say to you, but you cannot bear them now.*[10] The Lord was understanding towards his disciples. He had patience with their defects and their less than perfect ways. He did not give up on them. In the years to come these same men would be the pillars of his Church.

Patience and constancy are necessary for any work of spiritual formation, whether aimed at ourselves or at others. Patience is closely allied to the virtue of humility. The patient person accepts the workings of God's Providence and operates within that general framework. He recognizes his own defects and is not dismayed by the defects of others. *A Christian who practises the manly virtue of patience will not become disconcerted at the fact that most people are indifferent to the things of God. The truth remains that there are a good many people who have deep longings to encounter God. Their inner desire may be compared to a wine cellar in which is locked away a very good wine. It so happens that souls are like arable land. The farmer must accommodate himself to the seasons and the soil. Hasn't the Master likened the Kingdom of God to a householder who went out to hire workers for his vineyard? (cf Matt 20:1-7).*[11] The Lord has been so incredibly patient with us. Let us be sure to exercise patience towards others in the apostolate. St Paul teaches us: *'Caritas omnia suffert, omnia credit, omnia sperat, omnia sustinet'. Love bears all things, believes all things, hopes all things, endures all things.*[12] If we live the virtue of patience we will be faithful. We will become holy and help others to become holy, as many as the Blessed Virgin entrusts to our care.

---

[10] John 16:12

[11] J. L. R. Sanchez de Alva, *The Gospel of St John,* Madrid 1987

[12] 1 Cor 13:7

95. *ALL YOU PEOPLES BLESS THE LORD*

95.1 The whole of Creation gives praise to the Lord. The Canticle of the Three Young Men.

Dews and sleet! Bless the Lord. Frost and cold! Bless the Lord. Ice and snow! Bless the Lord. Night and days! Bless the Lord. Light and darkness! Bless the Lord ...[1]

Today's *Responsorial Psalm* is taken from the *Book of Daniel.* This is the beautiful *Canticle of the Three Young Men,* also known as the *Trium puerorum.* For many centuries, the Church has used this hymn as a song of thanksgiving, both in the liturgy of the Mass and at its conclusion, that being the present arrangement.[2]

We may recall that King Nebuchadnezzar had built a gigantic image of gold which his subjects were compelled to adore. The punishment for disobeying this decree was cremation in a fiery furnace. Three young Jews refused to do so. They were tied up and committed to the furnace, where they sang this hymn to the God of their fathers, the God of the Covenant. *The Biblical text sounds like an appeal addressed to creatures to proclaim the glory of God the Creator.*[3] This glory exists in God himself beyond all time. *Creatures, called into existence by God in a fully free and sovereign decision, participate in a real, though limited and partial way, in the perfection of God's absolute Fullness. They differ from one another according to the degree of perfection they have received, beginning with inanimate beings, then up*

---

[1] *Responsorial Psalm,* Year I, Dan 3:68 ff
[2] cf A. G. Martimort, *The Church in Prayer,* Barcelona 1987
[3] St John Paul II, *Address,* 12 March 1986

to animate beings, and finally to man; or rather, higher still, to the creatures of a purely spiritual nature.[4]

The hymn begins with an invitation for all creatures to give glory to the Creator: *Bless the Lord, all you works of the Lord; praise and exalt him above all forever.* The angels of Heaven lead the chorus. The Heavens bless the Lord and so does the rain.[5] All Creation participates: the sun and the moon, the stars of heaven, every shower and dew, the winds, fire and heat, dews and sleet, frost and cold, ice and snow, nights and days, light and darkness, lightnings and clouds. The earth blesses the Lord with its mountains and hills, its rivers, its whales and all that move in the waters, the birds of the air and every beast imaginable. Every created thing blesses its Creator.

Man is lord of Creation. He appears in the latter section of the hymn, taking this order: all mankind in general, then the people of Israel, the priests and servants of the Lord, spirits and the souls of the just, holy men of humble heart, followed by the three young men who remained faithful to the Lord – Ananias, Azarias and Misael.[6]

The Church has added Psalm 150 to this prayer of thanksgiving. Psalm 150 is the last of the psalms, inviting all living beings to bless the Lord. *'Laudate Dominum in sanctuario eius'* ... *Praise the Lord in his holy place, praise him in his mighty heavens. Praise him for his powerful deeds, praise his surpassing greatness. O praise him with sound of trumpet, praise him with lute and harp. Praise him with timbrel and dance, praise him with strings and pipes* ... Every living thing give praise to the Lord!

95.2 Preparation for Mass. Thanksgiving after Mass.

Our whole life is a time to give thanks to God,

---

[4] *ibid*
[5] cf Gen 1:7
[6] cf B. Orchard et al., *Verbum Dei,* II, notes to Dan 3:51-90

especially in those moments after we have received Holy Communion. If we are to give proper thanks to the Lord, we must have a care for our interior disposition. St Augustine has written: *We ought to praise God as much as possible in this life, for this activity will be our occupation for all eternity. If a person does not praise God in this way he will not be able to join the heavenly chorus. Let us sing the 'Alleluia' by saying to one another: give praise to the Lord. Prepare yourselves for giving praise to God in the glorified state.*[7] Give praise to the Lord! *And so, with all the choirs of angels in Heaven we proclaim your glory and join in their unending hymn of praise ...*[8]

Adoro te devote, latens Deitas.[9] This is our prayer to Jesus after we have received Holy Communion. We should try to be recollected in these moments when the Lord is one with us. There is nothing more important than to receive this guest of honour worthily. Let us mortify our impatience. If we are generous with the Lord, we will make room for ten minutes of intimate conversation with him. Eventually there will come a time when we will be impatiently yearning for Holy Mass and Communion. The saints of every age have had the same experience. *Something like this happened to St Josemaría. We know that during the morning he gave thanks for the Mass he had celebrated, and in the afternoon prepared for the Mass of the following day. And the awareness of the importance of the Mass – 'centre and root of the interior life' he called it – had penetrated so deeply into his being that if he woke up in the night his thought went immediately to the Mass he was going to celebrate the following day; and with the thought, the desire of glorifying God with and through that*

---

[7] St Augustine, quoted by D. de las Heras, *Ascetical and Theological Commentary on the Psalms*

[8] *Roman Missal*, Preface for the Mass

[9] Hymn, *Adoro te devote*

unique sacrifice. In this way, work, mortifications, aspirations, spiritual communions, details of charity with others or daily contradictions were always directed to God – either as a preparation or as an act of thanksgiving.[10]

Let us examine our conduct in today's prayer. Do we give our full attention during Holy Mass? Do we take special care to live those few moments of thanksgiving after Communion? This is a matter of supernatural courtesy which we should do our very best to fulfil.

95.3 Jesus comes to be with us in Communion. Using all the means we can to give him a good welcome.

Today's Gospel is an account of the last days and the Second Coming of Christ in power and glory: *There will be men fainting with fear and with foreboding of what is coming on the world; for the powers of the heavens will be shaken.*[11] This same *Son of man* comes to our heart in Holy Communion to strengthen us and fill us with his peace. He comes as the long-awaited Friend. *We read in the Gospel of St John that when Jesus went to Bethany, to the house of his friend Lazarus, one of his friend's sisters, called Martha, busied herself about the house. The other, Mary, gave her entire attention to the Lord. It seems that this was by far the more commendable kind of action: if you receive a friend as a guest into your house, you look after him – that is, you keep him company and converse with him. You do not leave him in the sitting room, or anywhere else in the house reading the newspaper to amuse himself until you have time to attend to him. Without doubt this would be a dereliction of good manners. And if the person were of such importance that the mere fact of his coming to your house would be regarded as an honour far surpassing your condition and deserts, the discourtesy would be tantamount*

---

[10] F. Suarez, *The Sacrifice of the Altar*, pp. 204-205
[11] Luke 21:20-28

to a gross insult.[12] Let us treat Jesus well. He wants so much to visit our soul. *It is not His Majesty's custom to pay cheaply for his lodging, when He is hospitably received.*[13]

Holy Mother Church has advised her children to take advantage of these wonderful prayers from Sacred Scripture and the writings of the saints: the Hymn *Adoro te devote,* the *Trium puerorum,* the *Prayer before a Crucifix,* the *Prayer of Self-Dedication to Jesus Christ* ... Whenever we receive Communion, let us be sure to have our Missal handy. These prayers will help us to use this time to the full. In a certain sense, the whole course of the day depends on the quality of this thanksgiving.

Let us be sure to use all the means available in order to prepare well for Mass and make a good thanksgiving. We can be confident that whatever effort we make will be richly rewarded. *When you receive Our Lord in the Holy Eucharist, thank him from the bottom of your heart for being so good as to be with you.*

Have you ever stopped to consider that it took centuries and centuries before the Messiah came? All those patriarchs and prophets praying together with the whole people of Israel: Come, Lord, the land is parched!

If only your loving expectation were like this.[14]

---

[12] F. Suarez, *op cit,* p. 201

[13] St Teresa, *The Way of Perfection,* 36, 18

[14] St. J. Escrivá, *The Forge,* 991

96. WORDS THAT WILL NOT PASS AWAY

96.1 Prayerful reading of the Gospels.

As we come to the conclusion of the liturgical year, we consider these words of the Master in today's Gospel: *Heaven and earth will pass away, but my words will not pass away.*[1] What Jesus has said will literally last forever. God has directed these words to every man and every woman who will walk the face of the earth. *In many and various ways God spoke of old to our fathers by the prophets; but in these last days He has spoken to us by a Son.*[2] Just as He spoke to our forefathers in the Faith, Jesus Christ speaks to us in our day. Because his message is divine, it cannot be limited by human constraints of time and place.

Sacred Scripture acquires the fulness of its meaning in the figure and preaching of Christ. St Augustine has stated this idea in a most graphic manner: *The Law was pregnant with Christ.*[3] On another occasion this holy Doctor of the Church affirmed: *To read the books of the prophets without seeing the coming of Christ is a most insipid practice. Seek therefore to find Christ in these words and they will prove not only delightful but stimulating.*[4] Christ will enlighten our minds about the riches within Sacred Scripture: *Then he opened their minds to understand the Scriptures.*[5] The

---

[1] Luke 21:33
[2] Heb 1:1
[3] St Augustine, *Sermon 196,* 1
[4] idem, *Commentary on St John's Gospel,* 9, 3
[5] Luke 24:45

Jews who refused to believe in the Gospel were left with a chest full of treasure – but without the key to unlock it. St Paul explained this situation to the first Christians at Corinth in this way: *But their minds were hardened; for to this day, when they read the old covenant, that same veil remains unlifted, because only through Christ is it taken away.*[6] *The economy of the Old Testament was deliberately so orientated that it should prepare for and declare in prophecy the coming of Christ, redeemer of all men, and of the messianic kingdom ... God, the inspirer and author of the books of both Testaments, in his wisdom has so brought it about that the New should be hidden in the Old and that the Old should be made manifest in the New.*[7] In this context, it is quite moving for us to read the dialogue between Philip the Apostle and the Ethiopian official from the court of Queen Candace. The Ethiopian was sitting in his chariot reading the Prophet Isaiah. Philip ran up to the man and asked him, *Do you understand what you are reading?* The Ethiopian replied, *How can I, unless some one guides me?* Philip took a seat in the chariot and *beginning with this scripture he told him the good news of Jesus.*[8] He explained the writings of Isaiah by means of the message of Jesus. His catechesis was wonderfully straight-forward: Jesus was the key concept.

St John Chrysostom has commented on this passage from the *Acts of the Apostles*: *Let us meditate on the importance of our reading the Scriptures with devotion, even during our travels ... Some people excuse themselves from this practice because they are busy with their family affairs, or because they have military drills, or because they have some worry or other. They think that such matters preclude any serious effort to read and meditate*

---

[6] 2 Cor 3:14
[7] Second Vatican Council, Constitution, *Dei Verbum,* 15-16
[8] cf Acts 8:27-35

upon Sacred Scripture ... This Ethiopian official is an
example for all of us: those who have a quiet life, those
who belong to the army, those who are officials, those who
have chosen a monastic life, those who care for their
families at home. Let everyone learn that no circumstance
should be an impediment for our divine reading. We can do
this at home or in the town square or the public park, or on
a trip or in the company of others or right in the middle of
our work. I beseech you, do not be careless with your
reading of the Scriptures.[9]

From her earliest days the Church has recommended
that the faithful read and meditate on Sacred Scripture,
especially the books of the New Testament. We will find
Christ coming out to meet us. Through these few minutes
each day we will become best friends with Jesus. Truly,
love depends on prior knowledge.

96.2 God speaks to us through Sacred Scripture.

The books of the Old Testament outlined in advance the
path which Christ marked out in his earthly sojourn.[10] Sacred
Scripture was, in a certain sense, a grand announcement of
the Messiah. The Prophets foretold the day of his coming
and they ardently desired to see it.[11] The disciples recognized
in Christ the fulfilment of all the prophecies.[12] When St Paul
had to defend himself before King Agrippa, he stated
simply: *So I stand here testifying both to small and great,*
saying nothing but what the prophets and Moses said
would come to pass.[13] Of course, Christ was not bound by
the patriarchs and prophets. It was God who inspired them
to describe the characteristics of the Son of God. As Jesus

---

[9] St John Chrysostom, *Homilies on Genesis,* 35
[10] cf Luke 22:37
[11] cf Luke 10:24
[12] cf John 1:41-45
[13] Acts 26:22

said to the leaders of Israel: *If you believed, Moses, you would believe me, for he wrote of me.*[14] At a later date He said to them: *Your father Abraham rejoiced that he was to see my day; he saw it and was glad.*[15]

Jesus took upon himself the types and figures of the Old Testament – the temple,[16] manna,[17] the rock,[18] the serpent raised up in the wilderness.[19] His biblical references are unmistakable. This perhaps explains the Lord's frustration with the scribes and the Pharisees: *You search the scriptures, because you think that in them you have eternal life; and it is they that bear witness to me.*[20]

We read in today's Gospel that the heavens and the earth will pass away, but that God's word will last forever. God's Revelation to man is fulfilled in the person of Jesus Christ. *But now that the faith is founded in Christ, and in this era of grace, the law of the Gospel has been made manifest, there is no reason to enquire of him in that manner, nor for him to speak or to answer as He did then. For, in giving us, as He did, his Son, He has said everything to us together, once and for all, in this single Word, and He has no occasion to speak further.*[21]

We read in the *Letter to the Hebrews*: *For the word of God is living and active, sharper than any two-edged sword, piercing to the division of soul and spirit, of joints and marrow, and discerning the thoughts and intentions of the heart.*[22] This word is directed to every person who receives it with faith. *In the sacred books the Father who is*

---

[14] John 5:46
[15] John 8:56
[16] John 2:19
[17] cf John 6:32
[18] cf Luke 12:10
[19] cf John 3:14
[20] John 5:39
[21] St John of the Cross, *Ascent of Mount Carmel*, II, 22, 3
[22] Heb 4:12

in Heaven comes lovingly to meet his children, and talks with them. And such is the force and power of the Word of God that it can serve the Church as her support and vigour, and the children of the Church as strength for their faith, food for the soul, and a pure and lasting fount of spiritual life.[23]

The teachings of Jesus are always 'up to date'. We are often amazed at the relevancy of the saga of the Prodigal Son, of the importance in every age of the leaven to transform the dough, of the reactions of the people cured by the Lord. How many times have we joined Bartimaeus in asking Jesus for his light: *ut videam! That I may see!* We also have used that plea of the publican: *My God, have mercy on me a sinner!* Our daily reading of the Gospel should be a source of strength and comfort.

96.3 The fruits to be gained by this practice.

How sweet are thy words to my taste, sweeter than honey to my mouth![24]

Monsignor Ronald Knox encouraged people to meditate on the Lord's Passion with this analogy from parish life: *When you have a lot of people singing without any organ accompaniment, there is a constant tendency for the note to drop all the time; it gets lower and lower as it goes on. And therefore, when the choir isn't accustomed to singing without accompaniment, every now and then the choir-master, who has a pitch-pipe concealed on his person, gives a little 'toot' in the background, to remind them of the higher note which they ought to be taking, and aren't.*

And, you see, we are rather like that. We go on living from day to day without thinking much about how we are living, or what we are here for, or whether the things that chiefly interest us are really worth living for; and we get

---

[23] Second Vatican Council, Constitution, *Dei Verbum,* 21
[24] Ps 118:103

accustomed to our sins, and feel vaguely that it is a pity we go on committing them, but after all, there doesn't seem to be much chance of our stopping; and our prayers get very languid and washed out, and we think of very little except our food and our amusements – do you see what I mean? All the time, the note on which our lives are lived is dropping, dropping, till it's ready to die away into our boots, and we don't notice, just as the choir doesn't notice when the note drops. So we want that sudden little 'toot' of the pitch-pipe, to pull us together and screw the note of our lives up again. And the pitch-pipe we use ... is meditation on Our Lord's Passion.[25]

Let us never turn the pages of the Holy Gospel as if it were just any old book. With what love did our forefathers in the Faith care for the Word of God! They went to great lengths to pass it on from generation to generation in all of its integrity. St Cyprian has written that the reading of Scripture is like the foundation for the building up of our hope. It is the means to consolidate our faith, the food for our charity and our unerring guide on the way of life.[26] St Augustine compares the teachings of Scripture to *lights shining forth out of the darkness.*[27] We can find no better beacon for our journey to the Father.

When you open the Holy Gospel, think that what is written there – the words and deeds of Christ – is something that you should not only know, but live. Everything, every point that is told there, has been gathered, detail by detail, for you to make it come alive in the individual circumstances of your life.

God has called us Catholics to follow him closely. In that holy Writing you will find the Life of Jesus, but you should also find your own life there.

---

[25] R. A. Knox, *A Retreat for Lay People,* pp. 122-123
[26] cf St Cyprian, *Treatise on prayer*
[27] St Augustine, *Commentary on the Psalms,* 128

too, like the Apostle, will learn to ask, full of love, *'...hat would you have me do?'* And in your soul you will hear the conclusive answer, *'The Will of God!'*

Take up the Gospel every day, then, and read it and live it as a definite rule. This is what the saints have done.[28]

This is how we can draw abundant fruit from Sacred Scripture. We will unite our prayer with the words of the Psalmist: *Thy word is a lamp to my feet and a light to my path.*[29]

---

[28] St. J. Escrivá, *The Forge*, 754
[29] Ps 118:105

97. ON OUR WAY TO THE HOUSE OF THE FATHER

97.1 Our yearning for Heaven.

Then he showed me the river of the water of life, bright as crystal, flowing from the throne of God and of the Lamb through the middle of the street of the city; also, on either side of the river, the tree of life with its twelve kinds of fruit ... There shall no more be anything accursed, but the throne of God and of the Lamb shall be in it, and his servants shall worship him; they shall see his face, and his name shall be on their foreheads.[1] Sacred Scripture draws to a close where it all began: in the Garden of Eden, in Paradise. The readings for this, the last day of the liturgical calendar, speak to us about our final destination: the House of the Father, our true homeland.

Through the rich use of symbols God teaches us in the *Book of Revelation* about the nature of eternal life. This is the fulfilment of mankind's deepest yearnings. We are to see God face to face and glorify him forever. In today's reading St John depicts the happy state of God's faithful servants in Heaven. The water is a symbol of the Holy Spirit who proceeds from the Father and the Son. It runs as a river from the throne of God and of the Lamb. The Name of God is to be found on the foreheads of the blessed. They belong to the Lord.[2] In Heaven *night shall be no more; they need no light of lamp or sun, for the Lord God will be their light, and they shall reign for ever and ever.*[3]

---

[1] *First Reading,* Year II, Rev 22:1-6
[2] cf *The Navarre Bible,* Revelation, *in loc*
[3] Rev 22:5

Death is an indispensable step towards our reunion with God. The children of God should view death as a transition to eternity. Once we are in God's company *night shall be no more.* To the extent that we grow in our sense of divine filiation, we should become more desirous of meeting our loving Father. We should, therefore, look at death without fear, but with holy expectation. After all, *life is a journey toward eternity ... Every moment becomes precious precisely through this perspective. We must live and work in time bearing within us the nostalgia for Heaven.*[4]

Nevertheless, we are well aware that many, many people do not share this *nostalgia for Heaven.* They have grown accustomed to their prosperity and material comfort, as if these things will last forever. They have forgotten that fundamental truth: *For here we have no lasting city, but we seek the city which is to come.*[5] Our hearts were made to last for all eternity. The things of this world cannot satisfy our nature. They can therefore become an obstacle to our eternal happiness.

We Christians have a great love of life and of all noble earthly realities – friendship, work, joy, human love. As a consequence, we should not be surprised that the prospect of death frightens us. This is quite natural. But our body and soul were created by God to be united with him forever. Thus, the Church prays in the *Preface* for Masses said for the dead: *Indeed, for your faithful, Lord, life is changed not ended, and when this earthly dwelling turns to dust, an eternal dwelling is made ready for them in heaven.*[6]

The true child of God *expresses his joy in seeing at last the transcendent perfections of the Father in all his holiness. The child recognizes the condescension of Infinite Majesty in adopting him on earth, in guiding, training,*

[4] St John Paul II, *Address,* 22 October 1985
[5] Heb 13:14
[6] *Roman Missal, Preface I for Mass for the Dead*

sanctifying and preparing him for Heaven. Now He has invited that child to enter Heaven, to be with his father for all eternity. God has had regard for his littleness and given him the power to glorify the Trinity forever.[7]

So, we have good reason to exclaim: *We shall never die! We will only be changing our lodgings, nothing more.* In conjunction with faith and hope, we Christians also need to have this sure hope. At our death we make only a temporary farewell. We should want to die in the spirit of these words: *'Until we meet again'.*[8]

97.2 The divinization of the soul, its faculties, and our glorified body.

But the saints of the Most High shall receive the kingdom, and possess the kingdom for ever, for ever and ever.[9]

We will find that everything appears new and young in Heaven. The old universe will seem to have *vanished like a scroll that is rolled up.*[10] And yet Heaven will not be a complete surprise to us. It is, after all, the focus of the deepest yearnings of every person, even of the most depraved sinner. Heaven is the new community of the children of God who have attained to the fulness of their adoption. We will have a new heart and a new will. In the time of Christ's glory our bodies will be transfigured. Interestingly enough, this felicity based on the vision of God will not override personal relations. *There in Heaven will be found all authentic human love: the love between spouses, the love between a father and his children, friendships, family relations, noble camaraderie ...*

We are all travelling in this life. As the years go by, we find that more and more of our loved ones are now on the

---

[7] B. Perquin, *Abba, Father*, p. 314

[8] St. J. Escrivá, quoted in *Newsletter* No. 1

[9] *First Reading*, Year I, Dan 7:18

[10] Rev 6:14

other side of that barrier. This knowledge might be a source of fear, but can also be a cause for joy. This is possible if we believe that death is the door to our true home. It leads to our definitive homeland which is inhabited by 'all those who have gone before us marked with the sign of faith'. Our common homeland is not a forbidding tomb; it is the bosom of the Lord.[11]

While we are here on this earth we find it quite difficult to imagine what Heaven will be like. The Old Testament compares our condition in Heaven to that of the Promised Land: *They shall not hunger or thirst, neither scorching wind nor sun shall smite them, for He who has pity on them will lead them, and by springs of water will guide them.*[12] Jesus frequently spoke of the incredible happiness that lies in store for us if we are faithful.

The soul and its faculties, along with our glorified bodies, will be *divinized,* though there will still remain an infinite difference between creature and Creator. We will contemplate God as He truly is. In addition, the blessed will delight in the knowledge of other people in God, for example, parents, relatives, spouse, children and friends. St Thomas teaches that the blessed will know in Christ everything that pertains to the beauty and integrity of the world. Because of our membership in the human community, the blessed will know the objects of Christ's love on earth. The blessed will have a clear understanding of the truths of the Faith regarding our salvation: the Incarnation, the divine maternity of Mary, the Church, grace and the sacraments.[13]

Think how pleasing to Our Lord is the incense burnt in his honour. Think also how little the things of this earth are worth; even as they begin they are already ending.

In Heaven, instead, a great Love awaits you, with no

---

[11] C. Lopez-Pardo, *On life and Death,* Madrid 1973

[12] Is 49:10

[13] cf St Thomas, *Summa Theologiae,* 1, q. 89, a. 8

*betrayals and no deceptions. The fulness of love, the ful-
ness of beauty and greatness and knowledge ... And it will
never cloy: it will satiate, yet still you will want more.*[14]

97.3 Accidental glory. Being vigilant.

In Heaven we will see God. This will fill us with a
great joy. The extent of this joy will be related to our
holiness here on earth. Yet the mercy of God is so great
that he has prepared additional motives for our joy in
Heaven. Theologians have termed these goods *accidental
glory*. They include being in the company of Jesus Christ
glorified, Mary our Mother, St Joseph, the Angels,
particularly our Guardian Angel, and all the saints. We will
have the joy of being with our loved ones – parents,
brothers and sisters, friends, those people who showed us
our vocation ...

In Heaven we shall also be capable of acquiring new
knowledge using our faculties.[15] We shall have the joy of
seeing new souls enter Heaven. We shall be able to see the
progress of our friends on earth. We shall see the fruits of
our apostolic efforts and sacrifices. At the time of the Last
Judgment we shall possess our resurrected and glorified
body. *Accidental glory* can increase up to the time of the
Last Judgment.[16]

We have to foster the virtue of hope so that it will
strengthen us in moments of difficulty. So much is at stake.
We have to be vigilant in our struggle to be detached from
the things of earth. The Lord has given us ample warning.
In today's Gospel Jesus tells us: *But take heed to
yourselves lest your hearts be weighed down with
dissipation and drunkenness and the cares of this life ...
But watch at all times, praying that you may have strength
to escape all these things that will take place, and to stand*

---

[14] St. J. Escrivá, *The Forge*, 995
[15] cf St Thomas, *op cit,* 1, q. 89, ad 1 ad 3, aa 5 and 6; 3, q. 67, a. 2
[16] cf *Catechism of the Council of Trent*, I, 13, 8

before the Son of man.[17]

Let us meditate on these consoling words of the Lord: *I go to prepare a place for you.*[18] Heaven is our definitive homeland. There we will enjoy the company of Jesus and Mary. Here we are but wayfarers. *And when the moment comes when we are to give an account to God, we will not be afraid. Death will be only a change of lodgings. It will come when God wants, being that liberation, that point of entry into the fulness of Life. 'Vita mutatur, non tollitur' (Preface I, Mass for the Dead). (...) Life changes; it does not come to an end. We have a firm hope that we will live in a new way, very united to the Blessed Virgin, as we adore the Most Holy Trinity, Father, Son and Holy Spirit. This is the reward that awaits us.*[19]

Tomorrow we begin the season of Advent. Advent is a time of expectation and hope. We await the arrival of Jesus while staying close to Mary his Mother.

---

[17] Luke 21:34-36
[18] John 14:2
[19] Bl. A. del Portillo, *Homily*, 15 August 1989 in *Romana*, 9, June-December, 1989, p. 243

INDEX TO QUOTATIONS FROM THE FATHERS, POPES AND THE SAINTS

Note: References are to **Volume**/Chapter.Section

SUBJECT INDEX